About This Book

Why is this topic important?

Today's organizations feel both external and internal pressures to test the competence of those who work for them. The current global, competitive, regulated, and litigation savvy economic environment has increased external pressures, while the resulting increased investment in training and the escalating cost of high-tech instructional and human performance systems create internal pressure for accountability. Many products are now so complicated that human testing systems to ensure the product's correct operation and maintenance have become virtually part of the product marketed to buyers. Valid, informative, and legally defensible competence testing has become essential to many organizations, yet the technology for creating these assessments has historically been shrouded in academic circles impenetrable to those without advanced degrees in measurement sciences.

What can you achieve with this book?

This book presents a straightforward model for the creation of legally defensible criterion-referenced tests designed to determine whether or not test-takers have mastered job-related knowledge and performance skills. Exercises with accompanying feedback allow you to monitor your own proficiency with the concepts and procedures introduced. Furthermore, the issues that are most likely to be encountered at each step in the test development process are fully elaborated to enable you to make sound decisions and actually complete and document the creation of valid testing systems.

How is this book organized?

This book is divided into five main sections. The first two introduce essential, fundamental testing concepts and present an overview of the entire CRTD Model. Part Three includes a chapter devoted to the elaboration of each step in the CRTD Model. A thorough discussion of the legal issues surrounding test creation and administration constitutes Part Four. Examples and exercises with feedback are used liberally throughout the book to facilitate understanding, engagement, and proficiency in the CRTD process. The final piece in the book is a brief epilogue reflecting on the profound and often unforeseen impact that testing can have on overall organizational performance.

About Pfeiffer

Pfeiffer serves the professional development and hands-on resource needs of training and human resource practitioners and gives them products to do their jobs better. We deliver proven ideas and solutions from experts in HR development and HR management, and we offer effective and customizable tools to improve workplace performance. From novice to seasoned professional, Pfeiffer is the source you can trust to make yourself and your organization more successful.

Essential Knowledge Pfeiffer produces insightful, practical, and comprehensive materials on topics that matter the most to training and HR professionals. Our Essential Knowledge resources translate the expertise of seasoned professionals into practical, how-to guidance on critical workplace issues and problems. These resources are supported by case studies, worksheets, and job aids and are frequently supplemented with CD-ROMs, websites, and other means of making the content easier to read, understand, and use.

Essential Tools Pfeiffer's Essential Tools resources save time and expense by offering proven, ready-to-use materials—including exercises, activities, games, instruments, and assessments—for use during a training or team-learning event. These resources are frequently offered in looseleaf or CD-ROM format to facilitate copying and customization of the material.

Pfeiffer also recognizes the remarkable power of new technologies in expanding the reach and effectiveness of training. While e-hype has often created whizbang solutions in search of a problem, we are dedicated to bringing convenience and enhancements to proven training solutions. All our e-tools comply with rigorous functionality standards. The most appropriate technology wrapped around essential content yields the perfect solution for today's on-the-go trainers and human resource professionals.

Pfeiffer *Essential resources for training and HR professionals*
www.pfeiffer.com

About ISPI

The International Society for Performance Improvement (ISPI) is dedicated to improving individual, organizational, and societal performance. Founded in 1962, ISPI is the leading international association dedicated to improving productivity and performance in the workplace. ISPI represents more than 10,000 international and chapter members throughout the United States, Canada, and forty other countries.

ISPI's mission is to develop and recognize the proficiency of our members and advocate the use of Human Performance Technology. This systematic approach to improving productivity and competence uses a set of methods and procedures and a strategy for solving problems for realizing opportunities related to the performance of people. It is a systematic combination of performance analysis, cause analysis, intervention design and development, implementation, and evaluation that can be applied to individuals, small groups, and large organizations.

Website: www.ispi.org
Mail: International Society for Performance Improvement
1400 Spring Street, Suite 260
Silver Spring, Maryland 20910 USA
Phone: 1.301.587.8570
Fax: 1.301.587.8573
E-mail: info@ispi.org

Pfeiffer™

CRITERION-REFERENCED TEST DEVELOPMENT

TECHNICAL AND LEGAL GUIDELINES FOR CORPORATE TRAINING

3rd Edition

Sharon A. Shrock

William C. Coscarelli

BICENTENNIAL
1807
WILEY
2007
BICENTENNIAL

Published by Pfeiffer
An Imprint of Wiley
989 Market Street, San Francisco, CA 94103-1741
www.pfeiffer.com

Wiley Bicentennial logo: Richard J. Pacifico

For additional copies/bulk purchases of this book in the U.S. please contact 800-274-4434.

Pfeiffer books and products are available through most bookstores. To contact Pfeiffer directly call our Customer Care Department within the U.S. at 800-274-4434, outside the U.S. at 317-572-3985, fax 317-572-4002, or visit www.pfeiffer.com.

Pfeiffer also publishes its books in a variety of electronic formats. Some content that appears in print may not be available in electronic books.

Library of Congress Cataloging-in-Publication Data

Shrock, Sharon A.
  Criterion-referenced test development : technical and legal guidelines for corporate training / Sharon A. Shrock and William C. Coscarelli. – 3rd ed.
    p. cm.
  Includes index.
  ISBN 978-0-7879-8850-0 (pbk.)
1. Employees–Training of–Evaluation.   2.   Criterion-referenced tests.
I. Coscarelli, William C. C. II. Title.
  HF5549.5.T7S554 2007
  658.3′12404–dc22   2007019607

Acquiring Editor: Matthew Davis	Production Editor: Michael Kay
Marketing Manager: Jeanenne Ray	Editorial Assistant: Julie Rodriguez
Director of Development: Kathleen Dolan Davies	Editor: Rebecca Taff
Developmental Editor: Susan Rachmeler	Manufacturing Supervisor: Becky Morgan

Printed in the United States of America

Printing 10 9 8 7 6 5 4 3 2 1

Dedicated to
Rubye and Don
and to Kate and Cyra and Maybeline

CONTENTS

List of Figures, Tables and Sidebars

Sidebars

A Little Knowledge Is Dangerous

Why Test?

Why Read This Book?

A Confusing State of Affairs

Testing and Kirkpatrick's Levels of Evaluation

Certification in the Corporate World

Corporate Testing Enters the New Millennium

What Is to Come . . .

Why Test?

Today's business and technological environment has increased the need for assessment of human competence. Any competitive advantage in the global economy requires that the most competent workers be identified and retained. Furthermore, training and development, HRD, and performance technology agencies are increasingly required to justify their existence with evidence of effectiveness. These pressures have heightened the demand for better assessment and the distribution of assessment data to line managers to achieve organizational goals. These demands increasingly present us with difficult issues. For example, if you haven't tested, how can you show that those graduates you certify as "masters" are indeed masters and can be trusted to perform competently while handling dangerous or expensive equipment or materials? What would you tell an EEO officer who presented you with a grievance from an employee who was denied a salary increase based on a

test you developed? These and other important questions need
to be answered for business, ethical, and legal reasons. And they
can be answered through doable and cost-effective test systems.

So, as certification and competency testing are increasingly
used in business and industry, correct testing practices make possible the data for rational decision making.

WHY READ THIS BOOK?

Corporate training, driven by competition and keen awareness of
the "bottom line," has a certain intensity about it. Errors in instructional design or employees' failure to master skills or content can
cause significant negative consequences. It is not surprising, then,
that corporate trainers are strong proponents of the systematic
design of criterion-referenced instructional systems. What is surprising is the general lack of emphasis on a parallel process for the
assessment of instructional outcomes—in other words, testing.

All designers of instruction acknowledge the need for appropriate testing strategies, and non-instructional interventions also
frequently require the assessment of human competence, whether
in the interest of needs assessment, the formation of effective work
teams, or the evaluation of the intervention.

Most training professionals have taken at least one intensive course in the design of instruction, but most have never
had similar training in the development of criterion-referenced
tests—tests that compare persons against a standard of competence, instead of against other persons (norm-referenced tests).
It is not uncommon for a forty-hour workshop in the systematic
design of instruction to devote less than four hours to the topic of
test development—focusing primarily on item writing skills. With
such minimal training, how can we make and defend our assessment decisions?

Without an understanding of the basic principles of
test design, you can face difficult ethical, economic, or legal
problems. For these and other reasons, test development should
stand on an equal footing with instructional development—for
if it doesn't, how will you know whether your instructional

objectives were achieved and how will you convince anyone else that they were?

Criterion-Referenced Test Development translates complex testing technology into sound technical practice within the grasp of a non-specialist. And hence, one of the themes that we have woven into the book is that testing properly is often no more expensive and time-consuming than testing improperly. For example, we have been able to show how to create a defensible certification test for a forty-hour administrative training course using a test that takes fewer than fifteen minutes to administer and probably less than a half-day to create. It is no longer acceptable simply to write test items without regard to a defensible process. Specific knowledge of the strengths and limitations of both criterion-referenced and norm-referenced testing is required to address the information needs of the world today.

A CONFUSING STATE OF AFFAIRS

Grade schools, high schools, universities, and corporations share many similar reasons for not having adopted the techniques for creating sound criterion-referenced tests. We have found three reasons that seem to explain why those who might otherwise embrace the systematic process of test design have not: misleading familiarity, inaccessible information, and procedural confusion. In each instance, it seems that a little knowledge about testing has proven dangerous to the quality of the criterion-referenced test.

MISLEADING FAMILIARITY

As training professionals, few of us teach the way we were taught. However, most of us are still testing the way we were tested. Since every adult has taken many tests while in school, there is a mis-leading familiarity with them. There is a tendency to believe that everyone already knows how to write a test. This belief is an error, not only because exposure does not guarantee know-how, but because most of the tests to which we were exposed in school were poorly constructed. The exceptions—the well-constructed tests in our past—tend to be the group-administered standardized tests, for example, the Iowa Tests of Basic Skills or the SAT. Unfortunately for corporate trainers, these standardized tests are good examples of norm-referenced tests, not of criterion-referenced tests. Norm-referenced tests are designed for completely different purposes than criterion-referenced tests, and each is constructed and interpreted differently. Most teacher-made tests are "mongrels," having characteristics of both norm-referenced and criterion-referenced tests—to the detriment of both.

INACCESSIBLE TECHNOLOGY

Criterion-referenced testing technology is scarce in corporate training partly because the technology of creating these tests has been slow to develop. Even now with so much emphasis on minimal competency testing in the schools, the vast majority of college courses on tests and measurements are about the principles of creating norm-referenced tests. In other words, even if trainers want to "do the right thing," answers to important questions are hard to come by. Much of the information about criterion-referenced tests has appeared only in highly technical measurement journals. The technology to improve practice in this area just hasn't been accessible.

PROCEDURAL CONFUSION

A final pitfall in good criterion-referenced test development is that both norm-referenced tests and criterion-referenced tests share some of the same fundamental measurement concepts, such as reliability and validity. Test creators don't always seem to know how these concepts must be modified to be applied to the two different kinds of tests.

Recently, we saw an article in a respected corporate training publication that purported to detail all the steps necessary to establish the reliability of a test. The procedures that were described, however, will work only for norm-referenced tests. Since the article appeared in a training journal, we question the applicability of the information to the vast majority of testing that its readers will conduct. Because the author was the head of a training department, we had to appreciate his sensitivity to the value of a reliability estimate in the test development process, yet the article provided a clear illustration of procedural confusion in test development, even among those with some knowledge of basic testing concepts.

TESTING AND KIRKPATRICK'S LEVELS OF EVALUATION

In 1994 Donald Kirkpatrick presented a classification scheme for four levels of evaluation in business organizations that have permeated much of management's current thinking about evaluation. We want to review these and then share two observations. First, the four levels:

- Level 1, or Reaction evaluations, measure "how those who participate in the program react to it … I call it a measure of customer satisfaction" (p. 21).
- Level 2, or Learning evaluations, "can be defined as the extent to which participants change attitudes, improve knowledge, and/or increase skill as a result of attending the program" (p. 22). Criterion-referenced assessments of competence are the skill and knowledge assessments that typically take place at the end of training. They seek to measure whether desired competencies have been mastered and so typically measure against a specific set of course objectives.
- Level 3, or Behavior evaluations, "are defined as the extent to which change in behavior has occurred because the participant attended the training program" (p. 23). These evaluations are usually designed to assess the transfer of training from the classroom to the job.
- Level 4, or Results evaluation, is designed to determine "the final results that occurred because the participants attended the program" (p. 25). Typically, this level of evaluation is seen as an estimate of the return to the organization on its investment in training. In other words, what is the cost-benefit ratio to the organization from the use of training?

We would like to make two observations about criterion-referenced testing and this model. The first observation is:

- Level 2 evaluation of skills and knowledge is synonymous with the criterion-referenced testing process described in this book.

The second observation is more controversial, but supported by Kirkpatrick:

- You cannot do Level 3 and Level 4 evaluations until you have completed Level 2 evaluations.

Kirkpatrick argued:

> Some trainers are anxious to get to Level 3 or 4 right away because they think the first two aren't as important. Don't do it. Suppose, for example, that you evaluate at Level 3 and discover that little or no change in behavior has occurred. What conclusions can you draw? The first conclusion is probably that the training program was no good, and we had better discontinue it or at least modify it. This conclusion may be entirely wrong … the reason for no change in job behavior may be that the climate prevents it. Supervisors may have gone back to the job with the necessary knowledge, skills, and attitudes, but the boss wouldn't allow change to take place. Therefore, it is important to evaluate at Level 2 so you can determine whether the reason for no change in behavior was lack of learning or negative job climate. (p. 72)

Here's another perspective on this point, by way of an analogy:

> Suppose your company manufactures sheet metal. Your factory takes resources, processes the resources to produce the metal, shapes the metal, and then distributes the product to your customers. One day you begin to receive calls. "Hey," says one valued customer, "this metal doesn't work! Some sheets are too fat, some too thin, some just right! I'm never quite sure when they'll work on the job! What am I getting for my money?" "What?" you reply, "They ought to work! We regularly check with our workers, who are very good, and they all feel we do good work." "I don't care what they think," says the customer, "the stuff just doesn't work!"

Now, substitute the word "training" for "sheet metal" and we see the problem. Your company takes resources and produces training. Your trainees say that the training is good (Level 1—What did the learner think of the instruction?), but your customers report that what they are getting on the job doesn't match their needs (Level 3—What is taken from training and applied on the job?), and as a result, they wonder what their return on investment is (Level 4—What is the return on investment [ROI] from training?). Your company has a problem because the quality of the process, that is, training (Level 2—What did the learner learn from instruction?) has not been assessed; as a result, you really don't know what is going on during your processes. And now that you have evidence the product doesn't work, you have no idea where to begin to fix the problem. No viable manufacturer would allow its products to be shipped without making sure they met product specifications. But training is routinely completed without a valid and reliable measure of its outcomes. Supervisors ask about on-the-job relevance, managers wonder about the ROI from training, but neither question can be answered until the outcomes of training have been assessed. If you don't know what they learned in training, you can't tell what they transferred from training to the job and what its costs and benefits are! (Coscarelli & Shrock, 1996, p. 210)

In conclusion, we agree completely with Kirkpatrick when he wrote "Some trainers want to bypass Levels 1 and 2. ... This is a serious mistake" (p. 23).

CERTIFICATION IN THE CORPORATE WORLD

In the 1970s, few organizations offered certification programs, for example, the Chartered Life Underwriter (CLU), Certified Production and Inventory Management (CPIM). By the late 1990s certification had become, literally, a growth industry. Internal corporate certification programs proliferated and profession-wide certification testing had become a profit center for some companies, including Novell, Microsoft, and others. The Educational Testing Service opened its first for-profit center, the Chauncey Group, to concentrate on certification test development and human resources issues. Sylvan became known in the business world as the primary provider of computer-based, proctored, testing centers. There are many reasons why such an interest has developed. Thomas (1996) identifies seven elements and observes that the "theme underlying all of these elements is the need for accountability and communication, especially on a global basis" (p. 276). Because the business world remains market-driven, the classic academic definitions of terms related to testing have become blurred so that various terms in the field of certification have different meanings. While a tonsil is a tonsil is a tonsil in the medical world, certification may not mean the same thing to each member in a discussion. While in Chapter 6 we present a tactical way to think about certification program design (The Certification Suite), here we want to clarify a few terms that are often ill-defined or confused.

Certification "is a formal validation of knowledge or skill ... based on performance on a qualifying examination ... the goal is to produce results that are as dependable or more dependable than those that could be gained by direct observation (on the job)" (Drake Prometric, 1995, p. 2). Certification should provide "an objective and consistent method of measuring competence and ensuring the qualifications of technical professionals" (Microsoft, 1995, p. 3). Certification usually means measuring a person's competence against a given standard—a criterion-referenced test interpretation. The certification test seeks to measure an individual's performance in terms of specific skills the individual has demonstrated and without regard to the performance of other test-takers. There is no limit to the number of test-takers who can succeed on a criterion-referenced test—everyone who scores beyond a given level is judged a "master" of the competencies covered by the test. (The term "master" doesn't usually mean the rare individual who excels far beyond peers; the term simply means someone competent in the performance of the skills covered by the test.) "The intent of certification ... normally is to inform the public that individuals who have achieved certification have demonstrated a particular degree of knowledge and skill (and) is usually a voluntary process instituted by a nongovernmental agency" (Fabrey, 1996, p. 3).

Licensure, by contrast, "generally refers to the mandatory governmental requirement necessary to practice in a particular profession or occupation. Licensure implies both practice protection and title protection, in that only individuals who hold a license are permitted to practice and use a particular title" (Fabrey, 1996, p. 3). Licensure in the business world is rarely an issue in assessing employee competence but plays a major role in protecting society in areas of health care, teaching, law, and other professions.

Qualification is the assessment that a person understands the technology or processes of a system as it was designed or that he or she has a basic understanding of the system or process, but not to the level of certainty provided through certification testing. Qualification is the most problematic of the terms that are often used in business, and it is one we have seen develop primarily in the high-tech industries.

Qualification as a term has developed in many ways as a response to a problematic training situation. Customers (either internal or external to the business) demand that those sent for training be able to demonstrate competence on the job, while at the same time those doing the training and assessment have not been given a job task analysis that is specific to the organization's need. Thus, the trainers cannot in good conscience represent that the trainees who have passed the tests in training can perform back at the work site. So, for example, if a company develops a new high-tech cell phone switching system, the same system can be configured in a variety of ways by each of the various regional telephone companies that purchase the switch. Without a training program customized to each company, the switch developer will offer training only in the characteristics of the switching system, or perhaps its most common configurations. That training would then "qualify" the trainee to configure and work with the switch within the idiosyncratic constraints of the particular employer. As you can see, the term is founded more on the practical realities of technology development and contract negotiation than on formal assessment. Organizations that provide training that cannot be designed to match the job requirement are often best served by drawing the distinction between certification and qualification early on in the contract negotiation stage, thus clarifying either formal or informal expectations.

Corporate Testing Enters the New Millennium

By early 2000 certification had become less a growth industry and more a mature one. A number of the larger programs, for example, Hewlett-Packard and Microsoft, were well-established and operating on a stable basis. In-house certification programs did continue, but management more acutely examined the cost-benefit ratio for these programs. Meanwhile, in the United States the 2001 Federal act, No Child Left Behind, was signed into law and placed a new emphasis on school accountability for student learning progress. Interestingly, the discussion that was sparked by this act created a distinction in testing that was assimilated by both the academic and business communities and helped guide resource allocations. This concept is "often referred to as the *stakes* of the testing," according to the *Standards for Educational and Psychological Testing* (AERA/APA/NCME Joint Committee, 1999, p. 139), which described a classification of sorts for the outcomes of testing and the implied level of rigor associated with each type of test's design.

High Stakes Tests. A high stakes test is one in which "significant educational paths or choices of an individual are directly affected by test performance. ... Testing programs for institutions can have high stakes when aggregate performance of a sample or of the entire population of test-takers is used to infer the quality of service provided, and decisions are made about institutional status, rewards, or sanctions based on the test results" (AERA/APA/NCME Joint Committee, 1999, p. 139). While the definition of high stakes was intended for the public schools, it was easily translated into a corporate culture, where individual promotion, bonuses, or employment might all be tied to test performance or where entire departments, such as the training department, might be affected by test-taker performance.

Low Stakes Tests. At the other end of the continuum, the *Standards* defined low stakes tests as those that are "administered for informational purposes or for highly tentative judgments such as when test results provide feedback to students..." (p. 139).

These two ends of the continuum implied different levels of rigor and resources in test construction. This distinction was also indicated by the *Standards:*

The higher the stakes associated with a given test use, the more important it is that test-based inferences are supported with strong evidence of technical quality. In particular, when the stakes for an individual are high, and important decisions depend substantially on test performance, the test needs to exhibit higher standards of technical quality for its avowed purposes than might be expected of tests used for lower-stakes purposes ... Although it is never possible to achieve perfect accuracy in describing an individual's performance, efforts need to be made to minimize errors in esti-mating individual scores in classifying individuals in pass/fail or admit/reject categories. Further, enhancing validity for high-stakes purposes, whether individual or institutional, typically entails collecting sound collateral information both to assist in under-standing the factors that contributed to test results and to provide corroborating evidence that supports the inferences based on test results. (pp. 139–140)

What Is to Come ...

- In the following chapters, we will describe a systematic approach to the development of criterion-referenced tests. We recognize that not all tests are high-stakes tests, but the book does describe the steps you need to consider for developing a high-stakes criterion-referenced test. If your test doesn't need to meet that standard, you can then decide which steps can be skipped, adapted, or adopted to meet you own particular needs. To help you do this *Criterion Referenced Test Development* (CRTD) is divided into five main sections:

- In the Background, we provide a basic frame of reference for the entire test development process.

- The Overview provides a detailed description of the Criterion-Referenced Test Development Process (CRTD) using the model we have created and tested in our work with more than forty companies.

- Planning and Creating the Test describes how to proceed with the CRTD process using each of the thirteen steps in the model. Each step is explored as a separate chapter, and where appropriate, we have provided summary points that you may need to complete the CRTD documentation process.

- Legal Issues in Criterion-Referenced Testing is authored by Patricia Eyres, who is a practicing attorney in the field and deals with some of the important legal issues in the CRTD process.
- Our Epilogue is a reflection of our experiences with testing. In fact, those of you starting a testing program in an organization may wish to read this chapter first! When we first began our work in CRTD, we thought of the testing process as the last "box" in the Instructional Development process. We have since come to understand that testing, when done properly, will often have serious consequences to the organization. These can be highly beneficial if the process is supported and well managed. However, we now view effective CRT systems as not simply discrete assessment devices, but as systemic interventions.

Periodically, we have provided an opportunity for practice and feedback. You will find that many of the topics in the Background are reinforced by exercises with corresponding answers and that, throughout the book, opportunities to practice applying the most important or difficult concepts are similarly provided.

We are also including short sidebars from individuals and organizations associated with the world of CRT, when we feel they can help illustrate a point in the process. Interestingly, most of the sidebars reflect the two areas that have developed most rapidly since our last edition—computer-based testing and processes to reduce cheating on tests.

PART ONE

BACKGROUND: THE FUNDAMENTALS

CHAPTER ONE

TEST THEORY

WHAT IS TESTING?

There are four related terms that can be somewhat confusing at first: evaluation, assessment, measurement, and testing. These terms are sometimes used interchangeably; however, we think it is useful to make the following distinctions among them:

- *Testing* is the collection of quantitative (numerical) information about the degree to which a competence or ability is present in the test-taker. There are right and wrong answers to the items on a test, whether it be a test comprised of written questions or a performance test requiring the demonstration of a skill. A typical test question might be: "List the six steps in the selling process."
- *Measurement* is the collection of quantitative data to determine the degree of whatever is being measured. There may or may not be right and wrong answers. A measurement inventory such as the *Decision-Making Style Inventory* might be used to determine a preference for using a Systematic style versus a Spontaneous one in making a sale. One style is not "right" and the other "wrong"; the two styles are simply different.
- *Assessment* is systematic information gathering without necessarily making judgments of worth. It may involve the collection of

quantitative or qualitative (narrative) information. For example, by using a series of personality inventories and through interviewing, one might build a profile of "the aggressive salesperson." (Many companies use Assessment Centers as part of their management training and selection process. However, as the results from these centers are usually used to make judgments of worth, they are more properly classed as evaluation devices.)

• *Evaluation* is the process of making judgments regarding the appropriateness of some person, program, process, or product for a specific purpose. Evaluation may or may not involve testing, measurement, or assessment. Most informed judgments of worth, however, would likely require one or more of these data gathering processes. Evaluation decisions may be based on either quantitative or qualitative data; the type of data that is most useful depends entirely on the nature of the evaluation question. An example of an evaluation issue might be, "Does our training department serve the needs of the company?"

PRACTICE

Here are some statements related to these four concepts. See whether you can classify them as issues related to Testing, Measurement, Assessment, or Evaluation:

1. "She was able to install the air conditioner without error during the allotted time."

2. "Personality inventories indicate that our programmers tend to have higher extroversion scores than introversion."

3. "Does the pilot test process we use really tell us anything about how well our instruction works?"

4. "What types of tasks characterize the typical day of a submarine officer?"

FEEDBACK

1. Testing

2. Measurement

3. Evaluation

4. Assessment

WHAT DOES A TEST SCORE MEAN?

Suppose you had to take an important test. In fact, this test was so important that you had studied intensively for five weeks. Suppose then that, when you went to take the test, the temperature in the room was 45 degrees. After 20 minutes, all you could think of was getting out of the room, never mind taking the test. On the other hand, suppose you had to take a test for which you never studied. By chance a friend dropped by the morning of the test and showed you the answer key. In both situations, the score you receive on the test probably doesn't accurately reflect what you actually know. In the first instance, you may have known more than the test score showed, but the environment was so uncomfortable that you couldn't attend to the test. In the second instance, you probably knew less than the test score showed due now to another type of "environmental" influence.

In either instance, the score you received on the test (your observed score) was a combination of what you really knew (your true score) and those factors that modified your true score (error). The relationship of these score components is the basis for all test theory and is usually expressed by a simple equation:

$$X_o = X_t + X_e$$

where X_o is the observed score, X_t the true score and X_e the error component. It is very important to remember that in test theory "error" doesn't mean a wrong answer. It means the factor that accounts for any mismatch between a test-taker's actual level of knowledge (the true score) and the test score the person receives. Error can make a score higher (as we saw when your friend dropped by) or lower (when it got too cold to concentrate).

The primary purpose of a systematic approach to test design is to reduce the error component so that the observed score and the true score are as nearly identical as possible. All the procedures we will discuss and recommend in this book will be tied to a simple assumption: the primary purpose of test development is the reduction of error. We think of the results of test development like this:

$$X_o = X_t + x_e$$

where error has been reduced to the lowest possible level.

Realistically, there will always be some error in a test score, but careful attention to the principles of test development and administration will help reduce the error component.

PRACTICE

See if you can list at least three situations that could inflate a test-taker's score and three that could reduce the score:

Inflation Factors   **Reduction Factors**

1. Sees answer key   1. Room too cold
2. ——————   2. ——————
3. ——————   3. ——————
4. ——————   4. ——————

FEEDBACK

Inflation Factors   **Reduction Factors**

1. Sees answer key   1. Room too cold
2. Looks at someone's answers   2. Test scheduled too early
3. Unauthorized job aid used   3. Noisy heating system in room
4. Answers are cued in test   4. Can't read test directions

RELIABILITY AND VALIDITY: A PRIMER

Reliability and validity are the two most important characteristics of a test. Later on we will explore these topics and provide you with specific statistical techniques for determining these qualities in your tests. For now, we want to provide an overview so that you will see how these ideas serve as standards for our attempts to reduce error in testing.

RELIABILITY

Reliability is the consistency of test scores. There is no such thing as validity without reliability, so we want to begin with this idea.

There are three kinds of reliability that are typically considered in CRT construction:

- equivalence reliability
- test-retest reliability
- inter-rater reliability

Equivalence reliability is consistency of test scores between or among forms. There are several reasons why parallel forms of a test (different questions that measure the same competencies) might be desirable, for example, pretest/posttest comparisons. Equivalence reliability is a measure of the extent to which test-takers receive approximately the same scores on Form B of the test as they did on Form A. Forms that measure the same competencies and yield approximately the same scores are said to be "parallel." If each of your test-takers has the same score on Form B as he or she had on Form A, then you have perfect reliability. If there is no relationship between the test scores on the two forms, then you have a reliability estimate of zero.

Test-retest reliability is the consistency of test scores over time. In other words, did the test-takers receive approximately the same scores on the second administration of the test as they did on the first (assuming no practice or instruction occurred between the two administrations and the administrations were relatively close together)? If your test-takers have the same scores the second time they take the test as they had the first, then you have perfect reliability. Again, if there is no relationship between the test scores, then you have a reliability estimate of zero.

Inter-rater reliability is the measure of consistency among judges' ratings of a performance. If you have determined that a performance test is required, then you need to be sure that your judges (raters) are consistent in their assessments. In Olympic competition we expect that the judges' scores should not deviate significantly from each other. The degree to which they agree is the measure of inter-rater reliability. This agreement will also vary between perfect and zero.

VALIDITY

Validity has to do with whether or not a test measures what it is supposed to measure. A test can be consistent (reliable) but measure the wrong thing. For example, assume that we have designed a course to teach employees how to install a new telephone switchboard. We could devise an end-of-course test that asks learners to list all the steps for installing the new equipment. We might find that the learners can consistently list these steps, but that they can't install the switchboard, which was the intended goal of the course. Hence, our test is reliable, but not a valid measure for the installation task.

Figure 1.1 illustrates the relationship between reliability and validity. Let's consider that a marksman's job is to hit the center of a shooting target, i.e., the bulls-eye. In Figure 1.1a, the marksman has fired all of her shots in a tight group. Her shooting might be termed "reliable" because the shots are all in the same place, but her shooting isn't valid since she missed the bulls-eye.

FIGURE 1.1A.   RELIABLE, BUT NOT VALID.

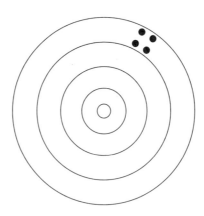

The marksman who produces Figure 1.1b is neither reliable, nor valid.

FIGURE 1.1B.   NEITHER RELIABLE NOR VALID.

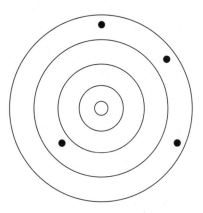

In Figure 1.1c the marksman's shots are both reliable and valid (she consistently hit the bulls-eye). Notice that it is not possible for the marksman's shots to be valid without also being reliable. Validity requires reliability. Hence, the truism that a test cannot be valid if it is not reliable.

FIGURE 1.1C.   RELIABLE AND VALID.

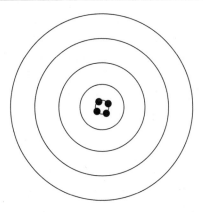

PRACTICE

1. "Bob, I don't know if this test should be considered a reliable measure of performance. What do you think?"

Person	Week 1 Score	Week 2 Score
Sid	89	90
Indrani	92	90
Atena	75	79
Pui Yi	65	68

2. "Lorie, here's the test you wanted to see. We selected the items to match the job descriptions for our participants. The test scores are highly reliable from one test administration to the next. Do you think this will work?"

FEEDBACK

1. The test appears to be reliable. The scores are very close between each administration. The time lapse of one week is probably a good choice. Waiting too long encourages forgetting or additional learning of the content; not waiting long enough allows pure memorization of the test items.

2. The test may well be valid. The items are linked to the job descriptions, which should increase the likelihood that the items are valid measures of expected performance. Furthermore, the test has demonstrated reliability, a prerequisite for validity. However, it would be impossible to know for sure whether the test were valid without running a job content study as described in Chapter 5.

As mentioned above, test reliability is a necessary but not sufficient condition for test validity. Establishing reliability assures consistency; establishing validity assures that the test consistently measures what it is supposed to measure. And while there are several measures of reliability (which we will discuss in Chapters 14 and 15), it is more important as you begin the CRTD process that you have a basic understanding of four types of validity:

- face validity
- content validity
- concurrent validity
- predictive validity

Of these four, only the latter three are typically assessed formally.

Face Validity. The concept of face validity is best understood from the perspective of the test-taker. A test has face validity if it *appears* to test-takers to measure what it is supposed to measure. For the purposes of defining face validity, the test-takers are not assumed to be content experts. The legitimate purpose of face validity is to win acceptance of the test among test-takers. This is not an unimportant consideration, especially for tests with significant and highly visible consequences for the test-taker. Test-takers who do not do well on tests that lack face validity may be more litigation prone than if the test appeared more valid.

In reality, criterion-referenced tests developed in accordance with the guidelines suggested in this book are not likely to lack face validity. If the objectives for the test are taken from the job or task analysis, and if the test items are then written to maximize their fidelity with the objectives, the test will almost surely have strong face validity. Norm-referenced tests that use test items selected primarily for their ability to separate test-takers, rather than items grounded in competency statements, are much more likely to have face validity problems.

It is important to note that, while face validity is a desirable test quality, it is not adequate to establish the test's true ability to measure what it is intended to measure. The other three types of validity are more substantive for that purpose.

Content Validity. A test possesses content validity when a group of recognized content experts or subject-matter experts has verified that the test measures what it is supposed to measure. Note the distinction between face validity and content validity; content validity is formally determined and reflects the judgments of experts in the content or competencies assessed by the test, whereas face validity is an impression of the test held among non-experts. *Content validity is the cornerstone of the CRTD process and is probably the most important form of validity in a legal defense.* Content validity is not determined through statistical procedures but through logical analysis of the job requirements and the direct mapping of those skills to a test. The detailed procedures for establishing content validity are found in Chapters 5, 6, and 9.

Concurrent Validity. Concurrent validity refers to the ability of a test to correctly classify masters and non-masters. This is, of course, what you *hope* every criterion-referenced test will do; however, face validation and even content validation do not actually demonstrate the test's ability to classify correctly. Concurrent validation is the technical process that allows you to evaluate the test's ability to distinguish between masters and non-masters of the assessed competencies. The process requires that subject-matter experts identify known masters and non-masters. The test is then administered to each group, and a statistic is calculated to determine that the test can separate these performers of known competence. Concurrent validity procedures are often difficult to apply in the corporate world, although we have seen them used relatively easily in the right circumstances. Chapter 14 lists the steps of this process.

Predictive Validity. Predictive validity is frequently confused with concurrent validity. There is an important conceptual distinction between the two and the procedures for calculating them. Whereas concurrent validity means that a test can correctly classify test-takers of currently known competence, predictive validity means that a test can accurately predict future competence. Predictive validity is important for many personnel selection devices that are used to choose persons for specific job responsibilities. Tests used to help persons select careers also require high predictive validity. In both of these cases, the test is taken first, while the demonstration of competence—job performance or successful career achievement—comes later; hence the term *predictive* validity. The procedures for calculating a test's predictive validity are also found in Chapter 14.

CONCLUDING COMMENT

As you begin the CRTD process, bear in mind the following observation and let it guide your choices: *An invalid test is not worth anything, to anybody, at any time, for any purpose.*

CHAPTER TWO

TYPES OF TESTS

CRITERION-REFERENCED VERSUS NORM-REFERENCED TESTS

There are two major philosophical differences in the interpretation of test scores: criterion-referenced versus norm-referenced interpretation. While some tests can be interpreted both ways, this is usually not the case. Tests should be constructed in order to facilitate either their criterion-referenced or their norm-referenced interpretation. Basically, norm-referenced tests need to be composed of items that will separate the scores of test-takers from one another, while criterion-referenced tests need to be composed of items based on specific objectives, or competency statements. To understand these differences in test interpretation it is helpful to understand frequency distributions (graphic representations of test scores).

FREQUENCY DISTRIBUTIONS

Figure 2.1 shows a frequency distribution for twenty-five people who have taken a test. The range of possible test scores is listed on the horizontal axis; the number of people who might obtain a given score is listed on the vertical axis. In this figure, five people

FIGURE 2.1. EXAMPLE FREQUENCY DISTRIBUTION.

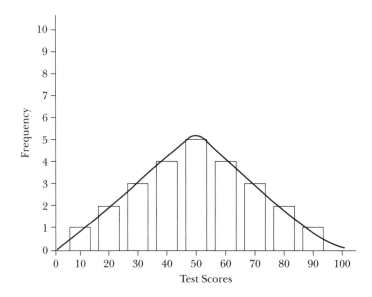

scored 50, two people scored 20 and 80, while nobody scored 100. These points are connected to create a smooth curve.

A norm-referenced test (NRT) interpretation defines the performance of test-takers in relation to one another. If you wanted to rank people to select the top performers, your ideal frequency distribution would look like Figure 2.2 because in this situation each test score was attained by only one person. The ranking of these test-takers would be easy because there are no tied ranks.

Now you will rarely have a test that separates everyone quite so perfectly. Instead, most NRTs will have distributions that look like Figure 2.3. Figure 2.3 is the classic shape of the NRT distribution; you may have heard it called the "bell curve" or "the normal distribution."

A normal distribution is what typically results from the administration of a NRT. Unlike our ideal in Figure 2.2, people will tend to cluster in the middle ranges. However, the scores still represent a wide spread, that is, the test scores have been successfully separated from one another. This spread of scores is ideal for NRT interpretation because it increases the confidence with which we can decide that one test-taker scored better than another. And the

FIGURE 2.2.   IDEAL NRT FREQUENCY DISTRIBUTION.

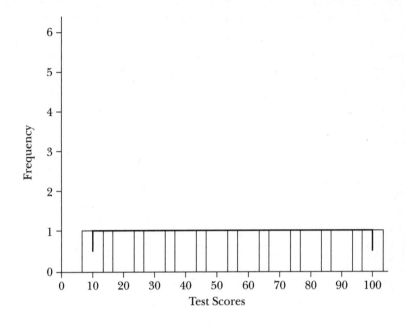

FIGURE 2.3.   THE NORMAL DISTRIBUTION.

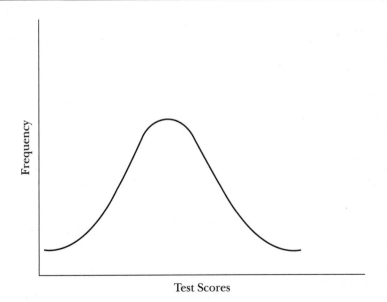

comparison of test-takers to one another is what NRT interpretation is all about.

Norm-referenced tests can be very useful. Medical schools use the Medical College Aptitude Test (MCAT) to help predict success in medical school. Because of the large number of people applying for medical school and the limited number of openings, medical schools have chosen to use the MCAT as one way of ensuring that the best students are admitted. (As a patient, you would probably prefer to know that only the best students are being admitted.) Norm-referenced tests are ideal for making this kind of selection decision, when we must choose the best test-takers among a group.

CRITERION-REFERENCED TEST INTERPRETATION

In contrast to NRTs, the criterion-referenced test (CRT) defines the performance of each test-taker without regard to the performance of others. Unlike the NRT, where success is defined in terms of being ahead of someone else, the CRT interpretation defines success as being able to perform a specific task or set of competencies. There is no limit to the number of people who can succeed on a criterion-referenced test, unlike the NRT. Very often the CRT frequency distribution looks like the one in Figure 2.4. This distribution is often called a mastery curve.

FIGURE 2.4.   MASTERY CURVE.

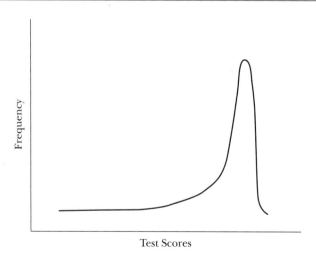

Test Scores

Unlike NRTs, the shape of the CRT distribution is not essential to its interpretation, since the scores are interpreted in terms of the competencies the scores represent rather than in terms of the scores' relationship to one another. The reason that a CRT frequency distribution often looks like Figure 2.4 is that the test items are based on specific competencies, and the instruction that the test-takers receive in anticipation of the test is usually addressed specifically to these competencies. Therefore, many test-takers do well on the CRT, resulting in a distribution with most test-takers clustered near the high end.

Criterion-referenced tests should be used whenever you are concerned with assessing a person's ability to demonstrate a specific skill. The medical boards licensing exam is an example of a test that is criterion-referenced. If you are being operated on, you should want to know that your surgeon is competent to perform the operation, not just that he or she is better than 90 percent of those who graduated. The reason is that merely knowing more than the others in the class doesn't guarantee that your surgeon can perform the operation; maybe nobody in the class mastered the operation. The danger of NRTs in corporate training situations is that, without reference to specific competencies, what test-takers can actually do is unverifiable.

PRACTICE

Here are four scenarios; decide which type of test—norm-referenced or criterion-referenced—is required for each one.

1. Many foreign countries administer tests as early as eighth grade to determine who among test-takers will be eligible to attend schools of different types, for example, vocational, engineering, medical, and so forth. Scores on these tests correlate with subsequent achievement in advanced classes. There is never enough space in each of the schools for all of the students who want to attend.

2. A number of years ago, England developed a national program called the Open University. By using television and textbooks keyed to objectives, anyone in the country is able to take instruction in his or her home that will

lead to a degree from the University. Students must master a given percentage of the objectives for the courses they take.

3. To be considered for a position as an Emergency Medical Technician, applicants must score at least 95 percent on each of ten major emergency procedures.

4. The city's sixth grade students from all schools were eligible to participate in a spelling bee; the winner would receive a $2000 savings bond for college. However, participants in this city-wide spelling bee would be selected by finishing among the top five in a spelling bee held at the students' individual schools.

FEEDBACK

1. Norm-referenced testing

2. Criterion-referenced testing

3. Criterion-referenced testing

4. Norm-referenced testing

SIX PURPOSES FOR TESTS IN TRAINING SETTINGS

Before we construct a CRT, we need to know what the purpose of our test will be in the instructional setting. There are six basic purposes for criterion-referenced tests in corporate training:

• *Prerequisite tests* are used to ensure that the learners have the background knowledge required for success in the course. If there are minimum skills required for the course, the prerequisite test is designed to assess mastery of these skills.
• *Entry tests* are used to identify skills taught in a course that the entering student may already possess. The entry test can be used to allow students to bypass a module of instruction, if the students demonstrate the skills covered in the module in advance.

This test can also be used to identify the range of skills the students have, beyond the prerequisite skills.

• *Diagnostic tests* are used to assess mastery of a group of related objectives in an instructional unit. Whereas entry and prerequisite tests are used before instruction, the diagnostic test will typically be used during instruction (when it is often called an embedded test) or as part of the posttest process to determine exactly where a learner is having difficulty.

• *Posttests* are administered after instruction to assess the test-taker's mastery of terminal objectives, that is, end-of-course objectives.

• *Equivalency tests* are used to determine whether a learner has already mastered the course's terminal objectives without going through instruction. These tests are used to determine if a test-taker can bypass—"test out of"—an entire course.

• *Certification tests* are usually voluntary processes "instituted by a nongovernmental agency in which individuals are recognized for advanced knowledge and skill" (Fabrey, 1996, p. 3). Certification tests are similar in design to equivalency tests, but usually exist independent of instruction. However, many businesses have also created and integrated certification procedures internal to the organization (Hale, 2000; Robertson, 1999).

You will find that the same questions often can appear on different types of tests. For example, items on the posttest can be the same as or similar to the items on the equivalency test. In fact, these tests are relative—a prerequisite test for one course could be a posttest for a previous course. These types of tests are determined by the purposes they serve (not by the text of the items they contain).

PRACTICE

Here are six quotes; determine which type of CRT would be recommended for each situation:

1. "Look, I already know this stuff. There is no need for me to travel to headquarters, lose time in the field that I can use for sales, and take some irrelevant class." _____

2. "I've got to teach a class of thirty people from all over. I have no idea who knows what." _____

3. "Well, you've been through five days of training; now let's see how you do." _____

4. "I think I have the general idea about how to install the switchboard, but there seems to be a couple of areas I can't quite do right." _____

5. "If I'm going to have thirty people in each of my classes, then we really need to make sure they have all the basic skills they will need to get through without always asking me for help." _____

6. "I have 230 resumes from all over the country in response to an information technology ad we placed. Everybody claims to be an expert in server installation. I wish I could be certain they really knew something without having to interview them all." _____

FEEDBACK

1. Equivalency	4. Diagnostic
2. Entry	5. Prerequisite
3. Posttest	6. Certification

THREE METHODS OF TEST CONSTRUCTION (ONE OF WHICH YOU SHOULD NEVER USE)

There are three basic methods for constructing a test: topic-based, statistically based, and objectives-based. You should never use the topic-based approach.

TOPIC-BASED TEST CONSTRUCTION

The topic-based approach is the way in which most tests are created. Almost all teacher education classes have recommended this strategy, and it is probably the only approach commonly used in most classrooms today. Essentially, the instructor takes a given number of questions from Chapter 3 or Topic 1, some number of questions from Chapter 4 or Topic 2, and so on, loosely basing the number of questions on the perceived importance of the topic. This practice is imprecise and certainly doesn't allow for criterion-referenced interpretation; usually the test score distribution is not widespread enough to allow for norm-referenced interpretation either. In other words, topic-based construction frequently will not separate test-takers as required for norm-referenced tests, nor will it verify specific competencies as does the CRT.

Statistically Based Test Construction

Norm-referenced tests are constructed using a statistically based method. This means that items are chosen for inclusion on the test because they have been shown to separate test-takers. There are item statistics that will indicate quite clearly which items can perform this separation. The SAT separates test-takers and can be used to predict some types of success in college. However, the SAT doesn't define specifically what is measured in the precise way required for criterion-referenced interpretation.

If you were constructing an NRT, you would look for items that separate people for whatever reason along the dimension of interest to you. Consider this: In one nationally recognized NRT, the test-taker is asked, "Who do you think was a better president—Washington or Lincoln?" If a test-taker chooses "Washington," the response will support his or her classification as "abnormal." This basis of classification has nothing to do with an objective criterion of being abnormal, that is, the item does not specify clinically abnormal behaviors against which the test-taker's behavior can be judged. Rather, the classification is warranted because people who have been classified as "abnormal" due to their verifiably abnormal behavior tend to select "Washington" over "Lincoln" when given this item. If the relationship between abnormal behavior and the preference for "Washington" is strong enough, preferring "Washington" (along with "abnormal" responses to other such items) is enough to make the classification. Finding a group of such items that separate people is the heart of NRT development. Since this book is about the creation of criterion-referenced tests, we will not discuss these statistically based item selection methods in great detail.

OBJECTIVES-BASED TEST CONSTRUCTION

In contrast to the NRT construction process, a CRT is based on items that assess a specific competency. Most corporate training philosophies specify an objectives-based system. After all, most airline companies, and passengers, want to know that the pilot can land the plane, not just that she was better than everyone else in the class. Look at Figure 2.5.

FIGURE 2.5. EXAMPLE OF AN OBJECTIVE WITH CORRESPONDING TEST ITEM.

Objective: Given a selection of previously unseen geometric figures, the student will identify a triangle.

Test: Which of the following is a triangle?

Notice how the test item follows directly from the behavior specified in the objective. With the "Washington/Lincoln" example item above, the test item doesn't logically follow from any known description of clinically abnormal behavior. To sum up the process of test construction and interpretation, avoid topic-based test construction, use a statistically based approach to develop NRTs, and use an objectives-based approach to develop CRTs.

PRACTICE

Here are three scenarios. Read each and classify it according to the test construction process each describes.

1. "The new switching system is critical to our success with this project. We can't afford to have any errors with its installation. We need to make absolutely certain that our trainees can perform this task quickly and flawlessly."

2. "We have a lot of candidates for the position of shuttle pilot. Before investing in the expensive training of those few who will become pilots, we need to select carefully those with strong general analytical abilities."

3. "Let's see, we've covered a lot of territory in the workshop. I thought the stuff on management styles was well done, so I'll put about five questions on that, another three or four might go to performance appraisal techniques...."

FEEDBACK

1. Objectives-based, criterion-referenced test construction.

2. Statistically based, norm-referenced test construction.

3. Topic-based test construction.

PART TWO

OVERVIEW: THE CRTD MODEL AND PROCESSES

CHAPTER THREE

THE CRTD MODEL AND PROCESS

RELATIONSHIP TO THE INSTRUCTIONAL DESIGN PROCESS

The process for the systematic design of instruction has become well established in most corporate training programs. Even if not always implemented, there is a common awareness that effective instruction usually follows from a process that considers the nature of the content, the context, and the learner in applying the principles of learning theory and evaluating outcomes. However, companies (and graduate programs) most often concentrate on the creation of training and relegate the testing and evaluation components to a superficial effort. For these organizations, testing is seen as just a box in the instructional design process—one that isn't necessarily needed or attended to once the deliverable of instruction has been completed. We find this a disturbing situation for professional practice. One can hardly imagine a physician prescribing a treatment and not evaluating its effectiveness or an investor committing millions of dollars to a new strategy without assessing the outcome of the investment. Yet companies routinely invest large amounts to train and educate people without taking the time to assess the outcomes of training at its most basic level: Did the learner's learn? It has been our experience that this omission is unnecessary.

The systematic design of instruction is a process that is no more complex (nor simple) than the systematic design of tests. The practice of testing is easily within the grasp of professionals who are conversant with instructional design processes. The CRTD process is not about complex statistical calculations, but rather about analytical thinking. Good tests can be developed in a nearly seamless manner along with the development of instruction. Good testing takes very little additional time and resources when you understand how it is done. In many instances, training professionals feel it may double the development process time and costs; it won't. Our experience has been that good, basic test development can be integrated into the ID process and may add no more than 10 percent to the timelines and resource requirements. Of course, other factors such as legal concerns or computer-based testing strategies will add to the cost and complexity of a testing project though the return attributed to such factors may easily be justified in some circumstances.

SIDEBAR: THE STAKES OF AN ASSESSMENT

THE CRTD PROCESS

Before examining how assessments can most effectively be used in the learning process, it's important to understand that not only is there more than one kind of assessment but they can be categorized in terms of the stakes involved in taking the test. These stakes are identified as:

- High

- Medium

- Low

The level of an assessment's stakes refers to the consequences to the candidate. For example, an exam normally has a higher consequence, while a survey has low or even no consequence.

In low-stakes assessments, such as quizzes and surveys, the consequences to the candidate are low, and so the legal liabilities are low. These low-stakes assessments are often taken alone, since there isn't any motivation to cheat or share answers with others. Therefore, proctoring or invigilating is not required. This means that test administrators wouldn't normally check the ID or watch someone taking a low-stakes assessment, whereas with a high-stakes exam, they would.

The requirement for validity and reliability is low for a quiz or a survey, but a high-stakes test must be reliable and valid. These higher-stakes assessments require more planning. The general rule for a test or exam is that in a work setting they should look like the job; at an academic institution the test or exam should look like the curriculum.

Very little planning goes on with regard to a low-stakes assessment. Subject-matter experts (SMEs) simply write the questions and make them available to students. However, a high-stakes test requires a great deal of planning, such as job task analysis, setting the pass/fail scores, specifying the methods and consistency of delivery required, and how results will be stored and distributed. Job task analysis discovers what tasks are associated with the job, how often they are completed, and how important they are to the job. Test developers plan which questions should be in the test by topic, which subjects are more important, which have less importance, and the depth of competency required. The pass/fail score or cut score determines the threshold between passing and failing.

Finally, in a high-stakes assessment psychometricians will analyze the resulting statistics and provide guidance on how to improve the wording of questions, the wording of choices, or how to improve the overall test. In a low-stakes one, however, it's rare to involve psychometricians.

Factors Determining the Stakes of an Assessment

The stakes of an assessment also determine a number of other factors, from the overall consequences to the validity of the test itself.

	Low	**Medium**	**High**
Consequences	Few	Some	Major
Decisions	Few and easily reversed	Can be reversed	Very difficult to reverse
Options for participant	Refine studies	Pass, fail, or work harder	Pass or fail
Motivation to cheat?	Low	Medium	High
ID individual	Not important	Maybe important	Very important
Proctoring required	No	Sometimes	Always and constant
Development effort	Minor	Medium	Major
Check reliability and validity	Rarely	SME	Psychometrician

As you can see in the chart above, the consequences of different types of assessments vary. A high-stakes exam might determine whether or not a person is hired or fired or will graduate from college. As would be expected, decisions in response to low-stakes tests are few and easily reversed. If someone receives a poor score on a quiz, he or she can very easily appeal it, but if he or she receives a failing score on a nursing certification exam, appealing it would be very difficult, if not impossible. The options for the participant vary in direct relation to the stakes.

Obviously, on a survey there's no motivation to cheat, and on a low-stakes quiz very little. Quizzes are really learning aids, so a person would only be cheating him- or herself. However, on a nursing, architectural, or engineering exam, the stakes are much higher, so there certainly is a motivation to cheat. As a direct consequence, it becomes more important to identify each test-taker. In fact, for high-stakes tests related to national security, such as for the CIA or the military, these organizations might use biometric screening, such as retinal scans, to ensure that test-takers are who they say they are.

Obviously, if there's a low motivation to cheat, there's no need to proctor an assessment, but if there's a high motivation to cheat, then there should be constant and continuous proctoring.

THE COSTS OF ASSESSMENT STAKES

The development effort for a quiz is quite minor. Not so for medium- and high-stakes assessments. A rule of thumb for a medium-stakes test is that the average subject-matter expert will develop three questions an hour, and of those, one will go into the test. High-stakes questions take far more time to develop. The average cost of a high-stakes question, by the time an SME develops a question and it is put into a high-stakes exam, is between $500 and $1,500—each! It's important, when the stakes are high, to make sure that each question resonates with the whole test, that it's valid, and that good, more knowledgeable candidates tend to get it right, while poor, less knowledgeable candidates tend to get it wrong. Consequently, it takes time, effort, and thought to get the right mix of questions into a high-stakes test or exam.

EXCERPTS FROM THE QUESTION*MARK* WHITE PAPER

ASSESSMENTS THROUGH THE LEARNING PROCESS

Question*mark* provides testing and assessment software for creating, administering, and reporting on surveys, quizzes, tests, and exams. Question*mark* CEO Eric Shepherd has advised corporations, government departments, universities, and schools on the deployment of computerized assessments. Janet Godwin, Dr. William Coscarelli, Dr. Sharon Shrock, and Dr. Will Thalheimer, president of Work-Learning Research, assisted with this paper.

THE CRTD PROCESS

For all the reasons we discussed earlier, many organizations are now turning to testing as a means to identifying and verifying competence. In the past, organizations may have been willing to assume that their tests were reliable and valid when, in reality, they were not. For professional and legal reasons, organizations are now rethinking these assumptions. Where once companies could accept token attempts at assessment, they now look for professional practice in testing. Simply writing tests that look like the tests everyone had in school is not a substitute for designing and developing tests that match real jobs. In this chapter we will provide an overview of the model we have created and seen used in developing tests that are linked to job content and performance as well as to a curriculum plan.

There is a systematic, although rarely documented, process for designing certification tests. We have identified thirteen major steps that are often used in the process (Shrock & Coscarelli, 1998, p. 279) and in this section we will provide an overview of the process. Figure 3.1 shows these steps. As you review the figure, you will see that the steps that are common to both cognitive and performance tests are in the middle row of the model. The steps on the top address issues primarily associated with cognitive testing. The steps immediately below are primarily for performance tests. And the role of documentation is shown to apply to all steps.

PLAN DOCUMENTATION

You must plan to document the test development process. Documentation becomes a special concern with testing because of its potential to precipitate internal and external disputes, for example, lawsuits, grievances, and so forth. Documenting the entire test development process is essential, especially from a legal point of view. You could have perfectly valid measurement instruments, the reported scores appropriate for the job skills assessed, but if you did not document the process you followed to ensure that validity, you have nothing with which to put together a legal defense of the test. You can create specific forms to match each of the stages we describe or summarize each in a memo; either way, the information should be complete and contemporaneous.

ANALYZE JOB CONTENT

The most important part of the CRTD process is establishing content validity, ensuring that the test items match the job.

FIGURE 3.1. DESIGNING CRITERION-REFERENCED TESTS.

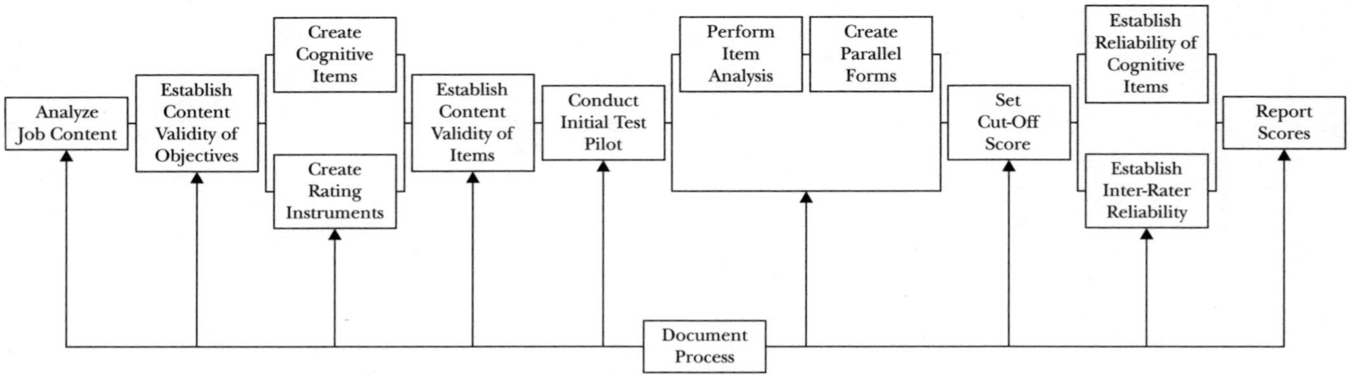

Content validation is a process that formally determines and reflects the judgments of experts regarding the content or competencies assessed by your test. Content validity demonstrates a logical link between the test items and job skills. Completing this validation process is a fundamental step in building a legal defense for reporting certification results. To accomplish this goal, you will identify subject-matter experts for the content to be tested. Then, in the formal process, the experts will be asked to review what is expected of the employee on the job and identify the range of duties and tasks that might be encountered.

ESTABLISH CONTENT VALIDITY OF OBJECTIVES

With the judges identified, and having completed a job task analysis, the tasks selected for instruction are converted into instructional objectives, if tests are being developed in conjunction with a curriculum plan. Terminal and enabling objectives are usually described and often organized in a hierarchy. It makes no difference who creates the objectives (the test developer, the instructional developer, or the subject-matter expert); what does matter is that the experts review the objectives and formally record their concurrence that the objectives match job competencies.

Note: If a test is being developed, such as a certification exam offered by an independent agency, with no anticipated course design, then the entire step "Establish Content Validity of Objectives" would be skipped, as there would be no instructional objectives to examine.

CREATE ITEMS

Once the objectives are written, the test items themselves must be developed and reviewed for concurrence. Test items are often divided into two categories (although in many high tech-fields the distinctions are blurring): cognitive items for assessing primarily intellectual knowledge and rating instruments for assessing behaviors or products.

Create Cognitive Items

We refer to the items that were commonly known as "paper-and-pencil" items as "cognitive items" because frequently they are no longer administered on paper. The process for creating these items for computer-based testing is essentially the same as for paper administration, unless you are considering computer adaptive testing—a system that most companies don't use because of its complexity. (Computer adaptive testing systems seek to determine test scores with a minimum number of items by using statistical probabilities. They work best for stable content areas with large numbers of test-takers, such as the Graduate Record Exam. We rarely recommend such systems for corporate training assessment.) Relying on the validated objectives for guidance, the cognitive items are written. With the items created, the experts must then formally concur that there is a match between the objectives and the items.

Create Rating Instruments

Performance tests always involve the rating of a behavior or product. A valid performance test is based on a detailed and thorough analysis of the skills needed to perform the job or the characteristics of a completed product. We generally recommend the use of checklists as the most reliable type of rating instrument. The subject-matter experts review the checklists, as they did the cognitive items, to determine their fidelity to the objectives.

ESTABLISH CONTENT VALIDITY OF ITEMS AND INSTRUMENTS

Whether creating a test with a curriculum plan or a certification exam that would not have a matched course plan, the subject-matter experts review all cognitive items and performance-rating instruments in light of the job task analysis. Consensus among the judges that the items and instruments match the job competencies must be reached and documented.

CONDUCT INITIAL TEST PILOT

Just as instructional designers allow for a time to try out an initial course design to gauge its effectiveness, test designers need to conduct a test of the test as well. Piloting a test has two purposes: (1) to find the major flaws in the test or the testing system and (2) to begin to establish the statistical validation of the test. With careful planning, both purposes can be accomplished at the same time, although often the first phase is conducted with smaller numbers that mirror the typical class size.

The effort devoted to the second phase varies depending on the criticality of the test and the demand for precision in testing. The more critical the test or the larger the scope of an item bank, the greater the need for large numbers of test-takers to establish the test's statistical credentials. A well-designed second phase of the initial test pilot will significantly increase the quality of the item analysis data that is needed in the next step.

PERFORM ITEM ANALYSIS

The data most corporate test designers need to collect for cognitive tests are gathered from three measures: (1) the difficulty index, (2) the distractor pattern, and (3) the point-biserial correlation. In this stage you will need to have a larger sample of test-takers—at least fifty to one hundred test-takers. This process is part of the item analysis procedure and must be completed to help assure that the test will function as designed.

Difficulty Index. This statistic is simply a measure of the number of people who answered a given item correctly. It really should be called the "easy index" because it indicates how many test-takers got the item correct. This statistic is usually expressed as a decimal; for example, .80 means that 80 percent of the people taking the test answered the item correctly. The difficulty can range from .00 (nobody got the item right) to 1.00 (everyone got the item right).

Distractor Pattern. The distractor pattern is used in conjunction with the difficulty index. In this assessment you look at the test-takers' responses to your distractors. If test-takers consistently eliminate an incorrect choice as wrong, your distractor may be too easy. If this happens, you have changed the odds of guessing the correct answer and thus introduced error into the test.

Point-Biserial. The point-biserial is the most sophisticated technique of the three for analyzing a test item's value. A point-biserial correlation really requires computer support. It is, however, a very powerful tool that easily allows you to identify items that test-takers with the highest scores consistently missed and that low scoring test-takers consistently got right. Such items are generally poorly written and require modification.

CREATE PARALLEL FORMS OR ITEM BANKS

Parallel forms of a given test are different versions of the test that measure the same objectives and yield similar test results. This means that parallel forms of a test are composed of different items but have the same number of items covering each of the same objectives; the items are of the same difficulty and have similar discrimination power (similar point-biserial coefficients); and all forms have similar mean (average) scores and yield similar master/non-master classification results. The main reason for creating parallel forms of a test is test security. If the security of a test is breached, the loose or circulated form can be destroyed and a parallel form put into service.

The concept of parallel forms applies directly to the creation of computerized item banks. Each test generated by the computer should be equivalent. However, the most common error in the use of item banks in corporate testing is to simply select items on a random basis from a pool of items. Simple random item selection does not guarantee that the different tests will have the same difficulty, similar discrimination, and similar means yielding similar master/nonmaster decisions. In this case, the entire testing process may be invalid.

ESTABLISH CUT-OFF SCORES

One of the most difficult, yet important, tasks required of CRTD is determining the standard for passing, that is, the cut-off score which separates masters from non-masters. With the final test item selection complete (including the elements on the performance instruments), the cut-off to determine mastery can be established. There are several techniques available, but three are typically identified. These can be used individually or, even better, in conjunction with each other. The techniques are: (1) Informed Judgment, (2) the Angoff Approach, and (3) Contrasting Groups. Regardless of which procedure you choose to determine the cut-off score, human judgment will enter the process at some point. Although some of the procedures available are highly quantified, one should not be deluded into believing that the numbers somehow replace the judgment process. There is no formula for determining the cut-off score that eliminates the sticky business of trying to achieve consensus among human beings. This point will become clearer as we discuss the various standard-setting procedures.

Informed Judgment. This process systematically solicits the opinions of stakeholders—for example, supervisors, employees, customers, and others—in setting the score. It asks each group to review the test and identify a cut-off score. However, the process is best used when performance data are also included in the review, such as average scores of incumbents, newly trained personnel, and so forth.

Angoff. This technique, named after its creator, is one of a class of techniques called conjectural methods. These are based on professional conjecture by subject-matter experts who review each item on the test and assign a probability estimate that a minimally competent master will succeed on the item. The Angoff is one of the most practical of the standard-setting techniques and is widely used.

Contrasting Groups. This approach is probably the strongest technique of the three because of its use of performance data; however, it is also logistically more difficult because it requires the identification of known masters and nonmasters by subject-matter experts and a relatively large sample size of each. Both groups are given the test and their scores plotted. A cut-off score can be established at the intersection of the usually overlapping distributions with some adjustment up or down made in light of the consequences of misclassifying masters and non-masters.

DETERMINE RELIABILITY

Once a cut-off score has been determined, you have the information to determine the consistency of the master/nonmaster decisions made possible by your test. This process will be different for cognitive and performance tests.

Determine Reliability of Cognitive Tests

Reliability for paper-and-pencil or computer-delivered tests can be thought of as the consistency of master/non-master decisions yielded by parallel forms of a test (equivalence reliability) or as the consistency over time of the master/non-master decisions that you make based on a single test (test-retest reliability) or a combination of both of these types of reliability. It is important to note that the establishment of test reliability is a time-consuming, and therefore expensive, quantitative process. While important and useful, for the creation of criterion-referenced tests a formal calculation of reliability should not be considered an absolutely essential step like the establishment of content validity. Formal reliability calculation should be addressed for tests that affect large numbers of test-takers or that assess critical objectives.

The reliability of a test is usually expressed as a number called the reliability coefficient. For criterion-referenced tests, one of the most commonly recommended statistics in this process is the correlation coefficient Phi. Perfect consistency would result in a phi coefficient of +1.00. Under no circumstances should tests with coefficients below +.50 be considered reliable tests. **Note:** Unlike norm-referenced tests, we do not typically establish the reliability of criterion-referenced tests with a single test administration. It can be done, although we do not recommend doing so with high-stakes tests.

Equivalence Reliability. To determine equivalence reliability, the same group of test-takers is asked to take two or more versions of the same test. Equivalence reliability for two parallel "paper-and-pencil" tests is a relatively straightforward procedure. Each person takes the different forms of the test, and the scores are correlated. Ideally, the test-taker should achieve about the same score on each test. For computer-based testing with item banks, the concept is the same, but the process is somewhat more complicated, as the possible range of items that can be drawn will affect the possible number of equivalent test forms.

Test-Retest Reliability. To determine test score consistency over time, a sample of test-takers will take the test twice. Two test administrations are scheduled somewhat closely together in time—between two and five days apart. Test-takers are not supplied with any additional instruction pertinent to the objectives during the time between the test administrations. Test-retest procedures are usually cumbersome and difficult to apply in the corporate world, so this approach is rarely seen. Because learning is vulnerable to both forgetting and additional learning, cognitive test score reliability over time becomes problematic. You are more likely to see this kind of reliability calculated for attitude or personality measures that are more stable over time.

Determine Reliability of Performance Tests

Raters and the instruments they use are the focus for establishing that you have consistent and accurate ratings of a performance. Because reliability is a prerequisite for validity, if the judges are inconsistent, their decisions cannot be valid. The reliability and validity problems associated with performance tests differ from those associated with cognitive tests because the test-taker's behavior must be rated by an observer. Therefore, you must be concerned about the consistency of the test-taker's performance as well as reliability and validity of the judges' observations and quality of the rating instrument.

To establish inter-rater reliability you will most likely need to first train the raters and then measure their consistency. Training the raters is a surprisingly easy task for most organizations due to the common, but often unstated, expectations of the company's culture. This entire process of training the raters and documenting their reliability either through a percent of agreement or through a Phi calculation can often be completed in less than a day. Remember though, you are establishing the reliability of the rater and the rating instrument in tandem. The rating instrument by itself cannot be considered reliable in the sense that a paper-and-pencil test can be.

REPORT SCORES

Only after these steps have been completed can a reliable and valid test score be reported. However, it is important to remember that the only legitimate score to report is "master" or "non-master." There is often strong pressure from managers within the organization to report raw scores (or some variant), but such reporting confuses criterion-referenced testing with norm-referenced testing. CRTs are designed to measure specific competencies and to sort test-takers into two classifications, that is, masters and non-masters. These tests are not designed to separate test-takers reliably into gradations of master or levels of non-master. In other words, these tests (unlike norm-referenced tests) are not designed to separate and compare test-takers to one another. Therefore, it is inappropriate to compare masters against one another or non-masters against one another based on their scores on a criterion-referenced education test, especially if the scores are close together.

SUMMARY

As we said when we introduced the model in 1998, the process of creating criterion-referenced tests "is a systematic one, based on the foundation of job performance. While it may appear to be a complicated one, it is not. Nor is it necessarily a time-consuming one. With experience, the test design and course design process progress smoothly together, requiring relatively few additional resources or time demands" (Shrock & Coscarelli, 1998, p. 293).

PART THREE

THE CRTD PROCESS: PLANNING AND CREATING THE TEST

CHAPTER FOUR

PLAN DOCUMENTATION

Why Document?
What to Document
The Documentation

WHY DOCUMENT?

Patricia Eyres (1997, pp. 6–19) lists ten of the most common legal problems for trainers, consultants, and speakers. Of these ten, number nine, "You find your documentation is ineffective or nonexistent" (p. 17), is particularly important to the test developer. As she observes:

> In any legal dispute … the decision maker must make several determinations: what happened, who was injured or damaged, how it occurred, who is responsible, and what penalties or damages should be assessed. As in most conflicts, memories fail, recollections differ, and stories definitely change. To reach a reasonable conclusion on the issues, the agency representative or civil jurors must ultimately determine whose recollections are most credible. The existence of effective, accurate, and consistent documentation helps immeasurably. Conversely, the absence of documentation can destroy even the best technical defense.

> Documentation is a written record of an event, discussion, or observation by one or more individuals. … Any written information, whether formally or informally generated can be considered documentary evidence if it is pertinent to a legal action or regulatory

proceeding. Why is documentation so important? Simply because a written record of events is the best evidence of what actually occurred ... a common thread throughout the reported cases in all aspects of training liabilities reveals that the absence of documentation hinders an effective defense, *even when the facts would otherwise support your position.* (pp. 17–18)

To that, we would add these words from *The Uniform Guidelines on Employee Selection Procedures* (1979), "Validation studies begun on the eve of litigation have seldom been found to be adequate" (p. 12,002).

SIDEBAR: USING ASSESSMENTS FOR COMPLIANCE

Although assessments are not always required to prove compliance, they are often used as part of an effective compliance strategy. Assessments offer an excellent way to identify knowledge gaps, measure learning, and help individuals master the material they need to learn in order to perform successfully on the job.

This paper explains how computerized or online assessments can play a vital role in helping organizations ensure that personnel understand what is required of them with regard to compliance. It also demonstrates how such assessments can help organizations move beyond compliance to improve organizational performance.

THE GROWING ROLE OF COMPLIANCE

The past few years have brought an ever-increasing number of compliance requirements and more intensive scrutiny of business activities. In response, organizations in a broad array of sectors are increasingly compelled to design and implement defensible compliance strategies. A common thread found in many such initiatives includes the collection and processing of data to document compliance efforts that ensure—often through extensive training—their employees' practices are keeping within industry and/or governmental requirements. In many cases, it is no longer sufficient for employees to understand processes and procedures; employers must be able to document and demonstrate this comprehension as well.

Keeping pace with compliance requires investment, but non-compliance is far more costly. A growing risk of negative publicity, fines, and costly litigation resulting from failure to comply with government regulations is driving organizations to establish credible, comprehensive, and defensible policies and procedures for compliance and to document them accurately.

COMPLIANCE AFFECTS EVERYONE

Compliance affects virtually every enterprise in one way or another. Organizations must comply with diversity and harassment regulations, safety procedures, and financial regulations. Globally, anti-terrorism legislation and international banking practices aimed at stemming money laundering have been widely reported and drive many compliance efforts. Yet for many businesses, compliance with less publicized, comparatively mundane requirements—whether local, national, or international—can be just as critical and costly.

In the United States, business headlines have been dominated by the impact of regulations stemming from recent legislation such as Sarbanes-Oxley, the Health Insurance Portability and Accountability Act (HIPAA), and the Patriot Act. However, the headline grabbers often comprise only a sliver of the compliance initiatives mandated by federal regulatory bodies within the U.S. federal government such as the Occupational Safety and Health Administration (OSHA), the Securities and Exchange Commission (SEC), the Environmental Protection Agency (EPA), the Food and Drug Administration (FDA), the Department of Transportation (DOT), the Nuclear Regulatory Commission (NRC), and many more. In addition to federal guidelines, a myriad of state and local requirements also contribute to the scope and complexity of compliance demands.

An array of regulations and regulatory bodies exist in countries around the world, such as the United Kingdom's Financial Services Authority (FSA) and the Australian Securities and Investment Commission (ASIC) or the Occupational Health and Safety Act (OHSA) in South Africa. Some regulations can span the globe. For instance, the International Conference on Harmonization of Technical Requirements (ICH) has been working to blend the approval process for new pharmaceutical drugs from Europe, the United States, and Japan into one set of standards.

Compliance initiatives can involve many individuals and departments: the training department, HR, safety, compliance officer, risk management, corporate governance, legal teams, and sometimes, outside consultants. Training and compliance departments often work hand-in-hand with government regulatory bodies in designing their compliance training and assessments. Some of the most effective compliance strategies seek to do more than merely obey the letter of the law; they use compliance training as code of conduct education, seeking to establish extremely high standards of ethics that reflect the organization's sense of good corporate citizenship.

How Assessments Can Help

The process of compliance involves aligning operations to be predictable, consistent, and validated. By implementing and maintaining an assessment management system, an organization can accurately track and report the state of compliance and respond promptly to requests for compliance audits.

Here are some specific ways in which assessments can play a critical role in a comprehensive compliance program:

- identify and remediate knowledge gaps
- measure knowledge gained from compliance training
- analyze results in order to improve future training
- document employees' mastery of required knowledge
- create an effective and accurate audit trail
- reinforce learning and knowledge
- provide opportunities for self-assessment
- deliver practice assessments

What Types of Assessment Should Be Used

Depending on the situation, assessments used in connection with compliance are generally summative or formative assessments, as highlighted in the table below.

PURPOSE	ASSESSMENT TYPE	ASSESSMENT USE	ASSESSMENT STAKES
Measure knowledge and skills for issuing certifications	Exam	Summative	Medium, High
Confirming knowledge and skills are sufficient	Test	Diagnostic	Low, Medium
Practice memory recall	Quiz	Formative	Low
Confirm that you are providing the right environment	Survey	Course evaluations	Low
Determine certification and learning requirements	Survey	Needs analysis	Low
Skill surveys to determine learning and certification requirements	Survey	Diagnostic	Low
Employee satisfaction surveys to confirm working environment is appropriate	Survey	Reaction	Low

MANAGING COMPLIANCE ASSESSMENTS

A good assessment management system should offer the following capabilities that will make it a practical answer for organizations that need to test employees on a wide variety of subjects.

- workflow management that allows organizations to define and enforce processes and rules to control the development and deployment of questions. This feature also helps create an audit trail essential for legally defensible high-stakes exams.

- on-demand reports that can be viewed by an unlimited number of administrators

- coaching reports that can be viewed by participants to understand what they have missed and where they need to focus future study. They can see detailed information, including the answers and scores for each question.

- item analysis reports that help administrators identify which questions are most effective and which need to be modified or retired.

- a question statistics report that provides an analysis of scores and outcomes for questions about a given topic, including the difficulty and correlation between questions.

- in high-stakes situations, a security system that can be used to prevent the test-taker from printing questions, using the right-click on the mouse, saving the HTML, viewing the source, opening new applications, switching tasks, or accidentally exiting an assessment in a proctored environment.

- assessment results safely stored within a central repository, serving as a system to simplify any inspection process

- randomized assessments that can be created from item banks to give employees multiple and varied questions on the same subject

- the delivery of assessments that present scenarios simulating real-world working situations; these require that an employee apply what he or she has learned instead of just memorizing facts

- storing results centrally, giving geographically dispersed workforces a clear view of what people know and areas in which interventions are required

- if an employee fails an assessment, use of the data gathered to channel the person into an appropriate training program that addresses knowledge deficits

Organizations that must demonstrate compliance can use computerized assessments to help boost employees' learning and knowledge and to demonstrate that employees have mastered required topics.

Question*mark* provides testing and assessment software that enables educators and trainers to create, securely administer and report on surveys, quizzes, tests, and exams. Businesses, governments, awarding bodies, schools, colleges and universities in fifty countries use the Question*mark*™ Perception™ assessment management system. Question*mark* provides extensive online learning resources for anyone interested in assessment best practices.

WHAT TO DOCUMENT

Nearly every organization with which we have worked has espoused differing opinions about what steps in the test creation process, if any, need to be documented. Our first piece of advice, then, is to check with your own legal department if you are beginning a test development process that may have an employment effect on an individual test-taker, such as hire-fire, promote-don't promote, etc. Keep in mind, too, that most legal and human resources staffs are probably unfamiliar with criterion-referenced test assumptions. If they have had any training in test development at all, it is almost certainly only in norm-referenced testing procedures. Make sure all staff involved in the documentation discussion have a common understanding of the purpose of the test and the underlying assumptions of the two testing models—using norm-referenced techniques on a criterion-referenced test will prove meaningless at best, but likely lead to misleading and misguided testing outcomes that will prove detrimental to all.

If you are beginning the test development and documentation process, we think you should review both *Certification: A NOCA Handbook* (Browning, Bugbee, & Mullins, 2006) and *The Legal Handbook for Trainers, Speakers and Consultants* (Eyres, 1997)—particularly pages 430 and 431, which list "15 steps to effective documentation in a legal context." We have reviewed both, as well as *The Uniform Guidelines on Employee Selection Procedures* (1978; 1979) and the *Standards for Educational and Psychological Testing* (AERA/APA/NCME Joint Committee, 1999). In particular, we would recommend that anyone who is concerned about legal challenges—or truly professional testing—consider the need to document the six standards that Wang, Schnipke, and Witt (2005, p. 17) found were "particularly applicable for licensure/certification exams" after they reviewed credentialing standards and their implementation in nursing certification and real estate licensure programs. The standards listed below are taken verbatim from the 1999 *Standards for Educational and Psychological Testing:*

> **Standard 1.1.** A rationale should be presented for each recommended interpretation and use of test scores, together with a

comprehensive summary of the evidence and theory bearing on the intended use or interpretation. (p. 17)

Standard 1.6. When the validation rests in part on the appropriateness of test content, the procedures followed in specifying and generating test content should be described and justified in reference to the construct the test is intended to measure or the domain it is intended to represent. If the definition of the content sampled incorporated criteria such as importance, frequency, or criticality, these criteria should also be clearly explained and justified. (p. 18)

Standard 3.2. The purpose(s) of the test, definition of the domain, and the test specifications should be stated clearly so that judgments can be made about the appropriateness of the defined domain for the stated purpose(s) of the test and about the relation of the items to the dimensions of the domain they are intended to represent. (p. 43)

Standard 3.11. Test developers should document the extent to which the content domain of a test represents the defined domain and test specifications. (p. 45)

Standard 14.9. When evidence of validity based on test content is a primary source of validity evidence in support of the use of a test in selection or promotion, a close link between test content and job content should be demonstrated. (p. 160)

Standard 14.14. The content domain to be covered by a credentialing test should be defined clearly and justified in terms of the importance of the content for credential-worthy performance in an occupation or profession. A rationale should be provided to support a claim that the knowledge or skills being assessed are required for credential-worthy performance in an occupation and are consistent with the purpose for which the licensing or certification program was instituted. *Comment:* Some form of job or practice analysis provides the primary basis for defining the content domain. (p. 161)

THE DOCUMENTATION

If you follow the model of this book, you will be on the path toward developing a valid test; if you document the process by answering the questions we pose for each part of the model, you will be on the path toward developing a defensible test. What follows is a list of basic questions you should consider addressing as you document your test development process. (**Note:** We are not attorneys and do not claim these questions to be legal requirements. Once again, consult with your organization's legal staff if you have any concerns.)

Purpose of the Test

What is the need for the test?
How was the need determined?
Who sponsored the effort? Why were they the sponsor(s)?

Analyze Job Content

What job/duty/task is being analyzed?
If a duty or a task, of what job(s) is it a part?
What is the hierarchical relationship of job/duty/task elements?
Include a copy of the analysis.
Who performed the job analysis?

Establish Content Validity of Objectives

For what job/duty/task were the objectives derived?
In what course(s) are they covered?
What are the names, titles, and credentials of the subject-matter experts who validated the objectives?
When was the validation performed?
Include a copy of the objectives and the job analysis.

Create Cognitive Items/Rating Instruments

For what job and objectives were the items/rating instruments created?
For what course is the test intended?
Who wrote the items/rating instruments?
What are the titles and credentials of those who wrote the items/rating instruments?
When were the items/rating instruments written?
Include a copy of the items/rating instruments.

Establish Content Validity of Items and Instruments

For what job and objectives were the items/rating instruments created?
For what course is the test intended?
Who validated the items/rating instruments?

What are the titles and credentials of those who validated the
items/rating instruments?

When were the items/rating instruments validated?

Include a copy of the form on which subject-matter experts indicated the match between the items/rating instrument and the
objectives or the job elements.

Initial Test Pilot

When was the test pilot conducted?

Where was the pilot conducted?

Who conducted the pilot?

Who were the sample test-takers?

How were the sample test-takers chosen?

What were the pertinent characteristics of the sample test-takers?

What was the process used to conduct the pilot?

What changes were made to the test as a result of the pilot?

Item Analysis

Who were the test-takers whose test data were used in the
item analysis?

What were the relevant characteristics of this sample of
test-takers?

How were the sample test-takers chosen?

When were the item analysis data collected? By whom? Where?

What program was used to analyze the test data?

What were the results of the item analysis?

What changes were made to the test as a result of the item analysis?

Include a copy of the item analysis printout.

Parallel Forms and Item Banks

For what job/objectives were the parallel forms or item banks
created?

How many parallel forms were created? When were they created?

How was a decision made about the number of parallel forms to
be created? Who made this decision?

What software was used to create the item banks? Who chose the
software and why was it chosen?

What are the sizes and structure of the test item banks?

How are items selected from the banks?

What process was used to create the parallel forms?

What is the equivalence reliability of the parallel forms? How was it established?

Cut-Off Scores

How is the test scored?

What is the cut-off score for the test?

When was the cut-off score determined?

What procedure(s) was (were) used to set the cut-off score?

Include all data pertinent to the procedure(s) used, including a description of test-takers and how they were chosen; judges and their credentials; item difficulty estimates; stakeholders and their suggested cut-off scores.

Who decided what the cut-off score would be? What are their titles and credentials for making this decision?

Reliability of Cognitive/Performance Tests

What procedures were used to establish the reliability of the test/raters?

When were the data collected upon which the reliability was calculated?

What is the reliability of the test/raters?

Include all pertinent data used in the calculation of the reliability coefficient.

Report Scores

To whom are scores reported?

In what form are the scores distributed?

Are the scores accompanied by course means? Medians? Other descriptive statistics?

Are reported scores composites of sub-scores? If so, what are they and are they differentially weighted? If so, how? How were the weights determined?

What guidance regarding the use of the scores is provided with them?

In summary, complete documentation must be viewed as a necessity for any high-stakes test; basic documentation of each step is simply the best practice. Figure 4.1 shows another way to think of the CRTD model integrated with the documentation process.

FIGURE 4.1.   THE CRTD PROCESS AND DOCUMENTATION.

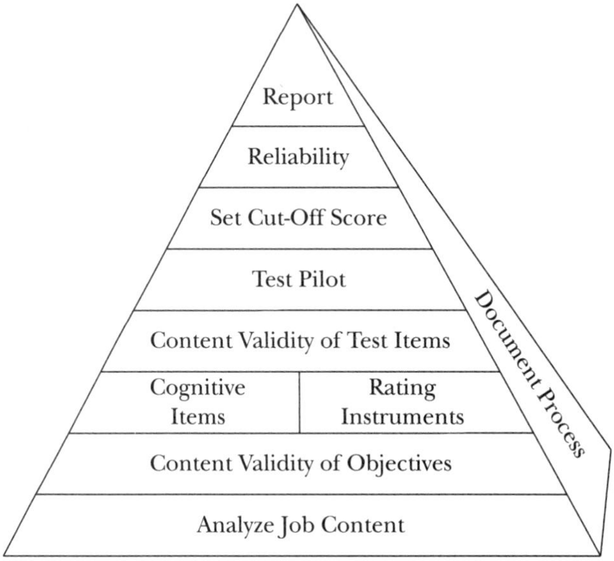

SIDEBAR: DOCUMENTING A TEST SECURITY PLAN

One of the best ways to deal with the problem of cheating is by preventing it from happening in the first place. How you document your test security processes for areas such as test and item design, test administration, and test security incidents will not only provide you with the tools to prevent test security breaches, but will allow you to act swiftly when testing misconduct arises.

WHAT IS IT?

A test security plan describes the processes, procedures, and policies a testing program will use to prevent, manage, and remediate test theft and fraud. It describes the process to be followed, who will be involved in making decisions, and the outcomes to be administered, depending on the severity of the test security incident.

According to the Association of Test Publishers' guidelines for Test Security Planning (see www.testpublishers.org) and Caveon Test Security (see www.caveon.com), a test security plan may contain the following topic areas:

1. *Security Goals and Objectives*—The goals, objectives, and measures for test security activities are defined. They have been approved by management.

2. *Roles and Responsibilities*—The security roles are adequately described and all responsibilities are covered. Security training has been provided to staff, suppliers, and contractors.

3. *Budget and Funding*—There is sufficient security budget and funding for the remediation of security breaches and for legal actions.

4. *Legal Agreements*—Confidentiality and conflict of interest agreements with employees and contractors have been executed properly.

5. *Test Design*—Secure item and test design principles are used to protect the test's intellectual property and prevent the overexposure of items.

6. *Test Development*—Measures are put in place to make sure items are secure and protected from unauthorized access.

7. *Test Publication*—The test content is protected during test publication and distribution.

8. *Test Administration*—During test administration, adequate security procedures are in place. Test site administrators and proctors are trained sufficiently on security procedures.

9. *Test Scores and Results*—Test scores and other results (that is, candidates' identification, site, proctor demographic information) are protected during transmission between temporary and permanent storage sites, and while stored.

10. *Physical Security*—The physical location(s) where test items are developed and stored are secure at all times.

11. *Internet and Media Monitoring*—The testing program monitors the Internet and other media (such as test preparation materials) for disclosure of test content.

12. *Security Training and Awareness*—Individuals in the organization are trained/retrained on security procedures.

13. *Information Security*—The program information (test scores, item answers, candidate information, etc.) is secure from hackers and other unauthorized access.

14. *Security Incident Response Planning*—Procedures are in place and consistent sanctions are applied when a test security breach occurs.

A test security plan, like many other test development documents, should be a living manual that exists beyond the individuals who work in the testing organization. It is a means of providing consistent implementation of security standards, practices, and sanctions.

The test security plan should be owned and managed by the individual in the testing organization who has responsibility for test security management. In some organizations, this will be someone's full-time responsibility. In others, test security may be one responsibility among others for a manager. Regardless, this individual provides the structure, administration, and management of a consistent test security program.

Last, a test security plan, like other testing program documentation, should take into consideration its stakeholders. Considerations such as buy-in, legal defensibility, and usability of the plan should be evaluated. Stakeholders may include upper management, legal counsel, boards of directors, and related departments. It will be important to identify these stakeholders and gain the appropriate approvals.

Although a brief description of a test security plan outline is provided above, it is useful to run through a scenario on how such a plan might be of use in the event of a test security breach.

Consider the following scenario: Review and analysis of test scores from a recent test administration indicates a ring of eight individuals have similar passing scores and their item response patterns are shown to be nearly identical; that is, both the correct responses and incorrect responses are the same. This data-driven evidence, along with a statement from another test-taker, leads you to the conclusion that a proctor was coaching some of the students during the administration of the test.

What happened? This scenario is all too common. Many testing organizations lack the proper documentation and controls to remedy a situation such as this one when it arises. Frequently when this circumstance occurs, a testing program is thrown into a panic:

- Legal agreements aren't in place to hold individuals accountable for their actions.

- Policies are not in place to take appropriate, consistent actions on behalf of the testing organization.

- Test results are suspect and place the validity of the test and its results in jeopardy.

What could have happened? We can look at this situation using the test security plan from a perspective of a tiered test security matrix. This matrix looks at test security from a test development perspective—from planning and design to monitoring and managing.

On the first tier, agreements and policies are put in place to provide a framework for consistent test security administration.

On the second tier, more advanced policies as well as systems are in place, for example, making sure all items are developed using a secure, systematic process.

On the third tier, integration of systems and technology provide enhanced abilities to catch theft and fraud through data-driven activities.

Test Security Matrix

With a test security plan in place, as outlined on the table on the next page, you are prepared to handle this problematic scenario by doing the following:

- Follow specific procedures for de-escalating the breach when it occurred (Tier 1)

- Take consistent actions against candidates and proctors (Tiers 1 and 2)

- Use data-driven analyses to provide objective assessment of the likelihood of the scores being obtained in a valid manner (Tier 3)

TIER	PLAN AND DESIGN	DEVELOP	PUBLICATION AND DELIVERY	MONITOR AND MANAGE
One	• Program policies • Non-disclosure agreements	• Item access • Confidential disclosure agreements	• Secure transmission • Password protection • Non-disclosure agreements	• Ad hoc web monitoring • Monitor pass rates • Pulse on prevalence of fraud
Two	• Advanced program policies • Secure test design	• Item access and item development systems • Auditing	• Secure transmission and auditing • Onsite shredding • Bonded warehouse	• Ongoing web monitoring • Item statistics review
Three	• Security plan • Additional program policies • Innovative test design and item formats	• Item banking system • All policies active • Hardware scrub	• Real-time delivery • Media-based surveillance • Biometrics	• Test content match analysis • Data forensics analysis

Caveon, Copyright © 2005

- Replace the test form with a new one and "rest" the form that has been overexposed (Tiers 2 and 3)

- Make sure proctors are trained and aware of their responsibilities to manage the security of the exam administration (Tier 2)

- Use the following as evidence to support claims of misconduct: signed candidate agreements, signed proctor agreements, eye-witness testimony, and videotapes. (Tiers, 1, 2, and 3)

Like other testing processes that need to be documented, creating a written test security plan provides testing organizations with a roadmap for administrating consistent test security processes, practices, and agreements. It allows the testing organization to communicate the criticality of maintaining the security of the program's test and its content to staff, stakeholders, and the testing community.

Caveon is a test-security firm that offers protection against test piracy and cheating. Using proprietary software Caveon identifies breaches, offers remediation services to halt and prosecute abuses of sensitive test information, and provides prevention services to help secure testing programs from further compromise. Jamie Mulkey, Ed.D., senior director, is responsible for business development, client consultation, and services management

ANALYZE JOB CONTENT

JOB ANALYSIS

This chapter assumes that you are skilled in the techniques of job analysis in general, and offers a way of thinking about how to use a hierarchical analysis of tasks for the purpose of efficient testing. However, we want to begin with a review of the job analysis process, as it is fundamental to creating valid tests. Then we will concentrate on two of the most common techniques used to plan both a course of instruction and its tests: hierarchical analysis of tasks and hierarchical analysis of levels of learning.

An analysis of the content to be tested, or more significantly, the content of a job to be assessed by a test, is an absolutely critical foundation to the testing process. In *Standards for Educational and Psychological Testing* (1999), Standard 14.10 provides the fundamental underpinning to test development in the corporate setting.

> When evidence of validity based on test content is presented, the rationale for defining and describing a specific job content domain in a particular way (e.g., in terms of tasks to be performed or knowledge, skills, abilities or other personal characteristics) should be stated clearly. (p. 160)

If you are creating a test that is not linked specifically to a job, but to a content domain for purposes of certification, the need for careful analysis of skills is the same. Standard 14.14 and its associated comment summarize this concern.

> The content domain to be covered by a credentialing test should be defined clearly and justified in terms of the importance of the content for credential-worthy performance in an occupation or profession. A rationale should be provided to support a claim that the knowledge or skills being assessed are required for credential-worthy performance in an occupation and are consistent with the purpose for which the licensing or certification program was instituted *Comment*: Some form of job or practice analysis provides the primary basis for defining the content domain. (p. 161)

The *Uniform Guidelines on Employee Selection,* which have become the primary standard for adjudication of testing issues in the courts, state in part:

> There should be a job analysis which includes an analysis of the important work behavior(s) required for successful performance and their relative importance and, if the behavior results in work product(s), an analysis of the work product(s). Any job analysis should focus on the work behavior(s) and the tasks associated with them. If work behavior(s) are not observable, the job analysis should identify those aspects of the behavior(s) that can be observed and the observed work products. The work behavior(s) selected for measurement should be critical work behavior(s) and/or important work behavior(s) constituting most of the job. (p. 38302)

The courts' response to inadequate job analysis is typified by the opinion in *Kirkland v. Department of Correctional Services* (cited in Thompson & Thompson, 1982):

> The cornerstone in the construction of a content valid examination is the job analysis. Without such an analysis to single out the critical knowledge, skills and abilities required by the job, their importance relative to each other, and the level of proficiency demanded as to each attribute, a test constructor is aiming in the dark and can only hope to achieve job relatedness by blind luck. (p. 867)

As you can see, there are compelling professional and legal reasons for attending to a careful task analysis of the job or content to be assessed. Also, as you begin your test development process you may wish to visit the *Epilogue* to this book. We have found that when testing is taken seriously, the role of the test designer or the test's advocate within the organization needs to expand to include change management; tests that have substantive consequences will also tend to foment resistance in the organization. (To help guide this change management process, Hale [2000] provides a discussion of business drivers, the business case, and some strategies for change management of the test development, implementation, and maintenance processes.)

JOB ANALYSIS MODELS

Job analysis is a "systematic procedure involving gathering, documenting, and analyzing information about job content, job requirements, and/or the context in which the job is performed," according to Bemis, Belenky, and Soder (1983, p. 60). They go on to add: "While this definition is broad, we believe that most personnel professionals and writers in the area of job analysis would embrace the definition after some consideration" (p. 60). How you conduct a job analysis probably depends on a number of factors ranging from a theoretical belief in the learning process, for example, behaviorism versus cognitivism, to operational, legal, or business needs. We don't know exactly how many job analysis models have been created to guide the professional in determining the "job," but we can account for at least another eleven approaches beyond the ten Bemis, et al. surveyed in 1983 simply by reviewing the *Handbook of Task Analysis Procedures* (Jonassen, Hannum, & Tessmer, 1989), not to mention the detailed discussions in *The Job Analysis Handbook for Business, Industry, and Government* (Gael, 1988).

Summary of the Job Analysis Process

The essence of most business-related job analysis models is to provide a process to decompose the job into its component parts—with a variety of terms used to represent the various components or levels of performance, such as Job, Duty, Task, Skill, etc. Henderson (1996) provides a succinct overview of the characteristics of a good job analysis. He begins by dividing the process into two phases: Obtaining and Describing Job Information and then Validating the Job Description. In the first phase the analyst seeks to identify the "tasks to be performed and the knowledge, skills, and other abilities needed to carry out work activities" (p. 45). The most common methods used in this phase are interviews of job incumbents, questionnaires, direct observation, review of relevant job performance documents, and perhaps most importantly, focus groups of subject-matter experts. In the second phase "it is necessary to verify the accuracy of the compiled task list" (p. 53). It is this phase that establishes the content validity of the analysis. The tasks that were identified in Phase One are listed and submitted for review to job subject-matter experts. The experts review the task list and verify that each task is job-related and often rank the importance of each task on a scale as well, for example, from "Not Important" to "Extremely Important." (The rankings can help determine which areas should receive the most emphasis in the test itself.) The output of this process is the content validation document.

If all of this analysis sounds like a time-consuming and difficult process—it needn't be. It is a process you must engage in to create a defensible test, but it can be done very efficiently and effectively. One respected and long-established model for job analysis, DACUM (Norton, 1997), uses a facilitator and focus group strategy to complete the Phase One process in two working days. Phase Two is then completed within two to four weeks after that.

If test designers did nothing more than add two days to the test development process to achieve Phase One, they would increase the quality of their tests a quantum level (or two)! Since DACUM is so well established, we want to describe it in more detail and recommend that it or a similar systematic analysis process be used to determine the job content.

DACUM

DACUM is an acronym for **Developing A Curriculum** and was first developed in 1966 as a means to describe occupational training needs. DACUM begins with several premises:

- Expert workers can describe and define their job/occupation more accurately than anyone else.
- An effective way to define a job/occupation is to precisely describe the tasks that expert workers perform.
- All tasks, in order to be performed correctly, demand the use of certain knowledge, skills, tools, and positive worker behaviors.
- While the knowledge, skills, tools, and worker behaviors are not tasks, they are enablers which make it possible for the worker to be successful... Because these attributes are different and distinct from the tasks, it is very important to keep them separate if a high quality analysis of job performance requirements is to be obtained. (Norton, 1997, pp. 1–2)

While DACUM actually refers to a five-step model for curriculum development, most practitioners equate the term with the highly visible two-day job analysis workshops that are offered across the globe. So will we.

DACUM uses a process of brainstorming and analysis guided by a facilitator to identify the major job Duties ("A cluster of related tasks. Usually six to twelve per job"), the Tasks ("Specific meaningful units of work. Usually six to twenty per duty and 75 to 125 per job"), and the Steps ("Specific elements or activities required to perform the task. Always two or more per task") (Norton, 1997, p. D-17).

DACUM is highly structured and requires a facilitator to manage the group process. Guidance is given for almost every detail from pre-DACUM planning to room design (e.g., entrance, doors, windows, blackboards) to follow-up. DACUM draws on a group of five to twelve expert members in a group process to analyze the job. Rules of communication are clarified as are the various stages of the process. A two-day DACUM workshop begins at 8:00 A.M. with a continental breakfast, a welcome, and introductions completed by 8:30; the official DACUM begins at 9:00. Fifteen-minute breaks are scheduled for the morning and afternoon with an hour for lunch and conclusion at 4:30 P.M.

The structure of the workshop begins with a description of the roles each will play in the workshop and then definitions for the major terms, e.g., Job, Duty, Task, Step, etc. Several sample charts are then reviewed as quality examples of the DACUM process. The facilitator then reviews the ground rules for group conduct and begins with an initial brainstorming session to develop Duty statements. After about an hour of discussion, most of the Duty statements will have been generated. A phase of analysis then follows until consensus is developed for the Duty statements. A similar cycle continues for Tasks and Steps. By 1:00 P.M. of the second day a nearly finished job analysis is complete. The group then moves on to develop lists of: General Knowledge and Skills, Worker Behaviors, Tools, Equipment, Supplies and Materials, and Future Trends/Concerns. Following a break, a final review and refinement of the DACUM Chart is completed. Table 5.1 is a partial DACUM chart for Computer Applications Programmer that identifies the Duty and Task levels. Table 5.2 is a partial analysis of Steps for the Task "Mow the Lawn."

With the job analysis complete, we often find that it can be viewed, figuratively and literally, as a hierarchy. We have found working with hierarchies in test development to be one of the most powerful tools a test writer can use. In the perfect world, a formal job analysis will have been completed before test development begins. In the real world, where compromises must be made, learning to think about the hierarchical nature of tasks will provide guidance in creating worthwhile tests.

TABLE 5.1.   DACUM RESEARCH CHART FOR COMPUTER APPLICATIONS PROGRAMMER.

Duties	Tasks				
A: Analyze Business Requirements	A-1: Interview customers	A-2: Study existing process	A-3: Conduct focus groups	A-4: Bench-mark "best practices" companies	A-5: Determine project benefits
B: Develop Conceptual Design	B-1: Diagram process flow	B-2: Create logical model	B-3: Evaluate multiple solutions	B-4: Present recommended solution	B-5: Identify project costs
C: Develop Detailed Design	C-1: Design data flow diagram	C-2: Design data files	C-3: Diagram program flows	C-4: Define screen requirements	C-5: Define menu requirements
D: Develop Business Applications	D-1: Validate program specifications	D-2: Create application data files	D-3: Develop application screens	D-4: Develop application reports	D-5: Develop application menus
E: Test Business Applications	E-1: Develop system	E-2: Set up test environment	E-3: Execute system test	E-4: Review customer feedback	E-5: Perform necessary modifications
F: Implement Business Applications	F-1: Publish implementation time line	F-2: Conduct customer training	F-3: Coordinate implementation activities	F-4: Archive existing environment	F-5: Convert production data files
G: Maintain Business Applications	G-1: Provide customer support	G-2: Provide application enhancements	G-3: Resolve reported problems	G-4: Optimize system performance	G-5: Perform routine file maintenance
H: Continue Professional Development	H-1: Review trade journals	G-3: Attend professional seminars	H-3: Maintain professional certification	H-4: Participate in cross training	H-5: Participate in professional associations

TABLE 5.2. STANDARD TASK ANALYSIS FORM.

Duty: MAINTAIN THE HOME YARD Expert Workers: Steve Brown, Glenn Maxon

Task: MOW THE LAWN Recorder: Robert E. Norton Date: 9/22/95

Steps (Required to Perform the Task)	Performance Standards (Observable & Measurable Criteria)	Tools, Equipment, Materials, & Supplies (Needed)	Required Knowledge (Math, Science, Language, & Technology)
1. Remove mower from storage	1.	1. Mower	1.
2a. Check/add oil b. Check/add gas	2a. 1) Checked oil level 2a. 2) Added correct amount and type of oil, if needed 2b. 1) Checked gas level 2b. 2) Filled gas unit, if desired	2a. 1) Rag or paper towel 2a. 2) Correct type oil 2b. 1) Gas can 2b. 2) Correct type gas	2a. 1) Location of oil level measure (dipstick) 2a. 2) Read oil level measure 2a. 3) Type of oil needed 2b. 1) Location of gas tank 2b. 2) Determine gas level 2b. 3) Type of gasoline appropriate, or gas/oil mixture ratio
3a. Check/adjust cutting height 3b. Attach bagger, if desired	3a. Adjusted mower to desired cutting height 3b. Attached bagger unit, if desired	3a. Ruler 3b. Bagger unit	3a. Read ruler/owner's manual 3b. Attach bagger unit correctly

Performance Steps (Required to Perform the Task)	Tools, Equipment, Standards (Observable & Measurable Criteria)	Materials, & Supplies (Needed)	Required Knowledge (Math, Science, Language, & Technology)
4. Determine mowing pattern	4. Mowed lawn in pattern requested	4.	4. Available patterns and benefits of each
5. Start mower	5a. Choked engine, if cold 5b. Adjusted gas to recommended setting 5c. Started engine quickly	5. Owner's manual	5a. Basic principles of engine operation 5b. Location and operation of choke and throttle
6. Guide mower safely over the lawn	6a. Guided the mower safely by 1) wearing proper clothing 2) removing any objects from lawn 3) keeping children animals at safe distance 4) proceeding at safe speed for conditions 6b. Mowed the entire lawn	6.	6a. Safe lawn mowing Procedures 6b. What objects constitute danger

(continued)

TABLE 5.2. (CONTINUED)

Duty: MAINTAIN THE HOME YARD Expert Workers: Steve Brown, Glenn Maxon

Task: MOW THE LAWN Recorder: Robert E. Norton Date: 9/22/95

Steps (Required to Perform the Task)	Performance Standards (Observable & Measurable Criteria)	Tools, Equipment, Materials, & Supplies (Needed)	Required Knowledge (Math, Science, Language, & Technology)
7. Shut off mower	7. Turned off engine properly	7.	7a. Location of off switch 7b. Appropriate cleaning procedure
8. Dispose of clippings	8a. Properly disposed of clippings 8b. Prepared mower for storage	8a. Container for clippings 8b. Broom and rags	8. Clipping disposal options
9. Return mower to storage	9. Returned mower to storage area	9.	9. Store mower safely
10. Collect mowing fee (if appropriate)	10. Collected appropriate fee for services	10.	10. Calculation of correct mowing fee

© Norton, 1997, p. H-11.

TABLE 5.2. (CONTINUED)

Safety (Concerns)	Attitudes (Important to Worker Success)	Decisions (Made by the Worker)	Cues (Needed for Making Correct Decisions)	Errors (Will Result if Incorrect Decisions Are Made)
1. Do not damage car or other items	1. Cautious and careful	1.	1.	1.
2a. 1) Be careful not to spill or waste oil	2. Cautious and careful	2a. Whether to add oil, and if needed, amount and type	2a. Reading from the oil dipstick	2a. Could damage or destroy engine
2a. 2) Be careful not to overfill engine		2b. Whether to add gas, and, if needed, how much	2b. Gas gauge or other measure	2b. 1) Run out of fuel
2b. 1) Be careful not to spill gasoline				2b. 2) Clog fuel system
2b. 2) Avoid sparks or touching hot surfaces				
3. Avoid cuts	3. Concern for quality	3a. Determine best cutting heights	3a. Owner's manual and customer preference	3a. 1) Dissatisfied customer
		3b. Whether to bag clippings	3b. Owner preference	3a. 2) Damage to lawn health
				3b. Dissatisfied customer

(continued)

TABLE 5.2 (CONTINUED)

Safety (Concerns)	Attitudes (Important to Worker Success)	Decisions (Made by the Worker)	Cues (Needed for Making Correct Decisions)	Errors (Will Result if Incorrect Decisions Are Made)
4.	4.	4. Decide on best mowing pattern	4. Owner's manual and owner's preference	4. Dissatisfied customer
5. Locate on flat surface free of objects	5. Concern for safety of self and others	5.	5. Owner's manual and condition of engine	5. Engine won't start
6. Watch for safety of children, adults, other animals	6. Safety conscious	6. How to operate safely	6. Owner's manual	6. Loss of customer
7. Avoid touching hot surfaces	7. Safety conscious	7.	7.	7.
8.	8.	8. Determine how to best dispose of clippings	8. Owner's preference	8. Dissatisfied customer
9. Avoid damage to mower and adjacent objects	9. Safety conscious	9.	9. Owner' preference or previous location	9. Dissatisfied customer
10.	10. Courteous, appreciative	10. Determine reasonable and correct fee	10. Going rates in the area	10a. Worker loses money 10b. Customer unhappy with excessive fee

© Norton, 1997, p. H-1.

Hierarchies

Learning theorists have found that many learning goals can be thought of as hierarchical in nature; that is, subordinate skills are prerequisites to the final task. More specifically, some of the assumptions of this approach are:

- A final goal can be analyzed into component skills that are quite distinct from each other.
- The component skills are mediators of the final goal, that is, mastery of a lower-level skill is necessary to achieve the next level of performance; non-mastery of a subordinate skill significantly reduces the probability that the next level task will be mastered.

A hierarchical analysis can be approached from a variety of perspectives to include both mental and physical performances on the job.

Hierarchical Analysis of Tasks

As you may know, one of the most important steps in a complete course planning process is the creation of the content hierarchy. The hierarchy identifies the basic instructional units for the course as well as suggesting a logical sequence for instruction. Figure 5.1 is an illustration of the relationship of the components that mediate the final goal.

Figure 5.2 illustrates a relationship where the three skill components have been further analyzed and additional components identified.

Finally, Figure 5.3 provides a partial task hierarchy for the skills required by a production-operations manager—someone responsible for the planning, scheduling, and controlling of the production of goods or services.

FIGURE 5.1. HIERARCHICAL RELATIONSHIP OF SKILLS.

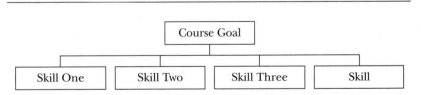

FIGURE 5.2.   EXTENDED HIERARCHICAL ANALYSIS.

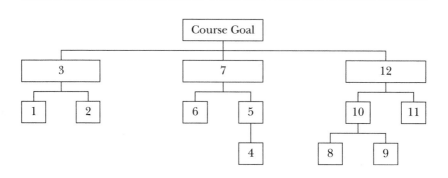

FIGURE 5.3.   HIERARCHICAL TASK ANALYSIS, PRODUCTION-OPERATIONS MANAGER.

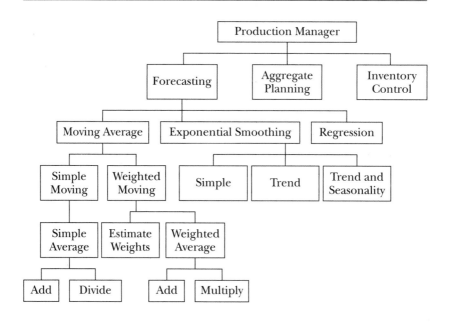

MATCHING THE HIERARCHY TO THE TYPE OF TEST

Let's assume we are planning to teach a unit for which the objective is:

- Given a set of data, apply the correct formula to forecast product demand (represented by the "Forecasting" box in Figure 5.3 above).

To master this goal, there are three subordinate quantitative skills that need to be mastered:

- Moving Average
- Exponential Smoothing
- Regression

With the course hierarchy in hand, we can now select objectives to be covered by each of the six types of tests described in Chapter 2.

Prerequisite Test. If we wanted to assure that everyone who entered the course possessed the minimal skills needed to succeed in this unit—skills that will not be covered in the course—we would probably test at the lowest level of the hierarchy for this unit. In this instance, we would want to be certain that all participants can add, divide, and multiply.

Entry Test. Once we determined that all of our participants possessed the basic skills needed to succeed in this unit, we might want to know whether they all have the same skill levels, or if some members of the class have already learned some of the material on the job. We might then select objectives that represent skills in each of the boxes two levels below our final objective, that is, "Simple Moving," "Weighted Moving," "Simple," "Trend," and "Trend and Seasonality." In a fully individualized course, this test would allow students to bypass instructional units the objectives of which they have already mastered.

Diagnostic Test. To determine the exact skill levels of each participant, as well as those areas in which they may be having problems, you would design a diagnostic test based on *all* of the skills represented by the boxes below your final objective. Whereas the entry test would typically be used before instruction, the diagnostic test would typically be used in conjunction with the instruction or as part of the posttest process.

Posttest. At the end of your unit of instruction on Forecasting, you would want to assess student mastery. This type of test would focus on the skills found in and just below our final objective, that is, "Forecasting," "Moving Average," "Exponential Smoothing," and "Regression." Test items would be drawn from this level because these skills represent the accumulation of all prior skills. Thus the assumption is that if a learner can pass the final objective, then all sub-skills have been mastered.

Equivalency Test. If a manager claimed that one of his or her employees didn't need the course because he or she "knows it already," you might then ask the employee to take an equivalency test. This test will be composed of items based on the same objectives as the Posttest. (However, because having students participate in mastery-based instruction provides a "cushion" in your confidence in their abilities to perform a skill, the equivalency test may need to contain more items in order to establish a similar level of confidence. We will discuss the issue of how test length affects test reliability, and hence validity, in Chapter 7.)

Certification Test. If the American Production and Inventory Control Society decided to create a test to assess competency in production operations skills to credential members of the profession at large, then the test design would begin with the same objectives and assumptions as those underlying the equivalency test. However, as a credentialing exam, it might also broaden the content to include issues of ethics, law, portfolio review, etc.

As you plan your test, there are three points pertinent to using content hierarchies that we want you to keep in mind:

- If you are designing a test used in a course, you can't design a good test without good objectives. A fuzzy set of objectives means not only fuzzy instruction, but also fuzzy (and therefore invalid) testing.
- Different content hierarchies will result in different specific levels being chosen as the source for items for the different test types. For example, it would be foolish to suggest that items for a prerequisite test will always come from the lowest two levels of the content hierarchy. However, prerequisite items will nearly always come from the lower levels, posttest and equivalency items from the highest levels, and diagnostic and entry test items from nearly all levels.
- You may find yourself using some of the same test items on the different types of tests. That's normal. Just be careful that your

learners don't discover that all they have to do is memorize the answers to the pretest items because the same items will be on the posttest.

USING LEARNING TASK ANALYSIS TO VALIDATE A HIERARCHY

One question that always arises when creating a course hierarchy is: Is this hierarchy right? A valid hierarchy is especially important in testing because, without this blueprint, it will be nearly impossible to create an efficient and valid test for any of the five types of tests we have just discussed. A hierarchical sequencing of the objectives can only be formally validated through somewhat complex statistical procedures. However, another more workable approach to validating the hierarchy is to identify the learning level of each objective and then to see if the levels are in the proper sequence from a learning theory viewpoint.

A number of important learning theories might be used to help validate a hierarchy; we have selected three approaches that have been used in a variety of training settings. These are Bloom's Taxonomy, Gagné's Learned Capabilities, and Merrill's Component Design Theory. If you are familiar with these approaches, you will understand that there is some overlap among the theories; for example, Merrill's "Remember," Gagné's "Verbal Information," and Bloom's "Knowledge" levels are similar. However, while each theory makes sense in and of itself, you can't easily (or most likely, usefully) shift back and forth among approaches. Our advice is to pick an approach and stay with it. Then, analyze your hierarchies in light of your chosen approach.

BLOOM'S ORIGINAL TAXONOMY

Bloom (1956) and the other psychologists who worked on the taxonomy project sought to create a system for describing in detail different levels of cognitive functioning so that the precision of testing cognitive performance could be improved. The result of this extensive effort was a classification scheme that breaks cognitive processes down into six types—knowledge, comprehension, application, analysis, synthesis, and evaluation. (See Figure 5.4.)

FIGURE 5.4. COGNITIVE LEVELS OF BLOOM'S TAXONOMY.

Evaluation
Synthesis
Analysis
Application
Comprehension
Knowledge

The scheme is called a "taxonomy" because each level is subsumed by the next higher level. For example, it is assumed that in order to function at the application level, a person must also be able to function at all levels below application, that is, comprehension and knowledge. Tasks, objectives, or test items are classified at the highest level of cognitive functioning that they require. Therefore, even though analysis-level tasks also involve application, comprehension, and knowledge, they are said to be "at the analysis level."

Since its creation, the taxonomy has been widely used to classify the cognitive level of learning objectives and test items. Having a thorough understanding of Bloom's taxonomy is very useful, not only for classifying objectives to validate hierarchies, but also for writing objectives and test items that measure them. Because the taxonomy provides a test developer with a language for describing different kinds of cognitive operations, it therefore provides much guidance in how one might construct test items at these different cognitive levels.

Let's look now at the six levels of Bloom's taxonomy in a little more detail.

Knowledge Level. This is the lowest level of the taxonomy and simply indicates the ability to remember content in exactly the same form in which it was presented. Learning objectives that require learners to memorize material—definitions, procedures, formulas, poems, and so on—are said to be written at the knowledge level. Note that the recall of the material is identical to the original presentation in a knowledge level objective. For example, a test item that asks learners to *conduct* a procedure that has been presented only verbally to learners is not a knowledge level test item. The knowledge level item would ask learners to *state* the steps in the procedure.

Comprehension Level. Most tasks at this level are one of the following four types. Learners restate material in their own words *or* translate information from one form to another *or* apply designated rules *or* recognize previously unseen examples of concepts. Notice that at the comprehension level more than simply remembering is required. If learners have to use their own words, they must do more than rote memorization. Similarly, translation and simple rule application is a form of representing material using other words or symbols than were used in the original presentation of the material. Obviously, the correct identification of *previously unseen* examples cannot be memorized. If learners are asked to classify examples that have previously been identified for them, the classification task is reduced to the knowledge level because only recall is then involved.

Application Level. This task level requires learners to decide what rules are pertinent to a given problem and then to implement the rules to solve the problem. If learners are told what rules to use, the task is reduced to the comprehension level. For example, providing a learner with the formula, Area = πr^2, and a circle's radius and asking the learner to calculate the area is a comprehension level task. Success requires only recall of the value of π, translating the formula given into the values provided, and multiplication, which is a succession of recall-level and comprehension-level tasks. At the application level, the learner is presented with problems, but not told which rules or formulas to use in solving them. This feature makes application-level objectives more complex than comprehension-level ones.

Analysis Level. At this level learners are required to break complex situations down into their component parts and figure out how the parts relate to and influence one another. In other words, at the analysis level learners are discovering for themselves what rules explain and govern a given situation. Analysis level tasks ask learners to solve problems after being provided extensive scenario descriptions and data, only some of which are pertinent to the solution.

Synthesis Level. Objectives at this level require the creation of totally original material—original products, designs, equipment, and so on. Objectives at this level can only be assessed with open-ended kinds of test questions or assignments;

multiple-choice or other closed-ended questions cannot measure the attainment of synthesis-level objectives.

Evaluation Level. The highest level of Bloom's taxonomy, the evaluation level requires learners to judge the appropriateness or worthwhileness of some object, plan, design, and so on., for some purpose. True evaluation-level objectives are extremely complex, requiring demonstration of all five lower levels, including the synthesis of original criteria for making judgments. Like synthesis-level objectives, evaluation-level objectives cannot be assessed via closed-ended test questions.

USING BLOOM'S ORIGINAL TAXONOMY TO VALIDATE A HIERARCHY

As we just saw, a basic assumption of Bloom's taxonomy is that one level subsumes another; that is, an application-level objective would require preceding objectives at the knowledge and comprehension levels. Therefore, when you develop a hierarchy of objectives, you can classify each objective according to Bloom level and then determine whether the sequence reflected in your hierarchy matches Bloom's sequence. For example, the hierarchy in Figure 5.5 is correct because lower Bloom levels are taught first. The hierarchy in Figure 5.6 shows a situation in which you could expect to have significant instructional and testing problems because higher level skills are taught before the prerequisite lower level skills.

Figure 5.7 shows how Bloom's levels might be applied to the hierarchy we illustrated in Figure 5.3.

FIGURE 5.5. HIERARCHY ILLUSTRATING CORRECT BLOOM SEQUENCE.

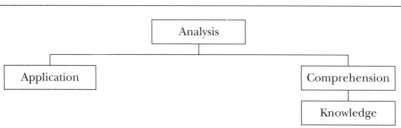

FIGURE 5.6. HIERARCHY ILLUSTRATING INCORRECT BLOOM SEQUENCE.

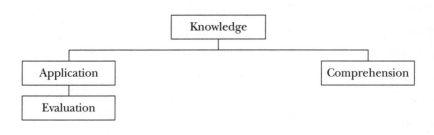

FIGURE 5.7. BLOOM'S LEVELS APPLIED TO THE PRODUCTION MANAGER
CONTENT HIERARCHY.

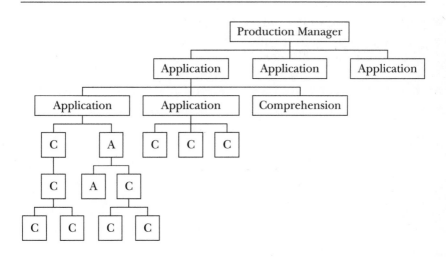

BLOOM'S REVISED TAXONOMY

Bloom's original taxonomy was based on a content analysis of thousands of test items. As such, it was never designed to provide a prescriptive process for the design of instruction. Over the years a number of educators felt that the model should be reconceptualized to provide more guidance for instructional tactics. A revised taxonomy was presented in 2001 by Anderson, Krathwohl, et al. (Krathwohl was the second author with Bloom of the original taxonomy.) A review of the revised taxonomy shows a strong

TABLE 5.3. SUMMARY OF THE REVISED BLOOM'S TAXONOMY.

The Knowledge Dimension	The Cognitive Process Dimension					
	Remember	Understand	Apply	Analyze	Evaluate	Create
Factual						
Conceptual						
Procedural						
Meta-Cognitive						

similarity to the work of Merrill in that it separates objectives into a Knowledge Dimension and a Cognitive Process Dimension. The Cognitive Process dimension is: Remember, Understand, Apply, Analyze, Evaluate, and Create. The Knowledge Dimension is: Factual, Conceptual, Procedural, and Meta-Cognitive. We have used the original Bloom's taxonomy throughout this book because it is simpler, yet elaborates the cognitive processes dimension most relevant to the construction and analysis of tests. Table 5.3 summarizes the relationship of the two dimensions of the revised taxonomy.

What is important to see here, and as we will elaborate and emphasize in Chapter 7 in the section "The Single Most Useful Improvement You Can Make in Test Development," is that the fundamental division of learning processes is still the same between taxonomies: there are memory level items and there is everything else.

GAGNÉ'S LEARNED CAPABILITIES

Gagné (1985) divided learning outcomes into five classes of behavior that describe Cognitive Skills as well as Motor Skills and Attitudes.

Intellectual Skills. These skills are the ones that enable persons to interact with the environment in terms of symbols and conceptualizations. Intellectual skills are broken down into a hierarchy of five skills. Listed hierarchically from lowest to highest, these five skills are:

- Discriminations—an ability to make different responses to stimuli that differ from each other along one or more physical dimensions, e.g., distinguish between a "red light" and a "green light."
- Concrete Concepts—the ability to identify a stimulus as a member of a class having common characteristics, e.g., a "chair."
- Defined Concepts—demonstrating understanding of the meaning of some particular class of objects that has no physical referent, e.g., "freedom."
- Rules—using a sequence of steps that transforms or identifies a class of objects, e.g., long division transforms a number into its component parts.
- Higher Order Rules (Problem Solving)—using complex combinations of simple rules that are created for discovering a solution to a new and previously unencountered situation.

Cognitive Strategies. These are internal processes by which a learner selects and modifies his or her ways of attending, learning, remembering, and thinking, for example, practice, paraphrase, note taking, and so on.

Verbal Information. This is the ability to learn specific facts or organized items of information, such as stating the steps in filling out a service request form.

Motor Skill. Any learned behaviors that lead to movement are motor skills, such as changing an oil filter or landing a plane.

Attitudes. Attitudes are internal feelings or emotions that affect choices of action, for example, an attitude of professionalism may lead to civility in communications during a performance appraisal.

USING GAGNÉ'S INTELLECTUAL SKILLS TO VALIDATE A HIERARCHY

If you have developed your instructional objectives using Gagné's model, then you can also review your instructional plan through a hierarchical analysis. Since Gagné argues that lower-order skills must be learned before higher-order ones (as Bloom argues, Knowledge is prerequisite to Comprehension, and so on), any course hierarchy should reflect this prescribed pattern. As a result, any pattern of objectives, when the objectives are converted to their type of learning, should show that lower level skills, for example, Discriminations, must be taught before the higher-level skills like Concepts. Figure 5.8 illustrates how a set of objectives have been converted to their Intellectual Skill levels. In this example, the hierarchical structure has been validated by its match with Gagné's prescribed sequence.

FIGURE 5.8.   APPLICATION OF GAGNÉ'S INTELLECTUAL SKILLS
TO HIERARCHY VALIDATION.

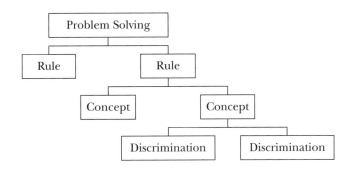

MERRILL'S COMPONENT DESIGN THEORY

Merrill (1983) has developed a method of classifying learning tasks as part of an instructional design process called Component Design Theory. (Originally called Component Display Theory, Merrill broadened "Display" to "Design" in recognition of the theory's utility beyond computer display systems.) Merrill's work is very explicit in making one of the most important distinctions in test creation—the difference between memorizing and applying. Component Design Theory describes two dimensions: the task to be performed and the type of learning.

The Task Dimension. A learner's final performance is divided into three levels. Those tasks or relationships the learner must:

- Remember—repeat exactly as instructed
- Use—apply to new situations
- Find—create new rules or solutions

Types of Learning. The tasks to be performed can be classified as:

- Facts—simple associations between names, objects, symbols, and so forth.
- Concepts—categories or classifications defined by a common set of characteristics
- Procedures—a sequence of specific steps or operations performed on a single type of object
- Principles—explanations or predictions of why things happen based on cause-effect relationships

Thus in using Component Design Theory, objectives are matched to the type of learning in light of the desired task dimension. For example, an objective such as "The learner will classify a leadership style as Authoritarian, Democratic, or Laissez-Faire" describes concept (type of learning) using (task dimension) behavior. An example test item might be described as:

- Given a previously unencountered description of a leader's behavior, classify the style as Authoritarian, Democratic, or Laissez-Faire.

USING MERRILL'S COMPONENT DESIGN THEORY TO VALIDATE A HIERARCHY

As you can probably see, Merrill's work shares stronger similarities to Gagné than to the original Bloom taxonomy. This is due to a common foundation in learning theory. And while Component Design Theory would also argue that Concepts must be taught before Principles, the theory is stronger in pointing out the differences between being asked to repeat something (Remember) and applying it (Use). Thus, in reviewing your objectives from a

Component Design perspective, one of the most elegant uses of the theory is to simply make sure that no Use-level task is presented before a Remember-level task. For example, don't expect sales trainees to practice the six steps of a sales call before they have been taught what the six steps of a sales call are. While this example seems self-evident, more complex course designs, especially those created by subject-matter experts, are more likely to fall into the trap of using before remembering. Figure 5.9 illustrates how a hierarchy might be viewed from Merrill's perspective.

FIGURE 5.9.   APPLICATION OF MERRILL'S COMPONENT DESIGN THEORY
TO HIERARCHY VALIDATION.

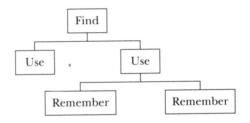

DATA-BASED METHODS FOR HIERARCHY VALIDATION

As we said earlier, more formal, data-based methods exist for validating a hierarchy. These approaches require that data be collected at the end of each instructional module identified by the hierarchy; the data are then analyzed to validate the learning sequence. A real difficulty in this process, however, is deciding whether learner failures are the result of a faulty hierarchy or faulty instruction. In other words, if 100 percent of the learners pass the first level of instruction and then 50 percent fail on the second level, is this result due to an improper placement of the instruction in the hierarchy or to poor design of the instructional module?

Because data-based analyses of the hierarchy will require well-designed unit tests keyed to each stage of the hierarchy and a relatively large sample of learners, these approaches are usually reserved for highly critical areas of training such as nuclear power plant operation. The most sophisticated approaches will use Guttman scalogram analysis to calculate a coefficient of reproducibility (a perfectly scaled hierarchy would have a coefficient of 1.0) as well as Multiple Scalogram analysis to examine the hierarchy for a given optimal sequence of tasks. The underlying theory to these techniques, however, can be demonstrated and used by almost any course designer through the simple analysis of posttest data percentages.

In Figure 5.10, the posttest scores are shown for each level in a simple hierarchy. As you can see, the pattern of success is about what we would expect for a valid hierarchy with good (not perfect) instruction. There are high levels of performance at the bottom, indicating mastery of the content, with some attrition in performance as the task becomes more complex at the top of the hierarchy.

FIGURE 5.10. ANALYSIS OF POSTTEST SCORES TO VALIDATE A HIERARCHY,
EXAMPLE OF A VALID HIERARCHY.

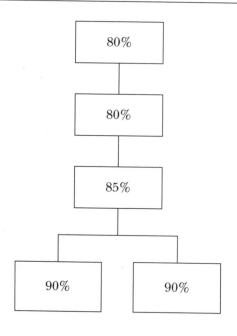

In Figure 5.11, there was success at the lowest levels, but the pattern of performance in the higher levels is confusing. The "40–75–25" pattern could indicate a number of problems, but a first reaction might be that the unit where learners scored 40 percent is unnecessary, as many scored much higher at the next level (75 percent). The drop in performance at the top of the hierarchy may also be due to a needed but missing unit of instruction, or to weak instruction in the unit itself.

FIGURE 5.11. ANALYSIS OF POSTTEST SCORES TO VALIDATE A HIERARCHY,
EXAMPLE OF AN INVALID HIERARCHY.

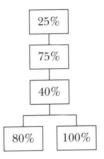

WHO KILLED COCK ROBIN?

In the end, it is important to remember that, while a hierarchy provides the test designer with a blueprint for making efficient testing decisions, the hierarchy itself may be internally logical and correctly sequenced but not be valid for the job skills to be assessed. In other words, a hierarchy could be analyzed through a task analysis, a learning analysis, and then verified through empirical techniques invoking the most sophisticated Guttman scaling analysis to determine that the sequencing of tasks is correct—and yet remain invalid because the wrong tasks were analyzed. In *Fire Fighters Institute for Racial Equality v. City of St. Louis* (cited in Barrett, 1981) the court examined the content validity of an exam for the position of fire captain and noted the following:

Constructing a content valid exam and proof of its validity requires as a first step a thorough analysis of the job to be performed. … It is in fact the fatal flaw in the validation study that the test…devised did not reflect [the] findings in the job analysis. The captain's exam admittedly failed to test the one *major* job attribute that separates a firefighter from a fire captain, that of supervisory ability… The job analysis here may have appeared impressive in relation to those challenged in other cases, but a good analysis in any situation is of little use when the examination fails to reflect what is found in the job analysis. The test is not *content* valid. … Here, where the exam failed to test a job component comprising over 40 percent of the employee's time, the inference of discrimination has not been rebutted with a finding of the exam's "job relatedness." (p. 591)

Barrett's article, "Is the Test Content-Valid: Or, Who Killed Cock Robin?" summarizes the courts' attitudes toward job relatedness and test items. The article illustrates the role of job relatedness with an item the courts found to be content-invalid for assessing the skills required of elementary school principals:

Of the following characters in the nursery rhyme, "The Burial of Poor Cock Robin," the one who kills Cock Robin is the

1. Lark
2. Thrush
3. Bull
4. Sparrow

Such an item reflects what the test creator thinks good elementary school principals know, rather than an analysis of what these principals actually do on the job. Hence, it is invalid for the job performance to be assessed.

CHAPTER SIX

CONTENT VALIDITY OF OBJECTIVES

OVERVIEW OF THE PROCESS

Establishing the content validity of your objectives appears to be a relatively straightforward process: you've identified the job-task skills, now it should be a simple matter to create objectives that match the skills. So, for example, if the task requires the performer to weld two metal bars at a 90-degree angle, the objective might be: "Given an arc welder, rods, and two iron bars, weld the bars at a 90-degree angle with no gaps in the weld." There should be a close match between the objective and the task (and later the test item). However, in the corporate world, such seemingly simple prescriptions have a way of becoming harder to fulfill as the demands of technology, time, costs, law, health, and safety issues enter into the planning process. The "real world" sometimes forces compromises from this ideal. If for any reason you decide *not* to match the job to the objective and subsequently to the test item, you need to be aware of the consequences of teaching and testing in a way that does not reflect the job.

This chapter is about those compromises and is written to help you think about them and then make professional decisions about them. We begin with an overview of the role of objectives in testing and then enter into discussion about how to classify the types of compromises you may be considering and the consequences of these compromises. Then, we conclude with a description of the process of matching the job-task to the objective.

THE ROLE OF OBJECTIVES IN ITEM WRITING

It is difficult to overstate the usefulness of good instructional objectives in the creation of sound tests. Most instructional designers are aware of how important objectives are to the creation of instruction; many are less familiar with the role of objectives in testing. It is not the purpose of this book to treat comprehensively the techniques for writing instructional objectives. However, we do want to focus briefly on the critical roles objectives play in testing and the components of well-written objectives most essential for item writing.

Instructional objectives serve three fundamental purposes for criterion-referenced test developers:

- Objectives ensure that a test covers those learner outcomes important for the purposes that the test must serve. Remember that there are several different types of tests (See Chapter 2) and that the content for these tests is derived by task analysis procedures that order objectives hierarchically. Matching test items to the appropriate course objectives within these hierarchies guarantees that all essential content is assessed.
- Objectives increase the accuracy with which cognitive processes in particular can be assessed. A well-written objective is a blueprint for the creation of test items that will assess the specific competency described by the objective. In this way, objectives make it much easier for test writers to create so-called parallel test items, that is, different test items that assess the same objective. Parallel test items are essential for the construction of reliable tests, as we shall see later in this chapter,

as well as for the creation of equivalency tests and different forms of any given test. Hence, objectives are essential to the construction, maintenance, and security of an organizational testing process.

- The size of the domain covered by the objectives and the homogeneity of the objectives the test is designed to assess are important factors in determining how many items will need to be included on the test. These characteristics of objectives are discussed later in this chapter in the section on determining test length.

Characteristics of Good Objectives

Of course, not all objectives are equally well written. Numerous authors have provided course developers with advice about how to write objectives. Most authorities agree, however, that good objectives have four parts:

- Who the learner is
- What behavior or competency the learner will perform
- Under what conditions the learner will perform the competency
- To what standard of correctness the learner will perform the competency

We will examine briefly the latter three components of the objective—the behavior, the conditions, and the standard. An understanding of the learner is, of course, an extremely important part of the instructional design process, but for our purposes we are assuming that this learner analysis has already been completed and as test designers we know the pertinent characteristics of those for whom our learning objectives and our tests are intended.

Behavior Component. It is essential that the competency that the learner is to perform be described in observable, measurable terms, hence the term "behavioral objective" used to describe the most useful statements of learner outcomes. When writing objectives, choose the most precise verb you can to state what the learner will be able to do. For example, the words "list," "categorize," "draw," and "evaluate" are better than "understand," "appreciate," "know," and "really understand" as verbs in behavioral objectives. The more descriptive the verb in an objective, the easier it will be to write test items that accurately assess the objective.

Conditions Component. If well written, this part of the objective provides useful information to test writers, since the test essentially presents learners with a series of conditions under which they must demonstrate their achievement of the instructional objectives. Unfortunately, the conditions component of an objective is frequently omitted by designers who do not realize how critical it is for clearly communicating the intent of the objective. Changing the conditions under which a behavior is to be performed can dramatically alter the difficulty and nature of the competency assessed.

For example, the behavior "assemble the milk shake machine" is significantly altered depending on whether the corresponding condition is "given the unassembled parts and the repair manual" or simply "given the unassembled parts." The latter behavior can be expected to be significantly more difficult than the former, and in fact, the very nature of the intended competency specified by the objective changes depending on which condition is used. The former condition causes the objective to describe skills in reading and using a repair manual, whereas the latter specifies mechanical analysis skills.

Standards Component. Complete objectives include a statement of how well the learner must perform the indicated behavior. This component, however, is probably the most difficult component to write. It frequently takes the form "with 90 percent accuracy" or "correctly 80 percent of the time." It is helpful to realize that all standard statements need not be in the form of percentages. In fact, many competencies do not lend themselves to percentage standards at all. Other forms of standards are in terms of:

- number of allowable errors
- time limits
- expert judgments
- negative consequences avoided ("remove pizza from oven to boxing counter *without burning the fingers.*")

If available, the standards component can be useful to test writers in setting the cut-off score for mastery of a criterion-referenced test. However, as we shall see in Chapter 13, the setting of the cut score is a somewhat complex procedure. Test writers need to be careful of objectives with hastily written, ill-thought-out standards statements. Test developers cannot afford simply to adopt the standards dashed off by course designers who do not understand the enormous significance the cut-off score has to the test's effectiveness and its ability to withstand legal challenge.

A WORD FROM THE LEGAL DEPARTMENT ABOUT OBJECTIVES

For trainers, the essence of an objective is the behavior and condition components. The classic objective template reads something like "Given … the student will. …" We have now seen several companies whose legal departments have intervened in this classic model. The issue? The word "will." The word "will" (or its variants) has proved problematic in a few instances, as it *promises* an outcome. Outside purchasers of training who send participants to training, or internal trainees whose job promotions might be at stake, have grieved or litigated when the trainees did not achieve the "promised" skills. Those giving the training argued that the participants didn't fully engage in the training and hence the failure was with the participants and not the training. But the lawyers focused on the word "will" as a promise that was not kept and thus lack of learning constituted a breach of contract. If you think you might be in such a position, you should visit your legal department and ask for their advice. Changing the words "the student will" to "the student will be given materials and instruction that is designed to enable" may make the legal department happier.

THE CERTIFICATION SUITE

There are some important points we feel are relevant to writing the objectives that form the link from job task statements to the test items themselves. Jobs rarely, if ever, depend on the sole memorization of facts. Unfortunately, the vast majority of Level Two assessments regularly test for memorization-level skills. Whether constructing a criterion-referenced assessment for a course or a certification program, it is imperative to recognize that there are systematic, ordered deviations from the ideal of matching the test to the real-world job performance. If an organization feels that it cannot meet the ideal standard in testing, it should at least be cognizant of the tradeoffs in validity that each deviation in fidelity brings with it, the consequences in stating the objectives, and the meaning that can be made of performance on the test.

"The Certification Suite: A Classification System for Certification Tests" (Coscarelli, Robins, Shrock, & Herbst, 1998) proposed a classification system for certification tests based on learning theory and the purposes of the tests. The article began with a definition of certification and a discussion of Bloom's Taxonomy (see Chapters 5 and 7) as a theoretical basis for classifying certification tests. It then described six types of certification tests and concluded with a discussion of how this model might best be used when balancing decision-making criteria for certification test development.

The Certification Suite is divided into two categories: Certification and Quasi-Certification tests. With the permission of the International Society for Performance Improvement, we are presenting a major summary of this article as a way to help you think about matching objectives to the job-task statements—and to the test.

CERTIFICATION LEVELS IN THE SUITE

Level A—Real World. Level A represents the highest level of certification. First, to achieve this level a complete certification process would be used that begins with subject-matter expert review of the job, moves through a comprehensive sampling of the job for item creation, and concludes with reliable and valid tests that match the job. This level would require access to and testing on equipment or in situations configured to match job characteristics and would be completed in "real time." Level A would be the ultimate "real-world" test of skills and knowledge, similar to an airplane pilot flying solo in a range of conditions or a salesperson demonstrating skills in a variety of sales situations. As one can imagine, such tests would clearly demonstrate the examinee's skill level, but in most situations an organization is unable to muster the resources, variety of skills samples, and time to complete such a comprehensive assessment—not to mention the potential costs and safety risks often inherent in real world performance.

Level B—High-Fidelity Simulation. Recognizing that full access to equipment in a real-world setting can be very costly, difficult, or perhaps life-threatening, for example, a nuclear power control room, one could construct high-fidelity simulations that systematically assess a range of skills required for job performance. Level B is a compromise in fidelity, but could nonetheless prove to be a very accurate reflection of job duties. An example would be an airplane pilot passing a flight test using a state-of-the-art simulator. In fact, in many job tasks (especially in the high-tech world) there is very little difference between the tasks assessed in a high-fidelity simulation and the job itself. For example, asking a candidate to configure a business letter from raw text, in a specified time period, using a specific word processing package is very close to a real job task. Another example is asking a new sales person to perform a "closing" with trained actors as customers who evidence one or more common objections to be surmounted by the candidate.

Level C—Scenarios. With Level C, the certification program moves yet further from the real world in that tests are constructed not on performance directly, nor on a high-fidelity simulation. Level C tests are best characterized as scenarios that require the test-taker to select a best option at levels of performance above the memorization level, that is, comprehension, application, or analysis. In Level C, the test would be analogous to asking the airplane pilot questions such as: "What should you do if …?" or "If the instruments show X and you are doing Y, what would you do next?" Depending on the ability of the test designer to construct well-crafted scenarios, Level C can be quite sophisticated.

Level C represents the last level of certification that can be considered to assess an ability to perform on the job. Movement to Level D is often characterized as a compromise between operational demands and test validity. Level D represents the first quantum jump away from fidelity in assessment and should be used with caution. In fact, considering our experiences since publication of the second edition of this book, and at the urging of

Will Thalheimer (personal communication, 2006), we think it best to raise the bar, so to speak, and move Level D from Certification to Quasi-Certification.

QUASI-CERTIFICATION

Quasi-certification is best described as a process that leads to an endorsement not linked to job performance. While Level D shows some job relatedness not found in Levels E and F, its continued use in organizations as a means toward certification or level two assessment has proven dysfunctional and should be applied only with a full understanding of its weakness as an assessment of performance.

Level D—Memorization. It is easy for subject-matter experts to generate memorization-level test questions; in all likelihood, unfortunately, that is the most common corporate testing strategy. Very few jobs require the employee simply to identify memorized content, for example, "True or False: To establish rapport, ask a customer for his or her name." Therefore, simply selecting the correct answer to a memorization level question does not mean that a competency can or will be executed properly on the job. Level D asks questions that demand an ability to remember facts, definitions, rules, or steps in a procedure, but not necessarily the ability to apply them. However, from a business perspective, this level of test may lead to a significant improvement of knowledge and motivation on the part of the performer that could lead to on-the-job transfer of knowledge.

Level D may represent legitimate certification of job content knowledge, for example, memorization of word processor commands may be essential, but Level D represents only the acquisition of information, not the conditional knowledge of when to apply the information on the job.

Level E—Attendance. Many companies do not support a formal assessment of participants in training. For them, testing becomes a very informal process that, at best, guides people in assessing their own skills. Testing at Level E is often more of an instructional tool, rather than an assessment tool, and all too often does not represent a systematic assessment of skills. Rather, it becomes a series of memorization-level questions lifted directly from the material taught or a team project (without consequences) using the equipment that was the subject of the course. At this level, certification is typically a certificate of verified attendance in a class or a curriculum.

Level F—Affiliation. In some areas, such as working with business partners, certification can become a symbol of maintaining a close partnership or relationship. Such certification may mean quicker access to technical support or an earlier notification of system enhancements. Certification here tends to be a demonstration of the partnership or relationship and can be based on a number of factors such as sales, number of years in the partnership, and so forth, and would not need to involve any of the general guidelines for certification described above. Certification at this level is usually made with a minimal investment of time and energy on the part of both partners. Indeed, certification may simply refer to a partner having sold a specific number of products or a dollar volume over a time period and the certificate (perhaps a decal) may be posted near the point of sale. Table 6.1 summarizes the Certification Suite.

TABLE 6.1. SUMMARY OF CERTIFICATION SUITE.

Certification	Level A—Real World
	Level B—High Fidelity
	Level C—Scenario
Quasi-Certification	Level D—Knowledge
	Level E—Attendance
	Level F—Affiliation

HOW TO USE THE CERTIFICATION SUITE

There appear to be two basic ways in which the Suite might be used: finding a common understanding about testing levels and making a professional decision about which level to use.

FINDING A COMMON UNDERSTANDING

First, as we have argued, the Suite can be helpful in positioning the meaning of "certification" or "testing" in discussions. It is one way of getting everyone to speak the same language and to grasp a better understanding of what exactly is needed. Certification as a concept among professionals does mean different things to different people. For example, employee certification is now often an important benefit offered to buyers of high-tech equipment. If I as a customer want my employees certified as evidence that they can use the new equipment I have purchased, I am probably envisioning an A- or B-Level certification. However, most end-of-training tests assess at a D-Level certification. D-Level assessment for A-Level certification is invalid; the learner may have demonstrated the necessary memorization skills required to pass the end-of-course test but may be unable to perform on the job. The decision about the level of certification should be made at the beginning of such contract negotiations so that all parties are aware of what is to be created and delivered and what the consequences of those decisions will be.

MAKING A PROFESSIONAL DECISION

In choosing a level of testing, the professional must balance three dimensions: the correct level for assessment to match the job, the operationally correct level for implementation, and the consequences of testing at a level of lower fidelity than the job calls for.

The correct level to match the job. The best strategy in selecting a certification level is to match the job as closely as possible. Tests at this level will look a great deal like the job, but will require more sophisticated thinking about item sampling and creation. (Tests created to match the job often do not take as long to create and administer as many think; we have seen valid, high-fidelity paper-and-pencil tests for job certification that take less than half a day to create and no more than twenty minutes to administer. These tests operate at the Analysis level and are a direct match to the job.)

The operationally correct level. The degree of fidelity that one brings to the testing setting is probably the most important predictor of success on the job following training and testing. Therefore, tests should be developed to match the job setting as well. As Gronlund observed:

> ... the degree of realism to be incorporated into a performance
> situation depends on the purpose of instruction, the location of the

performance assessment in the instructional sequence, the practical constraints operating (such as time, cost and availability of equipment), and the nature of the task being measured. We shall always favor the performance measure with the highest degree of realism, but these numerous mediating factors may force us to settle for a degree of realism that falls far short of the ideal. (1988, pp. 85–86)

To balance these factors, we suggest the following guidelines:

1. Go as high as necessary to ensure effectiveness,
2. Go as low as possible for efficiency in testing, and
3. Seek to match the test stimuli to the job stimuli.

Figure 6.1 summarizes this relationship.

FIGURE 6.1. SELECTING THE CERTIFICATION LEVEL.

| Level A—Real World |
| Level B—High Fidelity |
| Level C—Scenario |

Go as High as Necessary
to Ensure Effectiveness

Go as Low as Possible
to Ensure Efficiency

The consequences of lower fidelity. Having chosen a level for certification testing that may not match the job's cognitive or operational requirements (for example, access to equipment), the test designer must consider what the consequences of this loss in fidelity will be. In some instances the loss of fidelity is intolerable (for example, flight training); thus major resources must be garnered to create an acceptable certification system. In other instances a business decision will be made that realizes there will be less than 100 percent transfer, but the perceived gain is worth the investment of resources; for example, requiring engineers to answer memory-level questions on content may not be what they do on the job, but it is a foundation for what they do.

Blair (1997, personal communication) argued that in many business training settings Level D certification would provide a real but hard-to-document increase in competence on the job and might be justified on that basis. On the other hand, Level C, Scenario-Based testing is usually no more costly than Level D. If the job competencies require more than memorized information, a better business decision would be Level C, since transfer of the competencies to job performance would be enhanced. Organizations that frequently fret about on-the-job transfer from training might best be served by reviewing the testing or certification process that follows training and by comparing the certification level of that instrument with the job's demands. Any large gap between the certification level and the job's required competencies (for example, Level D testing in place of a Level B test) is likely to lead to dissatisfaction with certification of competence when that competence doesn't appear in the workplace.

CONVERTING JOB-TASK STATEMENTS TO OBJECTIVES

A task-to-objective-to-item link is the best progression in test development and is the one the courts will examine. If you find that you can't complete that match, then you need to make a professional decision about your compromise with the reality of the job. In Chapter 7 we will look at item creation in detail, but to help you get a feel for how objectives and test items can vary from the ideal, we will present one job task, its objective, and four different testing levels with their corresponding objectives. As you read each one, ask yourself the question: "If the learners answered this item correctly, how certain am I they could perform the task on the job?" You will see, we hope, that with each step away from reality, you become less certain of the answer. Yet at the same time you might also see that approximating reality may be easier than you thought.

The Job Task. Think of the water that is piped to your home or business. A technician working at the water company needs to control the flow of water so that there is enough pressure for everyone to shower in the morning, but not so much that the shower becomes the fire hydrant. For this job, there is probably a task description that reads: "Control the flow of water to specific standards." From that task, one objective that could be created is: "Given a pressure reading and flow rate at specific pumps, the performer will identify and perform the corrective action to meet the standards." This objective, which matches the task, subtly changes as you move through the various levels in the Certification Suite, to the point where you may think you have an item that matches the task, but in reality it does not complete the job-to-objective-to-item link.

Let's look at test items and their related objectives at the four certification levels of the Suite.

The job task: "Control the flow of water to specific standards."

Level A—Real World

- The objective is: "Given a pressure reading and flow rate at specific pumps, the performer will identify and perform the corrective action to meet the standards."
- The test is: Place the performer in the water plant and systematically vary the water pressure. With each variation, the performer would read the real gauges and make the correct pressure adjustments.

Level B—High-Fidelity Simulation

- The objective is: "Given a simulated pressure reading and flow rate at specific pumps, the performer will identify and perform the corrective action to meet the standards."
- The test is: Place the performer in a simulated, three-dimensional control room of a water plant and systematically vary the water pressure. With each variation, the performer would correct the pressure using simulated gauges and valves that are based on the underlying relationships of the water plant.

or

- The test is: Place the performer in a simulated, multi-media control room of a water plant and systematically vary the water pressure. With each variation, the performer would correct the pressure using simulated gauges and valves that are based on the underlying relationships of the water plant.

or

- The test is: Place the performer in a simulated, computerized two-dimensional control room of a water plant and systematically vary the water pressure. With each variation, the performer would correct the pressure using simulated gauges and valves that are based on the underlying relationships of the water plant.

Level C—Scenarios

- The objective is: "Given a description of the pressure readings and flow rates at specific pumps, the performer will select the corrective action."
- The test item is: Customers serviced by pumps 6, 7, 8, and 9 complain they have low or no water pressure. The pump readings are:

Pump	Pressure Reading	Flow Rate
6	55	2—1
7	45	2—1
8	45	2—1
9	90	2—2
10	110	2—2
12	45	3—1

What corrective action should be taken?
a. Adjust pump 6 pressure up to 20 pounds.
b. Lower pump-level parameters for pumps 10 and 12 by 20 pounds.
c. Change the flow rate at Pump 10 to 100.
d. Increase flow rate at Pump 12.

Level D—Memorization

- The objective is: "The learner will state the correct pressure level for water flow at a pump."
- The test item is: The correct pressure level for water flow at pump 10 is:
a. 55
b. 60
c. 90
d. 120
e. 140

IN CONCLUSION

In this chapter we have tried to show how matching end-of-course tests or certification exams and the objectives that guide instruction to real workplace activities is the best strategy for test design. We described how to think about compromises in test fidelity to the workplace and classified these compromises into four categories of assessment for objectives-based tests. As you write your objectives and design your tests, you should continue to ask yourself the question we posed earlier: "If the learners answered this item correctly, how certain am I they could perform the task on the job?" The less certain you are that they can perform on the job, the more certain you can be that your objectives and your test lack content validity.

CHAPTER SEVEN

CREATE COGNITIVE ITEMS

WHAT ARE COGNITIVE ITEMS?

The answer to the question "What are cognitive items?" used to be easily understood by test designers. "They are the paper-and-pencil items," most would reply. The traditional distinction was that you assessed intellectual skills with "paper-and-pencil" items, and you used performance scales to observe a behavior or to judge a product. As computer-based technology has evolved, the distinction between the two domains has blurred in many areas.

The first wave of change was simply to move the paper-and-pencil items to the computer screen as a delivery strategy. However, as computer processing power evolved, it became possible to create items that could simulate the job in a manner that "thinking about" the task and "doing it" were indistinguishable; for example, the simulated configuration for installing a Local Area Network and the reality of doing it were essentially the same. In some fields the distinction between "thinking" and "doing" is not easy to reconcile; for example, listing the steps to install an electrical amplifier is not the same as installing it twenty-five feet above ground. However, in an increasing number of information-age jobs you may find it useful to consider how the computer can be used not just as a delivery vehicle—but rather a near-perfect simulation of real-world performance.

CLASSIFICATION SCHEMES FOR OBJECTIVES

As we have seen, good objectives are an essential precursor to sound testing systems. Translating objectives into rating scales for performance tests (Chapter 8) is usually easier than translating objectives into test items for paper-and-pencil tests. One strategy that can be helpful in this regard is to classify the objectives first according to the types of cognitive behavior they require. Classifying objectives by cognitive skill assists item writers in:

- Choosing which item type—multiple-choice, essay, or other— will most accurately and efficiently assess the objective, and
- Deciding what the text of each item will be.

Several different classifications of cognitive behavior have been developed over the years. We discussed three of them, the systems written by Gagné, Merrill, and Bloom, in Chapter 5. In this chapter, however, we will first discuss specific item types in relation to Bloom's original classification system and then explore two other ways to think about item writing.

We are going to concentrate on Bloom's work for a specific reason. Gagné and Merrill based their classifications on learning theory approaches. The systems are, therefore, very useful for instructional designers because they provide instructional prescriptions for each type of learning task. In contrast to the learning theory approaches of Gagné or Merrill, Bloom and his colleagues developed their system through an intensive content analysis of thousands of instructor created test items. As a result, Bloom's Taxonomy provides a particularly comfortable fit with and support to cognitive assessment. You may find the other schemes helpful for test writing as well as instructional design, and all three do share some commonalities, but Bloom's Taxonomy probably provides more refined guidance for test-item construction.

BLOOM'S COGNITIVE CLASSIFICATIONS

In Chapter 5 we described Bloom's Taxonomy of cognitive objectives in some detail. As you will recall, the Taxonomy was created to improve precision in the testing of cognitive processes. The classification scheme consists of six levels with each given level subsuming all levels beneath it as follows:

- Evaluation
- Synthesis
- Analysis
- Application
- Comprehension
- Knowledge

Each of these cognitive levels is described in great detail in the book *Handbook I: Cognitive Domain* (Bloom & Krathwohl, 1956) that originally presented the Taxonomy, *Taxonomy of Educational Objectives*. Understanding the nature of the cognitive performance to be assessed is a good first step to being able to write an appropriate test item. In the *Handbook* the description of each cognitive level is accompanied by many examples of test items that assess that particular cognitive behavior. If a test writer can correctly identify the Bloom level of an instructional objective, a wealth of ideas about how to measure the objective becomes available.

Another important result of understanding Bloom's Taxonomy is an increased awareness of all the cognitive behaviors beyond simply memorizing, that is, beyond the knowledge level. Most of the tests we take in school at all grade levels, and even at the college level, are composed of knowledge-level questions. This circumstance is not difficult to explain, since knowledge-level items are by far the easiest to write. However, developing tests that truly reflect on-the-job performance requires the ability to distinguish among different cognitive behaviors and skill in writing items at the higher cognitive levels, particularly the comprehension, application, and analysis levels.

Table 7.1 is an extensive example of Bloom's Taxonomy that elaborates the six levels within a stimulus and response context.

TABLE 7.1. BLOOM'S TAXONOMY ON THE BATTLEFIELD: A SCENARIO OF HOW BLOOM'S LEVELS OCCUR IN A COMBAT ENVIRONMENT.

Bloom	Stimulus	Response	Elaboration
Knowledge	An infantry squad is sent out on a night recon patrol. The squad encounters a group of enemy tracked and wheeled vehicles. Through Night Vision Goggles, the squad leader identifies each vehicle and reports his findings to the platoon leader.	The squad leader reports seeing four T-72s, three BTRs, and two BMPs. The T-72s are dug-in with the BTRs and BMPs spread out behind the T-72s.	The squad leader is operating at the recall level. He can identify the vehicles based on the armored vehicle recognition flashcards he has studied. He also *describes* the vehicles' positions, he does not *interpret* the positions.
Comprehension	The platoon leader receives the radio transmission. The platoon leader reports the enemy sighting to the company commander.	The platoon leader reports four enemy tanks and five light armored vehicles positioned defensively to the front of the platoon's position at particular grid coordinates.	The platoon leader *interpreted* the patrol's findings. He did not repeat the specifics but *translated* the information for the company commander.
Application	The company commander receives the message from the platoon leader. He understands he is facing enemy armor that is set up defensively at a certain grid coordinate.	Doctrinally, the company commander knows that armor fights armor. He orders 1st platoon to ready their Bradley Fighting Vehicles to engage enemy; orders 2nd platoon to do the same. He calls battalion commander, reports the enemy	The company commander *uses* the information and *applies* it in a new situation. He follows a doctrinal rule and begins to *develop* a plan based on that rule. He knows that Bradleys cannot kill tanks, but can kill light armor, therefore he needs

Bloom	Stimulus	Response	Elaboration
		sighting, and that two platoons are preparing to engage, requests tank support.	tanks to support his light armored vehicles.
Analysis	The battalion commander receives the message from the company commander. He understands that there is enemy armor that is set up defensively at a particular grid coordinate. He also understands that light armor assets are being prepared to engage the enemy and that heavy armor is being requested to support the mission.	The battalion commander knows that he does not have heavy armor in his unit. He must request heavy armor from another unit. Given the information he has, he calls the brigade commander to report the situation and request two platoons of heavy armor. One platoon to help the Bradleys complete the mission and one held in reserve should they need it.	Battalion commander knows his unit is but one part of the brigade. He knows he needs another part from the brigade to complete the mission. He has *identified* what his unit needs and where he can get it. He also understands the *relationship* between units and how they can work together in this new situation to accomplish the mission.
Synthesis	The brigade commander receives the message from the battalion commander. He understands that a small enemy armored force has	The brigade commander calls his tank battalion commander and orders two platoons be sent on the mission. He tells him to call the light armored	The brigade commander brings the parts of the brigade together to *form a whole* that can accomplish the mission. He understands that the units are

(*continued*)

TABLE 7.1. (CONTINUED)

Bloom	Stimulus	Response	Elaboration
	been sighted at particular grid coordinates and that light armored vehicles are preparing to attack and awaiting heavy armor support.	battalion commander and coordinate a rendezvous point for the tanks and Bradleys to link up, and to let him know what it is, and what their battle plan will be. The brigade commander then calls Division Artillery to request support for the mission. He gives them the grid coordinates of the enemy position and the name of the units involved in the attack so direct coordination can occur. The Brigade Commander then calls Division to report the situation.	complementary and must work together to defeat the enemy. He *organizes* the units involved and provides them with additional support. He has *designed* a combination of units that should accomplish the mission in this previously unencountered situation.

Bloom	Stimulus	Response	Elaboration
Evaluation	The chain of command reports that the battle was fought and won. All enemy armor was destroyed, with twenty-five enemy soldiers KIA and ten wounded. Two Bradleys were destroyed and two were damaged. Five soldiers KIA, fifteen wounded.	The brigade commander meets with the two battalion commanders and two company commanders involved. They discuss the battle in detail. What worked, what did not work? Did the artillery land where it was supposed to? Why were five of our soldiers killed? What tactics did the enemy use? What other tactics could we have used? What did we learn from the battle?	The soldiers in this meeting are trying to *make a judgment* about the battle. They are using costs vs. benefits as their criterion. The costs of the battle were five lives lost and two vehicles destroyed. The benefit was the enemy was destroyed. Do the benefits outweigh the costs? What can be done next time to reduce or eliminate the costs? Was the battle a success?

© 1993, Shrock, Coscarelli, and Burke.

PRACTICE

Here are six instructional objectives. Indicate the Bloom cognitive level at which you think each objective is written. Remember that objectives are classified at the highest level of cognitive functioning that they require.

1. Given an historical account of a working task force, identify the major characteristics of the group's functioning and describe the causal relations between these characteristics that explain the group's behavior.
   Bloom Level: _____

2. Shown a videotape of a business meeting, use principles of group behavior to predict the likely outcomes of the meeting.
   Bloom Level: _____

3. Given access to a job description, a subject-matter expert, and other supporting documentation regarding job responsibilities and employee characteristics, design an appropriate course of instruction to train an employee to perform the job.
   Bloom Level: _____

4. Given an oral description of a procedure, depict the procedure as a flowchart.
   Bloom Level: _____

5. List the criteria presented in class for judging the effectiveness of an oral presentation.
   Bloom Level: _____

6. Given a marketing plan for a new product, a description of the product, and access to the product's designers, determine the likely effectiveness of each major stage of the plan.
   Bloom Level: _____

FEEDBACK

1. Analysis   4. Comprehension

2. Application   5. Knowledge

3. Synthesis   6. Evaluation

TYPES OF TEST ITEMS

The classic notion about a test item is that it poses a question and either provides possible answers or distractors (called closed-ended items) or allows for a free-form response (open-ended items):

- Closed-ended questions are often used when you are looking for a response that would have a predictable correct answer. Common item types are multiple-choice, true/false, and matching. Closed-ended items are easily scored by a computer and will provide the best chance of establishing an acceptable level of reliability for a test.
- Open-ended questions are used when you are gathering information or looking for a response that is not easily classified as right or wrong. Common types of open-ended items are essay, short answer, fill-in, and numeric. Open-ended questions are difficult for humans to score reliably, but even more difficult to score using computers. Establishing test reliability and validity for tests composed of open-ended items typically requires greater effort on the part of the test designer.

NEWER COMPUTER-BASED ITEM TYPES

Computer-based testing has had the effect of increasing the number of test item types and response modes now available to test designers. Most of them are closed-ended in nature. There are some advantages to these new item formats, although it has been our experience that many of them are used primarily for memory-level assessments and that practice should be avoided. We want to provide a brief survey of these item types, but then concentrate our discussion on the six item types that are most commonly used by item writers. Four of the newer item formats are:

- *Animated.* Using software technology such as Macromedia Flash, an item can be created that introduces motion as part of the posed question.
- *Drag and Drop.* A list of options is presented to test-takers, and they use their computer mouse to select an option and move it to an appropriate place on the screen.

- *Hotspot.* The test-taker is directed to answer a question by clicking on a place on the screen or touching the screen depending on the type of screen.
- *Pull Down.* A selection of options is presented by a mouse click on a chosen field.

Caution should be used in introducing novel item types or response modes because confusion regarding how to respond to an item would certainly introduce error into test scores. Be sure test-takers are thoroughly comfortable with an item format before employing it in a test.

THE SIX MOST COMMON ITEM TYPES

There are six types of test items most commonly used in cognitive tests. These item types are:

- True/False
- Matching
- Multiple-Choice
- Fill-In
- Short Answer
- Essay

Of these six, multiple-choice is the preferred item type for most cognitive tests. It has the advantage of being able to assess most of Bloom's cognitive levels, yet it can be reliably scored by hand or machine. Therefore, throughout our discussion of item types we will frequently make comparisons between a given item type and multiple-choice. For each of these six item formats we present:

- A description of the item type and the kind of content for which the format is best suited
- The Bloom levels assessable by the item type
- The major advantages and disadvantages of using the item type
- A summary of the guidelines for writing each item type correctly

True/False Items

Description. The true/false item presents the test-taker with a statement that he or she must indicate is either true or false. This type of item is a sensible choice for "naturally dichotomous" content, that is, content that presents the learner with only two plausible choices. For example, assume your objective requires that given blood-composition data, learners will classify the blood as that of a male or a female. You might construct true/false questions asserting that a given blood composition is male or female to which the test-taker would respond "true" or "false." Content that is not naturally dichotomous is usually best assessed using the multiple-choice format because true/false questions have some distinct limitations that will be discussed below.

Bloom Levels. True/false items can assess the knowledge, comprehension, and application levels. However, unfortunately they are most often used to assess only the knowledge level.

Advantages. The primary advantage of true/false items is that they are typically easier to write than other types of closed-ended questions, that is, matching or multiple-choice. However, the reputed ease of construction is partly because most of these items are written at the knowledge level; it requires more thought to write true/false items at higher cognitive levels. Their other advantages are that, like all closed-ended questions, they are easily and reliably scored, and test-taker responses can be submitted to statistical item analysis that can be used to improve the quality of the test. (These item analysis procedures are discussed in Chapter 11.)

Disadvantages. The biggest disadvantage of true/false items is that test-takers have a 50–50 chance of getting the items correct simply by guessing. However, if the true/false item covers content that is truly dichotomous, it will be very difficult to write a multiple-choice item with more than two choices anyway, resulting in an item that also allows test-takers to guess correctly half of the time. Before writing true/false items, always examine the content and instructional objectives carefully to be sure that they are not more appropriately addressed by multiple-choice items. The key to using true/false items effectively is to use them only when the content is naturally dichotomous and to write true/false items that require more than mere memorization of content.

Matching Items

Description. Matching items present test-takers with two lists of words or phrases and ask the test-taker to match each word or phrase on one list (hereafter referred to as the "A" list) to a word or phrase on the other (the "B" list). These items should be used only when assessing understanding of homogeneous content (types of wire, types of clouds, types of switches, etc.). The matching item most frequently takes the form of a list of words to be matched with a list of definitions.

Bloom Levels. The matching item can assess the knowledge and comprehension levels. However, like the true/false item, we very rarely see them written beyond the knowledge level.

Advantages. Matching items are relatively easy to write. Note, however, that one reason for this feature is that they do not assess beyond the comprehension level. Matching items can be scored quickly and objectively by hand and frequently also by machine. Responses to matching questions can be submitted to statistical item analysis procedures.

Disadvantages. Matching items are limited to the two lowest levels of Bloom's Taxonomy. Another disadvantage is that if these items are constructed using heterogeneous content, that is, if the words or phrases appearing on the "A" list are essentially unrelated to one another, matching items become extremely easy. For example, a list that contains a type of software, a type of fuse, a type of icon, or whatever, will be easier to match to a corresponding "B" list than will a list that contains only names of different types of software. Another difficulty with matching items results from test writers including equal numbers of entries in both lists and allowing items from the "B" list to be used only once. Under these circumstances, test-takers can use the process of elimination to figure out cues to the correct matches. A better practice is to include more items in the "B" list and allow each item in the "B" list to be used more than once.

Multiple-Choice Items

Description. The multiple-choice item presents test-takers with a question (technically called a "stem") and then asks them to choose from among a series of alternative answers (a single correct or best answer and several distractors). Sometimes the question takes the form of an incomplete sentence followed by a series of alternative completions among which the test-taker is to choose. Sometimes the stem is a relatively complex scenario containing several pieces of information ending in a question. Dichotomous content can be assessed using multiple-choice questions with two optional answers; thus, most true/false items can be converted to the multiple-choice format.

Bloom Levels. Multiple-choice questions can assess all Bloom levels except the two highest ones, synthesis and evaluation. The reason that these two levels are beyond multiple-choice questions is that they require totally original responses on the part of the test-taker. Because multiple-choice questions are closed-ended—the correct answer appears before the test-taker who must recognize it—the test-taker's response is necessarily not original. However, multiple-choice allows assessment of more Bloom levels than any other closed-ended question format.

EXAMPLES OF MULTIPLE-CHOICE ITEMS AT DIFFERENT BLOOM LEVELS

Here are four multiple-choice items, one written at each of the four Bloom levels assessable by items of this format.

KNOWLEDGE LEVEL

According to Gagné, the association of an already available response with a new stimulus is called:

A. instrumental conditioning

B. learning

C. signal learning

D. front-end analysis

Discussion. The answer is "C." The item is knowledge level because it simply asks the student to remember the definition of signal learning.

COMPREHENSION LEVEL

According to the definition of "refugee" used by the United Nations, what group below would NOT qualify as refugees?

A. Vietnamese boat people in Indonesia.

B. Ugandan Christians who fled to Tanzania during Idi Amin's rule.

C. Cambodian followers of Pol Pot who fled to the northwestern mountains of Cambodia when the Vietnamese invaded Cambodia in December 1978.

D. Palestinians now living in Lebanon.

E. Jews who came to the United States from Europe in the 1930s.

Discussion. The answer is "E." This item is written at the comprehension level because the test-taker has been asked to translate information from one form to another. In this item the test-taker must translate from one level of abstraction to another; that is, the student has been asked to recognize a specific non-example (the word "not" is emphasized) of the more abstract concept "refugee." For an item to be at this level, the test-taker must not be able to simply remember the correct answer. This item would not be a comprehension-level item if the students had previously been shown these examples of refugees or told that Jews who came to the United States during the 1930s were not refugees.

Many times a test designer *cannot* tell whether an item is at the knowledge or any other level without knowing the content of the students' previous instruction. *Any* item that has been encountered previously will be a knowledge-level item regardless of the test designer's intent.

APPLICATION LEVEL

Amy, age three-and-a-half, spills her milk at the table. According to current principles of child development, her parents should:

A. Tell her she shouldn't waste milk, and refuse to let her have any more at the meal.

B. Wipe up the milk in silence and serve her again.

C. Have Amy get the cloth to help wipe it up. Serve her again.

D. Dismiss Amy from the table.

E. Tell Amy that she is a baby when she spills, and that the next time she will be served milk from a bottle.

Discussion. The answer is "C." This is an application item emphasizing the application of child development principles in a new context. It is assumed that the students have never before been confronted with Amy's milk-spilling behavior. They are being asked to apply a principle of child development having to do with encouraging children to accept responsibility for the consequences of their behavior. In choosing the correct answer, the test-taker must consider the situation, decide how it is similar to the context in which he or she learned relevant principles, and then apply the correct principles to get the right answer.

ANALYSIS LEVEL

Susan, a student in Mr. Stepp's statistics class, asks Mr. Stepp what her average score is for the three exams he has given the class. Breaking with his usual manner of reporting scores, he replies that her average is +1.7. Which of the following assumptions about the student's scores on these tests is most plausible?

A. The standard deviations of scores on all three tests were similar.

B. None of the tests produced extremely skewed distributions.

C. All of the students did poorly on at least one of the tests.

D. The correlations between the three sets of test scores were restricted.

Discussion. The answer is "D." This is an analysis item because it requires the test-taker to recognize unstated assumptions. In this item the test-taker must first recognize that Mr. Stepp has converted the students' raw test scores to standard Z scores, a type of score based on the student's position relative to other test-takers. The test-taker must them remember that this conversion is usually made before averaging the scores from tests that have resulted in very unlike distributions, or in a lack of variation in the scores on one or more tests.

It is this assumption of lack of variation in the scores that provides the clue to the correct answer. The only choice that makes a true statement about test scores generally lacking in variation is "D." The correlations between tests when students tend to score alike—when there is a lack of variation in their scores—will be low, or more technically speaking, be "restricted." Hence "D" is the correct answer. "A" is wrong because similar standard deviations on tests indicate like distributions. "B" is wrong because the absence of extremely skewed scores increases the likelihood that adequate variation was present in the scores. "C" is wrong because all of the students could have done well on one of the tests and the variation would still be lacking. In other words, "C" is an assumption too specific to be warranted by the facts given.

Note the differences between application and analysis. In application, the emphasis is on remembering and bringing to bear upon given material the appropriate principles. In analysis, the emphasis is on breaking complex material down into its component parts and detecting the relationships of the parts to one another. Remember, analysis does involve application, as it does comprehension and knowledge. Such is the hierarchical nature of Bloom's Taxonomy.

Advantages. Multiple-choice is the most flexible of all closed-ended item formats. Multiple-choice items can assess any kind of content at a variety of Bloom levels. Because the test-taker must choose among several optional answers, the probability of simply guessing the correct answer is lower than with true/false items. Furthermore, multiple-choice items are ideal for diagnostic testing. In other words, the distractors can target learners with specific problems; knowing what wrong answers test-takers chose can be important and useful information for instructors and course designers. In addition, multiple-choice questions are quickly and reliably scored either by hand or by machine and are ideally suited to statistical item analysis procedures that can lead to improved test quality (see Chapter 11).

Disadvantages. The major disadvantage of multiple-choice questions is that they are difficult and time-consuming to write. Most testing authorities agree that well-written multiple-choice questions are usually worth the effort, especially if they can be used repeatedly with a large number of test-takers. An additional weakness is that multiple-choice questions cannot assess objectives that require test-takers to recall information unassisted, since the correct answer does appear before the test-taker among the options. Their only other disadvantage is their inability to assess directly the synthesis and evaluation cognitive levels.

Avoiding the Multiple Response and Combined Response Variants. Finally, we want to caution against two variations of the multiple-choice item:

- The multiple-response item that presents a stem and a series of responses, and then asks the test-taker to select *more than one* choice from the list of distractors.
- The combined-response item that presents a stem and a series of options and then asks the test-taker to select the correct combination of responses to answer the question, for example, a) 1 and 2; b) 1, 2 and 4; c) 1 only if 2 is not present, etc.

Here is a sample item (italics preserved) from this variant class about which Case and Swanson (2001, p. 24) noted: "Sometimes, item writers can take a perfectly easy question and turn it into something so convoluted that only the most stalwart will even read it. This item is a sample of that kind of item."

Arrange the parents of the following children with Down's syndrome in order of the highest to lowest risk of recurrence. Assume that the maternal age in all cases is 22 years and that a subsequent pregnancy occurs within 5 years. The karyotypes of the daughters are:

   I. *46, XX, -14, +T (14q21q) pat*
  II. *46, XX, -14, +T (14q21q) de novo*
 III. *46, XX, -14, +T (14q21q) pat*
 IV. *46, XX, -21, +T (14q21q) pat*
  V. *47, XX, +T (21q21q) (parents not karyotyped)*
 VI. *III, IV, I, V, II*

  A. *IV, III, V, I, II*
  B. *III, I, IV, V, II*
  C. *IV, III, I, V, II*
  D. *III, IV, I, II, V*

You should avoid using these two types of items unless there is some very strong evidence from the job task analysis that this format reflects important job skills. Quoting from a summary of guidelines for creating multiple-choice items, Burton, Sudweeks, Merrill, and Wood (1991) observed:

> In a survey of forty-six authoritative references in the field of educational measurement, thirty-two of the thirty-five authors that discussed how many correct answers to include in an item recommend using only one. ... (In addition) numerous studies indicate that items of the combined-response variety have been found to be lower in reliability, higher in difficulty, and equal in validity when compared to similar items of the single-correct answer and best-answer varieties. (pp. 13–14)

SIDEBAR: THE MAN WITH THE MULTIPLE-CHOICE MIND[1]

Murgatroyd stirred fitfully as the music beat upon his fuddled brain. Slowly, almost painfully, he formulated the question. He was:

1. At a disco with Miss Godwin

2. Asleep

---

[1]E.A. Reitan (1979, April). The Man with the Multiple-Choice Mind. *Academe: Bulletin of the AAUP,* LXV, 197–201.

3. Awake

4. Hearing his clock radio

As his brain cleared, Murgatroyd marked number 4 on his mental Op-Scan sheet. He rolled over on his back and tried to think. Today was:

1. Monday

2. Tuesday

3. Wednesday

4. All of the above

5. None of the above

Again, the last answer was correct. The day was Thursday, and today he was scheduled to do all of the following except:

1. Conduct his 8 o'clock class

2. See Miss Godwin

3. Meet with the departmental proficiency committee

4. Talk to the department chairman about tenure

Mentally he marked number 4 as the exception, since, with his dissertation topic unsettled, such a conference, although necessary, was too risky. Instead he turned his thoughts to breakfast. The possibilities were:

1. Eggs and bacon

2. Cereal and toast

3. Coffee and doughnuts after class

4. Nothing

Deciding that number 4 was insufficiently nourishing for such an important day, and number 1 was too high in cholesterol, Murgatroyd inclined to number 2 until a glance at the clock made it clear that number 3 was the only answer consistent with making his 8 o'clock Western Civ class. If he hurried he would be there in time to see Miss Godwin make her entrance, looking deliciously drowsy and sulky at the same time. As he showered, Murgatroyd hoped that Jones, the burly linebacker who sat next to Miss Godwin, would not appear. He began to feel sprightly and witty, and he preferred that Miss Godwin give him her undivided attention.

Looking ahead to the meeting of the departmental proficiency committee, which the department chairman would probably attend, Murgatroyd contemplated what he should wear. The choices were:

1. The tweed jacket with brown pants

2. The brown herringbone suit

3. The blue blazer with gray flannel pants

4. The green bush jacket with twill pants

Each alternative had advantages and disadvantages. The tweed jacket (number 1) seemed more scholarly, but it gave him a rumpled, relaxed look and he wanted a more businesslike appearance, since the proficiency test would be administered to hundreds of students using the latest technology. Miss Godwin seemed to like the blue blazer (number 3), but the chairman might think such an outfit more suitable for late afternoon or evening wear. The bush jacket (number 4) made him stand out among his drabber colleagues but seemed too dashing for a meeting of the proficiency committee. Thus he marked number 2 on his mental Op-Scan sheet and proceeded to dress.

Murgatroyd was a young assistant professor with rather unusual mental processes. His genius for multiple-choice had first displayed itself in European history during his freshman year in college. After the hour exam on the Renaissance-Reformation period, he had argued with the professor—successfully—that one of the foils in the question on Luther's doctrine of the Eucharist had discriminated insufficiently between transubstantiation and consubstantiation. The professor had given him credit for the question, which raised his grade from a B plus to an A minus, and he made Murgatroyd's triumph complete when he carefully marked the question for revision. For the rest of the course, Murgatroyd studied furiously, hoping to repeat his earlier success. Although the professor's subsequent multiple-choice questions contained many flaws, all of which Murgatroyd pointed out, the professor never again conceded a point and Murgatroyd ended the course with a low B. By that time Murgatroyd had concluded that all human problems could be reduced to one right answer and three wrong ones ("Which of the following is. . . ?") or to three right answers and one wrong one ("Which of the following is not. . . ?"). There were a few circumstances in which "all of the above" or "none of the above" might properly be used, but such occasions of unanimity (positive or negative) were rare.

From this humble beginning, Murgatroyd's multiple-choice mind had flowered. Thereafter he took large lecture classes, where his skill in interpreting multiple-choice questions stood him in good stead. In graduate school he honed his unique skill by developing a distinctive style for seminar papers. Murgatroyd's professors were impressed with the logic and order of his presentations, little realizing the mental habits that gave form to his work. A Murgatroyd seminar paper was like a symphony with four movements, each part corresponding, had the professor known it, to one of the foils of a multiple-choice question. A case in point was his seminar paper on historical interpretations of the causes of the civil wars in England. In the paper Murgatroyd reviewed the interpretations of (1) Macaulay, (2) Tawney, and (3) Trevor-Roper, taking about three pages to summarize the work of each historian and demonstrate why the interpretation was unsatisfactory. In part 4 of the paper, Murgatroyd argued for an ideological interpretation of the origins of conflict, which corresponded to the correct answer of a multiple-choice question. During the questioning that followed, Murgatroyd conceded that even the unsatisfactory interpretations had some value ("all of the above"), but stoutly resisted the nihilistic notion that no satisfactory interpretation ("none of the above") was possible. Later he reduced each of the four interpretations to one phrase, which he used with considerable success as a multiple-choice question in his freshman quiz section. Satisfactory as Murgatroyd's method was for seminars, he had yet to find a dissertation topic that would yield to his distinctive mode of thinking, although he sensed that the Court-Country, Whig-Tory polarizations of the early eighteenth century offered possibilities. However, until he found a suitable topic Murgatroyd was just another floundering A.B.D., which reduced his chances for tenure considerably. For that reason he held high hopes that the departmental proficiency test would redress the balance.

As is often the case with instructors who begin teaching before completing their dissertations, Murgatroyd's classes had generated a wide range of interests to which the narrow specialism of the Ph.D. seemed irrelevant. In the five years since taking his position, Murgatroyd had taught Western Civ from Ancient Times to 1700 and from 1700 to the present, plus a stint in a one-semester World Civ course that included the Middle East, India, China, Japan, and Africa. He had also substituted once in an interdisciplinary humanities class. These experiences had been stimulating to Murgatroyd's immature brain and he felt himself to be a junior Toynbee, seeing the full panoply of human history unroll before his eyes, as in a Charlton Heston Cinemascope spectacular. He avoided cranial indigestion in a manner natural to himself—by reducing textbook generalizations to multiple-choice questions. The ponderous textbooks used in these courses were usually supplemented by even bulkier collections of readings, to which Murgatroyd owed almost all his knowledge of the great creations of the human mind from Plato to Malraux. He found that readings could be put into multiple-choice form by skillful selection of key phrases. The end result was a beatific vision. Somewhere Murgatroyd had read of a Russian economist who had programmed the world economy in 144 simultaneous equations. Murgatroyd had an even more ambitious goal: to encapsulate all human achievement in one hundred perfect multiple-choice questions. With such a dream before him, identification of a dissertation topic seemed to be indefinitely delayed.

As he tooled along the Belt Line on his way to campus, Murgatroyd felt a rising buoyancy. The previous four days of rain and sleet had prolonged winter unbearably, but now the sky was clearing and there were signs that a warm April sun would break through the mist later in the morning. It seemed to Murgatroyd that the day held the prospect of all the following except:

1. Warm sunshine

2. A good lecture

3. A lovely Miss Godwin

4. Scornful rejection of his proficiency test

Murgatroyd did not hesitate to mark number 4 on his mental Op-Scan; youth may be excused optimism in early spring.

Turning into his usual parking lot (pleasingly empty at 7:55 A.M.), Murgatroyd's thoughts turned to Miss Godwin. On such a pleasant day he anticipated that she would wear:

1. A bright cotton frock

2. An off-shoulder print blouse with denim skirt

3. Jeans with shirt open at the throat

4. A tailored suit

Instantly dismissing number 1 as too girlish and number 4 as too ladylike, Murgatroyd for no very good reason settled on number 3. He was pleased to find that his instinctive mastery of multiple choice had not deserted him, for when he entered the classroom Miss Godwin was seated in the front row wearing well-washed jeans and a crisp white shirt with at least one button (possibly two) unfastened. Jones was not present at all. Murgatroyd sensed one of those days when everything was going his way.

Murgatroyd was in fine form that morning. He had developed the practice of lecturing from his multiple-choice questions, since the true answers embodied the points he wished to make and the false answers, as in Aquinas' Summa Theologica, were the alternatives that needed to be refuted. Thus the lecture included the material which, in terse multiple-choice form, would eventually appear on the test. Cunningly, Murgatroyd covered the early reign of George III without revealing the actual question to the students:

Which of the following statements concerning the personal influence of George III on the politics of the period 1700–1784 is true:

1. He was determined to exercise personally the legal powers of the king.

2. He desired to overthrow the Revolution Settlement and restore royal absolutism.

3. He preferred to entrust government to ministers chosen by the majority party.

4. He was interested in foreign policy but left domestic matters to the cabinet.

Murgatroyd began his lecture with an exposition of answer number 1, pointing out the constitutional ambiguities of the British monarchy in the mid-eighteenth century and commenting on the assessments of the king's intentions offered by Namier, Pares, and Butterfield. He then turned to refutation of number 2, waxing indignant as he showed how Horace Walpole and Edmund Burke had fabricated the canards that underlay the "Whig" interpretation of that unfairly maligned monarch. Foil number 3 gave him an opportunity to discourse on nineteenth-century misunderstandings of eighteenth-century cabinet government and political parties (decisively exploded by Namier). Foil number 4 led to the assertion that such a statement might apply reasonably well to George I, but completely ignored George III's determination to exercise a guiding hand in major policies and even minor patronage matters. Murgatroyd noted with satisfaction that most of the students, suspecting that one or two exam questions were concealed someplace in the lecture, were industriously taking notes. Even Miss Godwin was writing and, as she leaned over her desk, the deep V in her neckline made Murgatroyd even more aware that spring was at hand.

Murgatroyd's cup of delight ran over when Miss Godwin stopped after class to ask if she could speak to him in his office. As they walked together down the corridor, Murgatroyd pondered the possibility that she would ask him to:

1. Tutor her on Sunday evenings

2. Accompany her to her sorority formal

3. Help her decorate her apartment

4. All of the above

5. None of the above

Ominously the correct answer was number 5, for Miss Godwin simply wanted to take the next test on Monday instead of Friday. It turned out that Miss Godwin was a pom-pom girl and was expected to perform at the intra-squad spring football game, at which the well-muscled Jones would undoubtedly shine. Murgatroyd agreed, but with a sense that a cloud had passed over the day that had begun so auspiciously.

Murgatroyd spent the next hour preparing for the meeting of the departmental proficiency committee. The request of the department chairman for a Western Civ proficiency test consisting of one hundred multiple-choice questions had come to Murgatroyd as the opportunity of a lifetime. Perhaps departmental recognition of his unique talent would have some bearing on the decision concerning tenure, which had previously turned largely on his dissertation proposal, or lack of one. For the past five years Murgatroyd had struggled to select one hundred key movements, personalities, or ideas in Western civilization and reduce them to the essential points that could be stated in a multiple-choice question. Thus the question on Pericles captured the essence of Athenian democracy; the question on Machiavelli unraveled the subtleties of Renaissance statecraft; and the question on Luther (justification, of course) plumbed the depths of the Reformation. The method was not as confining as it appeared, for many other facets of Western civilization were included as wrong answers: Metternich's Concert of Europe in the question on nationalism and Montesquieu's separation of powers in the question on Rousseau. No topic was included, either as a right answer or a wrong answer, that was not found in three standard textbooks and two collections of documents. When the subject of a departmental proficiency test was raised, Murgatroyd understandably saw himself as the man of the hour.

Murgatroyd was both tense and confident as he entered the departmental conference room where the proficiency committee met. The next forty-five minutes were the most excruciating of his life. The department chairman, who used only essay tests graded by his graduate assistant, had decided that he was an expert on multiple-choice. Worst of all, he was a bare facts man. His proposed question on Pericles suggested nothing about Athenian democracy; it merely required selecting Pericles from three other names (Socrates, Aristotle, Plutarch) as the leader of Athens at the beginning of the Peloponnesian War. His question on Renaissance politics asked the student to identify Cosimo dé Medici with Milan, Venice, Florence, or the Papacy. And so it went. When his questions went beyond mere fact, his right answers were so loaded with pedantic qualifiers that they were twice as long as his wrong answers—a dead giveaway! His wrong answers had no deceptive plausibility whatever. For example, Thucydides was given as a wrong answer in a question dealing with Italian humanism when Francesco Sforza would have been perfect—obviously Italian, familiar enough to trigger recognition, but not important enough to be the subject of a question. Ambiguities abounded. Even his question on Luther used transubstantiation and consubstantiation!

Most distressing of all to Murgatroyd was the discovery that the other members of the committee invariably accepted the chairman's questions in preference to his own. Silently he contemplated defeat and the high probability that he would not be granted tenure. Instinctively, his inner turmoil took multiple-choice form.

This question about Pericles is:

1. Rote memory

2. Insignificant

3. Inane

4. All of the above (You better believe it!)

5. None of the above (Ha!)

Which of the following is not characteristic of our great chairman:

1. Windbag (Right on!)

2. Fathead (Meathead? Pighead?)

3. Scholarly, thoughtful, humble, helpful, open to other ideas, considerate, perceptive (Never make the correct answer too long!)

4. Pompous (Yeah! Yeah! Yeah!)

The reason this committee can't see that my question on Renaissance politics is meaningful while his is stupid is that:

1. They are lousy historians, indifferent teachers, and gutless toadies (Sometimes put the correct answer first. Students don't like to mark number 1.)

2. My question requires a level of perception that students cannot be expected to reach (Their contempt for students is an expression of their subconscious assessment of themselves!)

3. Geography is the key to Renaissance politics (Pretty far-fetched!)

4. If you have heard of Cosimo de' Medici, you can be assumed to understand Renaissance politics (Ha! And again a big fat Ha!)

Suddenly Murgatroyd felt his heart pound and his temples throb. His breath came in quick gasps, and for a moment he felt stabbing pain run along his left arm. When the committee rejected his question on justification by faith, accepting instead the chairman's muddled question on transubstantiation, Murgatroyd staggered to his feet. It seemed to him that his soul had parted from his body and he could scarcely recognize his voice in the hoarse rasps that issued in rising volume and intensity from his burning throat. What happened thereafter was a blur he was never able to recall.

When self-awareness returned, Murgatroyd was sitting in his office, dazed. As he looked up, he hardly realized that Miss Godwin was standing in the doorway. She was still wearing the white blouse with the open neck; Murgatroyd was totally indifferent to whether the buttons were fastened or not. She gave him an unusually shy smile and entered, seating herself on the edge of the chair by the desk.

"Mr. Murgatroyd," she began, "You know, I'm really enjoying your class. It's like, well, you know, it's really interesting. Even your tests. I mean, they're hard but they're fair, and they really make a person study."

"Fine, Miss Godwin," Murgatroyd replied faintly. "It really is OK for you to take that test on Monday if you wish."

"Oh, that's not what I came about," she replied. "It's just that my parents have this condominium in Sarasota, you know, by the beach, and I'm going there for spring vacation. They said I could bring a friend, and I thought, you know, that maybe you would like to:

1. Go to Florida for spring vacation

2. Come to Sarasota

3. Stay at our condo

4. All of the above

5. None of the above

Earl A. Reitan is Professor Emeritus of History at Illinois State University, Normal, Illinois. His specialties are English history and World War II (he is a veteran). His main publications are *The Thatcher Revolution: Margaret Thatcher, John Major, Tony Blair and the Transformation of Modern Britain, Politics, Finance, and the People: Economical Reform in England, 1770–1792, Politics, War, and Empire: The Rise of Britain to a World Power, 1688–1792, Riflemen: On the Cutting Edge of World War II*, and he is co-author with Roger Manning of *English Heritage*, a two-volume textbook.

Fill-In Items

Description. Unlike the first three item formats discussed, fill-in items are open-ended, that is, the answer does not appear before the test-taker. Rather, the fill-in item is a question or an incomplete statement followed by a blank line upon which the test-taker writes the answer to the question or completes the sentence. Therefore, fill-in questions should be used when the instructional objective requires that the test-taker recall or create the correct answer rather than simply recognize it. Objectives that require the correct spelling of terms, for example, require fill-in items. Fill-in items are limited to those questions that can be answered in a word or short phrase; short answer and essay questions require much longer responses.

Bloom Levels. Fill-in items can assess the knowledge, comprehension, or application levels. They most often are written, however, at the knowledge level.

Advantages. Fill-in items are typically easy to write. They are essential for assessing recall as opposed to recognition of information.

Disadvantages. There are two major disadvantages of fill-in items. One is that they are suitable only for questions that can be answered with a word or short phrase. This characteristic typically limits the sophistication of the content that can be assessed with fill-in items. The second major disadvantage is that, like all open-ended questions, fill-in items present scoring problems. Because test-takers are free to write any answer they choose, sometimes there can be a debate over the correctness of a given answer. Test-takers are marvelously unpredictable when it comes to concocting an unanticipated answer to an open-ended question. Unlike the scoring of closed-ended questions, the scoring of all open-ended questions requires judgment calls on the part of the scorer.

Short Answer Items

Description. These items are open-ended questions requiring responses from test-takers of one page or less in length. Short answer questions require responses longer than those for fill-in items and shorter than those for essay questions. Short answer questions are recommended when the objective to be assessed requires that the test-taker recall information unassisted (rather than recognize information) or create original responses of relatively short length.

Bloom Levels. Short answer questions can be used to assess all Bloom levels except possibly the highest one, evaluation; most responses to evaluation questions would necessarily be somewhat longer.

Advantages. The major advantage of short answer questions is that they are able to elicit original responses from test-takers. For some objectives at the higher Bloom levels, only short answer and essay questions are appropriate. Lower-level short answer questions are typically easier to write than multiple-choice questions covering the same content. It is important to remember, however, that changing the format of a question can significantly alter the cognitive skills assessed. Short answer items are best reserved for those objectives that cannot be assessed using closed-ended questions.

Disadvantages. The only disadvantages of short answer questions are, unfortunately, extremely serious ones. Most notably, short answer questions are very difficult to score reliably. The evaluation of short answer responses and essays is notoriously prone to error resulting from halo effects, placement of a given test in the scoring sequence, scorer fatigue, and especially, quality of handwriting. In addition to being unreliable, the scoring of short answer responses is time-consuming. Short answer questions also require far more time to answer than multiple-choice questions, thus sometimes limiting severely the content that can be covered by the test.

Essay Items

Description. Essay items are open-ended test questions requiring a response longer than a page in length. They are recommended for objectives that require original, lengthy responses from test-takers. Essay items are also recommended for the assessment of writing skills.

Bloom Levels. Essay questions can be used to assess all levels of Bloom's Taxonomy. They are the only item type with this capability, and the only item type that can truly assess the evaluation level.

Advantages. The essay question's major advantage is its capacity to assess the highest cognitive levels. Essay questions that assess the lower levels are usually not difficult or time-consuming to construct. Those that assess the higher levels can be very difficult to write, requiring the provision of a great deal of stimulus material to which the test-taker responds in the essay.

Disadvantages. The disadvantages of the essay item are identical in nature to those of the short answer item; however, these problems are aggravated by the additional length of the responses. Essay questions are even more difficult to score reliably, take even more time to score, and use up even more testing time than do short answer questions. For these reasons, essay items are to be avoided if at all possible. Use essay questions only when necessitated by the cognitive level of the objective.

THE KEY TO WRITING ITEMS THAT MATCH JOBS

The vast majority of test items are written at the memorization level. In contrast, the vast majority of jobs require performance that is above the memorization level. This disconnect between testing practice and job performance is what often leads management to question the value of training and turns testing into a misleading indicator of performance. "How come they passed the course but can't do the job?" is a common summary of the problem.

Matching the job to the objective to the test item seems to be common sense among trainers, but the execution of this idea has proven harder to accomplish than we first expected. It has been our experience that most of the time and money organizations spend on testing is wasted because the tests are invalid, that is, they don't measure what they are supposed to measure. Many organizations that are considering testing think that sophisticated testing is too expensive. As we stated earlier, we believe that in most instances testing correctly is no more expensive than testing incorrectly, and that testing incorrectly is a waste of resources and creates a culture of anxiety, avoidance, and often outright hostility among trainees who are tested.

THE SINGLE MOST USEFUL IMPROVEMENT YOU CAN MAKE IN TEST DEVELOPMENT

In the course of giving presentations on the CRTD process, we have talked with a number of participants who challenged us to further refine our advice about improving testing in organizations. After thinking about their questions and concerns, we offer our first piece of advice about the two most important things you can do to improve testing in your organization (The second piece of advice is covered in Chapter 13):

- In general, the single most useful improvement you can make in test development is to write items above the memorization level.

When you design your test, first consider the job, and then consider the level of learning your test assesses in light of this job performance. In Bloom's terms, design your test items above the "Knowledge" level. It is usually not productive to worry about precise classification of items beyond knowledge level; the critical distinction is between memorization and everything else above it. Let the job drive the cognitive level of the test items and the associated objectives.

Memorization-level items are usually items that ask the test-taker to define a concept or rule or remember exactly what was presented in a presentation or manual. "Everything else" types of items usually ask the performer to apply the definition of a concept or rule in test items that are composed of previously unencountered examples—items that provide job-related scenarios that test-takers must comprehend, solve, analyze or judge. It is essential that you distinguish between the tasks that require simple memorization, as opposed to those needing scenarios or simulations that show what the performer must face on the job.

In fact, we have found the advice to test above the memory level so powerful, we want to look at this idea in three different ways in the hope that one of these perspectives will "click" for you.

INTENSIONAL VERSUS EXTENSIONAL ITEMS

Hunt and Metcalf (1968, p. 89) proposed a distinction that we have found useful in our item-writing advice. "A precise definition states the meaning of a concept in terms of its characteristics." This is the "intensional" meaning of a concept or rule. The "extension" of the definition is the ability to apply the definition to examples of the concept or rule. Once again the concern about memorization emerges; "We may suspect that a student who can give a verbal definition of a concept, but cannot recognize or supply examples, does not understand the concept. Ideally, we want students to be able to define a concept intensionally, and then be able to illustrate it with concrete examples, indicating for each example why it qualifies as an instance of the concept" (Hunt & Metcalf, 1968, p. 90). Here are some examples that have been created using this frame of reference. We have tried to keep the content the same for both types of items to help illustrate the difference between the definition and the example.

Objective:	Intensional	Extensional
	List the function of each fuse in the KLS-1000 System.	Clear a "Blown Fuse" problem at the KLS-1000 System.
Test Item:	The 48V 5A fuse performs which of the following functions:	A customer on Maple Avenue reports that his telephone is "dead." The Operations Center dispatches you to the vault on Maple Avenue that contains the digital loop carrier equipment serving the area. After entering the vault, you visually discover a major alarm on the KLS-1000 system. A visual inspection of the system shows a 48V 5A fuse blown on the MDS Assembly. You replace the fuse, and it immediately blows again. What is your next step to clear the problem?

Intensional test item:

A. Feeds power to a specific quadrant of the MDS Assembly.
B. Feeds power to the display in the user interface panel.
C. Feeds power to the bandwidth management section of the access resource manager shelf.
D. Feeds power to the test head controller in the access resource manager shelf.

Extensional test item:

A. Replace the channel unit circuit pack associated with the customer outage.

B. Depress the UPDATE button on the user interface panel to reset the digital bit system.

C. Replace the VTU circuit pack that feeds the digital signal to the MDS Assembly.

D. Replace the PTU circuit pack in the affected quadrant of the MDS Assembly.

Objective:	Intensional	Extensional
	Describe common multimedia design flaws.	Given a multimedia scenario, identify the underlying flaws in the design.
Test Item:	The point of diminishing astonishment is reached when:	Roger has been reviewing a multimedia training course. He has returned from a break and started a new module. His attention wanders and not even the customary fireworks display gets him back on track. Roger is a victim of:
	A. Developers cannot complete a project due to ongoing aesthetic updates. B. The boss no longer flinches when you show him the expenses so far. C. Developers overuse special effects just because they are available. D. The text and graphics needed to make a specific point no longer fit on a single screen.	A. Too much text on the screen. B. Creeping elegance. C. The point of diminishing astonishment. D. Too much narration without any interaction.

SHOW VERSUS TELL

For some, a literary metaphor is more useful in conceptualizing the distinctions between memorization and "everything else." One of the things a good novelist does is create scenes that show us what is happening rather than simply telling us what happens. In some organizations we have found using the words "show versus tell" or "scenarios versus terms" useful to help test writers focus their efforts.

Moroz (2004) provides a useful discussion of the differences between show and tell: An attribute is said to be shown in a scenario when the scenario describes a situation with enough information for a reader to infer the attribute. In other words, a scenario should provide the clues that allow the reader to argue the existence of the attribute. In contrast, an idea is said to be told in a scenario when the idea is stated directly and thus the reader is not required to infer the existence of the attribute.

It is important to show and not tell the criterial attributes of a concept in a scenario because

- Presenting the attributes in an indirect fashion forces the learner to *determine* whether those attributes are really there. Therefore, showing attributes requires test-takers to think above the memorization level.
- Presenting the attributes in a direct fashion requires only that test-takers memorize attributes and *locate* them in the scenario. Therefore, telling attributes requires cognition only at the memory level.

Here are some examples of the contrast between tell and show:

- Tell: The girl was cold.
- Show: Juanita wrapped her arms around herself and shivered. She exclaimed, "Brrrr! I'll bet it's only 10 degrees out here!"
- Tell: The manager questioned Mark about his assignment.
- Show: Mrs. Jamison asked, "Mark, did you get the names of the sales team yet?"

Here is a more extended example of show. Let's say we want to write a scenario for teaching the concept of the "Artistic Approach to Teaching." The criterial attributes of this concept are as follows:

- The teacher has vague objectives.
- Guidelines for activities are flexible.
- Varied activities encourage diverse outcomes.

Ruth and Iris are colleagues and are taking a walk during their lunch break. Iris sees herself as an "artistic teacher."

Ruth: One of the things that I really like about this job is watching the new trainees draw their own conclusions about why a sale worked or didn't. I think they get more involved when they see that they can figure things out by themselves.

Iris: Oh, yes! Case in point: Just the other day, I decided at the last minute to take my class on a field trip to see a call center. I didn't know exactly what we would be looking for, although it worked out.

Ruth: Well, it was a beautiful day to get out. What did you ask them to focus on?

Iris: I suggested they choose something that interested them and just watch and listen.

Ruth: I'll bet they found all kinds of things!

Iris: They did! Some noticed how the new hires really just followed the rules. The older people seemed more likely to chat with the customer. Everybody liked to stand up and stretch now and then, so wireless headsets really helped there. And you could watch a supervisor's nonverbals, I swear, and tell what she thought of each person she helped—wonder if those employees sensed that? Some others thought this would be a horrible job for them personally to have to sit under the lights all day and just answer questions.

Ruth: Must have been an interesting debriefing.

Iris: Oh, it was!

In the above scenario we can see:

- Iris has vague objectives, evidenced when she indicates that she "didn't know exactly what we would be looking for... ."
- Guidelines for activities are flexible, indicated when Iris says she would let students "choose something that interests them."
- The varied activities provided diverse outcomes among students—we hear different observations of what went on (people like to "stretch") as well as how the students felt about what they saw ("this would be a horrible job").

Aside from these examples, if you review the items we included to illustrate intensional versus extensional domains, you will see that intensional items are the "tell" or "terms" items that require simple memorization. The extensional items are composed of previously unencountered examples that "show" or provide the "scenarios" that test-takers must judge. The difference is critical. Asking sales trainees to identify the steps of establishing rapport does not mean they would recognize whether or not those steps were followed after reading a previously unseen description of an interaction between a salesperson and a customer. The test item in this instance may be in the form of a video or perhaps a narrative description as a playwright might script.

THE CERTIFICATION SUITE

The Certification Suite that we presented in Chapter 6 deals with the levels of testing in a third way. Levels A, B and C ("real-world" performance, high-fidelity simulation, and scenario analysis) represent learning assessment strategies that will provide the best appraisals of job performance. We find Level D (memorization–level questions) problematic—the questions cover job-related content—but at the memory level.

PRACTICE

Here are four test items that might be used as assessments for training insurance professionals. Which are above the memorization level? What level from the Certification Suite would you assign to each item?

1. An endowment insurance policy:

   A. is death protection for a specific period of one or more years.

   B. gives death protection for as long as the policyholder is alive.

   C. pays a sum or income to the policyholder if he or she lives to a certain age.

   D. allows the amount of insurance (and the related premiums) to be increased or decreased as needs change, subject to evidence of insurability.

Is this question above the memory level? Yes/No

What Certification Suite level does it reflect? _____

2. Jay is a 28-year-old graduate student just beginning studies for a Ph.D. in philosophy. He has four children. His wife stays home to care for and school the children. His assistantship pays $920/month. The best type of policy for him would be:

   A. Term

   B. Whole Life

   C. Endowment

   D. Universal Life

Is this question above the memory level? Yes/No

What Certification Suite level does it reflect? _____

3. Michael was flying his plane when he encountered a fierce windstorm just as he was running out of gas on an approach to landing. Unable to make it to the airport due to the headwind, he landed on Saluki Way just as the student nightclubs were letting out. When students saw the plane and ran for safety, they trampled Dr. Post's four Bradford Pear trees valued at $1,200 each. Dr. Post has a $250 deductible on her homeowner's policy. Is Dr. Post entitled to recover damages? And if so, how much?

Is this question above the memory level? Yes/No

What Certification Suite level does it reflect? _____

4. Examine the screen image on page 157 and decide:

Is Dr. Post entitled to recover damages?

Is Question 4 above the memory level? Yes/No

What Certification Suite level does it reflect? _____

PROPERTY CLAIM

Policy Holder:	Dr. Post
Policy Number:	EDUC-315

Address/Contact Information

Policy Mailing Address

Address:	1 Saluki Way
City, State & ZIP:	Carbondale, Illinois 62901

Who is the Primary Contact
for this loss?

Name of Contact:	Dr. Post
Primary Phone:	(618) 123–4567
Secondary Phone:	

Loss information:

When did the loss occur?

Date/Time of Loss	11/23/2006 2:00 AM

Where did the loss take place?

Address:	1 Saluki Way
City, State:	Carbondale, Illinois
ZIP:	62901

Tell us about the loss:

Cause of Loss:	Other
Severity of Loss:	Light
Were you injured?	No
Were there any fatalities?	No
Was a police/fire report filed?	Yes

Persons Information

Add an Other Involved Person:

Name:	Michael Pilot
Address:	Aviation Way
City, State & ZIP:	Carbondale, Illinois 62901

Additional Information (234 characters)
A plane landed on the street outside my house just as the student nightclubs were letting out. When students saw the plane, they ran for safety and trampled my four Bradford Pear trees valued at $1200 each.

FEEDBACK

1. This is a memory level item. It is indicative of Level D of the Certification Suite.

2. This is above memory. It is a scenario—Level C of the Certification Suite. To move it up a level to Level B, you would need to create a role-playing simulation in place of the item.

3. This is above memory. It is a scenario—Level C of the Certification Suite.

4. This is above memory. It is a high-fidelity simulation—Level B of the Certification Suite. Notice that the difference between practice items 3 and 4 (Level C and Level B) is simply use of the screen image of the accident report used on the job by the underwriter in Question 4. This item is a high-fidelity simulation because it closely matches what is used on the job. Remember that high fidelity doesn't necessarily mean high tech. Further, the gap between this item and what is seen on the job is nearly zero; so it also approaches Level A—Real World—in the Certification Suite. Creating this type of item is almost as easy as creating a simple memorization-level item, but is much more accurate in assessing job skills.

GUIDELINES FOR WRITING TEST ITEMS

Before we examine the guidelines for writing items of different types, it is well to remember that there are some basic, cross-cultural, privacy, and diversity issues to consider for any items you create.

- Monetary references should be applicable to all potential test-takers (for instance, Euro, USD, etc.)
- Personal information should always be fictional, although references to Social Security, personal IDs, telephone numbers, mail codes, and so forth should be in the format applicable to the job performance assessed by the test [(123) 456–7890 for a U.S. phone number].
- Avoid slang, idioms, and abbreviations (for example, use "that is" instead of "i.e.")
- If you expect a cross-cultural use of a test written in English, plan to write the items at a reading level appropriate to those for whom English is a second language.
- If you use names, select them to reflect the cultural norms of the country where the test will be given.

GUIDELINES FOR WRITING THE MOST COMMON ITEM TYPES

The following section presents a summary of guidelines for writing each of the six most common types of test items—true/false, matching, multiple-choice, fill-in, short answer, and essay. There are three interesting technical sources you may wish to review on this topic, as well:

- Burton et al. (1991) provide a clear and understandable set of guidelines for creating multiple-choice items.
- Case and Swanson (2001) from the National Board of Medical Examiners provide comprehensive and detailed advice on a variety of item formats for the basic and clinical sciences. Their discussion of item formats is detailed and thorough.
- The Educational Testing Service (2003) summarizes a wide variety of fairness issues in test development that detail concerns about cultural diversity, changing social roles, contributions of various groups to the culture, and the role of language.

Guidelines for Writing True/False Items

- Use true/false items in situations where there are only two likely alternative answers, that is, when the content covered by the question is dichotomous.
- Include only one major idea in each item.
- Make sure that the statement can be judged reasonably true or false.
- Keep statements as short and as simply stated as possible.
- Avoid negatives, especially double negatives; highlight negative words such as **not, no, none** if they are essential.
- Attribute any statement of opinion to its source.
- Randomly distribute both true and false statements.
- Avoid specific determiners (such as always or never) in the statements.

Guidelines for Writing Matching Items

- Include only homogeneous, closely related content in the lists to be matched.
- Keep the lists of responses short—five to fifteen entries.

- Arrange the response list in some logical order, for example, chronologically or alphabetically.
- Clearly indicate in the directions the basis on which entries are to be matched.
- Indicate in the directions how often a response can be used; responses should be used more than once to reduce cueing due to the process of elimination.
- Use a larger number of responses than entries to be matched in order to reduce process of elimination cueing.
- Place the list of entries to be matched and the list of responses on the same page.

Guidelines for Writing Multiple-Choice Items

Guidelines for Writing the Stem:
- Write the stem using the simplest and clearest language possible to avoid making the test a measure of reading ability.
- Place as much wording as possible in the stem, rather than in the alternative answers; avoid redundant wording in the alternatives.
- If possible, state the stem in a positive form.
- Highlight negative words (**no, not, none**) if they are essential.

Guidelines for Writing the Distractors:
- Provide three or four alternative answers, in addition to the correct response.
- Make certain you can defend the intended correct answer as clearly the best alternative.
- Make all alternatives grammatically consistent with the stem of the item to avoid cueing the correct answer.
- Vary randomly the position of the correct answer.
- Vary the relative length of the correct answer; don't allow the correct answer to be consistently longer (or shorter) than the distractors.
- Avoid specific determiners (all, always, never) in distractors.
- Use incorrect paraphrases as distractors.
- Use familiar looking or verbatim statements that are incorrect answers to the question as distractors.
- Use true statements that do not answer the question as distractors.

- Use common errors that students make in developing distractors; anticipate the options that will appeal to the unprepared test-taker.
- Use irrelevant technical jargon in distractors.
- Avoid the use of "All of the above" as an alternative; test-takers who recognize two choices as correct will realize that the answer must be "all of the above" without even considering the fourth or fifth alternatives.
- Use "None of the above" with caution; make sure it is the correct answer about one-third to one-fourth of the times it appears.
- Avoid alternatives of the type "both a and b are correct" or "a, b, and c but not d are correct"; such items tend to test a specific ability called syllogistic reasoning as well as the content pertinent to the item.
- Items with different numbers of options can appear on the same test.
- If there is a logical order to options, use it in listing them; for example, if the options are numbers, list them in ascending or descending order.
- Check the items to ensure that the options or answer to one item do not cue test-takers to the correct answers of other items.

Organizing the Distractors:

The United States Nuclear Regulatory Commission (2005) provides guidance for writing items in the high-stakes world of nuclear power generation. One of the most useful elements is a discussion about the types of items that would be used in assessing an operator's skills, particularly the guidance about how to write the incorrect responses to these questions. Potential models for distractors in multiple-choice test questions can be inferred from their directions and might be represented as follows:

Pattern 1   a. correct answer
             b. incorrect answer
             c. incorrect answer
             d. incorrect answer

Pattern 2   a. correct answer
                b. plausible misconception
                c. incorrect answer
                d. incorrect answer

Pattern 3   a. correct answer with correct condition (such as, because, since, when, if, etc.)
                b. correct answer with incorrect condition
                c. incorrect answer with incorrect condition
                d. incorrect answer with incorrect condition

Pattern 4   a. correct answer
                b. incorrect answer
                c. correct answer with incorrect condition
                d. incorrect answer with incorrect condition

The placement of the correct answer in these models should be random; there should be no discernible pattern in the placement of the correct response within the test as a whole.

Guidelines for Writing Fill-In Items

- State the item so that only a single, brief answer is likely.
- Use direct questions as much as possible, rather than incomplete statements, as a format.
- If you must use incomplete statements, place the blank at the end of the statement, if possible.
- Provide adequate space for the test-taker to write the correct answer.
- Keep all blank lines of equal length to avoid cues to the correct answers.
- For numerical answers, indicate the degree of precision required (for example, "to the nearest tenth") and the units in which the answer is to be recorded (for example, "in pounds").

Guidelines for Writing Short Answer Items

- State the question as clearly and succinctly as possible.
- Be sure that the question can truly be answered in only a few sentences rather than requiring an essay.
- Provide guidance regarding the length of response anticipated (for example, "in 150 to 200 words").
- Provide adequate space for the test-taker to write the response.

- Indicate whether spelling, punctuation, grammar, word usage, and other elements will be considered in scoring the response.

Guidelines for Writing Essay Items

- State the question as clearly and succinctly as possible; present a well-focused task to the test-taker.
- Provide guidance regarding the length of response anticipated (for example, "in 5 or 6 pages").
- Provide estimates of the approximate time to be devoted to each essay question.
- Provide sufficient space for the test-taker to write the essay.
- Indicate whether spelling, punctuation, grammar, word usage, and other elements will be considered in scoring the essay.
- Indicate whether organization, transitions, and other structural characteristics will be considered in scoring the essay.

WRITING DIFFERENT TYPES OF TEST ITEMS: A SUMMARY

We have discussed six types of items. Here is a summary of the six types of items and their most appropriate applications:

- True/False—Naturally dichotomous content for knowledge, comprehension, and application levels

- Matching—Homogeneous material for knowledge and comprehension levels

- Multiple-choice—Most flexible item for any level except synthesis and evaluation

- Fill-in—Tests recall rather than recognition of a word or phrase at the knowledge, comprehension, or application levels

- Short Answer—Tests recall or original creation of relatively short length for all levels but evaluation

- Essay—Tests writing skill and original creation of some length for any level

PRACTICE

For each of the following objectives, write a test item of the indicated type:

1. Write a True/False item for the following objective: Given a description of an assessment, classify the assessment as norm-referenced or criterion-referenced.

   _____

   _____

2. Write a Matching item for the following objective: Given a list of characteristics that distinguish one breed of feline from another and a list of feline breeds, match each breed with its distinguishing characteristic.

   _____

   _____

3. Write a Multiple-Choice item for the following objective: Given consumption, government spending, investment and net foreign investment, calculate the Gross National Product.

   _____

   _____

4. Write a Fill-In item for the following objective: Given a brief description of the distinguishing attributes of a bacterium, write the correct spelling of the bacterium's common name.

   _____

   _____

5. Write a Short Answer item for the following objective: Given a description of a family seeking to purchase a pet, provide the rationale for the selection of an appropriate animal.

   _____

   _____

6. Write an Essay item for the following objective: Given the professional position of the buyer and the product brand or model purchased, evaluate the appropriateness of the purchase including the specification of criteria used in the evaluation.

   _____

   _____

   _____

FEEDBACK

1. T/F: 4-H competitions are norm-referenced assessments.

2. On the left below is a list of feline breeds. On the right are feline characteristics that distinguish one breed from another. Match each breed with that
   characteristic that serves as one of its primary indicators. Record the corresponding characteristic letter in the blank to the left of each breed. Characteristics may be used more than once.

   — 1. Siamese   a. blue eyes

   — 2. Abyssinian   b. mane

   — 3. Persian   c. rounded ears

   — 4. Himalayan   d. almond eyes

   — 5. Burmese   e. rough coat

                        f. tailless

3. If consumption is $600 billion, investment is $100 billion, net foreign investment is $8 billion, and government spending is $250 billion, what is the
   Gross National Product?

   a. $758 billion

   b. $858 billion

   c. $950 billion

   d. $958 billion

4. What is the name of a very dangerous spherical bacteria occurring in irregu-
   lar clusters?

5. The Larsens want to acquire a cat. Their annual income is $15,000. They
   live in a small apartment. They have two children, ages 5 and 7; the children
   will be taking care of the cat. Their living room furniture is navy blue. Select
   a feline breed for the Larsens, and in 100 to 150 words explain why you think
   your choice is appropriate.

6. The President of the United States has decided to purchase a pickup truck.
   Write a well-organized essay of no more than 1,500 words evaluating the
   appropriateness of this automobile for the President. Be sure to state clearly
   the criteria you used in making your evaluation.

HOW MANY ITEMS SHOULD BE ON A TEST?

There comes a point in the test-planning process when developers need to decide how many items will appear on the test. This is a question that, unfortunately, does not have a simple, numerical answer. It is an extremely important question, however, because the length of the test has a direct relationship with the test's reliability and, therefore, with its validity as well. The question of test length turns on at least four factors:

- The criticality of the mastery decisions made on the basis of the test
- The resources (time and money) available for testing
- The domain size described by the objectives to be assessed
- The homogeneity or relatedness of the objectives to be assessed

This section on test length begins with a brief discussion of test reliability and why more items are always better for test reliability than fewer items. Each of the four factors listed above is then discussed in terms of its influence on the decision of test length. The section closes with a brief look at the advice resulting from research into test length and a summary that integrates the factors that impinge on the test length issue.

TEST RELIABILITY AND TEST LENGTH

As you may recall from Chapter 1, test reliability for cognitive tests has to do with the test's consistency in results. Consistency for criterion-referenced tests means consistency in classifying test-takers as masters or non-masters. In other words, if an employee takes the test twice during the space of two weeks, a reliable test will classify the employee the same way both times. The longer the test, the more consistent it is likely to be.

To understand why longer tests are more reliable than shorter tests, consider this analogy. Pretend you are standing in front of a large opaque, black jar that is filled with three different colors of jelly beans—some red, some green, and some yellow—all mixed together in the jar. Your task is to estimate approximately what proportion of the beans is of each color. You are allowed to sample the beans, that is, you are allowed to take some out and examine them in order to help you make this decision. You reach in and take out a sample of three beans; two are red and one green. This result might lead you to think that there must be more red beans in the jar than any other color, probably more green than yellow. That would be a plausible guess, but as you might imagine, you would not have a great deal of confidence in your ability to specify the proportions of colors present in the entire jar based on so small a sample. So you draw another sample and another. Eventually you have drawn out about three-fourths of the beans. Based on a sample of this size, you would be fairly confident in estimating the proportions of beans of each color in the jar.

Test items are like your samples of jelly beans; they are your opportunity to sample what the test-taker can do. As in the jelly bean example above, the more samples you draw, that is, the more items you include, the more accurate your picture of the competence of the test-taker will be. Hence your decisions regarding the mastery or non-mastery status of your test-taker will be more consistent when based on a longer test than a shorter test.

While the generalization that "more is better" is valid, clearly some constraints must be placed on test length. Here is where the four factors mentioned above become important considerations.

CRITICALITY OF DECISIONS AND TEST LENGTH

We know that test reliability is a function partly of test length. Therefore, when trying to decide how many items to put on a test, it makes sense to ask the question, "How reliable does the test have to be?" Sometimes errors in master/non-master classification of test-takers can be tolerated. It is very useful to do a systematic analysis of what the consequences are of both types of errors that can be made by unreliable criterion-referenced tests.

Ask yourself and others who are knowledgeable about the responsibilities of the target test-takers, "What are the costs to this organization of erroneously classifying a non-master as a master?" (This error is sometimes called an error of acceptance or a false positive error.) Undeserved bonuses? Poor work performance? Lawsuits from clients? Deaths? And "What are the costs to the organization of erroneously classifying a master as a non-master?"

(This error is sometimes called an error of rejection or a false negative error.) Denial of deserved bonuses? Demoralized employees? Lost talent for the organization? Lawsuits from employees?

The point here is that, to the extent that errors in classification can be tolerated, tests can be shorter. However, if the consequences of classification errors are severe, the tests used to make master/non-master decisions will have to be longer as well as meet other conditions required for reliable and valid tests. Chapter 14 explains how to calculate the reliability of a cognitive, criterion-referenced test so that its adequacy can be examined.

RESOURCES AND TEST LENGTH

It will come as no surprise that the creation of tests takes time and, therefore, costs money. The longer and more sophisticated the test, the greater the development costs. There are also costs, of course, associated with maintaining and scoring tests. Test designers are perhaps less inclined to realize that tests also incur other costs to the organization—some dollar costs and others in the form of what are called "opportunity costs."

The dollar costs result from paying employees while they sit for tests. It is widely acknowledged that the greatest costs of training usually result from having to take employees off the job, while they are being paid, to take training. Testing results in similar costs. The opportunity cost of testing is time lost to instruction. If course designers have only two days in which to deliver a course, and test designers create a three-hour test, those three hours constitute precious time that cannot be used for instruction. It seems obvious that the more time, and hence money, that an organization can afford to spend on testing, the more reliable (longer) tests they can afford. Organizations on a tight budget will need to trade off carefully the cost of test development and implementation against the cost of errors in test results. Once again, knowing the consequences of testing errors is essential to balancing this trade-off wisely.

DOMAIN SIZE OF OBJECTIVES AND TEST LENGTH

The number of items required for a test is also influenced by the objectives the test is designed to assess. In general, the smaller the domain of content described by the objective, the fewer the items required to assess the objective adequately. For example, consider an objective such as, "Without assistance, list the six steps required to make a milk shake using the Presto-Malt machine." This objective describes a small content domain; in fact, it is difficult to imagine how one could write more than one item to assess this objective. Most objectives, however, require more than one item—parallel items—to assess them adequately.

For example, consider the following objective: "Given pertinent data and access to all essential technical manuals, diagnose the source of a radiation leak in a nuclear reactor." This objective describes a far larger content domain and, as you can imagine, would require far more items to instill confidence that it had been adequately assessed. Objectives that describe behaviors that must be performed under several different conditions on the job should be assessed by several items reflecting those different conditions. This discussion should make it clear why specific objectives are so important to test creation. It is very difficult to decide the issue of test length if the objectives are ambiguous.

HOMOGENEITY OF OBJECTIVES AND TEST LENGTH

Another characteristic of the assessed objectives that influences test length is the homogeneity of the objectives, that is, their relatedness to one another. Consider these two objectives. (1) "Without access to references, describe the steps in conducting a performance appraisal" and (2) "Without access to references, describe the four stages of interpersonal confrontation." These two objectives are related in that the content they cover is similar. In fact, the second objective is very likely a prerequisite objective to the first. As a result, test-takers are likely to perform the same way on the test items written for these two objectives; in more technical language, responses to items covering these two objectives will be positively correlated. If objectives are homogeneous to the extent that they result in test items to which test-takers respond similarly, fewer items need be included to assess each objective independently.

It is important to realize that it is very frequently difficult to tell simply by looking at objectives whether or not responses to their corresponding test items will be similar. This conclusion can only be drawn after actual test results are available and you can determine for certain how similar the responses were. Chapter 11 presents item analysis procedures that will explain how to make this determination. You may be able to reduce the number of items included for each objective on a test if you can confirm sufficient homogeneity of the underlying objectives. On the other hand, if the objectives covered by the test are largely unrelated— heterogeneous—you can expect that the test will have to be considerably longer since several items will probably be required for each objective.

RESEARCH ON TEST LENGTH

Research into the accuracy of assessments as a function of numbers of test items per objective routinely indicates that more items result in greater accuracy. However, the improvement in accuracy tends to level off, generally somewhere between four and six items per objective. This finding, however, refers to objectives in general, without regard for the *criticality* of the objectives assessed. The accuracy achieved with four to six items may not be good enough for some critical objectives. In other words, the assessment of objectives that describe behaviors essential to health, legal requirements, and organizational survival should be assessed by more than six items, possibly by as many as twenty items, and may need to be assessed several times, especially if the content domain of these critical objectives is large.

Multiple assessments are more frequently used in performance testing than in cognitive testing; however, for some essential skills multiple cognitive assessments may be appropriate. Often when multiple assessments are used, the standard for passing is extremely high; frequently, no errors are allowed. See Chapter 15 for a discussion of the importance of consecutive success when multiple assessments are used.

SUMMARY OF DETERMINANTS OF TEST LENGTH

The number of items that should be included on a test is primarily a function of the criticality of the master/non-master classifications that will be made based on the test results. This is the case because test length is directly related to test reliability. The more costly the consequences of classification errors, the longer the test should be. Time and money, of course, are always limiting factors. Objectives that specify small content domains and that are correlated with other objectives require fewer items than those that describe large content domains and are essentially unrelated to other objectives covered by the test. Research suggests that the balance between effectiveness and efficiency in item numbers is achieved at four to six items per objective, but we know that more items will be required for some critical objectives.

You might use the numbers presented in Table 7.2 as a first estimate of how many items to include per objective on your test. Remember, however, that the actual reliability and validity of the test can only be determined after some test results have been collected. Chapters 14 and 15 describe the procedures for establishing the test's reliability and validity. In the absence of actual test data, you can only estimate how many items you will need to include on the test.

TABLE 7.2.   DECISION TABLE FOR ESTIMATING THE NUMBER OF ITEMS PER
OBJECTIVE TO BE INCLUDED ON A TEST.

If the Objectives Are:	Critical	From a Large Domain	Unrelated	10–20
			Related	10
		From a Small Domain	Unrelated	5–10
			Related	5
	Not Critical	From a Large Domain	Unrelated	6
			Related	4
		From a Small Domain	Unrelated	2
			Related	1

A COOKBOOK FOR THE SME

Sometimes you will need to interact with someone who has to create the test items but doesn't want to think very deeply about the test development process. Often these are subject-matter experts who are fascinated and knowledgeable about a product or process, but less enthralled with the test development process. To get started with them, we often use a cookbook approach that depends on the existence of course objectives for instructional units. (**Note:** It is always useful to create more test items than you think you will need in case some of the items appear to be flawed after you review the item analysis data; see Chapter 11.) The seven steps we list below assume a single test administration; if you are going to create a parallel form or an item bank, you should plan to create at least twice as many items. Here, then, is test length determination in seven easy steps (with a running example from Figure 5.3, the task hierarchy for a production manager).

1. *Have the SMEs identify the number of chapters, units, or modules that need to be assessed.* In most courses this can be done by reviewing the course table of contents. For example, a five-day course might have three units, and you might be trying to create an end-of-course test for all those units. For example, if you look at Figure 5.3, there are three major units: (a) Forecasting, (b) Aggregate Planning, and (c) Inventory Control.

2. *Have the SMEs identify the objectives for each unit.* If you have precise objectives, you have a strong foundation for the test. Failing that, you may have to review the content in the manual to understand what was meant by "be familiar with." In Figure 5.3 the SME identified three major objectives under "Forecasting": (a) Be able to select the best Moving Average technique and calculate it, (b) Be able to select the best Exponential Smoothing technique and calculate it, and (c) Be able to select the best Regression technique and calculate it.

3. *Rate the objectives by criticality.* Each objective is rated on a scale ranging from "0" for "not relevant" to "5" for "critical." How you define the ends of this continuum and what points you use in between are usually matters of your corporate training culture. The SME rated: Objective 1 a "4" for "Very

Important—Fundamental Knowledge"; Objective 2 a "3" for "Important—Fundamental Knowledge"; and Objective 3 a "5" for "Critical Knowledge."

4. ***Rate the objectives by domain size.*** Again, each objective is rated on a scale from "0" to "5" with "5" representing the largest domain size, for example, "plan a sales strategy for nationwide marketing." The SME rated Objective 1, Moving Average, a "2" for "Limited Domain Size"; Objective 2, Exponential Smoothing, a "3" for "Medium Domain Size"; and Objective 3, Regression, a "5" for "Broadest Domain Size."

5. ***Draw the line.*** In most instances you can't test for every objective; for example, organizations may decide to test only objectives rated "3" or higher for criticality. Others may modify that rule to allow for a broader assessment. You need to decide where you will draw the line and why. In this instance, a line was drawn at "3" and all objectives in this unit were deemed important enough to assess.

6. ***Multiply the criticality by the domain size.*** For each objective that you will test, multiply its criticality by the domain size.

If you refer to Table 7.3, you can see how this first unit was assessed. There were three major objectives, each rated for criticality and domain size. The initial calculation showed that the SME

TABLE 7.3. SUMMARY OF SME ITEM RATING FOR UNIT 1 PRODUCTION
MANAGER TEST.

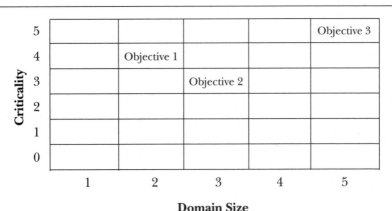

would need to write eight questions for Objective 1, nine questions for Objective 2, and twenty-five questions for Objective 3, for a total of forty-two questions.

7. *Adjust the proportions to fit the time allotted for testing.* Keeping in mind the advice that we gave in Chapter 6 from the Certification Suite—to select items as high as necessary in the Suite to ensure effectiveness while balancing the demands of efficiency—modify the final test size to meet your time constraints. Three strategies often help: (1) Write items that are at the higher levels of the hierarchy such that they subsume lower-level knowledge, (2) Test only those items rated "5," then "4, " and so on, until you meet the time constraint, or (3) Reduce the number of items for each objective by a constant percentage; for example, reduce the number of items for each objective by 10 percent; if that doesn't work, 20 percent, until you meet the demands of the time constraint.

By the time our SME completed the objective assessment for Units 2 and 3, the calculations suggested a complete test of more than 160 items. The SME estimated that each item would take approximately two minutes to complete; thus, the test would take about five and one-half hours. He was allowed only the last afternoon of training for testing, so he divided the item recommendations by an even 50 percent for all objectives to arrive at a test of eighty items, making a test of less than three hours in length (eighty items × 2 minutes = 160 minutes).

Keep in mind that this is only a cookbook process. It is designed to get you started. In the end, as with all of testing, there is no substitute for your professional judgment.

DECIDING AMONG SCORING SYSTEMS

As you are creating your test items, you should also consider the type of test scoring system you will use. There are two types of scoring systems that are traditionally used in cognitive tests: hand scoring and optical scanning (or OPSCAN). In addition, computer-based testing systems whereby the learner takes the test directly on a terminal and Computerized Adaptive Testing, which integrates statistical theory for item selection and test efficiency, are now entering the market. Deciding which system you will use probably depends on how many test-takers will be taking the test, how stable the content is, and how secure the test delivery system must be.

HAND SCORING

Most of us are familiar with the process of hand scoring a test. Hand scoring is easy for a short test with a small number of test-takers. However, it can become quite tedious and tiring (and thus lead to error) when there are a large number of items and/ or test-takers. To help reduce error in hand scoring, we suggest you consider using these techniques:

- Save time in the scoring process by locating the space for the correct answer at the left-hand margin of the test, next to the item number. Your directions to the test-taker would be to "place the letter of the correct answer in the blank next to the item." This practice prevents your having to hunt all over the page for the test-taker's answers.
- Do not instruct the test-taker to first circle the correct choice and then transfer the circled letter to the blank. Some test-takers will inevitably circle one letter and record another. Scoring controversies result when the test-takers assert that the circled answer was really what they meant, and that they just made a mistake in transferring the letter to the space.
- When you develop the answer key, place the answer for each item so that it lines up with the blanks on the left side of the form. Using a copy of the test to record the correct answers makes a useful key in this regard. All you need to do to score the test efficiently is line up the blanks on the answer key with those on the test.

OPTICAL SCANNING

With the increased power of personal computers, OPSCAN systems are becoming more accessible. OPSCAN systems use a lens to read the placement of marks made by the test-taker on a special answer sheet form. Because an OPSCAN system relies on precise location of answers on the scoring sheets, an OPSCAN answer sheet must be printed in a very precise manner, along with the addition of special "timing" codes, and usually using a vegetable-based or low-carbon (less than 40 percent) ink that won't interfere with the reading process.

While all of this may sound quite complex, OPSCAN scoring is a relatively inexpensive technology that is highly reliable. OPSCAN systems are fast (up to 10,000 forms an hour), accurate (virtually perfect), never tiring, but most of all, exceedingly informative. Once the computer has the test scores in memory, it can perform a number of analyses on the test that will help you interpret your test scores. In Chapter 11 we will look at some of the item statistics that you can easily create and use with an OPSCAN system.

OPSCAN formats vary with different systems. As a result it will be very important that you make certain the test-takers understand how the scoring sheet is to be filled out, and with what type of implement—usually a number 2 or softer pencil that the machine can read.

COMPUTER-BASED TESTING

While most training organizations primarily use hand-scored exams, and secondarily OPSCAN systems, a number of organizations have begun to use computers to deliver, analyze, and often provide feedback on tests. Recent advances in computer technology are opening the door to computer scoring of essays or other written performances (Wang, 2000). The computer-based testing system has a number of advantages. For example, Kelly Services, which provides temporary help, can assess keyboarding skills among job applicants for a number of different word processing systems while tracking error rate, speed, and accuracy by using a computer-based system to deliver their tests. Such data can also help diagnose areas in which training for employees is needed. In addition, using such a system allows an organization to test an employee at any time and any place there is a proper terminal (assuming there is adequate security).

Before deciding to invest in a software system, you should fully understand the assumptions behind it.

- First, check to see whether the system is designed to meet criterion-referenced assumptions. Most are not. We will discuss these issues and how to adapt to them in later chapters.

- Next, before deciding to use the software's item bank selection procedure, understand that simply putting related items into a test item bank doesn't mean you will have parallel tests as a result; for example, the SME who has the objective "Multiply two two-digit numbers" may write items of radically different difficulty. Asking test-takers to multiply 11 times 11 is not the same as having them multiply 59 times 98.
- Finally, it is quite likely that a well-designed test with a large item bank could have different cut-off scores for mastery, depending on the items selected. Most organizations prefer a single cut-off point for simplicity and political reasons. How you handle this issue is an important part of the planning and documentation process and is discussed in Chapter 13.

SIDEBAR: WHY COMPUTERIZED TESTING IS PREFERRED IN BUSINESS

In regulated industries as well as businesses, such as healthcare, where accurate knowledge and professional competency are a necessity, knowledge testing of employees becomes a key quality and/or compliance issue for the business. In these industries, employee knowledge testing, or certification, may be less of an option than a requirement, and meeting the needs of these regulations would be next to impossible in an organization with a large number of employees without the aid of a computerized testing system.

Computerized testing systems offer a variety of features to help facilitate and manage an effective testing program and respond to regulatory requirements. More advanced systems include:

- A variety of test item formats

- Complete recording and reporting of all testing activity

- Testing over the internet, LAN, or other distance learning options, such as testing centers

- A technology-secured environment, including system lock down and timed test delivery

- Archiving of all tests and test histories

- Test item analysis and other psychometric reporting to determine test validity and reliability

- Features to aid in test design and validation efforts, including subject-matter expert review

These features add efficiency and effectiveness to an otherwise daunting number of tasks that would have to be manually performed by trained personnel.

COMPUTER-BASED TESTING IS A COST-SAVING MEASURE

Businesses with a significant number of employees for whom tests must be frequently administered, maintained, and reported would be wise to implement a computer-based system as a cost-saving measure. There are a variety of ways a system could be implemented, either as an internal application or outsourced solution. At Bristol-Myers Squibb, a combination of internally hosted testing technology as well as outsourced solutions is employed to meet the needs of its diverse learning groups. Outsourcing is an attractive option when high-stakes tests are involved, since many outsourcing solution providers may also provide psychometric consulting services. Considering the number of tasks to be completed, including test delivery, grading tests, compiling grades, creating reports, filing test records, and performing even simple test item analysis, it quickly becomes cost-efficient to go the route of automation. Once automated, the task of delivering and maintaining tests for thousands of employees may be managed as part of the job of a single individual. A full testing service model is becoming more popular with organizations as they outsource their IT organizations, giving them cost savings not only in the testing solution but in the infrastructure to support it. Providing the opportunity for distance testing also saves expensive travel time of employees as well as learning team staff.

COMPUTERIZED TESTING FOR MEDICAL SALES TRAINING

At Bristol-Myers Squibb, development and delivery of an online cognitive test takes many steps from conception to completion: First, the decision to test is usually based on several factors, such as the need to identify knowledge gaps, assess the effectiveness of learning modules, reinforce learning, and to identify areas for future training.

Once an organization decides to conduct knowledge testing, business leaders from the affected divisions must work cooperatively to design a program that meets their goals. In a pharmaceutical sales organization, this means business leaders from training, sales, and marketing partner early in the process of assessment and testing.

The next step is to define the subject or topic area for the knowledge test. Marketing, in conjunction with sales, define the specific product knowledge required by the sales organization to perform their jobs. The training department, in conjunction with subject-matter experts from marketing and sales, writes the test items and stores them online in an item bank. The use of the item bank allows for an iterative process to continuously fine-tune the quality of the items.

Once the items are written and stored in the item bank, they can be assembled into various quizzes or tests. Quizzes have lower stakes and are used to check on learning and support the online learning throughout a module. The learner is presented with the question, answers the question, and then is provided specific feedback based on his or her choice, as well as guidance about why the choice is right or wrong and where the information comes from, usually within a specific learning module.

Tests may be medium or high stakes and administered to measure baseline product information and to follow up classroom training. The learner can only take the test once, the test is timed, and no feedback is given at the time of the test. A secure browser is used so that learners cannot print out the test or view other information on their computers as they take the test. In a regulated environment such as medical sales, the quiz or test must go through medical, legal, and regulatory review prior to use. Depending on the impact of the test, especially those that are medium or high stakes, a validation process may be applied. In high-stakes instances, additional validation and pilot testing will be required.

With final approval, the training department puts the quiz or test into the learning management system (LMS) and assigns the quiz or test to the students with a specific due date. Sales leadership communicates the quiz or test due date and the importance of completing the quiz or test on time.

The use of a timer and secure browser helps make the test more secure because learners do not have the time to find the answer in reference materials or the ability to refer to other materials on their computers. A password is used to access the test, and the learner must verify the test results with his or her electronic signature at the end of the test. Computer-based tools allow more secure testing with minimal impact on the learner having to be away from the job, especially geographically dispersed workers, such as those in a sales organization.

Quizzes and tests can be delivered, tracked, and reported through the use of an LMS. Various reports can be run and shared with business leaders. Completion/non-completion and pass/fail reports are shared with sales leadership. Item analysis reports are shared with sales leadership and marketing to review the common items that are missed. Item analysis data is used by the training department to identify knowledge gaps and design training to address these gaps. Individual coaching reports are used by the managers to review the test one-on-one with the learners who did not pass.

THE POWER OF COMPUTERIZED TESTING

Whether it is for a summative test, or for formative learning such as quizzes, computerized testing systems are putting the power of knowledge into the decision-making and budgeting hands of learning organizations. Smarter decisions around learning investment can be made more effectively than ever before. As the features of these programs continue to evolve and the testing and assessment process becomes more seamlessly integrated and accepted as a valuable aspect of all training efforts, the reports provided to the organization will form the foundation for the case that learning is a key business driver and competitive asset for the company.

Bristol-Myers Squibb is a global pharmaceutical company whose mission is to extend and enhance human life by providing the highest quality pharmaceuticals and healthcare products. Greg Sapnar, M.Ed., Associate Director, Metrics and Adaptation, Worldwide Medicines, is responsible for establishing and implementing learning measurement processes. Tracy Tinker, Senior Learning and Development Consultant, Bristol-Myers Squibb Medical Imaging is responsible for designing, developing, and implementing various training interventions.

COMPUTERIZED ADAPTIVE TESTING

Computers also allow for an approach called Computerized Adaptive Testing (CAT), a process whereby the computer scores the exam as it is taken and selects new items based on what is termed item response theory. Item response theory is a statistical technique that selects items based on their difficulty, their ability to discriminate among test-takers of various competence, and the probability of guessing a correct response. CAT is a new technique that is being developed primarily for traditional personality tests and for relatively stable domains, for example, math aptitude, with large numbers of test-takers. As such, there has been little use of the procedure in corporate settings. It is unlikely that you will consider using a CAT system, but we want to explain how it works because increasingly it is likely that you will encounter one.

A Computerized Adaptive Test does not work like the traditional paper-and-pencil tests most of us have seen. In a CAT test you will see only one item at a time—you must answer that item before the next one is presented *and* you cannot change your answer later. The computer begins with an item that about 50 percent of test-takers in the past answered correctly. If you answer that first item correctly, your score goes up in the computer, and it then selects a more difficult item. If you answer the item incorrectly, your score goes down in the computer, and it then selects an easier item. The statistical program driving the item selection process then continues in a similar manner, harder items if you have one correct, easier ones if you miss an item, until your performance stabilizes. Thus, unlike traditional testing, when you have an hour to answer sixty questions and can change your answers as you go, with CAT you might see only twelve questions. Because the computer adapts to each response based on statistical probabilities gathered from past administrations, your old one-hour paper-and-pencil test score would be essentially the same as your twenty-four-minute CAT score

CHAPTER EIGHT

CREATE RATING INSTRUMENTS

WHAT ARE PERFORMANCE TESTS?

Many corporate trainers feel that there is a "disconnect" in judging competence when people are asked "about" a task rather than asked to "do" the task. As Gronlund observed in 1988 (and in earlier editions):

> If you want to determine what an individual "knows about" a given performance, a knowledge test is perfectly appropriate. However, if you want to describe "proficiency in performing an activity," a performance test must be used. No matter how highly related the results of the two types of tests might be, the scores on the knowledge test obviously cannot be used to describe an individual's performance skills. (p. 85)

Performance tests seek to provide an objective rating of either a behavior or a product. Using them can help an organization in a number of ways. Performance tests:

1. Provide an objective and reliable measure of the trainees' actual ability to perform a task by distinguishing those who can meet the standards from those who cannot. At the same time, they allow trainees an additional opportunity for practice.
2. Provide a standard for performance against which all trainees can be evaluated consistently.
3. Reveal whether a trainee can deal with the stress and pressure of task performance under actual or closely simulated work conditions.
4. Indicate whether the instructional program is successful in producing workers whose performance meets job requirements.
5. Provide authoritative information on the maintenance of quality instruction and program effectiveness. (Campbell & Hatcher, 1989, p. 2)

It is not a conceptually difficult process to develop good performance tests, so we feel that the number of requests we receive to discuss this topic come because test developers think they must be missing something in the process. In fact, their read of the situation is usually accurate: A valid performance test is based on a detailed and thorough analysis of the skills required for the behavior or the desired characteristics of the product, or both. Creating performance tests and establishing their validity are often a straightforward part of the test development process; however, establishing the scoring and the reliability of the raters who will use the instruments (topics covered in Chapters 13 and 15) is usually the real challenge.

SIDEBAR: THE DIFFERENCE BETWEEN PERFORMANCE AND KNOWLEDGE TESTS

Much is being made in the testing world of "performance tests," but what exactly is a performance test? How will we know one when we see one? This question is actually a bit more complex than it seems at first, because performance tests lie on a spectrum of assessment types, in multiple dimensions. In constructing a taxonomy of testing, the Performance Testing Council (PTC, see www.performancetest.org) has created an illustration (shown below) that attempts to describe the terrain. Generally, knowledge-based tests assess useful knowledge and performance tests assess the demonstration of useful skills. There is a middle ground, referred to as "performance-based" testing, that attempts to measure job skills through indirect indicators. A well-rounded assessment that provides high concurrent validity (a high correlation between score on the assessment and the actual ability to do a job) would include measurements of both knowledge and skills (for example, a driving test).

The definition of performance testing used by the PTC is: "A test or assessment in which the response modalities required to demonstrate competence are identical to or closely approximate the response modalities required to apply that competence in its target context." Given that definition, what are the critical features of performance testing? We can look in four areas to illustrate these attributes.

Level of Fidelity

First, a response on a performance test has a high level of fidelity to the tasks that are performed on the job. Fidelity is the degree to which an assessment comes close to performing the actual task. Taxiing in a flight simulator for an X-14 fighter jet would be considered high fidelity, while identifying different airplane controls using a simple block diagram might be considered low fidelity. The experience of the individual and the level of assessment required will help determine the level of fidelity needed for the assessment. While it is certainly true that knowledge is required in any job, that knowledge is typically used within the performance of a task rather than simply declared, so declarative-knowledge-only tests tend to have low fidelity. To a lesser degree, the fidelity of "performance-based" assessments suffers because the response is constructed (for example, essays) but not performed in the modality of the job tasks.

Item Types

Second, and closely related to fidelity, are face and construct validity. The kinds of stimuli that act as the "questions" or "items" of a performance assessment typically require a constructed response, rather than a selected response. Selected-response assessments (multiple-choice) tend to have low face validity; they don't appear to measure a job "skill" because no one actually gets paid for selecting one of four choices all day. Selected-response tests can be seen as providing a description of how a person would do something, and as such there exists only a probabilistic relationship to the actual on-the-job performance. This "only-a-description-of" appearance also affects constructed-response performance-based tests, although to a lesser degree. An essay could well provide a very detailed description of how a task would be accomplished, yet it is still just a description. When a response on a performance test is essentially identical to what is done in the job task, that performance test is seen, rightly or wrongly, as a "better" (that is, more construct valid) test. (Note that it's not difficult to construct any kind of bad test, even performance tests.)

SUPPORTING PRACTICE ANALYSIS

Third, the classic job analysis typically has an added component for a performance test. Performance tests are almost always criterion-referenced; there is some defined performance that is considered competent. So, in addition to the standard job/task analysis, performance tests typically require a competency analysis that establishes "how well" the sample of tasks comprising a job sample needs to be performed to distinguish between masters and non-masters or competent and incompetent performers.

CORRELATION TO LEARNING THEORIES

Fourth, the job skills assessed by performance tests tend to represent the most cognitively complex areas described by learning theories, be they authored by Bloom, Gagné, Guilford, Krathwhol, or whomever. Not incidentally, these tend to be the most valued skills of a job, and so the ones most worth assessing. In areas in which human life is at stake, we already see performance testing in action. Whether it be a flight simulator for commercial airline pilots, residency programs for physicians, or a common automobile driving test, critical skills are assessed with a performance test. As businesses become more aware of the critical nature of measurable job skills, be they treating customers politely on the phone or making sure a wireless network is continuously available, performance testing will become more and more commonplace.

The Performance Testing Council is a non-profit organization dedicated to promoting fairness and equality in testing and the advancement and adoption of performance tests. The PTC unites test providers, developers, and deliverers to develop standards, best practices, and guidelines for performance tests based on scientific methods and foundations. For the Performance Testing Council: Tom Berry, MA Ed., Director and Jamie Mulkey, Ed.D., President.

PRODUCT VERSUS PROCESS IN PERFORMANCE TESTING

There is an essential distinction in performance testing: assessing the outcome of a procedure or process—the product—or assessing the way in which the outcome was achieved—the process. You may need to emphasize one aspect over the other or consider some combination of both as the job dictates.

The nature of the performance frequently dictates where the emphasis should be placed.

- Some types of performance do not result in a tangible product. Activities such as these require that the performance be evaluated in progress, special attention being paid to the constituent movements and their proper spacing.
- In some areas of performance, the product is the focus of attention and the procedure (process) is of little or no significance. Judging the quality of the product is typically guided by specific criteria that have been prepared especially for that purpose.
- In many cases both procedure and product are important aspects of a performance. For example, skill in locating and correcting a malfunction in a television set involves following a systematic procedure (rather than using trial and error) in addition to producing a properly repaired set. (Gronlund, 1988, pp. 86–87)

Again, how you manage the combination of process and product will be determined by the demands of the job.

FOUR TYPES OF RATING SCALES FOR USE IN PERFORMANCE TESTS (TWO OF WHICH YOU SHOULD NEVER USE)

Once the behavior (or final product) has been analyzed to define the essential characteristics of worthy performance, the next step is the creation of a rating scale to support a final evaluation. There are basically four types of rating scales: Numerical, Descriptive, Behaviorally Anchored, and Checklists. Of these four, we do not recommend the use of Numerical or Descriptive scales, as they allow for too much rater subjectivity. Both Behaviorally Anchored scales and Checklists are acceptable approaches to assessing a skill or product, but of these two, the Checklist is generally more reliable.

Numerical Scales

The numerical scale divides the evaluation criteria into a fixed number of points defined only by numbers, except at the extremes. In other words, there is no definition of what level of performance merits a particular numerical rating; for example, what does a "3" mean on a 7-point scale? These pure numerical ratings are inevitably highly subjective assessments that can introduce substantial error into the testing process. Figure 8.1 illustrates an example of a numerical scale.

Figure 8.1. Numerical Scale.

	Performance Rating
Behavior	Poor..................... Excellent
1. The quality of the response for directory assistance was... 1 2 3 4 5 6 7	
2. The statement of course objectives was...................... 1 2 3 4 5 6 7	

Descriptive Scales

Descriptive scales do not use numbers, but divide the assessment into a series of verbal phrases to indicate levels of performance. The descriptors may vary—"Very Good" to "Very Poor," "Strong" to "Weak"—but the resulting scale is deficient in that these words are open to many interpretations. Figure 8.2 provides an example of this second type of scale.

Behaviorally Anchored Rating Scales

The Behaviorally Anchored Rating Scale (sometimes called a BAR Scale) uses both words and numbers to define levels of

FIGURE 8.2. DESCRIPTIVE SCALE.

Behavior	Performance				
	Very Poor	Poor	Average	Good	Very Good
1. The quality of the response for directory assistance was					
2. The statement of course objectives was					

performance. However, the words that are used are not vague value labels, but terms that describe specific behaviors or characteristics that indicate the quality of the performance or the product. The use of specific descriptions tends to make these scales more reliable than the unanchored numerical or descriptive scales. Figure 8.3 provides an example of this type of scale. As you can see, the more specific the behavior interpretation, the more reliable the scale will be.

FIGURE 8.3. BEHAVIORALLY ANCHORED RATING SCALE.

Behavior	Performance	Rating
I. Response to directory assistance request	1. Curt voice tone; listener is offended	1
	2. Distant voice tone; listener feels unwelcome	2
	3. Neutral voice tone; listener is unimpressed	3
	4. Pleasant voice tone; listener feels welcome	4
	5. Warm, inviting voice tone; listener feels included	5

One issue that often arises with the use of these scales is, "How many points should there be on a scale?" While the selection of points is tied to the behaviors required for the task, research suggests that raters can reliably distinguish among five levels of performance. More than seven such points may stretch the limits of the rater's ability to quickly and accurately discriminate behaviors.

CHECKLISTS

Checklists are constructed by breaking a performance or the quality of a product into specifics, the presence or absence of which is then "checked" by the rater. Checklists may also have what are sometimes termed "negative steps" in them. These negative steps represent what should not be found, for example, "no extraneous holes in the wall" when evaluating hanging a picture.

Checklists tend to be the most reliable of all rating scales because they combine descriptions of specific behaviors or qualities with a simple "yes" or "no" evaluation from the rater. The checklist radically reduces the degree of subjective judgment required of the rater and thus reduces the error associated with observation. Remember, however, that while the checklist increases the reliability of the raters, a careful task analysis is required to assure the validity of the scale. Figure 8.4 is an example of a simple checklist.

Taken from Campbell and Hatcher (1989, p. 6), Figure 8.5 is an example of a performance test form for replacing a tire/rim assembly on a full-size half-ton pickup truck. Their complete test form incorporates job standards and examination directions in the left column, a checklist for the process of replacing the tire/rim assembly on the top right, and a single product checklist at the bottom-right column.

FIGURE 8.4. CHECKLIST.

Behavior *Statement of Objectives*	Performance	
	Yes	*No*
1. The course objectives specify the action required of a student to demonstrate an ability to perform		
2. The course objectives give the *conditions* under which the action will occur		
3. The course objectives specify the *criteria* by which the student and instructor will judge successful performance		

FIGURE 8.5. CRITERION-REFERENCED PERFORMANCE TEST.

Replacing a Tire/Rim Assembly on a Full-Size 1/2 Ton Pickup Truck

Elements.Steps	Standards	Yes	No
Process			
1. Remove hubcap	Such that no damage is done to hubcap or rim.	☐	☐
C 2. Loosen lug nuts	Loosen each nut before weight of vehicle is removed from ground.	☐	☐
CS 3. Position jack	At proper lift point on frame.	☐	☐
CS 4. Raise vehicle	Assure emergency brake is properly set. Tire must be raised to obtain a minimum 1½″ clearance from ground.	☐	☐
CS 5. Position jack stand and lower vehicle	Plus or minus 1″ behind center of lift point. Assure vehicle is lowered slowly and all weight is transferred to jack stand.	☐	☐
6. Remove and care for lug nuts	Lug nuts must be completely removed from all studs and placed in proper receptacle or upturned hubcap.	☐	☐
CS 7. Remove and install tire/rim assemblies	Such that no damage is done to stud thread. Assure tire pressure is 36 psi ± 2 psi. Lift with legs, holding from bottom of assembly.	☐	☐
CS 8. Replace lug nuts	100% replacement of lug nuts to studs as illustrated, starting with any nut as No. 1.	☐	☐
C 9. Tighten lug nuts	Torque all lug nuts in sequence to 80–90 ft/lbs.	☐	☐

(*continued*)

FIGURE 8.5. (CONTINUED)

Replacing a Tire/Rim Assembly on a Full-Size 1/2 Ton Pickup Truck

Elements.Steps		Standards	Yes	No
CS	10. Lower vehicle	Slowly with no jerky motions.	☐	☐
S	11. Replace hubcap	Such that hubcap is in a secure position.	☐	☐
S	12. Check tire pressure	To 36 psi ± 2 psi	☐	☐
S	13. Clean and stow tools	To assigned places, upon completion of task.	☐	☐
Product				
CS	1. Road test truck with replaced tire/rim assembly and make final adjustments	Stop vehicle after a maximum of three miles. Tire pressure should be no less than 36 psi. All lug nuts must remain fully torqued as specified. No visible misalignment of tire/rim assembly.	☐	☐

OPEN SKILL TESTING

In most instances, performance tests are used to assess either a static situation (a product) or a relatively straightforward, sequential process. However, there is a class of problems that may require a more intricate process of performance assessment. We won't try to describe the whole process here, but rather introduce you to the basic assumptions. Open skills require a performer to respond to novel situations according to principles by selecting proper procedures and modifying those procedures to fit the particular situation (Desmedt & Yelon, 1991, p. 16).

> Evaluators testing open skills must measure a trainee's ability to generalize and adapt the training to a complex array of situational, environmental, medical, legal, physical, temporal, and dynamic variables. The skills required in performing open job tasks may be of a relatively high order; that is, they are externally initiated, externally paced, and involve personal risk of varying degree from

possible embarrassment to injury. (Singer, 1975, as cited in
Desmedt & Yelon, 1991, p. 26)

As you might infer from these definitions, open skills require
some of the most complex thinking about how to assess performance. Open skills are demonstrated in dynamic situations and
usually require very high fidelity simulations or on-the-job situations to produce the proper assessment environment. Teaching
a police officer how to a handle a volatile and potentially dangerous domestic violence dispute, learning to negotiate a contract,
or simply driving a car on the freeway are all examples of situations that demand open skill assessment because of the range of
possible responses that should be made based on some stimulus
external to the performer that is constantly acting and reacting to
the performer's behavior. In other words:

> In an open task a worker must be ready to pick a procedure when
> the situation demands and must modify the steps as needed for the
> circumstances. The worker cannot merely apply special rules to
> cover exceptions to the usual situation; the worker must apply
> principles to create a variation of an acceptable response. In con-
> trast, in performing a closed skill, a worker responds with a routine
> application of prescribed procedures. The worker picks the time
> and performs the skill steps as specified. (Desmedt & Yelon, 1991,
> pp. 16–17)

Desmedt and Yelon go on to classify four elements that should be
considered in such testing: Critical elements, Style elements, Fluency, and Rate.

- *Critical elements* are the steps in a procedure that must be
  demonstrated (p. 18). [We use the term non-substitutable
  (Chapter 13) in a synonymous manner.]
- *Style elements* are the steps that are desirable in the performance. This usually means that some proportion of the steps
  must be present to demonstrate successful performance, but
  failure on one may be made up for by success on others
  (p. 18). [We use the term substitutable (Chapter 13) in a
  synonymous manner.]
- *Fluency* is the ability to demonstrate smoothness in transitions
  from one element of the procedure to another while responding to the external stimuli of the situation being assessed.

- *Rate* is the ability to accomplish the skill in the established time, for example, an officer draws a weapon quickly after the assailant pulls out a knife, but not so quickly that it is before the assailant draws the knife, and not so slowly that an assailant has an opportunity to strike. (p. 18)

Figure 8.6, taken from Desmedt and Yelon (1991, p. 21), is a sample form used to score the performance of a student driver learning to merge on an interstate in daylight. The elements of the performance are listed on the left; the assessment is recorded on the right for each of two tries. The Style points require mastery of three out of five elements.

FIGURE 8.6.   SAMPLE FORM USED TO SCORE THE TASK OF MERGING INTO TRAFFIC.

MERGING ONTO AN INTERSTATE IN DAYLIGHT	POINTS SUBTRACTED	
Critical Elements	TRY 1	TRY 2
• Accelerated to speed of traffic on interstate	FLUENCY	
• Visually checked position of vehicles in right lane of interstate		
• Positioned so merging did not begin abreast of a vehicle	RATE	
• Did not proceed past right lane prior to stabilizing		
• Left turn signal off upon stabilizing in right lane	STYLE 3/5	
Style Elements		
• Remained between marked lines on acceleration ramp	CRITICAL ELEMENTS	
• Activated left turn signal		
• Did not cross painted line prior to entering right lane		
• Merged at least one second behind vehicle in front-right lane	TOTAL POINTS	
• Merged so vehicle to rear in right lane not forced to brake		

CHAPTER NINE

ESTABLISH CONTENT VALIDITY OF ITEMS AND INSTRUMENTS

THE PROCESS

Validity means the test measures what it is supposed to measure. It is the fundamental assumption of criterion-referenced testing that the test matches the objectives you have established. The underlying process of establishing the validity of the test is conceptually quite simple. In most training settings the process will be one of showing a logical link between the job, the objectives of instruction, and the test items. In developing a certification test for which there may be no instruction offered by the sponsoring organization, the link will be between the job and the test. This process applies to both cognitive items and rating instruments used for performance assessment.

In this chapter we will discuss four types of validity: Face, Content, Concurrent, and Predictive. These are the four types that you are most likely to encounter in discussions with other professionals and in test planning, although it is only the latter three that are typically assessed formally and used to establish test quality.

If you are following our model to create your test, you now face two choices:

- If you feel that establishing only the content validity of your test is sufficient for your circumstances, then read the section Establishing Content Validity—The Single Most Important Step and continue with Chapter 10.
- If you are planning a more comprehensive approach to provide further evidence that your test is valid, you will need to add data-based evidence. Before you can establish the data-based evidence, you will need to read the section Establishing Content Validity—The Single Most Important Step, continue through Chapter 15 to create your item pool and determine the test's reliability, and *then* return to the section titled Two Other Types of Validity.

ESTABLISHING CONTENT VALIDITY—THE SINGLE MOST IMPORTANT STEP

You must establish the content validity of a test. It is the first evidence the courts will look for in any challenge to a test. It is also the primary property of a test that indicates the test's "job relatedness." However, before we introduce content validity we want to contrast it with face validity. The term "face validity" is sometimes encountered when you are working with colleagues who come from a norm-referenced testing background. Understanding the distinction between these two types of validity should help facilitate communication in the test planning process.

FACE VALIDITY

Description of Face Validity. The concept of face validity is best understood from the perspective of the test-taker. A test has face validity if it *appears* to test-takers to measure what it is supposed to measure. For the purposes of defining face validity, the test-takers are not assumed to be content experts. The legitimate purpose of face validity is to win this acceptance of the test among test-takers. This is not an unimportant consideration, especially among tests with significant and highly visible consequences for the test-taker.

Test-takers who do not do well on tests that lack face validity may be more litigation prone than if the test appeared more valid.

In reality, criterion-referenced tests developed in accordance with the guidelines suggested in this book are not likely to lack face validity. If the objectives for the test are taken from the job or task analysis, and if the test items are then written to maximize their fidelity with the objectives, the test will almost surely have strong face validity. Norm-referenced tests that use test items selected primarily for their ability to separate test-takers rather than items grounded in competency statements are much more likely to have face validity problems.

It is important to note that, while face validity is a desirable test quality, it is not adequate to establish the test's true ability to measure what it is intended to measure. The other three types of validity we discuss in the chapter are the substantive approaches you should rely on.

Content Validity

Description of Content Validity. A test possesses content validity when a group of recognized content experts or subject-matter experts (SMEs) has verified that the test measures what it is supposed to measure. Note the distinction between face validity and content validity; content validity is formally determined and reflects the judgments of experts in the content or competencies assessed by the test, whereas face validity is an impression of the test held among non-experts.

Determining Content Validity. The steps in the process of determining content validity are described below.

1. The first step in establishing content validity is to select three to five judges who are experts in the competencies assessed by the test. If the test covers sufficiently unrelated objectives, you might have to have a panel of judges for subsets of the items. You might have to have more judges if the test covers sufficiently general objectives. For example, if the test were an assessment of management skills, you might have to have judges who could represent the major divisions of the organization—technical, operations, sales, etc.—to ensure

that the test will be acceptable to managers throughout the organization. The identity of the judges and their credentials for serving as judges should be recorded for documentation purposes. This information could be important if the content validity of the test is ever challenged, especially legally.

2. The judges are presented with the objectives the test is supposed to assess and the items corresponding to each of these objectives. For each item, the judges must decide whether or not the item assesses the intended objective. We recommend asking judges to make a yes/no decision regarding whether or not the item matches the objective, rather than asking them to rate the objective on a scale. This recommendation simplifies the process for the judges, improves the reliability of their judgments, and facilitates the aggregation of the judges' opinions. Judges should also be asked whether they see any technical problems with the item—any cueing of the correct answer, more than one possible correct answer, and so on. Judges should also be provided with space to make any additional comments about the item that they think test developers ought to know.

3. It is suggested that judges review and rate the items independently first, then debrief their results together with the assistance of one of the test's writers. The test writer should be there to hear firsthand the judges' remarks and concerns; this person can also facilitate the reaching of consensus among the judges regarding the acceptability of each item.

It should be noted that it is important that the objectives given to judges be based on an accurate job analysis. Since judges are only matching items to the objectives presented to them, they cannot be expected to discover a faulty job analysis. If the job analysis reveals more skills than the planned test can assess, it is important that the objectives chosen for inclusion be representative of the job and that the procedure used to select the objectives be documented in the event of legal challenges to the test's validity.

Figure 9.1 illustrates a sample form that you might use to collect the content validity judgments.

Figure 9.2 illustrates how you might aggregate the opinions of the content validity judges.

FIGURE 9.1. TEST CONTENT VALIDATION FORM.

Judge:_____ Course:_____

Title:_____ Course Number:_____

Location:_____ Test Number:_____

_____ Date:_____

Please read each objective and its corresponding items. For each test item, please make two judgments.

1. Do you feel that the item assesses its intended objective? Circle "Y" for "Yes" or "N" for "No" to indicate your opinion. If you are uncertain, circle "N" and explain your concern in the comments section.
2. Do you see any technical problem with the item? For example, is there more than one correct answer among the alternatives? Is there a cue to the correct answer within the item? Is the indicated correct answer indeed correct? Circle "OK" if you see no problems; circle the "?" if you do see technical problems, and explain your concern in the comments section.

Please feel free to add any additional comments you think would be helpful to the designers of this test.

Item Opinion Record

Objective #	Item #(s)	Match	Technical Problems	Comments
1	3	Y N	OK?	
	8	Y N	OK?	
	10	Y N	OK?	
2	1	Y N	OK?	
etc.				

FIGURE 9.2. TEST CONTENT VALIDATION RESULTS FORM.

Objective #	Item #(s)	Judge 1, 2, 3	% of Matches	Technical Problems/ Comments
1	3	Y Y Y	100	None noted
	8	Y Y N	66	Stem is unrealistic
	10	Y Y Y	100	Cue in distractor 'b'
etc.				

Unlike the reliability calculations we will introduce and the other two validity procedures we will present, content validation does not typically result in a single numerical outcome that can be compared to a standard. As indicated above, if possible, it is advisable to have your judges reach consensus regarding the revisions required to make each item content valid. If the judges cannot be together to work as a group, it is recommended that you collect their individual opinions and examine any item that any judge felt did not match its objective and every item that was marked as technically flawed. You may, of course, have to call some of the judges back to get their approval on items that required substantial revision. However, there is an approach that helps define content validity with a numerical value, the Content Validity Index, and we will discuss that next.

The Content Validity Index. The technique we just described relies on a consensus approach to making the final decisions regarding content validity. As an underlying assumption, the idea of consensus is important to the content validation process. However, you may wish to use an alternative quantitative approach; better yet, combine the consensus approach with a quantitative one to generate a numerical estimate of agreement among judges.

1. The first step for the Content Validity Index (CVI) is the same as we explained before: Select the judges.
2. The judges are presented with the objectives the test is supposed to assess and the items corresponding to each of these objectives. For each test item, the judges must decide whether the item assesses the intended objective by rating the item on scales. In the original CVI work Waltz and Bausell (1983) and Lynn (1986) provided an approach to the CVI that used a four-part scale to quantify their assessment of an item: Relevance, Clarity, Simplicity, and Ambiguity. Because there appears to be some overlap in the meaning of the scales, especially Clarity, Ambiguity, and Simplicity, we would recommend using only the first two scales. Therefore, each item evaluated would have two Content Validity Indices—one for Relevance and one for Clarity. Figure 9.3 provides an example of these two scales.

FIGURE 9.3. CONTENT VALIDITY INDEX SCALES.

Relevance

Not Relevant	Needs Significant Revision	Needs Minor Revision	Relevant
1	2	3	4

Clarity

Not Clear	Needs Significant Revision	Needs Minor Revision	Very Clear
1	2	3	4

3. Ratings of 1 or 2 on the scale constitute "content invalid" items and ratings of 3 and 4 are classified as "content valid."
4. The CVI is the percentage of raters who judged the item to be valid, that is, rated it "3" or "4."

$$\frac{\text{Total number of "Valid" ratings}}{\text{Total number of ratings}}$$

Figure 9.4 illustrates this calculation for a test item's relevance as determined by three judges when one judge disagrees. The CVI-Relevance is 66 percent.

FIGURE 9.4. CVI-RELEVANCE FOR A TEST ITEM.

		Decisions Invalid	Valid
Judges	#1	x	
	#2		x
	#3		x
	Totals	1	2

$$CVI = 2/3 = 66\%$$

Wynd, Schmidt, and Schaefer (2003) discuss the CVI and summarize their concern about chance agreement inflating the CVI score. Any percent of agreement calculation—and the CVI is such a calculation—includes agreements among judges that are simply chance results. In other words, the three judges whose work is illustrated in Figure 9.4 would have agreed several times with each other, even if they were all merely guessing at an item's relevance. A technique that corrects for chance is the use of a correlation coefficient to express the extent of agreement among judges. We address this issue of adjusting for chance agreement in the next section's discussion of concurrent validity and the use of the phi correlation coefficient.

TWO OTHER TYPES OF VALIDITY

If you are developing a test using the linear approach of our model, then you have probably returned to this section to gather more evidence that your test does what it purports to do. You may want to gather this evidence if you feel that the test is likely to be grieved internally or legally or that the content covers risky or expensive behaviors. Or you just may want to fine-tune your test to get the best measurement possible. Concurrent validity is the technique you are most likely to use, and we present it next. You may also consider the value of the test to predict success in the future. Predictive validity is a concept most commonly used in the norm-referenced world, but it can also be applied in a criterion-referenced one.

CONCURRENT VALIDITY

Description of Concurrent Validity. Concurrent validity refers to the ability of a test to correctly classify masters and non-masters. This is, of course, what you *hope* every criterion-referenced test will do; however, certainly face validation and even content validation do not actually demonstrate the test's ability to classify correctly. Concurrent validation is the technical process that allows you to evaluate the test's ability to distinguish between masters and non-masters of the assessed competencies.

Determining Concurrent Validity. The process of calculating a test's concurrent validity is similar in some ways to the process used to assess its test-retest reliability. However, only one test administration is required to calculate concurrent validity. The success of the procedure depends heavily on your ability to form the group of sample test-takers correctly. The steps in the process are described below.

The first step is to identify a group of masters and a group of non-masters to serve as your validation sample test-takers. It is *not sufficient* to form a group that you think in all likelihood contains some masters and some non-masters. In order to establish concurrent validity, you must know before the test is administered the master/non-master status of every individual test-taker in the group. Furthermore, the sample test-takers should be representative of the masters and non-masters that you want the test to be able to distinguish between when it is finally implemented by the organization. Errors here are easy to make. For example, including non-masters in your validation sample that are far less competent than those non-masters who will ultimately take the test will not tell you whether your test will classify correctly when actually implemented. By including less competent non-masters in your validation sample, you have in effect made the classification task too easy for your test during the validation—easier than the classification decisions the test must make when actually used by the organization to distinguish between masters and non-masters.

It is also important that the validation sample be representative of the demographic characteristics (race, gender, national origin, and others) of the future test-takers. If the test's concurrent validity were legally challenged, it would be important to document that it is a valid instrument for all groups; this could be difficult to do if the test has been validated only on a sample of white males, for example.

This group of sample test-takers should be sizable—at least forty, more if you can get them—about equally composed of masters and non-masters. For documentation purposes you should keep a record of who the test-takers were and how they were selected; this information could be important if the concurrent validity of the test were challenged at a later date.

The next step is to administer the test to this group and record how the test classifies each test-taker. The test should be administered exactly as it will be when implemented.

A phi ϕ correlation coefficient is then calculated on the two sets of master/non-master classifications, that is, the known status and the status according to the test for each member of the sample.

Phi is a correlation coefficient used to determine the relationship between two dichotomous variables—two variables that have only two values each. In the case of concurrent validity the two variables are the test-taker's known mastery status and the test-taker's mastery status according to the test. The two values on each of these variables are "master" and "non-master." Like all correlation coefficients, the size of phi can range from $+1.00$ to -1.00. (If you are unfamiliar with correlations, see the section in Chapter 14 on correlation for an explanation of the meaning of direction and magnitude of correlation coefficients.) Table 9.1 contains an example of the results of concurrent validation procedures.

To calculate the phi coefficient, the data should first be placed in a phi matrix table set up like the one in Figure 9.5.

The values in the phi matrix for concurrent validity are: **B** is the number of test-takers who are known to be masters, but whom the test classified as non-masters; **A** is the number who are known to be masters and whom the test identified as masters; **D** is the number known to be non-masters whom the test identified as non-masters; and **C** is the number known to be non-masters, but whom the test classified as masters.

TABLE 9.1.   EXAMPLE OF CONCURRENT VALIDITY DATA.

Test-Taker #	Known Status	Test-Taker #	Test Status
1	Master	1	Master
2	Master	2	Master
3	Master	3	Master
4	Master	4	Master
5	Master	5	Master
6	Master	6	Master
7	Non-master	7	Non-master
8	Non-master	8	Non-master
9	Non-master	9	Non-master
10	Non-master	10	Non-master
11	Non-master	11	Non-master
12	Non-master	12	Master

FIGURE 9.5. PHI TABLE FOR CONCURRENT VALIDITY.

		Test Status		
		Non-Master	Master	
Known Status	Master	B	A	A + B =
	Non-Master	D	C	C + D =
		B + D =	A + C =	

FIGURE 9.6. EXAMPLE PHI TABLE FOR CONCURRENT VALIDITY.

		Test Status		
		Non-Master	Master	
Known Status	Master	B = 0	A = 6	A + B = 6
	Non-Master	D = 5	C = 1	C + D = 6
		B + D = 5	A + C = 7	

The formula for calculating phi using the values in this matrix is:

$$\phi = \frac{(AD) - (BC)}{\sqrt{(A+B)(C+D)(A+C)(B+D)}}$$

Figure 9.6 shows how the matrix (Figure 9.5) would appear correctly completed with the sample data from Table 9.1.

Substituting the numbers from the matrix into the phi formula, we can complete the calculation of the test's concurrent validity coefficient.

$$\phi = \frac{[(6)(5)] - [(0)(1)]}{\sqrt{(6)(6)(7)(5)}}$$

$$= \frac{(30 - 0)}{\sqrt{1260}}$$

$$= \frac{30}{35.5}$$

$$\phi = .845 \text{ or } .85$$

The concurrent validity of this sample test is .85. This outcome indicates a test with fairly high validity. By inspecting the sample data, you can see that only one test-taker was misclassified by the test. If all test-takers had been correctly classified, the phi coefficient would have been 1.00, indicating a perfect correlation between the known status of the test-takers and their classification by the test. The reason that a single misclassified test-taker lowers the validity coefficient so much is due to the small sample size. A single misclassification within a sample of forty test-takers would result in a far higher validity coefficient—.95, to be exact.

The required magnitude of the validity coefficient depends on the criticality of the assessment, that is, on what the consequences to the organization are of making classification errors. For critical objectives you would want your concurrent validity coefficient to be .95 or above. For important objectives, it should be above .75. Tests with coefficients below .50 should not be considered valid for any purpose.

PRACTICE

Table 9.2 contains practice data resulting from concurrent validation procedures. Using these data and the formula for phi above, practice calculating the concurrent validity coefficient for these example test data. A blank phi matrix (Figure 9.7) is provided to assist you.

TABLE 9.2. EXAMPLE OF CONCURRENT VALIDITY DATA.

Test-Taker #	Known Status	Test-Taker #	Test Status
1	Master	1	Master
2	Master	2	Master
3	Master	3	Master
4	Master	4	Non-master
5	Master	5	Non-master
6	Master	6	Non-master
7	Non-master	7	Non-master
8	Non-master	8	Non-master
9	Non-master	9	Non-master
10	Non-master	10	Non-master
11	Non-master	11	Non-master
12	Non-master	12	Master

Figure 9.7. Blank Table for Practice Phi Calculation: Concurrent Validity.

		Test Status		
		Non-Master	Master	
Known Status	Master	B =	A =	A + B =
	Non-Master	D =	C =	C + D =
		B + D =	A + C =	

FEEDBACK

Your correctly completed matrix should look like the one in Figure 9.8.

Figure 9.8. Answer for Practice Phi Calculation: Concurrent Validity.

		Test Status		
		Non-Master	Master	
Known Status	Master	B = 3	A = 3	A + B = 6
	Non-Master	D = 5	C = 1	C + D = 6
		B + D = 8	A + C = 4	

Placing the numbers in the formula, you should have written:

$$\phi = \frac{\left[(3)(5)\right] - \left[(3)(1)\right]}{\sqrt{(6)(6)(4)(8)}}$$

$$= \frac{(15 - 3)}{\sqrt{1152}}$$

$$= \frac{12}{33.9}$$

$$\phi = .353 \text{ or } .35$$

The result is that the concurrent validity coefficient for this practice test data is .35, indicating an invalid test.

Predictive Validity

Description of Predictive Validity. Another type of validity frequently confused with concurrent validity is predictive validity. There is an important conceptual distinction between the two and the procedures for calculating them. Whereas concurrent validity means that a test can correctly classify test-takers of currently known competence, predictive validity means that a test can accurately predict future competence. Predictive validity is important for many personnel selection devices that are used to choose persons for specific job responsibilities. Tests used to help persons select careers also require high predictive validity. In both of these cases, the test is taken first, while the demonstration of competence—job performance or successful career achievement—comes later; hence the term predictive validity.

Determining Predictive Validity. Predictive validity is determined in much the same way as concurrent validity. However, as indicated in the description above, the pool of test-takers must first take the test. At some later point in time, after their competence on the job can be determined, their achieved mastery status is correlated with their earlier performance on the test. A phi correlation coefficient could be used to calculate predictive validity in the same way as it was used to calculate concurrent validity above. The statistic would correlate test status—master or non-master—with future achieved status—master or non-master. Figure 9.9 illustrates the phi matrix for determining predictive validity. The formula for calculating phi is the same as above.

FIGURE 9.9. PHI TABLE FOR PREDICTIVE VALIDITY.

		Test Status		
		Non-Master	Master	
Future Status	Master	B	A	A + B =
	Non-Master	D	C	C + D =
		B + D =	A + C =	

Summary Comment About Validity

Establishing the content validity of the test is the single most important step you can take in developing your test. It is not difficult, nor a time-consuming process. We often notice how easily organizations could integrate this process into the instructional design process, but do not. Content validation requires relatively little time commitment from the subject-matter experts who were probably involved at the beginning of the job-task analysis process anyway. The data-based techniques are also more easily accomplished than one would first imagine. We have seen organizations integrate these techniques smoothly into the instructional development process once they stepped back and viewed the design of instruction and test construction as a single process. Doing testing right doesn't take much more time than doing it wrong.

CHAPTER TEN

INITIAL TEST PILOT

WHY PILOT A TEST?

Just as any systematic approach to course design includes a formative evaluation or course pilot, systematic test development means piloting your test. However, when designing a test, piloting is absolutely *essential* because the detection of faulty items *requires* real test data. The piloting process should identify potential problems with test organization, directions, logistics, and scoring, as well as with items, and lead to their correction. Additional test data gathering will also be required in order to establish the cut-off score that defines mastery (see Chapter 13) and to establish the reliability and validity of the test (see Chapters 9, 14, and 15). *The single most important purpose in the initial piloting of the test is to gather feedback for improvement of the test, not to rate the pilot test-takers.* Remember, almost any testing situation can be personally threatening. As you conduct the test pilot, you need to be particularly supportive and emphasize that your purpose is the evaluation of the test, not the test-takers. However, you should take the test pilot process very seriously, if you expect to create a test with significant consequences for the test-taker. As we discuss in Chapter 17, courts are very likely to support a challenge to a test if persons are not treated equally during its administration. The test pilot is the most informative opportunity to resolve any issues of fairness before the test becomes operational.

SIX STEPS IN THE PILOT PROCESS

The pilot test is a formative evaluation process that will parallel the course pilot process. You will need to determine the sample test-takers, orient the participants, give the test, analyze the test results, interview the test-takers, and synthesize the results. You may not be able to do all of these steps as the result of a single pilot test administration, but by adhering to these guidelines, you should be able to assess accurately the quality of your test.

DETERMINE THE SAMPLE

Your test pilot test-takers should mirror your intended test audience. Don't rely on a "sample of convenience" where you grab three people who are around the office and between projects. Nor should you be satisfied with just anyone sent to you from the field. If the pilot is to have meaning, the sample test-takers must be representative of future test-takers.

The size of the pilot test sample will depend on the scope of the test. A small sample will be useful primarily to gather qualitative reactions from the test-takers, that is, verbal comments about how the test might be improved. If you are designing a test for a limited-run workshop, then you could work with a smaller sample—even as small as three. If you are designing a test that will be used on an ongoing, company-wide basis, then you should invest the time and resources for a full pilot. So the next logical question is: "How do I decide whom I should pick for my pilot?" Let's start with the easy one first.

- If you have a test that will be used on a limited basis and you aren't concerned about legal or grievance issues, then you could go with a sample as small as three people (five would be better). We usually prefer that the three people be chosen to represent above-average, average, and below-average performers. This way we mirror, in a loose way, the total possible sample. If you can identify more than one person in each skill range, pick someone who is analytical and verbal over someone who would rather not talk; you will obtain more and better feedback.

- If you are trying to select your sample for a test that will have greater consequences, then you should choose a representative sample that will at least mirror the normal class size that might be associated with the test. Generally speaking, this means a test pilot of twelve to fifteen people.

- Don't try to establish test reliability or validity during an initial pilot of the test. The test is not likely to be ready for such measures at the pilot stage. The pilot process should always be completed in advance of these validation procedures. If you are under time pressure to complete the reliability and validity work, at least pilot the test on a small sample before bringing larger numbers together for the validation measures. You can imagine the frustration and wasted resources if you have selected a large test validation sample, planned to pilot the test and set the cut-off score at the same time, and then discover that words are missing from questions, questions are missing from the test, or the raters don't know how to use your checklist.

Finally, be sure to document the characteristics of the pilot test group. The sampling decisions you make for the pilot should be noted in a memo or other written form in case questions arise later about the test.

ORIENT THE PARTICIPANTS

Since your goal is to evaluate the test, not the test-takers, you need to make it clear to your pilot sample that it is the test that is being evaluated. Since the test-takers are, in effect, your colleagues in the test development process, they should be so informed and treated as such. You should begin the pilot process by establishing rapport with the test-takers and setting the collegial tone that will be needed to complete the pilot. Finally, be specific in terms of what you want the test-takers to do and what you will be doing during the test, for example: "I would like you to take the test just

as it is, but make a note anyplace on the form where you were confused or had a question. I'll be circulating during the test to see
whether there are any problems, but I don't want to get involved
in interpreting test items, unless clarifications are absolutely
necessary."

GIVE THE TEST

When you give the test, give it *exactly* as it would be given in the
field. This means you should give the directions verbatim, adhere
to the time limits, and avoid any hints, apologies, or interpretations of the test or any of its items. Any intervention on your part
during the pilot may jeopardize your understanding of how the
test will work later in the field. Smaller errors such as typos in
the test should be corrected just as you would during a field
administration. Gross errors may require immediate modifications
to the test in order to allow the pilot test-takers to proceed. In
either instance, it is important that you document your changes
and the reasons for the changes.

While the test is in progress, you should take careful notes to
document what the test-takers are doing. Watch for non-verbal
cues such as head scratching or frowning that might indicate
anger, confusion, or other issues. Don't allow any interaction
between test-takers unless it is called for in the test design. Don't
forget that you can exert a fair degree of control over the group
simply by maintaining a professional demeanor.

When the test taking is finished, be sure to thank the participants. You will still have other interactions with them during the
pilot process, but they have probably worked hard during the test
and deserve your recognition.

ANALYZE THE TEST

In an ideal setting, right after you administer the test, you would
complete the statistical analysis of the results. The test item analysis process allows you to identify any items that might be a problem; for example, nobody selected three of your distractors on
an item, effectively converting it from a multiple-choice item to
a binary-choice item (with a 50–50 chance of getting it right by

guessing). The data you gather from this analysis will help guide you in the next stage of the pilot process—your interviews with the test-takers.

Chapter 11 provides a detailed discussion of the statistical process of analyzing a test. These techniques are most commonly and easily applied to multiple-choice tests—although they can be used with other types of tests. We will just summarize the major techniques now:

- *Difficulty Index.* This is simply a report of the percent of test-takers who answered an item correctly.
- *Distractor Pattern.* This statistic is a report of the number of test-takers who selected each alternative option for each test item.
- *Point-Biserial Correlation.* A more sophisticated technique, the point-biserial correlation really requires computer support. It is, however, a very powerful tool that easily allows you to identify items that test-takers with the highest scores consistently missed while low scoring test-takers consistently got right. Such items are generally poorly written and require modification.

These techniques take very little time to complete with computer support, and the first two can be done by hand with a little advance planning. The results can then be reviewed and serve to guide your interviews with the test-takers; for example, "How come you didn't select any of these three options? Were they too far off? What would be a better choice for a distractor?"

INTERVIEW THE TEST-TAKERS

After the test you should interview the test-takers. We recommend that you conduct interviews on an individual basis. You should plan your interview based on two sources of data: your observations during the test and the test analysis data. When you begin the interview, first remind the test-takers of the formative nature of this experience and thank them for their cooperation. Then continue with your questions. Referring to the testing session, you might ask about difficulties they may have had; for example: "I saw you scratching your head at Question 9. Was that one a problem? Was it wording or content?" If your analysis has identified problems with specific items, ask test-takers how they interpreted the item. As they talk, take careful notes. Don't concentrate only on their performance. Be sure to explore their feelings about the test, for example: "How do you feel about this test? Would it be a fair test?"

A formative evaluation of the test should be pursued in the same manner as any other formative evaluation. Don't use a series of closed-ended questions; probe on responses, and summarize test-takers' comments to make sure you understand their thoughts. Whether they have volunteered or been volunteered for this experience, you should be sensitive to the fact that they may be anxious about the real purpose of the test. If you have developed rapport with the group and established that you are assessing the test and not the individual group members, your note-taking and discussion should proceed without difficulty.

SYNTHESIZE THE RESULTS

While your impressions are still fresh, you should synthesize your findings and document them. If your organization uses a standard form for course pilots, you might adapt it to meet your needs for testing. Some of the standard information that you may want to include would be:

- Time of test
- Location of the test
- Administrator
- Description of the participants
- The range of times it took to complete the test and the average time
- Any instructions or procedures that need to be modified
- Any test items that need to be modified
- Any format changes
- Any materials that need to be added or are unnecessary
- Overall impressions
- The item analysis report

PREPARING TO COLLECT PILOT TEST DATA

Before you can proceed with the final compilation of your test items, set the cut-off score that defines mastery and establish the reliability and validity of your test, you need to administer the test on a trial basis. These remaining steps in the test creation process require test data from real test-takers. Therefore, you need to organize the test as nearly as possible to its final form.

BEFORE YOU ADMINISTER THE TEST

Giving the test is often viewed as a perfunctory part of the testing process. Administering the test often seems to be a matter of logistics that are inevitably complicated by the hassles of room location, duplicating, and scheduling. Unfortunately, it is all too easy to become bogged down in these "details" and forget that the test administration process has to be viewed with the same philosophy that you have brought to bear on the entire test planning process; that is, the goal of a systematic approach to test development is to reduce the error component (X_e), not only in the test itself, but also in the way the test is administered. Thus, all those "details" have to be attended to and managed to reach our goal that the true score (X_t) equals our observed score (X_o).

Most of the issues we are now going to discuss apply to both cognitive tests and performance tests. However, there are some special considerations for performance tests on which we will comment at the end of this section.

SEQUENCING TEST ITEMS

Imagine how you would feel if you were taking a test that started with the most difficult items first, and to make matters worse, switched back and forth between test item formats such as essay, multiple-choice, and fill-in. If you weren't demoralized when you began, you'd soon be confused by the rapid succession of item formats. Demoralization and confusion are types of error, and should be avoided. So when you design the layout of your test, consider these two rules:

- *Keep item types together.* Don't mix fill-in items with multiple-choice items. The ability to move back and forth between different types of item formats is the result of a particular personality type, not the test-taker's degree of content knowledge.
- *Arrange items starting with the easiest and proceeding to the most complex.* Typically, this means beginning with true-false, moving to matching, short-answer, multiple-choice, and then essay. This format prevents test-takers from getting bogged down on hard items at the beginning and running out of time to answer the easier items at the end.

TEST DIRECTIONS

Your instructions to the test-takers must clearly describe, for each type of item, the action that is expected of the test-takers and any time or other constraints under which they must work. There are five common concerns in creating test directions:

- For multiple-choice questions, state very clearly that the test-taker is to select the "best alternative," rather than the "correct alternative." Failure to specify "the best alternative" will often lead to confusion on the part of test-takers. Good distractors are often "partly correct" but not "the best answer."
- List the time limits for the test, or each section if appropriate.
- Describe the method of recording responses. If scratch work will need to be turned in, indicate where the work is to be done.
- Provide a cover sheet (or initial computer screen for computer-delivered tests) that states the test's purpose. The cover sheet prevents test-takers from seeing the first test items while you are distributing the test and from becoming distracted while you are discussing test procedures.
- Provide sample test items (and a few minutes in which to practice them) if the learners are unaccustomed to the test format.

TEST READABILITY LEVELS

An often-overlooked area in test development is the readability level of the test. If the readability level either of an item or of the directions is too high for the test-taker, you may be testing reading level rather than the competence specified in course objectives. There are a number of methods to determine readability level, but they all focus on some relationship of words per sentence and the number of syllables per word. In general, readability level increases as sentence length increases. It also increases as you increase the number of multisyllabic words in each sentence. Conversely, it decreases as you decrease sentence length or the number of multisyllabic words.

The easiest way to examine the reading level of a test is to first analyze the directions for the test and then the items themselves. For multiple-choice items, analyze the stems and a randomly selected response if the response is in the form of a sentence completion. If the item stem is a question, analyze just the stem itself.

While there are a number of readability formulas, we have found that the formulas that calculate a reading level based on average syllables per word are somewhat more realistic than those that use a "percentage of hard words" (words of three or more syllables). Therefore, indices such as the Kinkaid or Flesch are probably better than the Gunning Fog Index. For example, the Fog Index for the Knowledge level example on page 133 in Chapter 7 calculates to grade 24, while the Kincaid Index is grade level 11. The Application-level question on page 134 is about a Grade 8 on the Fog and Grade 5 using the Kincaid. If this were a two-item test, the average readability level would be grade 16 for the Fog and grade 8 for the Kincaid. As you can see, there are differences in the indices, and you do need to average a number of items before the readability level stabilizes.

Whatever you do, don't just run your exam through the reading index in your word processing program. The short phrases in item alternatives, fill-ins, and so forth will lead to inaccurate estimates. Figure 10.1 provides a summary of the Kincaid Index procedures, which have been used extensively by the government. The index produces an approximate grade level based on the average syllables per word and the average words per sentence.

FIGURE 10.1.   KINCAID READABILITY INDEX.

Grade Level = .39 × (average words per sentence) + 11.8
× (average syllables per word) − 15.59

LEXILE MEASURE

The readability level of an item has little to do with its difficulty level. As we just saw, a simple knowledge level item can rate much higher in readability level than a more complex application item. This criticism of traditional measures of reading has led to the development of "a scientific approach to reading measurement that matches readers to text. The Lexile Framework measures both reader ability and text difficulty on the same scale. ..." (Lexile Framework for Reading, 2006). Stenner and Wright (2002) also provide a useful summary of the problem of assessing reading level. The Lexile system does seem to be a more accurate and sophisticated approach to establishing reading level, but it requires more complex calculations than the simple steps of the Kincaid. Suffice it to say that the most important thing is to match the reading level to the job task, but if you need to have a very precise measure of readability, you should explore the Lexile system.

FORMATTING THE TEST

Finally, as you prepare the test for administration, you should review it for editorial details that can affect error in testing. Ask yourself these questions:

- Are the directions clearly explained before each section?
- Are the items spaced to avoid crowding?
- Are questions and responses physically linked so that the test-taker does not have to flip back and forth between pages (or computer screens) to review the question being answered?
- Are the print or electronic characters legible? (Never use smaller than a 10-point font.)
- Are diagrams neat and accurate?

- Has the test been proofread? (One technique is to read the test from back to front—it's painstaking but generally accurate.)

Setting Time Limits—Power, Speed, and Organizational Culture

Trying to decide how much time to allow for a test can be tricky. From a purely psychometric perspective, you should first determine whether the test is to be a power test or a speeded test. However, test theory often takes a back seat to organizational culture, and you will often have to find a balance between theory and practice.

- *Power Tests.* Most of the tests we have taken in our lives have been power tests. A test to assess mathematical ability or one to determine knowledge of supervisory skills is usually a power test. These tests are designed to assess what you know, rather than how fast you can demonstrate what you know. Power tests usually have liberal time limits that assure that most people will finish the test. In theory, a power test would have no time limit, but in practice we usually need to put a limit to the allotted time. It's hard to estimate, but you might begin by allowing at least 45 to 60 seconds for each question, and possibly 2 minutes for more difficult items.
- *Speeded Tests.* When you have a situation in which you must consider how quickly a skill is performed, for example, a series of physical actions that must be completed in harmony with an assembly line or a clinical judgment about a severe drug reaction, then you need a speeded test. These tests are carefully timed, and the inability to perform satisfactorily within the time limits should result in a non-mastery decision. Time limits for a speeded test should be set to match the time limits for performance of the assessed skill on the job.
- *Organizational Culture.* By the time you have reached this point in the test-development process, you have conducted a very thoughtful analysis of item criticality and domain size, as well as hierarchical analysis to aid in item selection. You know that the more items you include on the test, the better the test will

likely be. However, and this is a big "however", you may find that your organization's norms just don't allow for tests that take longer than 50 minutes to complete, and you need 2 hours and 50 minutes! If you can't persuade the decision-makers to allow more time, you should consider documenting the tradeoffs that are being made so that the organization realizes it is making a business decision in contrast to an assessment decision.

In the end, the length of time for the test should be a data-based decision. You will need to pilot the test, and during the pilot, you should make certain that your time limits are appropriate. Thus, for power tests, you must budget enough time to assure that most test-takers can complete the test. If you don't, you convert it *de facto* into a speeded test with a probable increase in erroneous non-mastery decisions—not to mention an increased probability of lawsuits.

WHEN YOU ADMINISTER THE TEST

Test administrators have a responsibility to make sure that each test-taker has an equal opportunity to demonstrate what he or she knows. To help the test-takers to perform at their true levels, it is important to control both the physical and *the psychological environment*.

PHYSICAL FACTORS

When we first introduced the idea of error in testing, we listed a number of conditions that could reduce a person's true score. Factors such as room temperature, humidity, ventilation, noise, workspace, and lighting should all be checked—and adjusted if need be—right before the test is administered, to make sure they help contribute to test performance, not detract from it.

PSYCHOLOGICAL FACTORS

Most testing situations will create a certain level of anxiety for the test-takers. We know from research studies that people perform best when their anxiety level is neither too high nor too low. As a test administrator, you will need to establish an affective environment in which test-takers see the test as serious, but not excessively threatening. The best advice for controlling the psychological factors associated with the test is to act in a professional manner. You should be calm, friendly, but work-oriented. In fact, if you wish to be especially sensitive to the psychological environment of the test, you might want to consider that there has been some discussion in the literature that performance is facilitated with a same-sex or same-race test administrator. Matching administrator demographics to the test-takers may be somewhat extreme in most instances, but if you were administering a test affecting employment decisions to a group of people who were primarily of a protected minority, it might be good test policy to select an administrator with similar characteristics.

GIVING AND MONITORING THE TEST

Giving proper test directions is an integral part of the testing process. The test designer should clearly specify not only what the test-taker is to do during the test, but what the test administrator needs to do as well. In the course of the test administration, there are three stages you should attend to: (1) becoming familiar with test directions, (2) giving test directions, and (3) monitoring the test.

1. *Familiarize yourself with the test and its required procedures before the testing begins.* If you have never administered the test, or if it has been a while, then you should make certain that you understand what is required of the administrator. The test administrator should be given a checklist to make sure that test-takers have the appropriate support materials they need for the test, *but nothing more.* All should have equal access to reference materials if they are allowed or required for the test.
2. *Refrain from unnecessary talking before the test.* Most test-takers will be anxious, if not eager, to get on with the test. They are not likely to be in a frame of mind to listen to irrelevant chatter or information about future coursework. Right before a

test is perhaps the worst time to deliver any information, not pertaining to the test, that you want the test-takers to remember. (Under no circumstances should you administer a course evaluation before a test!)

3. *State directions* exactly *as prescribed by the test designer.* Giving test directions differently to different groups of test-takers can result in test scores that are not comparable across groups. Doing so can result in not only imprecise testing, but also litigation.

4. *Make sure that all test-takers know how to take the test.* Right after you have given the directions, ask whether there are any questions, and then pause long enough after asking to allow people who are thinking about what you said the time they need to respond with their questions.

5. *Keep talking to an absolute minimum.* The administrator needs to be available to deal with procedural questions, but these conversations should be as short and quiet as possible. If a test-taker discovers a flaw in an item that might cause confusion during testing, the confusing point must be clarified for the entire group of test-takers, as soon as possible after its point of discovery. Providing clarification only to the person who discovers the flaw will give that person an advantage over the others. Talking to each test-taker as the flaw is noticed will lead to a constant sense of distraction during the test.

6. *If someone asks about a question, do not provide hints to the answer.* Unless the item is genuinely flawed and in need of clarification for the whole group, instruct those who question to use their own best judgment. Remember that dropping hints is unfair, introduces error, and can lead to grievances or litigation.

7. *Do not allow talking among test-takers during the test (unless the test permits such interaction).* While it's common sense not to allow talking during the test, many administrators will forget that they too shouldn't be talking during the test. It is easy to become bored with the monitoring function and end up whispering to a colleague in the back of the room. However, such behavior can easily become distracting to anxious test-takers. If you expect to have time on your hands as a test administrator, we suggest taking some light reading to occupy your mind.

However, test administrators should remember that their role is an active one; they must remain alert to any factor during the test that would introduce error in the scores.

8. *The test should be monitored from different points in the room.* Moving around will help to ensure that the directions have been understood and are being followed. Attention to non-verbal cues can help identify confusing points even before a hand is raised to seek clarification; however, don't stand over anyone's shoulder. Many people find this behavior intimidating and anxiety producing.

9. *Adhere to time limits.* Consistency is fundamental in testing. If time limits have been specified, follow them. If you discover that the test-takers are having trouble completing the test as you expected, make a note for the test designer, but don't modify the situation on the spot. There are too many inter-related variables in a testing situation to expect that a modification in one part of the system won't affect other parts.

SPECIAL CONSIDERATIONS FOR PERFORMANCE TESTS

Most of what we have just discussed applies to performance tests as well as cognitive tests. Still, there are some special issues associated with conducting the performance test. These issues affect before-test planning and test monitoring.

1. *Carefully review the rating form.* The last thing you need during a performance test is to have to ask the test-takers to slow down so you can figure out how to use the rating form, or to ask them to repeat a performance because "I didn't see this other section." The rating form review will be especially important in those settings in which a series of rapid decisions and actions are likely. (As an instructional strategy, we also believe that students should have received copies of the rating form in advance of the test. This will not only allay anxiety, but also help the learners to focus on the competencies assessed by the test.)

2. *Determine that the test environment simulates the work environment.* With the rating form in hand, review the test setting to be

certain that whatever resources are to be available for the test (for example, electronic test equipment, reference manuals, and so forth) are in place. However, don't just review for the test itself. If you find there is a significant disparity between the work environment and the test environment, you should note this difference in the event that such a gap is a concern for the test-takers. If the gap is too large, then issues about the test's validity may be raised; for example, a simulation of air traffic direction without constantly moving radar images would be a serious breech of validity for air traffic controller assessment.

3. *Plan the schedule for testing.* Once you are comfortable with the rating form and the environment, determine how long it will take to test each person. The test administrator needs to develop a testing schedule that will minimize the effects of anxiety, and possibly unequal levels of instruction that result if some test-takers are allowed more study or practice time than others.

4. *Test-takers don't appreciate irrelevant assignments immediately before a test.* If you are in a setting in which there is limited equipment and/or raters to conduct the test, you should not keep the test-takers sitting around in the classroom area while they wait for the exams; this will only create anxiety or boredom. Nor should you provide additional instruction or opportunities for practice once testing has begun; this would be unfair to those who were tested first. Rather, the best approach would be to give each individual a specific testing time. You can then allow the test-takers to use the balance of the time as they wish—to read, jog, call the office—both prior to taking the test and while they wait for others to be tested after them.

5. *Monitor the setting.* During testing you may have a situation in which you can't schedule people one at a time. If you have to test several people at the same time, in the same space, be sure to spread them out as much as possible. Failure to do so will increase the likelihood of unwanted interaction among test-takers. If you don't want to make explicit your concern about unfair assistance, you may emphasize that the distribution of testing areas is to provide test-takers with enough room to work and avoid distractions (which is also true).

SIDEBAR: Should You Use an Independent Testing Center?

As any parent can tell you, no matter how much fun it is to have your children around, the time will come when they need to leave home. The same may be true for your tests. What would cause you to look for options to deliver tests outside your offices? What are the risks of letting them go? How do you decide where they should go? And what is it going to cost you to get them there (and home again) safely?

DECIDING TO SEND THEM AWAY

1. When your house is too small

2. When your kitchen is too hot

3. When your neighbors start talking

Find a better space and balance the load. The most common reason for moving a testing program beyond your office or classroom is to extend geographic reach. You may have a single location but offer training or need to recruit new students or employees from across the nation or around the world. Even if you have multiple locations, the cost of bringing people to a test is often much higher than the cost of taking the test to them.

There is also the "holiday meal effect" to consider. When the turkey must come out before the pies can go in but the green bean casserole is still not browning, you just don't have time for one more deadline. A performance test might best be administered in a real-world work environment, but cognitive multiple-choice tests, or even a high-fidelity simulation, might best be offered in a more controlled test center environment. What would be considered normal noise or temperature levels on a production floor or a busy office environment can create unwelcome distractions to nervous test-takers. You can protect both the test-takers and your own colleagues by separating testing from production when the heat is rising.

Offer more than a privacy screen. Privacy is becoming increasingly important in our busy, crowded lives. Taking a test to change jobs or move to another department or retaking a test to improve scores can be less threatening when offered away from the primary work or school environment. Whether your need is more locations, more seats in a limited administration period, a distraction-reduced environment, or just a bit more privacy, moving your tests to an outside delivery network may help.

SELECTING THE PERFECT CAMPUS

1. Exotic locale

2. Twenty-four-hour delivery service

3. Windows with a view

High adventure options. The ultimate in convenience is taking tests in the privacy of one's own home or office. This is not an unreasonable alternative in today's Internet-enabled society. Convenience needs must be balanced with security goals. High-stakes tests—those that will impact employment or promotion decisions—generally require proctor supervision. Competition among test-delivery networks is strong, and test sponsors have significant control in the current market. When it comes to selecting locations, however, more is not always better. Multi-national delivery, for example, means multi-cultural test management. Not all cultures have the same expectations regarding sharing of information. Test-security challenges will undoubtedly increase as you move further away from whatever you consider to be "standard." New college students may be seeking high adventure; testing programs should not.

Staying awake all night. Test delivery may be offered any day of the year, even around the clock in some independent testing networks. Consider the level of support you plan to provide before moving your tests to an any time/anywhere option. Be especially thoughtful about extended day testing if you are delivering electronically and hosting the tests on your own server. Don't assume that current technical and/or customer service support from your office help desk will be sufficient to handle the angst of high-stakes testing on nights and weekends.

Looking, and looking again. The cost of new technology that enhances test security dropped significantly in the last ten years. You should expect that your test delivery network will record and store an electronic picture of the person taking the test, just in case questions come up later about who was really there that day. You should also expect that testing sessions will be recorded (audio and video) and available for your review for weeks or months after each testing event. You may be able to collect electronic thumb prints, image files of the signature log, and in some locations even a retinal image scan. The various levels of security have value in both prevention and prosecution, but don't trade the flashing lights for a trained and attentive proctor.

COVERING THE COST OF TUITION

1. Beware the bargain

2. Sharing helps

3. Leather chairs cost more

Avoid financial aid from a loan shark. Surprisingly, the cost of buying a seat in a proctored test center has not gone down as technology has allowed us to do more work, faster and with fewer people than ever before. If anything, more and better technology allows us to create bigger and better tests, forcing out the test-delivery centers trying to get by with low bandwidth connections or older hardware. The "cheap" solutions are woefully substandard and quickly eliminated from the market mix, but even a brief experience with a bad delivery partner will be a very expensive mistake. Make sure you are getting value, not just a low price, by knowing what you are paying for.

Public institutions. Public universities and community colleges receive funding through tax dollars that many of them direct toward testing centers to serve their communities. Economic development grants also support lower-cost alternatives for local test centers. While free testing may be rare, tapping in to a subsidized network can significantly reduce the price. These networks tend to serve as "no frills" alternatives and may not have all the "flashing light" security options. Colleges, universities, and community-based economic development offices can generally be trusted to understand the requirements of a secure testing environment and offer well-trained and dutifully attentive proctors. Institutional testing centers are especially well suited to programs requiring only one or two locations beyond their own. Subsidized centers may offer testing for $10 to $30 per test, depending on the length of the test and complexity of administration requirements.

Private, but not exclusive. The addition of an automated registration and scheduling system is important if your program requires more locations. You should expect that automated system to accept electronic file rosters of people who are to take your tests. Such a system will help manage both who tests and when they are allowed to sit for specific exams. The system should also be configurable to bill the test sponsor directly or to collect fees from each test-taker. Remember, if you allow a testing company to collect fees from your test-takers, you must require the testing company to use appropriate security measures to protect against credit card fraud. Registration and scheduling systems require interaction from both test-takers and test centers. They usually require an initial fee to set up and enable continued access to a network-wide registration system. Expect this fee to be in the range of $5,000 to $10,000, which can be paid as a separate recurring fee or amortized across the population of test-takers.

Test centers in a national or multi-national network receive varying degrees of support from channel managers. At a minimum you should insist that management require each proctor and center administrator to sign a confidentiality agreement. To assure consistent and reliable test administration, the test center staff should also complete training in the use of any proprietary systems used to deliver the tests. Better testing companies will also provide ongoing customer service training and support for front-line test center staff. Nonexclusive networks accept tests that are published and hosted on third-party test platforms. Internet connections between the test center and your server offer reasonable security for nearly all tests. Connection to the Internet test driver is established and maintained by the test site using a standard or a secure browser to display test content. Testing appointments in secure nonexclusive center networks will probably cost $15 to $25 per hour, exclusive of start-up costs.

Ivy League. For those who need—and can afford—it, the most controlled and secure environment requires publishing tests to a proprietary testing system for periodic transmission to secure servers at hundreds or thousands of locations. The additional security comes at a significant reduction in convenience. Any modifications to the test content require redistribution to all network locations. The expense and security risks involved with wide network distribution will limit the number of times you modify test content. These networks are best utilized by very large programs that test more than 50,000 people each year. Start-up expenses may be quite high, in the range of $100,000, but will usually include not only item and test publishing, but also item banking and basic statistical reporting.

When the Time Is Right

A decision to put your tests in an independent test center or test center network shouldn't be painful. Just like sending a child off to college, when the time is right you (a) check out your options, (b) find the best match to your needs, and (c) send them off with some fanfare. Then you go to the kitchen table and start planning your next vacation, knowing you have one less obligation to worry about at home.

ACT, Inc. is an independent, not-for-profit organization that develops assessments of all types, provides information, and conducts research for the fundamental purpose of helping individuals attain their educational and career goals. ACT's flagship program, the ACT Assessment, is now administered to two million individuals each year. Terry Ausman, Director, has been in leadership positions relating to computer-based test delivery since 1990.

Honesty and Integrity in Testing

Honesty and integrity in testing have more than an ethical significance. Their lack contributes to the error component of test scores. We realize that testing can be a stressful event, the results of which may well affect employment or promotion. As a test administrator you may find yourself in the uncomfortable position of resisting pressures to "help" a friend, colleague, or even worse, an important executive. Clearly, a testing system has to be insulated from these pressures for ethical, political, and legal reasons. You should take precautions to protect the integrity of the test not only during a training-testing sequence, but on an organization-wide basis.

SIDEBAR: Cheating: It's Not Just for Breakfast Anymore

Would you want the pilot who is flying your airplane to have cheated his way through flight training? How about the nurse who administers a shot to you; would you be relaxed knowing that she cheated on her nursing exam? The answer to both of these questions is: "Of course not." Yet, if you've read any newspaper, listened to the radio, or watched TV recently, you know cheating is on the rise and heading toward epidemic proportions.

Students use cell phones and other electronic devices to cheat on tests. Hackers have illicitly accessed computer databases to change grades.

While others, like sophisticated cheating rings, steal test questions and answers to share or sell to interested parties. Widespread cheating has been found from Amsterdam to Zimbabwe. So severe and deep have been these accounts of test theft and fraud that scores have been withheld, test forms have been destroyed, and whole countries are concerned about the true proficiencies of their workforces.

Research studies reported by Greg Cizek, author of *Cheating on Tests: How to Do It, Detect It, and Prevent It* (1999), suggest that cheating has steadily increased over a thirty-year period. In one thirty-year longitudinal study, for example, college students who admitted to cheating on tests increased from 26 percent in 1961 to 52 percent in 1991. Another research study by the Josephson Institute (2006) suggests as many as 60 percent of high school students admit to cheating (see www.josephsoninstitute.org).

For a host of cheating stories, see Caveon's *Cheating in the News* repository (www.caveon.com).

WHY DO PEOPLE CHEAT?

In looking at the problem of cheating, it makes sense to try to understand the motivation to cheat. According to David Callahan, author of *The Cheating Culture: Why More Americans Are Doing Wrong to Get Ahead* (2003), there are a whole host of reasons why individuals cheat. However, there seem to be some reoccurring themes:

1. *Whatever it takes, I must win:* Rewards for performance have exponentially grown over the last twenty years, especially for those individuals at the top of the pyramid, be it in sports, school, or business. The result is that people will do whatever it takes to be a winner.

2. *A tough economy means greater financial anxiety:* Over recent years, there has been increased concern regarding the security of one's future. Individuals who should feel secure about their futures don't. As a result, individuals will cheat to save money, cheat on tests to get good grades, or fudge on their own job performance to gain a competitive advantage.

3. *Let sleeping dogs lie:* The incentives to cheat have grown as well. Watch dog agencies, such as the IRS, SEC, and state regulatory boards

have become complacent in the enforcement of monitoring and sanctions for cheaters.

4. *Go on, indulge yourself:* Last, Callahan (2003) suggests that there is more cheating in today's society because "our culture indulges it. We live in a more dog-eat-dog society, where greed and cutthroat competition are often encouraged by role models and television programming (for example, reality TV shows)."

Perceptions of cheating are even harder to swallow than the cheating itself. Most people who admit to cheating see little wrong with it. They rationalize cheating as a means of getting ahead: "Everyone is doing it, so why not?" Students justify cheating as a means to compete to get better grades. Professionals, such as lawyers, rationalize overcharging clients in order to make partner. Job applicants lie on their resumes to get a desired job. It's unfortunate, but the vast majority of individuals who cheat do not see a way to succeed without using dishonest approaches to work.

Why Should You Care?

Cheating on tests is prevalent and rampant, and it's not going away anytime soon. Why are we discussing cheating in a test development book? As a designer, developer, or project manager of tests, you want to make sure the assessments you develop validly assess skills and knowledge and provide a distinction between those who can and those who cannot perform on the job. You want to understand which items best tell you that important knowledge and skills are being assessed properly.

When individuals or groups of individuals cheat on tests, the validity and reliability of your tests are gone. The distinction between performers and non-performers disappears. The questions you use to make this distinction are rendered useless. In other words, you've just wasted your time creating a beautiful instrument that doesn't measure what you intended to measure.

In upcoming sections, this book will discuss policies, procedures, and practices to secure tests. There are item and test design strategies, test administration protocols, and analysis techniques that will allow you to frustrate cheating on the part of test-takers. It is important that you think about developing these test tools and practices as you go about designing and developing your exams so that cheating can be prevented before it occurs.

REFERENCES

Callahan, D. (2003). *The cheating culture: Why more Americans are doing wrong to get ahead*. Orlando, FL: Harcourt.

Cizek, G.J. (1999). *Cheating on tests: How to do it, detect it, and prevent it*. Mahwah, NJ: Lawrence Erlbaum Associates.

Josephson Institute (2006). 2006 Josephson Institute report card on the ethics of American youth: Part one–Integrity. Retrieved December 15, 2006, from: www.josephsoninstitute.org

Caveon is a test-security firm that offers protection against test piracy and cheating. Using proprietary software, Caveon identifies breaches, offers remediation services to halt and prosecute abuses of sensitive test information, and provides prevention services to help secure testing programs from further compromise. Jamie Mulkey, Ed.D., Senior Director, is responsible for business development, client consultation, and services management.

SECURITY DURING THE TRAINING-TESTING SEQUENCE

On a day-to-day basis when testing follows training, there are three safeguards you should use to avoid introducing error:

Test item security. Allowing some test-takers to see the items in advance is obviously unfair to the others. An instructor might feel that it's "okay" to talk about the test to a whole group, since that "wouldn't be unfair to any individuals," but this practice is still inadvisable for two reasons:

1. Such an action will be unfair to other groups of test-takers who were not allowed to preview the test.
2. A preview may well destroy the validity of the test items. It is sometimes felt in objectives-based testing circles that if instruction is based on a mastery model, then test-takers ought to be able to see the test in advance. However, whether or not this is the case depends entirely on what kind of objectives are assessed by the test. For instance, if you were testing a particular skill that required the test-taker to identify unassisted a previously unseen example of a concept, the item probably will be reduced to mere recall during the test administration for those test-takers who see the example in advance. If we were

testing to see whether TV technicians could, without help, correctly label previously unseen examples of different kinds of video shots, the validity of these test items would be destroyed for any test-taker who was allowed to see the examples in advance of the test, even if answers were not provided. Seeing the examples before the test might allow the test-taker to seek assistance with the answers. Providing answers to such items means that test-takers have only to *remember* answers during the test, which is not the same as classifying examples without help.

Interaction among test-takers should not be allowed. Unless the test requires group interaction (for example, a cockpit flight simulation) then the test-takers should not be allowed to talk during the test. Nor should they talk about the test afterward. During the test it is often difficult to enforce this "no talking" rule with adult learners. The best means to do so, as we discussed earlier, is through professional and serious demeanor. If your behavior and attitude demonstrate to the test-takers that you consider testing a serious process, you are less likely to have problems in winning the cooperation of the group.

After the test, the test-takers should be encouraged not to share information about the test items. Such sharing means introducing error into the testing process, that is, comprehension items reduced to recall as described above. The test-takers may be under pressure from colleagues to divulge information about the test. In this instance, a caution to the test-takers about the ethical or measurement issues surrounding sharing information may not be as powerful as a reminder that others are likely to outscore them if they know more about the test items.

For placement purposes, test-takers must do their own work. In many instances a test may be offered at the test-takers' work sites rather than in an instructional or formal test setting. Usually these tests involve an assessment for course equivalency, entry, or prerequisite skills. When these tests are offered at a work site, there is a real opportunity for supervisors or others to provide assistance to the test-taker. It is most important that you communicate with the test-taker and his or her supervisor to emphasize the importance of achieving valid test results for placement purposes.

ORGANIZATION-WIDE POLICIES REGARDING TEST SECURITY

Most organizations that are concerned about test policies concentrate on three points: Security, Access, and Destruction.

Security of the Test. Test materials should always be inventoried and kept in a physically secure area. Obviously, tests should not be left out where they could be seen. Any requests for tests that are to be administered outside the immediate training or testing areas (for example, an equivalency test mailed to a regional training office) should be logged and transmitted in a secure manner. An overnight delivery or a fax transmission can be received by any number of people. Be certain who is on the receiving end!

Access to the Test. A clear policy should be established and adhered to regarding who will have access to a test. A log system should be established that will provide for documentation of access to the test. If the test is available via computer, standard security measures (passwords, for example) should also be implemented to limit access. Tests shouldn't be made available to anyone not on the authorization list. Requests for access by those who are not authorized should be handled via prearranged procedures. Especially sensitive requests (unions or regulatory agencies, for example) should be referred to the legal department before any action is taken.

Destruction of Tests. An organization should have a policy on retention of tests; for example, how long should an individual's test be kept in the event you need to provide evidence of performance following a legal challenge or a grievance? However, tests may need to be destroyed for a number of reasons:

- Test forms or answer sheets have been written on.
- Test forms are worn out.
- Test copies are defective or incomplete.
- Tests are outdated as courses are modified, superseded, or replaced.

In these instances, be certain that the tests you sought to destroy are truly irretrievable. As any teacher will tell you, tossing an exam copy in the trash is no guarantee that the test has been taken out of circulation. Tests should be shredded or otherwise destroyed in the presence of a witness and so documented.

SIDEBAR: USING STATISTICAL METHODS TO DETECT CHEATING

No one likes to think that improper methods are used by test-takers to gain an unfair advantage in obtaining successful testing outcomes. Yet, we know from recent studies that test theft and fraud are on the rise (see sidebar on Cheating in this chapter) and that we need to do something to prevent and detect this malfeasant behavior.

For many years now, simple comparative analysis techniques have been used to detect answer copying (Bellezza & Bellezza, 1989), that is, looking at response patterns for similarities between two test-takers. For example, do we see individuals who are sitting next to each other with the same right answers and the same wrong answers? If so, it's likely one individual was copying from the other. This type of analysis assumes that only pairs of test-takers are copying, and, in some instances, it is difficult to detect who is copying from whom.

More recently, sophisticated, statistical analyses of test-response patterns have been developed to identify indications of test theft and fraud. These techniques, generically known as *Data Forensics,* look for clues in hard-to-detect patterns that can appear on individual tests. For example, is an individual getting the hard questions right and the easy questions wrong? Does a whole group of test-takers seem to have similar response patterns? And what is the impact of this cheating on the performance of the test itself? Are pass rates increasing? Are items being over-exposed?

WHAT ARE DATA FORENSICS?

Data forensics look for what are known as aberrant or unusual test-taking patterns. According to Dennis Maynes, Chief Scientist for Caveon Test Security, "Aberrance is a term used to describe something unusual about the way an examinee has responded to the test questions. The underlying assumption of the use of aberrance as an indicator of cheating is that the test responses of individuals engaged in test fraud will be quite different from normal test-taking patterns" (2003).

Now this is not to say that all aberrant test responses are those of cheaters. Aberrant test responses can arise in a variety of ways. However, these responses are usually a result of the test-taker's behavior. While aberrance is not synonymous with cheating on an exam or the theft of test questions, it is expected that behaviors such as these will leave an imprint and evidence in the data record. Suggests Maynes, "Aberrance is defined as a pattern of item responses that deviates from the statistical models describing normal test-taking patterns" (2003).

With the advent of computerized testing, another variable can be used to detect aberrance–latency. Latency or response time can give us additional clues about how an individual is taking a test. For example, if a test-taker completes exam questions at 5-second intervals, while the rest of the test-takers for that population take about 30 seconds per item, it is likely this individual had prior knowledge of the exam content.

Here are some examples of the type of test-taking behaviors data forensics can detect:

- **Collusion**—answer copying by one person or a collaboration between many individuals

- **Cheating**—having prior knowledge of some or all of the exam content and therefore responding in ways that are abnormal—missing easy items and answering hard items correctly

- **Piracy**—stealing test items by memorization or technology

- **Retake Policy Violations**—retaking the test outside the parameters or policies of the testing program

- **Volatile Retakes**—testing attempts that show extreme changes in scores from the most recent examination experience

What Can You Do with Data Forensic Results?

Data forensics can assist in the detection of testing misconduct in a multitude of ways. It can corroborate visual observation of possible misconduct. If, for example, a test proctor sees an individual who appears to be cheating from a neighbor's test, data forensics can support or refute the allegation.

Data forensics can act as a means to invalidate scores. More and more, testing programs use data forensic techniques to detect whether scores are achieved honorably. As such, a testing program may stipulate that test scores may be rendered invalid if program administrators feel they cannot certify that a test-taker's score represents a valid measure of knowledge or competence as sampled by the examination. (See the U.S. Medical Licensure Exam website: www.usmle.org/bulletin/2006/Indeterminatescores.htm as an example.)

Data forensics can provide entry into further investigation of strangely behaving testing sites or classrooms. For example, are there testing sites that show 100 percent of the test-takers passing? Do they show this type of result on an ongoing basis? Are these sites showing consistent patterns of responding? If so, could there be instructor "coaching" taking place? If the answer to any of these questions is "yes," policies can be invoked to shut down test sites and/or repeal proctoring duties to stop test theft or fraud from occurring.

Last, data forensics can verify honest test taking. It can exonerate possible testing misconduct as well as show process improvements in the testing process. By advising testing candidates and stakeholders that detection mechanisms are in place and enforced, the continued use of data forensics can show improvements in the reliability and validity of test-taking practices.

WHY ARE MORE ORGANIZATIONS RELYING ON DATA FORENSICS TO DETECT CHEATING?

With technology getting smaller and smaller, more and more cheating behaviors are becoming "invisible" to human proctors. As an example, consider the test-taker who is sitting for a computerized exam with a small camera hidden in a pair of his glasses and a small receiver in his ear. Outside, in a nearby van, another individual is picking up the camera transmission and providing the answers to the questions to the individual sitting for the test. Sound far-fetched? Well, it's already happened. Fortunately, these two were caught.

Additionally, there is wider use and procurement of stolen test content from sources on the Internet. It is easy to find alleged test content for sale or available at no cost on the Internet.

Unfortunately, the intrinsic benefits of high technology and the speed at which we can obtain information have decreased the effectiveness of human proctoring. Coupled with the fact that there are errors of observation, memory, and bias, other alternatives for cheating detection are needed. Data forensics help bridge this gap for many testing organizations wishing to corroborate evidence, monitor exam performance, and validate testing practices.

What Are We Likely to See in the Future?

What can we expect to see in terms of technological advances for data forensic analysis? We'll likely see more analysis done in real time, that is, catching an individual cheating while he or she is taking the exam. Imagine stopping a test half-way through its administration. As data forensic technology becomes more sophisticated, analysis tools will learn the response patterns of test cheaters and pirates and catch them "in the act," so to speak. The results will be less exposure of test items due to cheating and theft and a deterrent to would-be test cheaters—don't try this, you will be caught!

We know that test cheating and theft are on the rise. Analysis tools such as data forensics will provide the detection mechanisms to manage these maleficent behaviors. David Foster, CEO of Caveon Test Security suggests, "As the technological sophistication of cheaters increases, it must be met with an equal or greater improvement in our tools of detection. Better statistical measures of test aberrance will help make test security a reality" (2003).

References

Bellezza, F.S., & Bellezza, S.F. (1989). Detection of cheating on multiple-choice tests by using error similarity analysis. *Teaching and Psychology*, 16, 151–155.

Foster, D.F. (2003). Caveon Test Security website. Retrieved on December 15, 2006, from www.caveon.com

Maynes, D. (2003). Caveon Test Security website. Retrieved on December 15, 2006, from www.caveon.com

U.S. Medical Licensure Exam website: www.usmle.org/bulletin/2006/Indeterminatescores.htm

---

Caveon is a test-security firm that offers protection against test piracy and cheating. Using proprietary software, Caveon identifies breaches, offers remediation services to halt and prosecute abuses of sensitive test information, and provides prevention services to help secure testing programs from further compromise. Jamie Mulkey, Ed.D., Senior Director, is responsible for business development, client consultation, and services management.

CHAPTER ELEVEN

STATISTICAL PILOT

Standard Deviation and Test Distributions
Item Statistics and Item Analysis
Choosing Item Statistics and Item Analysis Techniques
Garbage In-Garbage Out

STANDARD DEVIATION AND TEST DISTRIBUTIONS

In this chapter we want to discuss how you can interpret the results of a test and use individual item statistics to improve the quality of the test. Before we describe and illustrate these item analysis techniques, however, there is one more concept that anyone trying to interpret a test must understand: the standard deviation. The standard deviation will tell you how spread out your test scores are (Did everyone tend to get the same score or is there a diversity of scores?) and can affect your interpretation of test data.

THE MEANING OF STANDARD DEVIATION

After a test has been given, you will want to examine the scores. Individual scores sometimes have great significance to individual test-takers because a score can determine a career path or other reward. However, analysis of the scores as a group will likely be of greater interest to course designers and test creators. Results of this analysis will tell you a great deal about the quality of your test

FIGURE 11.1. STANDARD NORMAL CURVE.

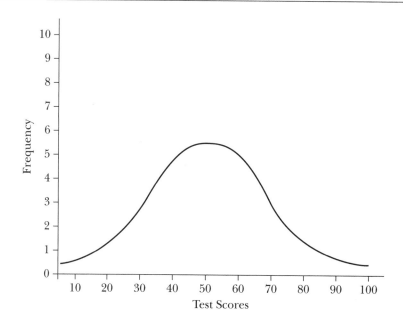

and provide guidance for test revision before you attempt to establish the test's reliability and validity.

The first step you want to take in examining your test results
is to construct a frequency distribution of the test scores. The
reason for plotting your scores is that the shape of the distribution can tell you something about how test-takers did on the test.
If, when you plot your scores, the distribution that results looks
like Figure 11.1, then the test results are said to be normally
distributed.

This bell-shaped curve is defined by the average deviation of
the scores from the mean; the mean is simply the average score.
In Figure 11.2 you can see that the curve is divided into sections.
Each of these sections represents one or more standard deviations
from the mean. In this instance, the average score or mean score
is 50 and the standard deviation is 15 points. The "0" point on
the standard deviations line represents the mean score. One positive

FIGURE 11.2. STANDARD DEVIATIONS OF A NORMAL CURVE.

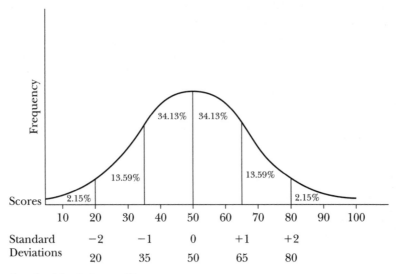

standard deviation from the mean is a score of 65 and one negative standard deviation is a score of 35. In any standard normal
curve, there will always be approximately 34 percent of the people
scoring in each of the first standard deviations, about 14 percent
in the second, and around 2 percent in the third.

Technically, the standard deviation is the average deviation of
the scores from the mean or average score. Calculating a standard
deviation is not complex, but it can be time-consuming. Any worthwhile test-scoring program will include this statistic automatically.
From our perspective, it's not terribly important that you know
how to calculate the standard deviation. What is important is that
you understand conceptually that the standard deviation is a measure of how widely the scores are distributed around the mean, and
that the percentage of scores (about 34 percent, 14 percent,
and 2 percent) that fall within the standard deviations from the
mean define the normal curve.

The Five Most Common Test Distributions

Any normal curve will be symmetrical in shape, and as we just saw, the standard normal curve has specific percentages of scores within a given standard deviation. Now, let's look at the impact of standard deviations on the shapes of curves. In Figure 11.3 there is a sequence of three curves.

The first curve is like the one we have just seen—a standard normal distribution that typically results from the administration of a norm-referenced test. This is also called a *mesokurtic* distribution. The next curve is one with a larger standard deviation. Notice how the scores are more spread out and the highest point on the curve is lower than in our first curve. (This curve is still a normal curve as long as the correct percentages of scores fall between the various standard deviations.) This flatter curve is called a *platykurtic* distribution. The final curve, a *leptokurtic* distribution, is one with a smaller standard deviation. Notice how the scores are closer together. The smaller standard deviation indicates less variation in the scores. Consequently, the highest point of the curve is much higher than in the other distributions.

You should be able to see from these examples that the smaller the standard deviation you obtain, the narrower the curve will be. Thus a leptokurtic distribution will have a smaller standard deviation, indicating that most people tended to score alike. Mastery distributions will tend to be leptokurtic, but they also have another characteristic—skew.

In Figure 11.4 the top curve is a typical mastery curve. In this curve most test-takers' scores are clustered near the high end of the scale. This clustering toward the extremes of the distribution is called the *skew*. Skewed distributions are not symmetrical and, therefore, are not normal distributions. The mastery curve is called a negatively skewed curve because the "tail" of the distribution is toward the low end of the scores. The bottom curve is a positively skewed curve.

Notice that the skew is labeled positive or negative based on the direction of the "tail." Thus, a "tail" to the right is a positive skew, a "tail" to the left a negative one. A positively skewed test distribution is usually cause for test developer depression, as it represents a situation in which most test-takers have scored poorly on the test.

FIGURE 11.3.   FREQUENCY DISTRIBUTIONS WITH STANDARD DEVIATIONS
OF VARIOUS SIZES.

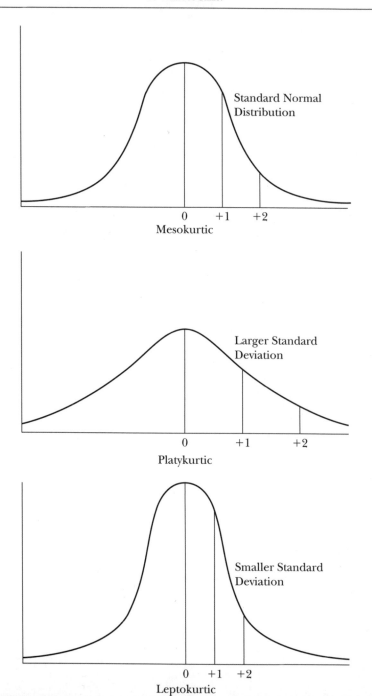

Standard Normal
Distribution

0   +1   +2
Mesokurtic

Larger Standard
Deviation

0   +1   +2
Platykurtic

Smaller Standard
Deviation

0   +1   +2
Leptokurtic

FIGURE 11.4. SKEWED CURVES.

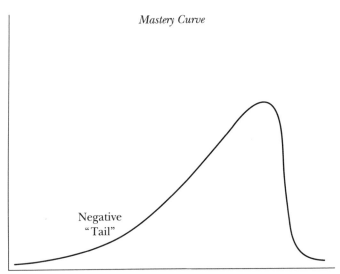

Mastery Curve

Negative
"Tail"

Negatively Skewed Curve

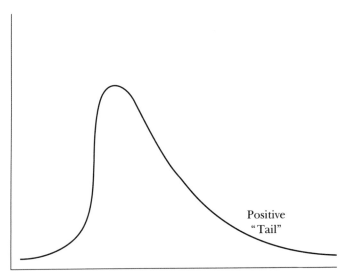

Positive
"Tail"

Positively Skewed Curve

Problems with Standard Deviations and Mastery Distributions

Some test designers consider a normal distribution of test results a reliable indicator of a good test. These test creators may have confused norm-referenced and criterion-referenced test philosophies. When creating a NRT, the normal distribution is highly desirable because it indicates spread in test-takers' scores—the spread that is essential to the reliable ranking of test-takers against one another. However, if your goal has been to create instruction based on specific competencies, and learners have largely mastered your objectives, your test distributions should look similar to Figure 11.5.

In this test, the mean is represented by the "0" on the horizontal axis where the standard deviations are listed. In a skewed distribution like this, you can calculate a standard deviation, but the result won't be meaningful because the percentage of scores within each standard deviation won't be like those of a normal curve, and in addition, will not be the same on both sides of the mean.

FIGURE 11.5. MASTERY CURVE.

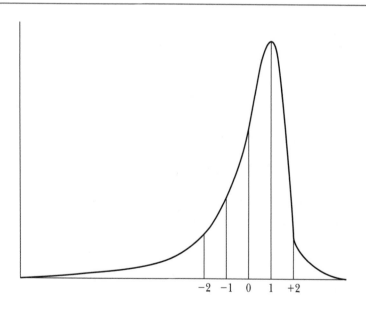

Remember, most of the traditional test statistics (point-biserial correlations presented in this chapter and internal consistency measures of reliability discussed in Chapter 14, for example) were designed for use with normal distributions. You can use some of them to guide you in developing a criterion-referenced test, but they are not as meaningful with non-symmetrical (skewed) distributions. In most instances involving CRTs, you can get a good feel for the standard deviation by plotting the scores. If most of your students have mastered most of your objectives, you should expect a negatively skewed distribution with a leptokurtic (tight) grouping of scores—this would be a distribution with a small standard deviation.

ITEM STATISTICS AND ITEM ANALYSIS

Once you have developed and administered your test, you need to review the test item statistics to help decide whether or not the test is "good." The process of reviewing each item and the way in which it contributes to the value of the test is called item analysis.

ITEM STATISTICS

There are four item statistics that are typically used to evaluate the quality of test items—the difficulty index, the p-values, the distractor pattern, and the point-biserial coefficient. The first three of these are expressed as percentages, while the point-biserial coefficient results from a correlation calculation.

Difficulty Index

The difficulty index is easy to understand once you realize it really should have been named the "easy index." The difficulty index is simply a measure of the number of people who answered a given item correctly. This statistic is usually expressed as a decimal, for example, .80 means 80 percent of the people taking the test answered the item correctly. The difficulty index can range from .00 (nobody got the item right) to 1.00 (everyone got the item right).

If you have a true mastery situation, you would expect to find high values for the difficulty indices since you expect everyone to pass. However, an alternative explanation for a high difficulty index is that the item is too easy or that people succeeded because of a technical flaw, for example, unrealistic distractors. Because of these problems, you should never use the difficulty index alone to decide about the quality of an item, as the value of the index varies depending on the test philosophy. In a norm-referenced test from which you want to separate the test-takers, you would create items that ranged in difficulty from .30 to .70. With a true mastery philosophy, you would create items that match job competencies and expect most items to have a difficulty index of .90 or higher.

P-Value

The p-value is similar in concept to the difficulty index. While the difficulty index refers to the percent of test-takers who answered the item correctly, the p-value refers to the percent of test-takers who selected each of the incorrect options. There is one difficulty index per item on a test. There are as many p-values per item as there are wrong answers; for example, if the difficulty index on a multiple-choice item with four options was .60, then the p-values for the distractors might be .10, .15, and .15 meaning that 10 percent selected the first incorrect option, 15 percent the next incorrect option, and another 15 percent the third incorrect option. Notice the p-values plus the item difficulty index sum to 1.00 or 100 percent of the test-takers. (**Note:** If you are familiar with basic statistical research design, you may have seen "p-value" defined differently. In research design p-value refers to the probability of incorrectly rejecting a null hypothesis. These p-values are two different statistics.)

Distractor Pattern

In conjunction with examination of the difficulty index and the p-values, you should also look at the pattern of test-takers' responses to your distractors. If you find that test-takers consistently eliminate one or more choices as wrong, then your distractors may be too unrealistic or otherwise too easy. If this happens, then you have changed the odds of guessing the correct answer. Where you might have expected the test-takers to have one chance in four of guessing the correct answer, one generally unused distractor will shift those odds to one out of three—a shift from a 25 percent to 33 percent probability of guessing the answer; two poor distractors will shift the odds from 25 percent to 50 percent. In the latter case, your multiple-choice item has become a binary choice item.

Point-Biserial Correlation

The point-biserial correlation is probably the single most useful statistic in item analysis. (If you are unfamiliar with the concept of correlation, you should read the section Correlation in Chapter 14 before trying to interpret point-biserial coefficients.) The point-biserial coefficient correlates the test-takers' performance on a single test item with their total test scores. What this means is:

- Each item will have a single point-biserial coefficient—a number ranging from $+1.00$ to -1.00.
- A positive coefficient means that test-takers who got the item right generally did well on the test as a whole, while those who did poorly on the test as a whole generally missed the item.
- A negative coefficient is an indication that those test-takers who generally did well on the test missed the item, while those who generally did poorly got the item right.
- Items with negative point-biserial coefficients are not useful for developing sound norm-referenced or criterion-referenced tests.
- If all test-takers answer an item correctly or all answer incorrectly, that item will have a point-biserial coefficient of 0.00.

If the point-biserial seems to be difficult, it isn't. It is just a particular correlation technique that follows the patterns of any correlation calculation, as described in Chapter 14. The point-biserial is a coefficient designed to measure the relationship between two variables, one of which is dichotomous (has only two values) and the other of which has a continuous range of values. In this item analysis application, the dichotomous variable is performance on a given item; the two values are "correct" and "incorrect." The variable with the continuous range of values is the total test score.

As a result, any item with a negative point-biserial correlation is immediately suspect! If the poorest performers got an item right that the best performers consistently missed, something is usually wrong. The most probable sources of the problem are:

- The scoring key is incorrect for this item.

- Some type of systematic misinformation is being disseminated in the instruction or the workplace.
- There is something about the item that causes those who know more to miss it, usually a subtle interpretation that the test designer missed in creating the item, but which better performers "read into" it.
- The sample size on which the item analysis is based is too small. This is not to say that under this circumstance the point-biserial incorrectly represents the relationship between test item performance and total test performance *for this sample.* The relationship is portrayed exactly as it is; however, if the sample size is smaller than fifteen to twenty, the negative finding might be due to chance error—some test-takers incorrectly coding a response or not paying attention—and might disappear as more test-taker data are collected.

When you review your tests, you will probably find that most items don't approach either extreme in point-biserial values—+1.00 or −1.00. This is especially so in mastery testing, where one expects most performers to do well. The lack of variation in test scores will limit how high the correlation figures will be. *Regardless of the size of your point-biserial coefficient, review every item with a negative or zero correlation for possible revision.* Keep in mind, though, that if every test-taker gets an item correct or incorrect, the item will have a point-biserial of 0. Thus in cases where the point-biserial is 0, you will also need to look at the difficulty index to determine how test-takers did and whether or not their performance represents trouble. For example, most test designers (course designers, too) would be more troubled if everyone missed an item than if everyone got the item correct.

ITEM ANALYSIS FOR CRITERION-REFERENCED TESTS

Item analysis is the most useful statistical application in the creation of criterion-referenced tests. However, remember that most item analysis techniques have been designed, developed, and studied for norm-referenced tests. Indeed, there are some problems in relying on norm-referenced techniques for criterion-referenced tests. Norm-referenced tests are designed to produce variation in the test scores (see Chapter 2), and most test and item statistics require score variation in order to show results. On the other hand, scores on criterion-referenced tests may not have much variation if most test-takers do well on the test. In that circumstance, most test and item statistics will have very low values.

However, the item analysis procedures we have discussed in this section are ones we believe are useful for CRT developers. Any computer testing software or standard statistical package you encounter will include these item statistics. The difficulty index, p-values, and distractor pattern statistics do not rely on score variance to be meaningful. We also recommend using the point-biserial coefficient because it has been our personal experience that any criterion-referenced test that assesses above the memory level will introduce enough variation in the responses to make the point-biserial correlation coefficient meaningful. In fact, the point-biserial coefficient will probably provide you with most of the item analysis information you need to evaluate your CRT. After the practice opportunity below, we introduce two additional statistics that were created specifically for criterion-referenced tests.

PRACTICE

Review the following sample test item analysis. What are the three best items? What are the three worst?

Item	Difficulty Index	Point-Biserial	Distractor Choices 1	2	3	4	5
1	1.00	.00	6*	0	0	0	0
2	0.17	.75	5	1*	0	0	0
3	0.33	.55	2*	0	1	3	0
4	0.83	−.88	5*	1	0	0	0
5	0.33	−.19	2*	4	0	0	0
6	0.33	.55	1	1	2	2*	0
7	0.50	−.71	3	3*	0	0	0
8	1.00	.00	6*	0	0	0	0
9	0.67	.46	4*	0	2	0	0
10	0.67	.22	4*	2	0	0	0

*Indicates the correct response
Number of Test-Takers = 6   Low Score = 2
Standard Deviation = 1.79   High Score = 10
Standard Error[1] = .41   Average or Mean = 5.8
Internal Consistency Reliability Estimate[1] = .16

[1]Standard error is explained in Chapter 13; internal consistency in Chapter 14.

FEEDBACK

1. The best items appear to be 2, 3, and 6. All have high point-biserials regardless of difficulty level. Item 6 has the best use of distractors.

2. The three worst items appear to be 4, 5, and 7. All have negative point-biserials.

THE UPPER-LOWER INDEX

A classic approach to examining an item's ability to discriminate between high performers and low performers has been to look at how the test-takers with the highest scores answered the item compared to the lowest scoring test-takers. The earliest NRT studies suggested that a comparison be made between the upper 27 percent and lower 27 percent of the test scores (Kelley, 1939). As CRT development emerged as an approach to testing, Brennan proposed a modification to this approach in 1972 that essentially substituted the master/non-master distinctions for upper and lower performance. As with the point-biserial, the index ranges from -1.0 to $+1.0$. The basic formula for the upper/lower index is presented in Figure 11.6.

FIGURE 11.6.   THE UPPER/LOWER INDEX FOR A CRT.

$$U/L\ INDEX = \frac{MC}{TM} - \frac{NMC}{TNM}$$

Where:

MC =   The number of masters who answered the item correctly

TM =   The total number of masters

NMC = The number of nonmasters who answered the item correctly

TNM = The total number of nonmasters

If we look at two examples of items using this index, we can see how it functions. Let's assume we have sixty test-takers. The results for one item yield these numbers:

$$MC = 35$$

$$TM = 40$$

$$NMC = 2$$

$$TNM = 20$$

Using the U/L index formula:

$$U/L \ INDEX = \frac{35}{40} - \frac{2}{20}$$

$$= .875 - .1$$

$$U/L \ INDEX = .775$$

So this item shows a high degree of differentiation between the masters and non-masters taking the test.

If an item were not working well to discriminate masters from non-masters, we might see numbers such as these:

$$MC = 2$$

$$TM = 40$$

$$NMC = 17$$

$$TNM = 20$$

Using the U/L index formula:

$$U/L \ INDEX = \frac{2}{40} - \frac{17}{20}$$

$$= .05 - .85$$

$$U/L \ INDEX = -.80$$

The discrimination power of this item is the near opposite of the first item we examined. Notice that the U/L Index shows a strong negative value because a majority of the non-masters succeeded on the item while most masters failed. Notice that the U/L Index provides the same type of information as the point-biserial.

Phi

We introduced phi in Chapter 9 as the preferred method for establishing concurrent validity for a test (using the known status of test-takers as determined by SMEs and their status as determined by the test). The same concept can be used for item analysis, as implied by Berk (1989) and Hambleton (1994) and proposed by Taylor and Lee (1995), by comparing performance on an item (pass/fail) with total test performance (master/non-master). The same calculation process illustrated in Chapter 9 is used again; the only change is that the vertical cell categories are labeled to reflect item performance. Figure 11.7 illustrates the change in the phi table.

FIGURE 11.7. PHI TABLE FOR ITEM ANALYSIS.

		Test Status		
		Non-Master	Master	
Item Performance	Pass	B =	A =	A + B =
	Fail	D =	C =	C + D =
		B + D =	A + C =	

Calculating phi "by hand" for the item analysis process would be tedious. If you determine that you need phi coefficients for each item (and we discuss whether you need to use phi in the next section), you will need some computing support.

Choosing Item Statistics and Item Analysis Techniques

The item statistics you gather and the subsequent item analysis will allow you to refine the accuracy of your test. The first point to remember though, is advice from Hambleton (1994, p. 1184):

> Criterion-referenced test items are only deleted from the pools of test items measuring objectives when it is determined that they are not consistent with the content specifications, violate standard

principles of item writing, or if the available item statistics reveal serious non-correctable flaws. Item statistics can be used to construct parallel forms of a criterion-referenced test or to produce a test to discriminate optimally between masters and non-masters.

With this advice in mind, we would suggest you proceed as follows:

1. Always review the three item statistics: difficulty index, p-value, and distractor pattern. These three techniques will help you to find quickly items that need attention.
2. You can use the point-biserial correlation for any low- or medium-stakes test with a fair degree of confidence. Sarvela (1986, p. 15) conducted a series of item analysis comparisons on normal and skewed test distributions. He found there were "no significant differences" between the values produced by an upper/lower index and the point-biserial.
3. If you are designing a high-stakes test with serious consequences, you may need to consider a more sophisticated approach to item analysis. Oshima, McGinty, and Flowers (1994, p. 196) point out that with a criterion-referenced test "developers should be extremely concerned about DIF (Differential Item Functioning) that occurs near the cut-off score but much less concerned when it occurs considerably above or below the cut-off score."

What this statement means is that techniques such as the upper/lower index will show you whether an item is discriminating between masters and non-masters in general. However, such a technique is too coarse an approach for dealing with test-taker scores that are near the cut-off point, for example, is there a real difference in mastery classification when a test-taker fails a test with a score of 84 percent when the passing score is 85 percent? We discuss this issue of borderline decisions in Chapter 13, but the advice from Oshima et al. (1994) is that the most sophisticated approach to reviewing an item's quality, especially at the borderline, is to use an approach from item response theory (IRT) to estimate the item's discrimination power. IRT attempts to identify the probability of a correct response to an item as a function of a test-taker's ability or trait levels (Baker, 2001). These approaches are not for the statistically faint-of-heart, and their full discussion is beyond the scope of this book. The good news is that corporate CRTs, based on a solid job-task analysis, are unlikely to require such precise item discrimination analysis— but we thought we'd at least give you a "head's up" here.

Garbage In-Garbage Out

Finally, remember that an item analysis, like any numerical technique, is only as good as what goes into it—as they say, Garbage In/Garbage Out (GIGO). The item analysis won't tell you anything about the quality of the objective being measured by the item. It doesn't tell you how accurately an item assesses a given objective. You could have an item with a high point-biserial, full use of the distractors, and a high difficulty index on a test of supervisory skills when the item is really measuring reading comprehension. Once again, there is no substitute for competent professional judgment in the testing process. An item analysis package will analyze response patterns for the most trivial as well as the most crucial items.

CHAPTER TWELVE

PARALLEL FORMS

Paper-and-Pencil Tests

Computerized Item Banks

Reusable Learning Objects

When a test is expected to be used a number of times or in a number of places throughout its life, the issue of parallel forms inevitably comes up. Parallel forms are different versions of a test that measure the same objectives and yield similar results. Whether you are thinking about two different forms of the same test in the tradition of Form A and Form B in the university large lecture hall exam, or preparing tests randomly created from a computerized item bank, parallel forms can be useful. Some arguments for creating them are:

- Parallel forms can be important if the security of a test is breached; the loose or circulated form can be destroyed and a parallel form placed into immediate service.
- Parallel forms are helpful in case an employee scheduled for group testing has to cancel and take the test at a later date; such an employee can be given a parallel form of the test without fear that the answers to the test may have been shared.
- Parallel forms allow for retesting of individuals who score too close to the master/non-master cut-off score to be classified with confidence.

Creating parallel forms of a test requires very careful matching of items in terms of the objectives they cover and the ways in which test-takers respond to them, that is, matched items should have the same difficulty level and the same discrimination index or point-biserial correlation (see Chapter 11).

In this short chapter we will first look at creating two or more paper-and-pencil parallel forms. If you are using a computer display to present electronic representations of the test (that is, you are not using a sampled item bank), the process is the same as for paper-and-pencil tests, as these computerized forms are just electronic presentations of the test. If you are using an item bank with a sampling algorithm, there are similar but more subtle considerations, and we will address those next. However, don't skip the paper-and-pencil section because it provides the best framework from which to think about sampling item banks.

PAPER-AND-PENCIL TESTS

The most common parallel testing situation in paper-and-pencil tests is the creation of two forms. Typically, organizations that have a concern about security for the exam or creating an alternative version for a test-taker who had to take the test apart from the original administration settle on two forms as the best balance between development time and testing flexibility. These are the steps in the process of creating two forms:

1. For each objective that is to be assessed, determine how many items you wish to have on the test.
2. Multiply that number by 2.5. If you are planning on two forms, you will usually need to create more than twice the number of items you expect to use because, as you analyze the item statistics, you will inevitably find that some items are not working as well as you planned.
3. Write the items. It is absolutely critical at this stage that you keep in mind the precision of your objective. If your objective is too broad, you will inadvertently create nonparallel forms. For example, if your objective were "multiply two two-digit numbers," the item "Multiply 11 × 11" is not parallel to the item "Multiply 78 × 96."
4. Administer the items to at least sixty test-takers. In test development, more is better. We pick sixty as a minimal number

for obtaining the item statistics based on a balance between the operational issue in corporate training of usual class sizes around twenty and statistical determinations. Thus you would need about three classes to achieve the number of test-takers needed to begin analysis of the data.

5. Analyze the test items by objective. You will review each item based primarily on the difficulty index and the distractor patterns (see Chapter 11.) Discard any items that you feel are not working, for example, a five-choice multiple-choice question where only two distractors are selected.

6. Distribute the test items to form each test. For each objective, place the items on the test to form an assessment of the objective by equal difficulty level; for example, if you had an objective for which you wanted to have two items on the test, you would now focus on the four items you have created that have similar difficulty indices and distractor patterns. If the item difficulty levels for the four items were .8, .9, .6, and .5, you would place the .8 and .6 items on one test and the .9 and .5 items on the other. This gives an average difficulty index of .7 for each form, as opposed to the possibility of an average difficulty level of .55 on one form and .85 on the other, for the same objective.

7. Set the cut-off scores and establish the reliability of the forms. In Chapters 13 and 14 we present three techniques for setting your cut-off score and then strategies for establishing the reliability of the test. We realize that in most corporate testing situations the test development process will stop after the cut-off score has been set. This actually doesn't worry us for most instances, as a well-designed job-task analysis with tightly matched objectives will inevitably lead to a valid and therefore reliable test.

However, in setting the cut-scores for the test, especially with the Informed Judgment and Angoff techniques, it is possible that two different cut-scores will result for each test. From a purely psychometric view, this is not a problem. From an organizational perspective, it can be. If the word goes out that the tests have different passing scores (though probably not by much) most will conclude there is an "easy" and a "hard" test. Thus, most organizations seek to standardize the cut-off point between the two tests—and that often means a political decision to set it at the lower score of the two. In any event, as we explain in Chapter 13, there is no substitute for professional judgment in setting the cut score, and you should make and document the decision using your best possible professional judgment.

Computerized Item Banks

With the increasing ease of finding testing software that will allow for randomization of item selection from a large pool of items, it becomes easier to create multiple forms of a test and thus makes it very difficult for someone to get a copy of "the test." (The Association of Test Publishers [2002] has provided detailed and useful guidelines for those using computers to create and deliver tests.)

The most critical issue by the time you have reached this stage of the CRT development process, though, is to recognize that most organizations that use item bank software do not consider the sampling procedures that should be used to develop a test from the item pool. The usual procedure is to write the items by objective and put those items in the item bank. From the banked items, a random selection is made by the computer and the test created. Simply following this process is a mistake for at least three reasons:

1. If you simply pull items out randomly, there is a good chance that some objectives will not be assessed on the test.
2. To create *equivalent* tests from the sampling procedure, you need to know at least the difficulty level for each item. If you haven't gathered the data as described in Steps 4 and 5 above, you can't be certain of equivalence among test forms.
3. As with creating just two forms, it is possible that each test could have a different cut-off score. However, the software we have seen does not track the necessary item data to allow for the calculation of the test cut-off score.

If you do decide to use an item bank system without the full statistical analyses needed, we have three pieces of advice:

1. Make sure the items for each bank are as similar in difficulty as possible. The easiest way to do this is to create precise objectives from which to create items.

2. Use a stratified random sampling technique. In other words, randomly draw the items from the bank by objective. This process will ensure that all objectives are assessed.
3. Set the average cut-off score for any randomly generated test based on the bank as a whole. This quick fix is best implemented in conjunction with the Angoff technique. You would begin by setting a probability level for each item, then determine the average probability level per objective, and finally, multiply the number of items per objective on the test by the average probability level. This sounds complicated, but it isn't. A simple example should help (but if you aren't familiar with the Angoff technique, you should turn to Chapter 13 and read about it now).

Table 12.1 summarizes a simple item bank of fifteen items assessing three objectives.

The average Angoff rating of the items for Objective 1 is .88, for Objective 2, .90, and for Objective 3, .86. If the test were to have two items on it for each objective, for a total of six items, you would set the cut-off score by multiplying .88 × 2, .90 × 2, and

TABLE 12.1. ANGOFF RATINGS FOR ITEMS IN AN ITEM BANK.

Objectives	Items	Angoff	Average
1	1	1.0	
	2	.9	.88
	3	.8	
	4	1.0	
	5	.7	
2	6	1.0	
	7	1.0	
	8	.9	.90
	9	.8	
	10	.8	
3	11	1.0	
	12	.9	
	13	.8	.86
	14	.7	
	15	.9	

.86 × 2. Thus, the initial cut-off score for passing on this six-item test would be 5.28, most likely adjusted to five out of six. (**Note:** This process assumes substitutability of the items, which is also discussed in Chapter 13. If you can't make that assumption, you will need to reconfigure this process to control for the non-substitutable items. It is not a conceptually difficult task to do so, but e-mail us via www.shrockandcoscarelli.com if you get this far and need help.)

REUSABLE LEARNING OBJECTS

Since about 2000, there has been a great deal of interest in reusable learning objects (RLOs) among the armed forces and some high-tech businesses (Advanced Distributed Learning, 1999; Barritt & Lewis, 2000). The RLO is made up of reusable instructional objects (RIOs). The idea of the RIO and the RLO is to create a repository of content, tagged electronically (RIOs), that can be archived and then recombined as needed for new purposes (RLOs). New RLOs can be created based on already developed RIOs thus saving time and effort in the design and development process. For example, a RLO on leadership style could use a RIO that also can be used in a RLO on management. Ruyle (2001, p. 1) draws the analogy of Lego blocks:

> You can think of RIOs as elements that have a high degree of granularity and are free from instructional connotations. A RIO is like a single Lego block. Put the Lego blocks together, add some gears, rubber bands, and wheels, and you have a simple machine. Put RIOs together and add instructional enablers (e.g., test and practice items) and elements to provide a context, and you create RLOs.

Our caution here is this: When you start to assemble RLOs from the RIOs, the instructional context of each RLO changes and thus any attempt to set a universal passing score for each RLO assessment (based on the individual RIOs) will prove invalid. It is difficult to foresee an elegant and usable solution to this problem in the near future.

CHAPTER THIRTEEN

CUT-OFF SCORES

DETERMINING THE STANDARD FOR MASTERY

One of the most difficult, yet critical, tasks required in CRT development is to determine the standard for passing, that is, the cut-off score that separates masters from non-masters. The CRT literature presents several methods for doing this, with Livingston and Zieky's work presenting the first manageable presentation of the techniques in 1982. Berk (1986b) reviewed thirty-eight methods for setting a cut-off score and provided standards for evaluation of their use. Shortly thereafter, he observed (1989, p. 1,116) that "Despite several extensive reviews of these methods, standard setting is still the stickiest technical topic."

Since 1989 there have been a number of refinements and additions to standard-setting processes, with the most recent work attempting to refine decisions made at the borderline between mastery and non-mastery. Kane (1994) offered a discussion about selecting passing scores, and Hambleton provided an update on criteria for evaluation of performance standards in

2001. Donath (2005, pp. 6–7) lists eight techniques that are currently used in various settings and situations: Angoff, Modified Angoff, Nedelsky's method, Ebel's method, Contrasting Groups, Jaeger method, Bookmark, and Direct Consensus. A number of these discussions are highly theoretical, but three techniques we discuss and illustrate in this chapter are still the most viable for corporate settings. In fact, the Angoff Technique is probably the most popular of all the techniques for corporate CRTs (Impara & Plake, 2000).

However, before we look at these procedures, we want to make you aware of a number of considerations that affect the standard-setting process, regardless of the method used.

The Outcomes of a Criterion-Referenced Test

Following the assumptions of criterion-referenced testing, the true status of every test-taker is either a master or a non-master. A reliable and valid test will lead to a judgment that matches the true status with the test-taker's performance. If the test-taker is a non-master and is classified as such, or the test-taker is a master and is classified as a master, then we have made the correct decisions. However, if the master is judged to be a non-master, we have made an error of rejection (also called a false negative because the negative decision on mastery is an error). If a non-master is judged to be a master, then we have made an error of acceptance (also called a false positive because the positive decision on mastery is an error). Figure 13.1 summarizes these relationships.

Figure 13.1.   Outcomes of a Criterion-Referenced Test.

| | | Test Decision | |
		Non-Master	Master
True Status	Master	Error of Rejection	Correct Decision
	Non-Master	Correct Decision	Error of Acceptance

The only way to minimize these errors is to ensure that your test is reliable and valid.

THE NECESSITY OF HUMAN JUDGMENT IN SETTING A CUT-OFF SCORE

Several of the techniques we are about to describe have the appearance of statistical precision in establishing a cut-off score. These methods, especially the contrasting groups process, can be appealing because they create the impression of certainty. Don't be deluded. *There is no simple, cookbook solution to establishing the standards for your test, and there is no formula for determining the cut-off score that eliminates the sticky business of human judgment in standard-setting procedures!* With this caveat, there are four considerations worth your attention:

CONSEQUENCES OF MISCLASSIFICATION

One of the first judgments you must make has to do with the consequences of misclassification of test-takers. If it is particularly important to prevent non-masters from being certified as masters, it makes sense to raise the cut-off score beyond what might be otherwise satisfactory. On the other hand, if greater damage is done by denying master status to those who may in fact be masters, then it might be advisable to lower the cut-off score.

For example, the consequences of passing a non-master during a surgical residency far outweigh the consequences of occasionally holding back a master. In other situations, such as minimal competency tests for high school graduates, the opposite may be true. It may be felt that denying diplomas to masters has such severe social and economic consequences for those individuals that these consequences outweigh the disadvantages to society of letting some non-masters erroneously graduate.

There are specific consequences to the organization of making both false negative and false positive errors. As a result of false negatives, the company may lose the services of a competent performer, or at the least, lower the morale of the employee. If the test-taker is from a legally protected group (see Chapter 17), there can also be legal costs associated with the erroneous classification of a master as a non-master. False positives can cost the company the dollar value of the employees' mistakes, as well as lost time on the job as incompetent employees learn the skills they need, usually inefficiently. Loss of reputation for the company due to a failure to perform, and thus a consequent loss of sales may result from certifying non-masters as masters. Lawsuits from clients are also a possible consequence of false positive errors. Thus, one of the first issues a test designer needs to address when setting standards is the consequences of misclassification resulting from the test whose cut-off score is to be determined.

STAKEHOLDERS

It is usually advisable for the standard setters to collect opinions from all groups who have a stake in the outcome of the test decision. In fact, this process is so important that it forms the basis for one of the cut-off score techniques we will cover. For a given corporate test, you might expect to find that the cut-off score you develop is of interest to the EEO officer, the test-takers' supervisors, the personnel department, and others. Thus, by using a process that not only recognizes your best professional judgment to set the cut-off score, but also involves those who will be affected by the results of the test, you will cultivate greater acceptance of the testing procedure and its resulting decisions.

REVISABILITY

Never assume that the initial cut-off score will remain unchanged, or that an established cut-off score will not need to be revised over time. Experience with the test, new data, or contextual changes over time may require an adjustment in the cut-off score. For example, a nuclear power company may have chosen one cut-off score to certify reactor operators. However, after a year, with data on critical operator errors, a new, higher score might be selected. In this instance, excessive allegiance to the original cut-off score may not only hamper efforts to improve the testing process, it may lead to a fatal error.

PERFORMANCE DATA

Standard setters should rely extensively on performance data in choosing the cut-off score. It is unwise to set a standard in the absence of hard data about how real test-takers perform on the test. An unrealistically high cut-off score can be particularly difficult to lower for political or legal reasons; for example, "How come I had to have a 94 percent to get a pay grade increase, and now people only need a 75 percent?" At best, an unrealistically low standard can create a sense of mockery for its graduates; at worst, low standards support a hazardous workplace with unskilled employees damaging equipment or jeopardizing the health and safety of others.

Three Procedures for Setting the Cut-Off Score

With these thoughts in mind, we are almost ready to turn to three different but complementary methods of determining the cut-off score for a criterion-referenced test. The Informed Judgment Method draws primarily on perceptions of various stakeholders in the organization. Conjectural Methods base cut-off scores on content-expert projections of competent performance on each test item. The Contrasting Groups Method uses performance data of masters and non-masters to establish the level of mastery. We recommend, and research shows (Impara & Plake, 2000), that you should use as many of these standard-setting methods as you can to establish the test cut-off score through a triangulation process. Here we include the *political* process of Informed Judgment, the *projected* outcomes of the Conjectural Method, and the *performance* process of Contrasting Groups. Each approach is based on a systematic collection and analysis of data from a different source, but each also requires that you consider an issue we call substitutability in setting your cut-off score.

The Issue of Substitutability

When establishing a cut-off score for a test, a common procedure is to set the score based on the test-taker's ability to pass a certain number of items (such as 85 out of 100). In doing so, however, a critical assumption is being made—one that you *must* consider if you are to develop a valid test. The assumption is that failure to perform on one item can be made up for by success on another item. For example, in our test of one hundred items, if all items are equally substitutable, it doesn't matter which of the eighty-five are answered correctly. However, if there are certain items that must be answered correctly for mastery performance, then failing on any of those items may mean failing the test—even if only one item is missed—for example, in constructing a test to assess skills in utility-pole climbing, a test-taker who fails to wear safety glasses fails the test. Efficient climbing, wire splicing, and descent cannot overcome the single failure of violating an essential safety rule. When using any of the three techniques covered in this chapter you may determine:

- That all items are substitutable and a single cut-off score is acceptable, or
- You can partial out the non-substitutable skills and establish a two tiered scoring system in which a score of 100 percent is required on the non-substitutable items, and a given percentage is required for the remaining items.

Again, we want to emphasize that the chosen cut-off score should not be considered as absolutely final. The operation of the chosen cut-off score should be monitored periodically to make sure that it is rendering decisions that are satisfactory to those involved and facilitating the achievement of the company's objectives. In the end, there is never any substitute for good professional judgment.

INFORMED JUDGMENT

The Informed Judgment Method acknowledges most explicitly that the standard-setting process is essentially one of human judgment. The steps of this method follow directly from paying attention to the four considerations we have just discussed.

1. Begin by analyzing the consequences of misclassification. The political, legal, but especially the performance consequences of test-takers on the job need to be analyzed.
2. Gather relevant performance data to see how different test-takers actually do on the test. It is preferable to collect

performance data from at least three different groups of test-takers:

- Those who have not taken instruction in the competencies covered by the test
- Those who have just finished such instruction
- Those who are doing the job

The idea here is to get a feel for how well naive test-takers can do on the test, and how long the test competencies are retained once the instruction is completed. These scores are also considered in the light of how actual job performers do.
3. The third step is to collect the preferences of other stakeholders. In other words, take the test to those who will be affected by the consequences of your test decisions, for example, the test-takers' supervisors, test-taker co-workers, the EEO office, and so on, and ask them what they think the cut-off score should be.
4. Finally, select the cut-off score based on consideration of all the accumulated data. There is no formula available to weight each component and then calculate the final cut-off score. The final decision is thus a professional, informed judgment regarding what level of test-taker competence constitutes mastery.

PRACTICE

Assume that a test was developed to assess the competencies to become an instructional evaluation specialist. Here are the data gathered by the test developer to reach an informed judgment about the cut-off score. What would you recommend as the cut-off score?

Average score of non-masters   34 percent

Average score of masters   79 percent

Preferred cut scores of various constituencies:

    Current evaluation specialists   70 percent

    Evaluators' supervisors   85 percent

    Instructional design staff   60 percent

Evaluators' clients	90 percent
Personnel department	50 percent
Cut-Off Score Estimate	___ percent

FEEDBACK

Because this is an informed judgment process, there will generally be variation in suggested cut-off scores due to different divisional responsibilities and different types of interactions with the employees the test will certify. The process of gathering the data and discussing the various constituency judgments is critical to the effectiveness of this technique.

The personnel department may wish to have a lower score (50 percent) to reduce its difficulties in recruiting or to protect itself from an EEO challenge (by viewing the risk of certifying a non-master as less than the risk of legal challenge for denying certification). The clients, of course, would prefer to deal only with the very best professionals and would prefer the instructional evaluation specialist to score at the top end (90 percent). The instructional design staff might feel threatened by the evaluation specialists and therefore lobby for a lower skill level. The evaluators' supervisors want to have strong colleagues, but probably have a more realistic view of what the meaning of a specific score on this test is, and have opted for a cut score of 85 percent, still higher than most, but lower than that of the clients. Finally, the current evaluation specialists have probably sought a balance between what is an adequate professional assessment and personal interests in not making their work life any more difficult than it currently is. Hence they have chosen a mid-range score of 70 percent. (FYI: Training professionals reviewing these data—as an exercise divorced from a real situation—have tended to set the cut-off score in the 70 to 75 percent range.)

A CONJECTURAL APPROACH, THE ANGOFF METHOD

There is a general class of techniques for estimating the cut-off score of a test by determining estimates of success for a minimally competent performer on each item. This class of techniques is often referred to as Conjectural Methods in that they rely on professional estimates or conjectures of success. Of the conjectural techniques that exist, the Angoff method (Zieky & Livingston, 1977) is perhaps the most useful and generally used technique of the conjectural methods and the one we want to discuss. Hurtz and Auerbach (2003) conducted a meta-analysis of the Angoff method and some modifications to it and provided this abstract of their findings:

> The Angoff method for setting cut-off scores on examinations has been researched extensively over the past thirty years, including investigations of several procedural modifications to the method. In the current study, the authors meta-analytically synthesized this research and evaluated the systematic effects of the most common modifications on the level of the resulting cut-off scores and the degree of consensus among judges. The authors found the following: (a) when judges use a common definition of minimally competent test-takers, this tends to increase judgment consensus; (b) when judges discuss their estimates, this tends to result in higher cut-off scores with increased consensus; and (c) when judges view normative data, this tends to systematically lower cut-off scores. In addition, the authors found an interaction effect which revealed that when judges use a common definition and later discuss their estimates, this tends to produce the highest standards on average, with the highest degree of consensus among judges. (p. 584)

Their findings have matched our experience with the technique. These are the steps in the Angoff method that we recommend you follow to enhance the validity of the results:

1. The first step is to identify judges who are familiar with the competencies covered by the test, and with the performance level for masters of these competencies. The number of judges you select will depend on availability of judges, criticality of the performance, and so forth. However, we think you would rarely need more than five, with three being the more typical number.
2. Plan a face-to-face meeting with the judges to set the cut-off scores. We recommend you conduct an Angoff session face-to-face instead of virtually, as critical subtleties of the process seem to be lost without the human interaction. We have had some success with virtual meetings, but only when all the judges had been engaged in an initial face-to-face meeting.

    You should also have a projection system with a spreadsheet program available and format it to identify the judges across the horizontal axis and to list the items by number along the vertical, left side of the spreadsheet. You will need to "program" the software to calculate an average across judges and items.

3. Have the judges come to a consensus regarding the definition of the borderline or minimally competent performer. It is important to point out that a "minimally competent" person is not an incompetent one. A minimally competent pilot, for example, is still very competent. Another common discussion at this stage focuses on whether the organization is comfortable with mastery levels of performance as they currently exist in the organization or as they might exist if higher standards prevailed. The outcome of that discussion will have an important impact on the definition of the minimally competent performer.

4. Print a copy of the test on a different colored paper for each judge; this will facilitate sharing estimates later in the meeting. Test items should also show the correct answer to each question.

5. Hold a discussion with the judges about the estimation process that addresses the following issues *before* beginning to assign estimates:

   - Make sure the judges understand that a probability estimate should never be lower than the probability of getting the item correct by chance; for example, if there are four alternatives in a multiple-choice item, the estimate should not be lower than 25 percent. These estimates are expressed as percentages and assigned a corresponding decimal value. For example, if a judge thinks there is a fifty-fifty chance of the minimally competent test-taker getting a given item right, that item is assigned a value of .50. If the judge estimates that an item is either so simple or represents content so critical that the minimally competent test-taker will almost surely get it right, then the item would be assigned a value of 1.0. Estimates need not be in increments of 25 percent or 20 percent; their value can vary anywhere from chance level to 1.0.

   - Tell the judges to examine each answer and the distractors. Decide how many distractors the minimally competent test-taker could surely eliminate. This would provide a floor to the rating of the item; for example, if one option on a four-choice item can almost certainly be eliminated by any competent performer, then the lowest estimate for this item will be 33 percent.

- If the choice between or among the remaining distractors is truly random, then estimate the Angoff weight as the chance probability between/among the remaining option(s). For example, if there are two choices remaining from four distractors, then the probability would be 50 percent or .50.
- If the choice among the remaining distractors in NOT random, then the decision is based on how far the judge believes the deviation from random should be.
- Judges tend to go through three stages while learning to estimate the probability for items:
  a. Their first reaction is to estimate the difficulty of the item for themselves. Since the judges are rarely at the minimally competent level, using this estimate will produce an artificially high estimate.
  b. Judges then tend to estimate the difficulty for the typical test-taker.
  c. Finally, judges see that they are setting a standard for how the minimally competent performer should be able to answer.

6. Start with a single item and have the judges independently estimate the probability that a minimally competent test-taker would get the item right.

7. Have the judges share their privately derived estimates and discuss why they decided as they did.

8. Clarify the process and content questions as needed until consensus is reached or until each judge feels comfortable with his or estimate on the first practice item.

9. Pick a second item; again, have the judges rate it privately and then discuss their estimates. Continue this process until the judges feel comfortable with their role.

10. Send the judges to private spaces to rate the entire test. When they have finished, have them return to the meeting room and dictate their estimates (to speed the process) for entry into the spreadsheet program.

11. Review the ratings and have judges discuss any Angoff weight for an item that varies by more than .20 among the judges' estimates. Judges can choose to change the weight for an item

in any direction based on the results of their subsequent discussion or maintain their original estimates.

12. The chosen cut-off score is the sum of the probability estimates. If more than one judge is used, the cut-off score is the average of the individual judges' sums.

Here is an example (Table 13.1) of the process illustrated with a five-item test:

TABLE 13.1.   JUDGES' PROBABILITY ESTIMATES (ANGOFF METHOD).

Item	Judge 1 Probability	Judge 2 Probability	Judge 3 Probability
1	.33	.50	.40
2	.80	.90	1.00
3	.20	.33	.20
4	.20	.90	.33
5	.50	.75	.50
Total	2.03	3.38	2.43

Averaging the Totals for Each Judge to Obtain the Cut-Off Score
2.03 + 3.38 + 2.43 = 7.84
7.84/3   = 2.61

Cut-Off Score   = 2.6 or 3 when rounded

PRACTICE

Assume you are a judge for a test designed to assess competencies to become an instructional evaluation specialist. For each item, estimate the probability that the minimally competent test-taker will get the item correct.

Item   **Probability**

1. Nearly every high school graduating class selects a valedictorian and a salutatorian. What kind of decision do these choices represent?

    a. Norm-referenced

    b. Criterion-referenced

    c. Domain-referenced

    d. None of the above   _____

2. Ann goes bowling. Every time she rolls the ball, it goes into the gutter. In testing terms, Ann's performance might best be described as:

   a. both reliable and valid

   b. neither reliable or valid

   c. valid, but not reliable

   d. reliable, but not valid   _____

3. Mr. Kinser is charged with determining the quality of finished cabinets produced by his employees. Which is the most reliable instrument he could develop for this purpose?

   a. A behaviorally anchored rating scale

   b. A checklist

   c. An objectives based test

   d. A descriptive scale   _____

4. The appropriate correlation coefficient for calculating the correlation between decisions based on a criterion-referenced test and IQ is the point-biserial correlation coefficient.

   a. True

   b. False   _____

5. Define the term validity.

   _____

   _____

   _____   _____

Cut-Off Score (sum of estimates)   _____

FEEDBACK

The estimates for each item can only be made as a function of the difficulty of the content and the relative level of sophistication of the minimally competent person in a given organization. Hence the need to employ qualified judges. Table 13.2 shows what might be one set of estimates for the minimally competent performer.

TABLE 13.2. POSSIBLE PROBABILITY ESTIMATES, ANGOFF METHOD.

Item	Probability
1	.75
2	.50
3	1.00
4	.75
5	.75
Sum of Estimates	3.75

Cut-Off Score Estimate = 3.75 or 4 when rounded

CONTRASTING GROUPS METHOD

The Contrasting Groups method has the aura of scientific precision about it. Indeed, it is probably the single strongest technique of the three, and one may be tempted to use it exclusively. However, there is no evading the necessity for human judgment in setting a cut-off score—even in the Contrasting Groups method—nor should one standard-setting technique be used alone. We feel the Contrasting Groups process is most appropriately an integral part of the data collected for the Informed Judgment method.

1. The first step in this technique is to choose judges who are familiar with employee performance and knowledgeable enough about the competencies tested to select a pool of definite masters and non-masters. It is important that the judges understand the definition of a "non-master."

   Non-masters are *not* those people who are totally ignorant about the topic to be tested. A non-master for testing word processing skills with a specific program would be someone who knows how to type and use a computer—not someone who has no skills with either the computer or the typewriter. Because this technique compares the performance of the two groups, defining a non-master as someone totally unskilled in the area may lead to an artificially low standard of mastery.

   If there are no other sources of data from which to choose, you can *approximate* master and non-master performance by administering a pretest and a posttest for a course (if one

exists that teaches the skills tested). However, this approach is
particularly susceptible to error introduced by poor teaching
or underestimating entry skills.

2. Have the judges identify masters and non-masters. There should
   be at least fifteen people in each group, preferably thirty or
   more. (As we discussed with test length in Chapter 7, more is
   usually better. The larger your sample, the more confidence
   you can have in your judgments about the cut-off score.)
3. Administer the test to both groups, that is, the masters and the
   non-masters.
4. Plot the scores of both groups as frequency distributions. Figure 13.2
   illustrates one such pair of frequency distributions.

FIGURE 13.2. CONTRASTING GROUPS METHOD OF CUT-OFF SCORE ESTIMATION.

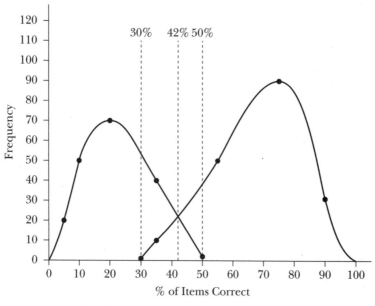

Non-Masters			Masters	
f	Score		f	Score
20	5		1	30
50	10		10	35
70	20		50	55
40	35		90	75
2	50		31	90

5. Make the initial cut-off score where the two distributions inter-sect. In Figure 13.2 this point would be around 42 percent. This intersection point is the cut-off score that minimizes the total number of misclassifications—both false positive and false negative—resulting from the test.

6. Adjust the cut-off score as necessary. Shifting the cut-off score to 50 percent would eliminate all non-masters as well as the lowest scoring masters. Shifting the cut-off score to 30 percent would create a situation in which all identified masters are passed as well as the higher-scoring non-masters. The final cut-off score could be adjusted to any point between 30 percent and 50 percent, depending on the severity of the consequences of false positive and false negative errors and the opinions of other stakeholders.

PRACTICE

A group of masters and a group of non-masters have been given a test developed to assess the competencies required to become an instructional evaluation specialist. The frequencies of the achieved scores (expressed as percentages of items correct) for both groups are given below in Table 13.3. Plot the frequencies and determine the cut-off score.

TABLE 13.3.   EXAMPLE TEST RESULTS FOR USING THE CONTRASTING GROUPS METHOD.

Non-masters		Masters	
Frequency	% Correct	Frequency	% Correct
8	10	1	40
23	20	4	50
30	30	8	60
26	40	17	70
17	50	30	85
8	60	23	90
2	70	1	100

Estimated Cut-Off Score: _____

FIGURE 13.3. FREQUENCY DISTRIBUTIONS FOR USING THE CONTRASTING
GROUPS METHOD.

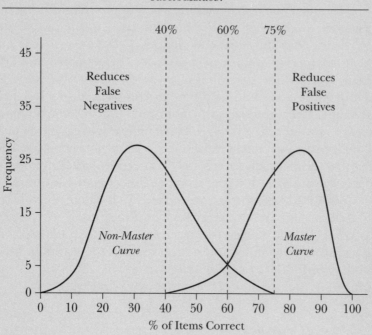

FEEDBACK

The graphs above (Figure 13.3) illustrate the results of plotting the two distributions resulting from this test.

As you can see, the initial cut-off would be set at 60 percent. By shifting the cut-off score to the right to 75 percent, you will reduce false positives and increase the chances that only masters will be certified by your test. Raising the cut-off score, however, increases the likelihood of false negative errors. A shift down the scale to 40 percent will reduce the false negatives but increase the chances that non-masters will be certified. The point at which the two curves intersect (60 percent) minimizes the total number of misclassifications (the false positive and false negative misclassifications added together.)

Having reviewed these distributions, you might go back to the Informed Judgment exercise and decide whether or not you would have made the same cut-off decision having seen the distributions rather than just relying on the average scores for masters and non-masters. When given this fictitious data as a learning exercise, most training professionals tend to shift their cut-off score estimates in light of the distributions—usually to no less than 60 percent and no more than 75 percent.

BORDERLINE DECISIONS

As previously mentioned, one of the assumptions of testing has been that any observed score is composed of two parts: true score and error. If you can reduce the error component to zero or near zero, then you can have a high degree of confidence that a person's observed score is equivalent to his or her true score. However, we know that it is impossible to eliminate the error component of a test score. At the same time, intuitively we understand that at some point people with two different scores really are different in skill level or the knowledge base assessed by the test. For example, most people would agree that two people with scores of 85 percent and 25 percent are probably at different levels of mastery. But what about two people with scores of 84 percent and 86 percent? Can you really feel confident that they are truly different? What if the cut-off score is set at 85 percent? Does it make sense to certify one of these test-takers as a master and one as a non-master? Most test designers wonder how to treat the borderline cases, but before we discuss this issue, we need to introduce the concept of standard error of measurement.

THE MEANING OF STANDARD ERROR OF MEASUREMENT

Beyond intuition, there is a statistical mechanism for estimating the probability that two scores are truly different. The estimate of the amount of variation to be found in a given test score is the standard error of measurement. *In criterion-referenced tests, the standard error of measurement should be considered as a conceptual framework for understanding the quality of the test. Traditional norm-referenced formulas will not be effective with mastery distributions.*

If we had a test of 100 points and one person had a 70 and another a 71, most people (test-takers and designers alike) would not feel comfortable in saying that the person with a 71 really did outperform the person with a 70. If one scored 60 and the other 70, then those involved would probably be more likely to agree there was some difference in performance. For a given score, the standard error provides an estimate of how far apart the scores have to be to be significantly different.

An example of the effect of standard error. If you knew that a test's reliability was .80 and the standard deviation was .15, by applying a statistical formula you would find that the standard error of measurement is .07 (the ideal standard error of measurement being 0.0). Knowing the standard error of measurement allows you to establish a confidence interval around the observed score. In Figure 13.4 below a calculation has been made for someone whose score is 60 percent on this test, for which you want a level of confidence of 95 percent. To achieve this level of confidence, you will have to establish a range of two standard errors of measurement on either side of the observed score. (If you are willing to accept greater risk of error, you can establish the interval at one standard error of measurement on either side of the observed score.)

FIGURE 13.4. APPLICATION OF THE STANDARD ERROR OF MEASUREMENT.

$$
\begin{aligned}
\text{Estimate of true score} &= \text{observed} \pm (\text{confidence} \times SE_m) \\
&= .60 \pm (2 \times .07) \\
&= .60 \pm (.14) \\
&= .46 \text{ to } .74
\end{aligned}
$$

In this instance, we would say that there is an approximately 95 percent probability that this person's observed score of 60 percent does not deviate from his or her true score by more than 14 percentage points on either side of 60 percent—by more than two standard errors in either direction. What is most important to remember is that a single test score should *always* be viewed as a point within a range—not a single, absolute point (see Figure 13.5).

FIGURE 13.5. THE TEST SCORE AS A RANGE RATHER THAN A POINT.

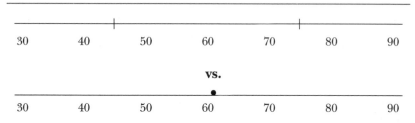

Problems with Standard Error and Mastery Distributions. The standard error of measurement is a useful concept to understand, but its application to most criterion-referenced tests is controversial. The controversy is centered on the argument that it should be applied only to those items that measure a single objective.

In other words, many authorities feel that reliability estimates need to be figured on subsets of test items that measure the same objective. This recommendation is usually impractical, as most tests will measure more than one objective, with each objective being assessed by a small number of items. Following this advice would result in a multitude of error estimates, none of them very accurate given the fact that they were based on so few items. So what should you do? *If you have any variability in your test scores, and you have access to a measure of internal consistency (see Chapter 14), the standard error of measurement would be a useful guide to the width of the border of indecision surrounding individual scores.* However, there is a practical and intuitive approach to dealing with the borderline cases.

REDUCING MISCLASSIFICATION ERRORS AT THE BORDERLINE

If you are particularly concerned about certification errors for test-takers who score near the cut-off (above *or* below the cut-off score) then you can follow a simple procedure we have adapted from Robert Lathrop (1986) to resolve this problem.

1. Establish a region of indecision, that is, the width of the border, around the cut-off score. Ideally this border would be defined as a function of the standard error of measurement; but an estimate of the width of this region can be made by selecting one-tenth of the total test range around the cut-off score. For example, on a test with 100 points, and a cut-off score of 85, the border would be between 80 and 90 (Lathrop favors one-fifth of the total test range, but estimates are primarily for norm-referenced tests with greater variability in scores than the criterion-referenced test.) The width of the border is still a matter of professional judgment associated with the test designer's assessment of the risks of misclassification. The greater the concern about misclassification, the larger the border may be.

2. For those test-takers who have scores in the borderline range, you should administer a second testing. With the second test, three outcomes are possible:
   • The test-taker will score above the cut-off score on both tests

- The test-taker will score below the cut-off score on both tests, or
- The test-taker will score above the cut-off score on one test and below it on the other.

When the scores are the same on both tests, that is, master/master or non-master/non-master, then the decision is made as indicated by the tests. If the scores are different on the two tests, then you are back to the issue of subjective judgment and the risk level you are willing to accept for misclassification. If the consequences of certifying a non-master as a master are great, then you may choose to classify the inconsistent test-taker as a non-master. If the consequences of classifying a master as a non-master are greater, then you might choose to certify the inconsistent test-taker as a master.

In the end, and once again, there is no substitute for professional judgment. However, if you are going to establish a procedure for borderline cases, do so in advance of the test and make this known to all test-takers. Inconsistency in testing procedures, especially if they affect a protected group, may well create negative professional, ethical, and legal consequences. For a more detailed discussion of this topic, including the recommendation and explanation of why cut-off scores should be raised for repeat test-takers, Millman's (1989) article "If at First You Don't Succeed" is particularly useful for anyone working with high-stakes tests.

PROBLEMS WITH CORRECTION-FOR-GUESSING

As we pointed out earlier, the multiple-choice test is one of the most powerful techniques in test design. One of its weaknesses, though, is that test-takers do not have to create the right answer, they just have to recognize it. While we have seen that "just recognizing" isn't always a simple task, test designers often wonder if there isn't some value in using a correction-for-guessing score adjustment to penalize getting a certain percentage of multiple-choice items right simply by guessing. While we think that the disadvantages of correction-for-guessing outweigh the advantages, it is useful for test developers to understand why, since they are frequently asked to apply such corrections. To understand the problems with adjusting scores for guessing, you need to know what the correction-for-guessing formula looks like and how to apply it.

If you give students a one-hundred-item multiple-choice test for which each item has four alternative responses, students will, on the average, get twenty-five items correct simply by guessing. (If there are five choices, they will get 20 percent correct.) What the correction-for-guessing formula does is to subtract from the test-taker's number of correct answers the estimated number of answers that were answered correctly simply by guessing. The number to be subtracted is estimated from the number of items that the test-taker answered incorrectly. A correction-for-guessing formula thus assumes that every wrong answer resulted from guessing incorrectly. Figure 13.6 illustrates a correction-for-guessing formula and its application on a test with ninety-five items and five choices per item.

As you can see from this example, the original score of 85/95 has now been reduced to 82.5/95 due to the subtraction of a portion of the number of items attempted but answered incorrectly.

FIGURE 13.6. CORRECTION-FOR-GUESSING FORMULA.

$$\text{Score} = R - \frac{W}{n - 1}$$

Where R = number right
W = number wrong
n = number of alternatives

Correction for Guessing Example

R = 85
W = 10
n = 5

$$\text{Score} = 85 - \frac{10}{5 - 1}$$
$$= 85 - \frac{10}{4}$$
$$= 85 - 2.5$$
$$= 82.5$$

Although the correction-for-guessing formula seems to make good sense intuitively, research has revealed a problem with its use. As it turns out, very few responses to multiple-choice test items are pure guesses. Most of the time, the test-taker has some partial knowledge about each item and is making a decision based on more than random chance. In such cases, the correction-for-guessing formula penalizes test-takers for applying partial knowledge, since it is not guessing that has led them to select the wrong answer. Furthermore, people differ widely in their willingness to take risks—in this case, the risk is associated with making a choice about which they are not completely certain, and knowing they will be penalized if they are wrong. The result is that low risk takers refrain from answering many items that they would in fact get correct if they marked them. Therefore, the resulting scores of these persons are substantially lower than they should be. In other words, much current research indicates that the threat of the application of the correction-for-guessing formula introduces more error into the test scores than is eliminated by correcting for guessing. As we said, we do not recommend the adjustment of test scores by using a correction-for-guessing formula.

THE PROBLEM OF THE SALTATORY CUT-OFF SCORE

As CRT test development has become more widespread, so too has the use of computerized test development tools. These tools allow for random selection of questions from a data bank and thus can generate many different tests from the same bank that would, in fact, make the number of forms combinatorially large—and thus reduce errors in testing due to familiarization with items or attempts at cheating. And thus, a new problem is created. Theoretically each form of the same test could have a different cut-off score because each item could have a unique Angoff weight. The idea that one person passed an exam with a score of 82 percent while another failed a test on the same content with a score of 83 percent would be hard to explain to anyone but a psychometrician. This saltatory (bouncing) score would be defensible from a statistical perspective, but would give organizations implementation challenges for political and perhaps legal reasons. Using a true data set from a certification test, Coscarelli, Barrett, Kleeman, and Shrock (2005) examined the consequences of selection procedures that relied on pure randomization from within an item bank, or stratified randomization based on Angoff weights. They concluded:

- For low-stakes tests you can randomly sample within the item bank (as most computer-based testing programs allow as a default).
- For medium-stakes tests, you can probably sample within the bank if the distribution is statistically normal; however, stratification is safer.
- For high-stakes tests, you should consider stratification of the sample by Angoff weight for increased precision.

Chapter Fourteen

RELIABILITY OF COGNITIVE TESTS

THE CONCEPTS OF RELIABILITY, VALIDITY, AND CORRELATION

Reliability and validity are two important characteristics of any kind of test—norm-referenced tests and criterion-referenced tests, cognitive tests and performance tests. Reliability and validity describe qualities that any good test must possess. They are important factors in defending a test against legal challenge. As indicated in Chapter 1, reliability refers to consistency in the testing results; validity refers to the test's accuracy in measuring what it is intended to measure. While it is possible for a test to be reliable but invalid, it is not possible for a test to be valid if it is unreliable.

An unreliable test doesn't measure anything—at least not the same thing every time it is taken, so it cannot possibly be a valid test of any competency.

While the concepts of reliability and validity are fundamental, there are in fact several different types of reliability and validity. (See Chapter 9 for a discussion of different types of validity.) A test's reliability, and frequently its validity, are expressed as numbers, that is, as reliability and validity coefficients. These coefficients differ depending on the type of reliability and validity being expressed. The concepts of reliability and validity are closely related to the concept of correlation, and most reliability and validity coefficients are correlation coefficients of some kind. Therefore, we begin this chapter with a discussion of the meaning of correlation. We next take up the topic of reliability as the concept is most often applied to cognitive criterion-referenced tests. (The concept of reliability as applied to performance tests is called *inter-rater reliability*. Procedures for establishing inter-rater reliability are presented in Chapter 15.) The chapter concludes with a discussion of reliability and validity in criterion-referenced testing.

CORRELATION

Correlation is simply a statistical procedure to determine the relationship between two or more variables. A positive correlation means that as one variable changes, the other changes in the same way. A negative correlation means that as one variable changes, the other changes in the opposite way. A zero correlation means there is no relationship between the variables. Figure 14.1 illustrates how these relationships would look if they were graphed.

The top figure is an example of two variables that are positively correlated. These variables could be high school grade point average and college board scores. As you can see, when the grade point average (Variable 1) goes up, the college board scores (Variable 2) also increase. In the next graph we have a situation in which the relationship is a negative one. This could be a drawing of the relationship between the annual average temperature of cities (Variable 1) and the average snowfall in each city (Variable 2). So when the average temperature is high, say 70 degrees, the

FIGURE 14.1.   GRAPHIC ILLUSTRATIONS OF CORRELATION.

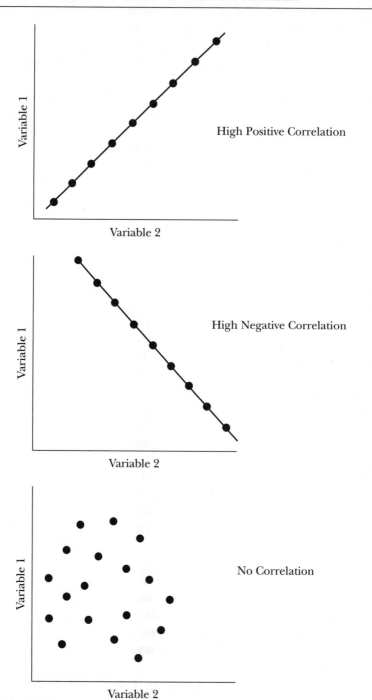

average snowfall will be low, less than 1 inch. Conversely, when the average temperature is low, say 40 degrees, the average snowfall might be 90 inches—with the points between falling on the line (or close to the line). The third correlation is a zero-order one. There is no discernible pattern to the relationship. This might be an example of plotting the variables of height and intelligence, two variables known to be totally uncorrelated.

Correlation coefficients are derived by plugging the corresponding values of the two variables to be correlated into a mathematical formula. The result is a number that expresses the strength and direction (positive or negative) of the correlation. The number will always be between -1.00 and $+1.00$. Correlations of, say, $+.98$ are very high positive correlations; correlations of $-.98$ are very high negative correlations. Correlations in either direction that are close to zero ($-.15$ or $+.09$, for examples) are termed low correlations.

Correlations depend partly on variance in the variables being correlated; that is, correlations are affected by the range of values held by the variables being correlated.

- A variable with a small range of values will tend to be only lowly correlated with any other variable. For example, if we were to correlate average monthly rainfall and temperature in a city that is basically the same temperature all year round, we would find the correlation is very low, even if a wide range of rainfall values is reported. This is logically (and mathematically) so because if rainfall varies while temperatures remain the same, there cannot be much of a relationship between them.
- Correlations between two variables, both of which have a small range of values, are also low for the same reason. This characteristic of correlations is important for understanding why some of the statistics that work with norm-referenced tests don't work well with criterion-referenced tests.
- Data sets where all values are alike, that is, have no variance, are not variables at all. Think about this example. You would not try to correlate any human variable like IQ or height or even gender with how many hearts a human has. We know intuitively that since everyone has only one heart, number of

hearts is not going to predict—be correlated with—any other human factor. Well, correlation has the same reaction to two data sets where one is composed of identical values; it automatically detects that there is no discernible relationship. This feature of correlation is why statisticians always advise those who gather data to be sure that the entire range of possible values of the correlated variables is present in the two data sets; at a minimum, there must be some variation in each.

Remember that NRTs "spread the scores of test-takers out" from one another, whereas CRTs are less likely to do so. Hence different correlation coefficients—different reliability and validity indices—are appropriate for the two kinds of tests.

TYPES OF RELIABILITY

It is frequently stated that test reliability refers to the consistency of test scores. In fact, there are several different kinds of reliability— several different ways in which test scores can be consistent. Some are more relevant to criterion-referenced tests in particular than are others. Each of these reliabilities is calculated differently, but most reliability coefficients are correlation coefficients of some type.

There are at least five different kinds of reliability that you might encounter in your work with tests in addition to inter-rater reliability discussed in Chapter 15. (There is a sixth—domain score estimation indices, but you are not likely to see these in corporate testing circles.) The five reliabilities we will discuss here are divided into two groups. The first group is a set of techniques that could be applied to a test using a single test administration; the second group requires two administrations of the test. These five techniques are:

Single-Test Administration Techniques

- Internal consistency
- Squared-error loss
- Threshold-loss

Two-Test Administration Techniques

- Equivalence reliability
- Test-retest reliability

SINGLE-TEST-ADMINISTRATION RELIABILITY TECHNIQUES

The reliability of criterion-referenced tests has historically been reported as a comparison of test-taker performance on two administrations of the CRT. However, as Taylor and Lee (1995, p. 90) observed, "It is not uncommon for test administrators to balk at the economic and political problems associated with providing two administrations of a test." Their survey of the complicated and abstruse literature on the topic led them to the same conclusion we have reached on single test estimates of reliability for CRTs, "the 'best' method is somewhat a matter of opinion and compromise—it involves a tradeoff among assumptions, computational practicality, and the ease with which it can be understood and trusted by users." Coscarelli and Shrock (2002) reviewed the state of the art of single test administration techniques for CRTs and recommended two approaches that would complement the time-honored and traditional approach to reliability estimates of internal consistency that are used for NRTs.

INTERNAL CONSISTENCY

This measure of reliability determines the extent to which a test measures one underlying ability or competency, that is, the extent to which the test is internally consistent in what it assesses. Tests with high internal consistency are composed of items that result in the same patterns of responses among test-takers. The most common NRT coefficients of internal consistency are the Kuder-Richardson 20 (K-R 20), Kuder-Richardson 21 (K-R 21), and Cronbach's *alpha* indices. These indices are very likely to appear on any computer-generated item analysis output (of the kind discussed in Chapter 11) or the output of any computer statistical package that calculates test evaluation data. Most of these item analysis and evaluation packages were designed for the evaluation of norm-referenced tests.

There are decided problems in using internal consistency coefficients with the test score results of criterion-referenced tests. These problems arise from two sources:

- Lack of spread (variance) in scores on CRTs
- The inclusion of items that measure unrelated objectives on CRTs

Unlike the results of norm-referenced tests (NRTs) that are designed to separate test-takers from one another, very often there is not much of a range in the test scores resulting from the administration of a CRT. The technical term for this situation is a *lack of variance* in the test scores. (As was pointed out in Chapter 2, it is this lack of variance that gives frequency distributions of CRT test results their typical tall, narrow shape, in contrast with the bell-shaped distribution resulting from NRTs.) This situation arises because CRTs are designed to measure specific competencies, and these competencies have usually been taught to the test-takers in anticipation of the test. Therefore, many of the test-takers will do well on the test, causing the range of scores to be small. Correlations between variables that lack a range of values—that lack variance—will tend to be low. Therefore, internal consistency measures of reliability when applied to a CRT will tend to make the test look unreliable.

Another reason why internal consistency measures of reliability are inappropriate for some CRTs is that these tests are usually not designed to measure a single, underlying ability anyway, especially in a corporate context. CRTs are composed of items that measure specific objectives; these objectives may or may not be related to one another. If they are unrelated, the items that measure them will not result in similar patterns of responses among test-takers. Since it is the relatedness of the items that internal consistency indices measure, it is questionable whether there is much meaning in them for CRTs. The squared-error loss and threshold-loss techniques evolved as a way to adjust for the lack of an underlying single construct (Feldt & Brennan, 1989).

You might ask why we have discussed these indices of internal consistency since their application to CRTs is problematic. We do so because a little knowledge is a dangerous thing. It is not unusual for someone in a corporate training department to have access to item analysis programs that routinely calculate and output these indices. Sometimes these indices are simply labeled "reliability coefficient." It is important for test developers to know that low internal consistency figures do not necessarily mean that their CRT is unreliable. These figures are best interpreted with caution from a position of knowledge regarding what they mean.

Squared-Error Loss

Squared-error-loss coefficients use the squared distance between a person's score and the cut-off score to establish a CRT's reliability. Livingston's Coefficient kappa (κ^2) first published in 1972 viewed CRT reliability as a generalization of traditional NRT reliability. It has the advantage of drawing on common internal consistency measures and statistics that are then mathematically adjusted for CRTs. Livingston offers two algebraically equivalent procedures for calculating his coefficient: one based on the integration of a norm-referenced index, the other based on common test statistics.

Threshold-Loss

The underlying concept to decision-consistency approaches is quite straightforward: Were test-takers classified the same way on each test administration? For example, was a test-taker who was classified as a master on the first test also classified as a master on the second test? For some, such as Hambleton and Novick (1973), the decision-consistency approaches are seen as superior to other approaches because they put the test to the test, so to speak. They argue that approaches such as κ^2 that emphasize deviations around the cut-off score are not as meaningful as deviations in classification, since proper classification is the goal of the test. Drawing on Swaminathan, Hambleton, and Algina (1974) and Cronbach, Schonemann, and McKie (1965), we proposed a new index, S_c that uses phi in conjunction with a split-half technique.

S_c simulates a test-retest situation by stratifying the test items by objectives and then measuring decision consistency (Coscarelli & Shrock, 2002). This stratification divides the test into two units and seeks to create similar underlying constructs for each test through the division of the test by instructional objectives.

Calculating Reliability for Single-Test Administration Techniques

Livingston's Coefficient kappa (κ^2)

Livingston's kappa relies on traditional NRT statistics that are readily available in most computer software and statistical packages.

$$\kappa^2 = \frac{\text{(the NRT reliability estimate) (observed variance)} + \text{(test mean} - \text{cut-off score)}^2}{\text{test variance} + \text{(test mean} - \text{cut-off score)}^2}$$

or, when using common test statistics,

$$\kappa^2 = \frac{\text{(observed variance)} + \text{(test mean} - \text{cut-off score)}^2}{\text{observed variance} + \text{(test mean} - \text{cut-off score)}^2 + \text{test error variance}}$$

In either instance, if all test-takers get perfect scores, there is no variance and the equations reduce

> to the fraction 0/0; the reliability of the test in this special situation is undefined. ... However, if all students attain the same score and this score is *not* equal to the criterion score, the equation reduces ... to 1.0. In this case, the test has reliability in the criterion-referenced sense. That is, it will give reliable information about these students' scores in relation to the criterion score, even though its norm-referenced reliability is undefined. (Livingston, 1972, p. 19)

The Index S_c

The phi coefficient (ϕ) is used when both variables being correlated are dichotomous (such as master/non-master) and is the basis of this technique. The process for calculating S_c (Coscarelli & Shrock, 2002) consists of three steps:

1. Divide the test into two equal or near equal "subtests" by dividing the items for each objective between the two. (**Note:** Unless the test has exactly an even number of items for each

objective, there will inevitably be an imbalance of one item in an objective category. When this happens, simply distribute the item into the next objective grouping. The next time the balance is off, keep the item in the group. This process will provide a test that is nearly evenly split.)
2. Designate the two subtests Test 1 and Test 2.
3. Calculate phi (ϕ) using the master/non-master classifications from each of the two subtests; the cut-off score for each subtest is determined by summing the Angoff weights assigned to the individual items on the respective subtests.

$$\phi = \frac{(AD) - (BC)}{\sqrt{(A + B)(C + D)(A + C)(B + D)}}$$

Where
A = the number of test-takers who were masters on both tests
B = the number of test-takers who were non-masters on Test 1 but masters on Test 2
C = the number of test-takers who were masters on Test 1 but non-masters on Test 2
D = the number of test-takers who were classified as non-masters on both test administrations

(**Note:** Phi can be calculated using other formulas. This interpretation relies on simple calculations whose variables are easily matched to the four possible test comparisons.)

OUTCOMES OF USING THE SINGLE-TEST-ADMINISTRATION RELIABILITY TECHNIQUES

In 2002 Coscarelli and Shrock analyzed a forty-four-item CRT using these three statistical techniques on the same test. The alpha, designed to measure internal consistency of NRTs, was .68. Using Livingston's kappa, the reliability estimate was .82. S_c resulted in an estimate of .41. Table 14.1 shows the outcomes.

The data are interesting in a couple of ways. If you were to use a standard software package, your estimate of reliability would be "acceptable" for most instances. But the kappa shows that

TABLE 14.1. COMPARISON OF THREE SINGLE-TEST
ADMINISTRATION RELIABILITY ESTIMATES.

Reliability Estimate		
Alpha	κ^2	S_c
0.68	0.82	0.41

alpha under represents consistency around the cut-off score and offers an estimate of .82, which is a more than "acceptable" reliability coefficient for most settings and purposes. S_c proves to be the most conservative probably because it attempts to partial out performance on each of the sub-scales. The distinctions here are reminiscent of the multiple-range tests used in analysis of variance models to identify statistically significant differences, some being more liberal than others and thus increasing or reducing the probability of error in making a decision. This same thinking seems to apply when choosing among these techniques, as we will discuss at the end of this chapter.

TWO-TEST-ADMINISTRATION RELIABILITY TECHNIQUES

The alternatives to internal consistency measures of reliability are what are termed equivalence and test-retest reliability measures. These measures indicate consistency of the test scores across forms or over time, respectively. Their calculation requires two test administrations, either of parallel forms of the same test in the case of equivalence reliability, or of the identical test with a time lapse between administrations in the case of test-retest reliability. (Parallel forms are constructed by carefully matching items on the two forms for objective assessed, difficulty level, and other response characteristics discussed in Chapters 11 and 12.)

EQUIVALENCE RELIABILITY

Equivalence reliability is calculated by correlating the scores from the first test administration (for example, Form A) with those from the second (Form B). Tests with high equivalence reliability will result in test-takers achieving nearly the same scores on both test administrations. Therefore, the resulting reliability coefficient will be a high positive correlation. Professionally developed, standardized, norm-referenced tests will have reliabilities above +.95. The correlation of scores from two forms of a criterion-referenced test will usually be considerably lower because of the lack of variance problem mentioned above. Remember that correlations between variables with a small range—in this case the two sets of test scores—will always tend to be low. Therefore, designers of CRTs should be cautious about drawing reliability conclusions based on a simple correlation of scores from two administrations of the test.

TEST-RETEST RELIABILITY

In the case of test-retest reliability, it is desirable that the two administrations be fairly close together in time—between two and five days apart. If too much time elapses, test-takers are likely to have acquired additional relevant information, forgotten information, or otherwise changed in ways that will cause their scores on the second administration to be different. It is important that test-takers receive no additional instruction pertinent to the objectives the test measures during the time between the two administrations.

Reliability for CRTs can be thought of as the consistency over forms or time of the master/non-master decisions that are made based on the test, rather than the consistency of the scores themselves. Here again, two test administrations are required, and all the precautions regarding matching items and elapsed time described above apply. With this modification, tests with high test reliability are tests that result in test-takers being classified consistently as masters or non-masters on both forms of the test (equivalence reliability) or on two consecutive test administrations (test-retest reliability).

Table 14.2 illustrates the results of two administrations of a criterion-referenced test—a test-retest reliability procedure. Notice that the resulting classifications are fairly consistent, but that two

TABLE 14.2.   EXAMPLE OF TEST-RETEST DATA FOR A CRT.

1st Test Administration		2nd Test Administration	
Test-Taker	Status	Test-Taker	Status
1. Diana	Master	1. Diana	Master
2. Sid	Master	2. Sid	Master
3. Tishika	Master	3. Tishika	Master
4. Mary	Master	4. Mary	Master
5. George	Master	5. George	Non-master
6. Kenneth	Non-master	6. Kenneth	Non-master
7. Jaime	Non-master	7. Jaime	Non-master
8. Walter	Non-master	8. Walter	Non-master
9. Polly	Non-master	9. Polly	Non-master
10. B.G.	Non-master	10. B.G.	Master

of the ten test-takers (numbers 5 and 10) were misclassified on one of the administrations.

CALCULATING RELIABILITY FOR TWO-TEST ADMINISTRATION TECHNIQUES

The different forms of reliability described above all have distinct procedures for calculating a reliability coefficient associated with them. We have recommended above that you view the reliability of a CRT as the consistency in master/non-master classifications. We follow with a section demonstrating three different ways to calculate reliability coefficients that meet three conditions: (a) applicability to criterion-referenced tests; (b) relative ease of computation; and (c) relative ease of interpretation.

We will now present three different ways of calculating reliability coefficients based on the two-test administration strategy. These three methods are:

- The Phi Coefficient (ϕ)
- The Agreement Coefficient (p_o)
- The Kappa Coefficient (κ)

THE PHI COEFFICIENT

Description of Phi. Phi is a correlation coefficient (ϕ) that indicates the relationship between two dichotomous variables. Dichotomous variables are simply variables that have only two values, such as male/female, plant/animal, pass/fail, etc. As you can see by examining Table 14.2 above, CRT results constitute such a variable because the status decisions resulting from the test are dichotomous—master/non-master. Therefore, one measure of test-retest reliability for CRTs is the phi correlation coefficient calculated on the master/non-master decisions from two consecutive administrations of the test.

Like all correlation coefficients, phi can have values from -1.00 to $+1.00$. A phi coefficient of $+1.00$ would indicate that the master/non-master classifications were perfectly consistent between the two test administrations, a highly desirable result. A phi coefficient of -1.00 would indicate that everyone who was a master on the first administration was a non-master on the second and visa versa! This, of course, is a very undesirable and unlikely outcome. A phi coefficient near 0 indicates no relationship between the scores on the two administrations. This is also an undesirable outcome, but not unlikely if the test is unreliable. Note that an unreliable test has a phi coefficient near 0, not a high negative correlation near -1.00. A correlation near -1.00 indicates a very strong relationship between two variables; the relationship just happens to be in the opposite direction. Lack of reliability means no or weak relationships between the two sets of test scores.

Remember that correlation coefficients are low when one or both of the correlated variables have a small range of values; if all of your sample test-takers are either masters or non-masters on either test administration, your phi reliability coefficient will be 0.

Calculating Phi. Now let's look at how phi is calculated. The illustration below is for a test-retest reliability calculation. The equivalence reliability calculation is identical except that the matrix labels are "Form A" and "Form B" instead of "1st Test Administration" and "2nd Test Administration." The arithmetic is extremely simple, even if you have only an inexpensive calculator. One

FIGURE 14.2. PHI TABLE FOR TEST-RETEST RELIABILITY.

		1st Test Administration		
		Non-Master	Master	
2nd Test Administration	Master	B =	A =	A + B =
	Non-Master	D =	C =	C + D =
		B + D =	A + C =	

begins by putting the results of the test administrations into a table—a two by two matrix as in Figure 14.2 above.

In Figure 14.2, cell B should contain the number of test-takers who were non-masters on the first administration but masters on the second. Cell A should contain the number who were masters on both test administrations. Cell D should contain the number who were classified as non-masters on both test administrations, while cell C should contain the number of test-takers who were masters on the first administration but non-masters on the second. Check your accuracy; adding the numbers in all four cells should equal the total number of test-takers in your sample. Note: Your test results must be placed in the table in exactly this way; reversing the positions of the letters in the matrix can result in your phi coefficient appearing to be in the opposite direction from what it actually is.

Once these totals have been placed carefully in these cells, add the numbers in the cells horizontally and vertically as indicated in Figure 14.2. The numbers in the four cells (B, A, D, and C) and the four cell totals (A+B, C+D, B+D, and A+C) must then be placed in the following formula which is the equation for calculating phi.

$$\phi = \frac{(AD) - (BC)}{\sqrt{(A + B)(C + D)(A + C)(B + D)}}$$

Figure 14.3 shows an example of a phi calculation using the data from Table 14.2 presented earlier. First the appropriate totals are placed into the matrix.

Then the numbers are moved into the formula. The product of B times C is subtracted from the product of A times D for the

FIGURE 14.3. EXAMPLE PHI TABLE FOR TEST-RETEST RELIABILITY.

		1st Test Administration		
		Non-Master	Master	
2nd Test Administration	Master	B = 1	A = 4	A + B = 5
	Non-Master	D = 4	C = 1	C + D = 5
		B + D = 5	A + C = 5	

numerator. The denominator is simply the square root of A + B multiplied by C + D multiplied by A + C multiplied by B + D, as illustrated below.

$$\phi = \frac{[(4)(4)] - [(1)(1)]}{\sqrt{(5)(5)(5)(5)}}$$

$$= \frac{16 - 1}{\sqrt{625}}$$

$$= \frac{15}{25}$$

$$\phi = .60$$

As you can see, the resulting phi coefficient is .60. This indicates that there is a positive correlation between the two sets of test classifications of +.60.

How High Should Phi Be? It seems appropriate to consider at this point how high a phi coefficient should be in order to indicate acceptable reliability for a criterion-referenced test. Unfortunately, there is no single, simple answer to this question, as we learned in Chapter 7 during our discussion of the numbers of test items that should be included on a test. When we ask how high phi should be, we are asking, "How reliable does my test have to be?" Remember that perfect consistency would result in a phi coefficient of +1.00. The answer to this question depends entirely on what the consequences of testing error are. (See Chapter 7.) A test that assesses highly critical competencies that determine health and safety of clients or employees or that are essential to organizational survival should have phi reliability estimates above +.85 (Subkoviak, 1988, p. 52). Tests of important competencies should have coefficients above +.70. Under no circumstances should tests with coefficients below +.50 be considered reliable tests.

PRACTICE

Table 14.3 shows example test data from two administrations of a criterion-referenced test. Practice using the formula presented above to calculate phi. A blank matrix (Figure 14.4) is provided to assist you.

TABLE 14.3.   SAMPLE TEST-RETEST DATA.

1st Test Administration		2nd Test Administration	
Test-Taker #	*Status*	*Test-Taker #*	*Status*
1	Master	1	Non-master
2	Master	2	Master
3	Master	3	Non-master
4	Master	4	Non-master
5	Master	5	Master
6	Master	6	Master
7	Non-master	7	Non-master
8	Non-master	8	Non-master
9	Non-master	9	Non-master
10	Non-master	10	Master
11	Non-master	11	Master
12	Master	12	Master

FIGURE 14.4.   BLANK TABLE FOR PRACTICE PHI CALCULATION.

		1st Test Administration		
		Non-Master	Master	
2nd Test Administration	Master	B =	A =	A + B =
	Non-Master	D =	C =	C + D =
		B + D =	A + C =	

FEEDBACK

Your correctly completed matrix should look like the one below in Figure 14.5.

FIGURE 14.5. ANSWER FOR PRACTICE PHI CALCULATION, TEST-RETEST RELIABILITY.

		1st Test Administration		
		Non-Master	Master	
2nd Test Administration	Master	B = 2	A = 4	A + B = 6
	Non-Master	D = 3	C = 3	C + D = 6
		B + D = 5	A + C = 7	

Placing the numbers in the formula, you should have written:

$$\phi = \frac{[(4)(3)] - [(2)(3)]}{\sqrt{(6)(6)(7)(5)}}$$

$$= \frac{12 - 6}{\sqrt{1260}}$$

$$= \frac{6}{35.5}$$

$$\phi = .169 \quad \text{or} \quad .17$$

The resulting phi coefficient is $+.169$ or $+.17$. This outcome indicates a very unreliable test.

THE AGREEMENT COEFFICIENT

Description of the Agreement Coefficient. Not all test reliability coefficients are correlation coefficients. One of the easiest reliability coefficients to understand is the agreement coefficient; the symbol for this statistic is p_o. Simply put, the agreement coefficient is the number of test-takers consistently classified on the two test administrations divided by the total number of test-takers. As such, the agreement coefficient is simply a percentage of consistent classifications achieved by the test.

Before we discuss the calculation of the agreement coefficient, it should be noted that it can result in deceptively high indices of reliability. A proportion of the consistent matches in the two test administrations would occur due to chance alone; these chance matches are included in the agreement coefficient. Remember that unlike phi, p_o is **not** a correlation coefficient and does not have the same range of values. A test that appears to have a decent agreement coefficient may have a very low phi coefficient. We will make such a comparison after we calculate p_o.

Calculating the Agreement Coefficient. The formula for calculating the agreement coefficient is:

$$p_o = \frac{(a + d)}{N}$$

where a is the number of test-takers classified as masters on both administrations; d is the number of test-takers classified as non-masters on both administrations; and N is the total number of test-takers.

Below is a calculation of the agreement coefficient for the test-retest data from Table 14.2 presented earlier.

$$p_o = \frac{(4 + 4)}{10}$$

$$= \frac{8}{10}$$

$$p_o = .80$$

PRACTICE

Use the p_o formula and the test-retest data from the practice phi calculation (Table 14.3) presented above to practice calculating the agreement coefficient.

FEEDBACK

The correct calculation of p_o for the test-retest data in Table 14.3 is as follows:

$$p_o = \frac{(4 + 3)}{12}$$

$$= \frac{7}{12}$$

$$p_o = .583 \quad \text{or} \quad .58$$

How High Should the Agreement Coefficient Be? Notice the sizable differences between the phi coefficients for the example data sets (the data in Tables 14.2 and 14.3) and their corresponding agreement coefficients. The phi coefficient for the first data set (Table 14.2) was .60 while the agreement coefficient was .80. The phi coefficient for the second data set (Table 14.3) was .17; the corresponding agreement coefficient is .58. It is essential for test developers who use these indices to realize that it would be inappropriate to compare the phi coefficient for one test with the agreement coefficient for another as if they were examining the two tests on a single reliability measure. The two statistics are quite different indices of reliability.

Of the two, we recommend phi because the agreement coefficient is inflated by matches in master/non-master status due simply to chance agreement alone. In other words, even a totally unreliable test will have a deceptively large number of matches due merely to chance. Therefore, the agreement coefficient can instill false confidence in the reliability of a test. The next coefficient presented, the Kappa Coefficient was designed to overcome this weakness in the agreement coefficient. Because agreement coefficients tend to be inflated, it is recommended that, for important master/non-master classification decisions, a test should achieve a p_0 reliability coefficient above .85. For critical assessments, an agreement coefficient above .95 should be sought. It is sobering to remember that even with an agreement coefficient of .95, five test-takers out of a hundred are being inconsistently classified—conceivably non-masters being certified as masters.

THE KAPPA COEFFICIENT

Description of Kappa. The kappa coefficient (κ) is a refinement of the agreement coefficient in that it represents the test's improvement in master/non-master classification accuracy beyond the level of chance classification matches (Cohen, 1960). The coefficient literally represents the proportion of possible improvement in classification accuracy achieved by the test.

The first task in figuring the kappa coefficient is to determine the agreement coefficient as already described. Subtracted from this agreement coefficient is the level of agreement expected due to chance. The result of this subtraction is then divided by 1 minus the agreement expected due to chance, which is the maximum possible improvement in accuracy that the test could make. Therefore, κ is a simple proportion; it is the actual improvement in classification consistency attributed to the test divided by the possible improvement in classification consistency.

Calculating the Kappa Coefficient. The formula for calculating the kappa coefficient is as follows:

$$\kappa = \frac{p_o - p_{chance}}{1 - p_{chance}}$$

The formula for p_o is as presented earlier:

$$p_o = \frac{(a + d)}{N}$$

The formula for p_{chance} is:

$$p_{chance} = \frac{[(a + b)(a + c)] + [(c + d)(b + d)]}{N^2}$$

Remember that N equals the total number of test-takers. The following matrix (Figure 14.6)—similar to the one used to assist in the phi calculation—will demonstrate how to determine quickly and accurately the values for a, b, c, and d for calculating p_o and p_{chance}. (**Note:** This table is similar to the phi matrix, but the positions of the test administrations have been reversed and the master/ non-master categories are located differently. Be careful to set up these matrices correctly for each of the two different reliability coefficients.)

FIGURE 14.6. MATRIX FOR DETERMINING P_0 AND P_{CHANCE}.

		2nd Test Administration		
		Master	Non-Master	
1st Test Administration	Master	a =	b =	(a + b) =
	Non-Master	c =	d =	(c + d) =
		(a + c) =	(b + d) =	

Using the test-retest data originally presented in Table 14.2, an example of a kappa coefficient calculation follows. We begin by filling in the p_o and p_{chance} values table, as illustrated in Figure 14.7.

FIGURE 14.7.   EXAMPLE MATRIX FOR DETERMINING P_0 AND P_{CHANCE}.

		2nd Test Administration		
		Master	Non-Master	
1st Test Administration	Master	a = 4	b = 1	(a + b) = 5
	Non-Master	c = 1	d = 4	(c + d) = 5
		(a + c) = 5	(b + d) = 5	

Next we figure p_o.

$$p_o = \frac{(4 + 4)}{10}$$

$$= \frac{8}{10}$$

$$p_o = .80$$

The calculation of Po follows directly

$$p_{chance} = \frac{[(4 + 1)(4 + 1)] + [(1 + 4)(1 + 4)]}{10^2}$$

$$= \frac{[(5)(5)] + [(5)(5)]}{100}$$

$$= \frac{(25 + 25)}{100}$$

$$p_{chance} = .50$$

Now that we have the values for p_o and p_{chance}, it is a simple matter to calculate the kappa coefficient.

$$\kappa = \frac{.80 - .50}{1 - .50}$$

$$= \frac{.30}{.50}$$

$$\kappa = .60$$

How High Should the Kappa Coefficient Be? It is important to remember that the coefficient of agreement and the kappa coefficient are two very different indices of reliability with distinct interpretations. The agreement coefficient is an indication of overall consistency in the test's classifications, whereas the kappa coefficient indicates the improvement in consistency over chance matches resulting from using the test. Therefore, one might expect that kappa values would be lower than coefficient of agreement values; however, when the test is perfectly reliable, both the agreement coefficient and the kappa coefficient will be equal to 1.00. (Kappa values and phi values tend to be similar, although kappa is not a correlation coefficient and so their interpretations are also distinct.)

Interpretations of how high a kappa coefficient should be differ among authorities. However, we tend to err on the side of higher standards than lower. Furthermore, we assume that the time and effort to establish test-retest or equivalence reliability will not be expended unless the objectives assessed by the test are important to the organization. Therefore, we recommend that a kappa coefficient be above .75 and higher as the objectives become more critical.

PRACTICE

Using the test-retest data from Table 14.3 and the formulas for calculating the kappa coefficient above, practice calculating kappa for these data. A blank p_o and p_{chance} values matrix is provided to assist you (see Figure 14.8).

FIGURE 14.8.   BLANK MATRIX FOR DETERMINING P_0 AND P_{CHANCE}.

		2nd Test Administration		
		Master	Non-Master	
1st Test Administration	Master	a =	b =	(a + b) =
	Non-Master	c =	d =	(c + d) =
		(a + c) =	(b + d) =	

FEEDBACK

Your correctly completed p_o and p_{chance} values matrix should look like Figure 14.9 below.

FIGURE 14.9.   COMPLETED PRACTICE MATRIX FOR DETERMINING P_O AND P_{CHANCE}.

		2nd Test Administration		
		Master	Non-Master	
1st Test Administration	Master	a = 4	b = 3	(a + b) = 7
	Non-master	c = 2	d = 3	(c + d) = 5
		(a + c) = 6	(b + d) = 6	

Your calculation of p_o should have been as follows:

$$p_o = \frac{(4+3)}{12}$$

$$= \frac{7}{12}$$

$$p_o = .58$$

The correct calculation of p_{chance} is:

$$p_{chance} = \frac{[(4+3)(4+2)]+[(2+3)(3+3)]}{12^2}$$

$$= \frac{[(7)(6)]+[(5)(6)]}{144}$$

$$= \frac{(42+30)}{144}$$

$$= \frac{72}{144}$$

$$p_{chance} = .50$$

Having the values for p_o and p_{chance}, the kappa coefficient should have been calculated as follows:

$$\kappa = \frac{.58 - .50}{1 - .50}$$

$$= \frac{.08}{.50}$$

$$\kappa = .16$$

This outcome indicates an unreliable test (and is consistent with the phi coefficient determination of reliability calculated earlier).

COMPARISON OF ϕ, P_o, AND κ

It is difficult to overstate the importance of understanding that these three reliability coefficients, while they all address test reliability, are different indices requiring separate interpretations. However, if all three indices are calculated on the same test data, the outcomes will, of course, be related. In other words, while a test with borderline reliability might clear the standard of acceptability for one of the indices and not for the others, tests will not look highly reliable on one index and totally unreliable on the next. Of the three, we recommend phi for the following reasons:

- While by far the easiest coefficient for most people to understand, the agreement coefficient, p_o, tends to be inflated by chance matches, as discussed in some detail above. This characteristic makes it a dangerous coefficient in the hands of those who do not realize this weakness and encourages the naive implementation of unreliable tests. (It is a sobering exercise to calculate the agreement coefficient on test results from a test with a phi equal to 0 and a kappa coefficient equal to 0; in other words, on a totally unreliable test, you will find that a deceptively high number of matches appear due solely to chance.)
- While the kappa coefficient corrects this weakness in the agreement coefficient by reflecting only the improved

accuracy attributable to the test, kappa thereby becomes, in our judgment, somewhat difficult to interpret intuitively. It just doesn't seem to make as much "common sense" as a correlation coefficient to most people, perhaps because so many instructional designers, human performance technologists, and human resource professionals have encountered the concept of correlation before.

This recommendation, however, also requires some qualification by noting one of phi's frequently mentioned weaknesses. For reasons the explanation of which are beyond the scope of this book, phi tends to be a conservative estimate of reliability, that is, its values tend to be lower rather than higher under some conditions dictated by the balance of the numbers appearing in the four cells of the phi matrix. However, given our tendency to higher rather than lower standards in testing, conservative measures may have some advantages in actual practice.

It is worth noting again that all of the coefficients discussed can be expected to yield unstable results when calculated on small samples of test-takers. One of the most important pieces of advice we can give you in establishing the reliability (and validity) of your test is to use a sample size of at least thirty if at all possible.

THE LOGISTICS OF ESTABLISHING TEST RELIABILITY

You will need to plan carefully to establish the test reliability of your CRT. Among the factors you must consider are:

- Choosing items for your trial test
- Choosing the type of reliability you wish to determine— internal consistency, test-retest, or equivalence (giving the same test once versus twice versus giving parallel forms of the test)
- The sample of test-takers who will take your test
- Testing conditions during test administrations

Choosing Items. Ideally you will have created a pool of items for each of your objectives in excess of the number you think you will actually need (see Chapter 7.) This is a recommended strategy because inevitably some items will not work when actually pilot tested. Flaws in the items such as ambiguities and cues will be revealed when the items are tested. Such items should be revised or eliminated from the pool. (Chapter 10 describes procedures for piloting your test; Chapter 11 presents information on item analysis statistics and procedures to assist you in identifying poor items.) It is recommended that you have already eliminated bad items from your pool and have selected the best items in appropriate numbers for your test before you attempt to establish its reliability. Otherwise, you may find that you have to conduct the reliability procedures again with a substantially revised test. The test should be assembled using the procedures described in Chapter 10.

Sample Test-Takers. You will need a group of at least thirty people who can take your test. Many organizations have difficulty getting a group of that size to take the test. Our feeling is that any test data is better than nothing, so use the largest group that you can arrange. However, be aware that statisticians recommend larger groups for good reasons. The data from small groups are likely to be misleading. With a small group, the performance of even one person can dramatically change your results. Small groups just do not give you the accurate picture of your test's reliability and your items' performance that a larger group will. Our advice is to make every effort to locate a group of thirty people.

The sample test-takers should be representative of the persons who will take the test under implementation conditions with one additional qualification. Try to ensure that your group includes some masters and some non-masters; you want to see if your test can reliably distinguish between these two groups. Compose the sample of the types of persons between whom you want the test to distinguish after it has been implemented in your organization. Many statisticians would recommend that you draw the sample of test-takers randomly from identified pools of appropriate employees. Most organizations do not have the scheduling flexibility to accommodate this advice. In our opinion it is better to forego the randomness of the sample than to settle for a sample that is too small.

For documentation purposes, you should keep a record of the composition of the test sample (names, titles, or job classifications) and how the sample was chosen. Such information could be important if the reliability of the test is ever challenged.

Testing Conditions. Parallel forms of a test can be administered one after the other unless fatigue is a problem. When determining the test-retest reliability, the two test administrations should be close together, between two and five days. As previously mentioned, it is essential that the sample test-takers not study or receive additional information regarding the content the test covers between the two testings. Conditions at each of the two test administrations should be as identical as possible. The test should be given at the same time of day under the same physical, environmental, and psychological circumstances.

RECOMMENDATIONS FOR CHOOSING A RELIABILITY TECHNIQUE

When all of this is said and done, the test designer needs to make a decision about how to proceed. As we have said on a number of occasions, there is no substitute for professional judgment—and you will have to interpret your needs in light of your own context to decide which technique is best. For most corporate tests, we would recommend you consider these options:

- Use phi to calculate reliability using the two-test administration technique. Phi is easy to calculate and is probably the easiest technique to explain. It would be the most powerful evidence of a test's stability should you find yourself in a high-stakes testing situation.
- To estimate a CRT's reliability using the easiest logistics, use Livingston's kappa, which can be determined from traditional test statistics in a single test administration.
- If you can't use a two-test design, and if the test is being used for a significant decision-making issue, then you may wish to rely more on S_c to demonstrate the consistency of test decisions. The S_c estimate will likely be lower than either Cronbach's alpha or Livingston's kappa, as it reflects the dual effects of removing chance agreement from the estimate as

well as the variation of performance around the cut-off score
(Coscarelli & Shrock, 2002, p. 85).

Summary Comments

It should be apparent that it requires an investment of time and
resources to establish the reliability and validity of a test. One way
to streamline the process is to form the sample test-takers for the
concurrent validation process—the group of known masters and
non-masters—and arrange to have them take the test twice or take
both forms of the test in order to establish the test's reliability.

It should also be noted, however, that it is difficult to overstate the importance of reliability and validity for tests of any kind.
Tests that are not reliable and valid are, by definition, not worth
giving. Many organizations are willing to assume that their tests
are reliable and valid. These organizations are in jeopardy from
two sources:

• Unreliable, invalid tests cannot be expected to be upheld in a
  court of law should the fairness of the tests be challenged.
• Even if the tests are never legally challenged, the costs of
  bad decisions resulting from unreliable, invalid tests can be
  extremely high; not only are such tests useless because they
  do not provide the information regarding competence that
  they are presumed to provide, but they actively encourage the
  organization to misplace people, resources, time, and talent.

CHAPTER FIFTEEN

RELIABILITY OF PERFORMANCE TESTS

RELIABILITY AND VALIDITY OF PERFORMANCE TESTS

The concepts of reliability and validity are as important in performance testing as in cognitive testing. However, the reliability and validity problems associated with performance testing are different from those associated with cognitive tests composed of closed-ended items. In some ways, the reliability and validity problems associated with performance tests are similar to those posed by essays and other types of open-ended questions; unlike closed-ended assessments that are even machine scorable, the test-taker's behavior on an essay test or during a performance test must be rated or judged by an observer. Therefore, the locus of reliability and validity shifts from the test itself to the consistency of the test-taker's performance and the reliability and validity of the judges' observations.

The reason for the creation of rating scales, as described in Chapter 8, is to improve the reliability and validity of these observers' judgments. The more specific the rating instrument, the better it supports reliable and valid observations. However, error in these judgments is always a concern and test designers should be aware of the types of errors that most frequently occur, how to assess the reliability of the judgments, and how to correct unreliable and invalid performance assessments when they are revealed.

The problem of consistency in the test-taker's performance is in many ways analogous to the reliability issue presented in Chapter 7 regarding how many items should be on a cognitive test. The issue is one of adequate sampling of the test-taker's ability.

Curiously enough, validity is usually not a problem with performance tests that have been shown to be reliable. A similar circumstance does not exist with cognitive tests. However, because performance tests deal with observable actions rather than indicators of mental processes, their validity is usually assured once consistency in the observations of raters has been achieved.

This chapter begins with a discussion of the six most common types of error associated with rating scales: Errors of Standards, Halo, Logic, Similarity, Central Tendency, and Leniency. Two different methods of determining the reliability of the raters' judgments are then explained, followed by procedures for training the raters to increase the reliability of their judgments. The chapter closes with a discussion of the role of repeated performance in performance testing.

TYPES OF RATING ERRORS

Error of Standards. In discussing checklists, we noted that the scale must contain descriptions of behaviors or characteristics that accurately reflect the desired performance or product outcome in order to be considered valid. A failure to define the standards in a precise manner on any scale is an error of standards. The major flaw with numerical and descriptive scales is their inability to provide definitions of behaviors specific enough to prevent raters from imposing their own interpretations on the standards, and subsequently rating the same performance or product differently.

Halo Error. The halo error is a tendency on the part of the raters to allow, usually quite subconsciously, a performance judgment to be influenced by the rater's opinion of the performer. However, despite its name, the halo error isn't always a positive one. A halo effect can occur when a person's behavior on a performance test is negatively affected by a rater's opinion. For example, if an instructor was to serve as a rater to assess an end of course performance and the "best" student in the class performed poorly on the performance test, a halo error would occur if the performance was rated higher than it actually merited. Subconsciously, the rater may be thinking, "She *really* knows this stuff; she just had an off day ... no point penalizing her." The opposite sentiment introduces just as much error into the testing process if a particularly difficult student performed well on the test, but was downgraded by the instructor because of a previously formed bias against the test-taker's competence.

Logic Error. A logic error occurs when a rater purports to be rating one characteristic but is really rating another. This type of error happens when the rater is confused about or unaware of the independence of the characteristics of the performance. For example, suppose an airline refueling supervisor assumes that haste is the cause of unsafe fueling practices. In fact, the time used by the technician and the number of safety violations may be unrelated. Under these circumstances, this supervisor will tend to assume incorrectly that technicians who take longer to perform this task are safer; he or she will rate as safer those who spend more time, instead of focusing specifically on safety procedures such as attaching a grounding strap. The confusion of time with safety is a logic error that is correctable by a task analysis that results in the creation of a valid and specific checklist.

Similarity Error. This error is sometimes called the "similar to me" error. There is some evidence that raters will tend to rate performers they perceive as similar to themselves more highly than those who are "different." Such frequently irrelevant characteristics as educational background, job experience, gender, race, and so forth, could thus lead to incorrect assessments of performance in the absence of carefully designed rating instruments and adequate rater training.

Central Tendency Error. There is a distinct pattern of behavior associated with any rating scale that allows a rater to choose points along a continuum, as with descriptive, numerical, or behaviorally anchored scales; raters avoid the extremes of the scale. Raters appear to have a tendency to group ratings in the middle of a scale. This finding is so consistent that for a given scale, the two extreme positions will likely be lost; thus, a 7-point rating scale becomes really only a 5-point scale. Perhaps the thinking is, for example, "Nobody is really perfect. If I rate them as that good, people will wonder about me. ... Better not stick my neck out."

When you are constructing rating scales, give thought to using only an even number of categories, thus removing the exact center point and forcing more spread in the ratings. (Exceptional scales are those where the end points define opposite and equally undesirable characteristics, such as too hot and too cold or too tight and too loose; the meaning of this type of scale requires a center point.) Another strategy is to use a larger number of points on the scale (say, eight rather than five) assuming that raters will tend not to use the extremes.

Leniency Error. Some organizations develop the norm of giving high ratings to their employees. This tendency may develop gradually as raters—usually supervisors or trainers—begin to see the ratings as a reflection of their own success; hence, they bias the ratings toward the favorable end of the scale. Once high ratings are routinely expected, the norm is difficult to counter without some performers feeling that they have been treated unfairly. In such circumstances the problem will have to be addressed across all raters—organization-wide perhaps—in order to change customary practice.

In the end, it is best to use a checklist or a behaviorally anchored scale. Error is reduced primarily by the precise specification of criteria. The precision of behavioral specification is as important in testing as it is in the design of instruction.

INTER-RATER RELIABILITY

It is important to establish the consistency with which raters are judging the performances of test-takers. The mastery/non-mastery decision made about each test-taker should be determined by what the test-taker does, not by differences among the judges either in what they see or in the value they place on what they see. Remember that, since reliability is a prerequisite for validity, if the judges are inconsistent, their decisions cannot possibly be valid. Hence, the importance of determining inter-rater reliability, the reliability among raters.

The two methods we shall demonstrate for assessing inter-rater reliability yield comparable results, but are conceptually different. One is based on a corrected percentage of agreement figure (kappa or κ), while the other is a correlation coefficient (phi or ϕ). Which one you decide to use really depends on which of the two statistics you find the easiest to understand or perhaps which of the two you think other interested parties will find the easiest to understand. Persons who have worked with correlation coefficients in the past will probably find phi conceptually more appealing. Those totally unfamiliar with correlation and the meaning of its range of values will probably prefer to use kappa.

These statistics are the same ones used to determine test reliability in Chapter 14. Their interpretation is explained in detail there. They will be modified in this chapter to be applicable to more than two judges. However, if the agreement coefficient or the kappa coefficient is unfamiliar to you, you should read the sections on Description of the Agreement Coefficient (page 306) and Description of Kappa (page 308) in Chapter 14 before calculating kappa. Likewise, if the concept of correlation or the phi coefficient is unfamiliar to you, you should read the sections on Correlation (pages 290 through 293) and Description of Phi (page 302) in Chapter 14 before calculating phi.

Calculating and Interpreting Kappa (κ)

The kappa coefficient was designed to measure the agreement between two judges; however, averaging procedures allow you to calculate kappa for more than two judges. This is an important point because we strongly recommend that you have more than two judges when trying to establish the reliability of your performance testing procedures. We will begin by showing how to calculate kappa for two judges and then extend the procedure to three. You will see how you can use the same process to extend the procedure to any number of judges.

The formula for calculating kappa is:

$$\kappa = \frac{p_o - p_{chance}}{1 - p_{chance}}$$

Let's begin by explaining what this formula means. The calculation of kappa begins by figuring the percentage of test-takers consistently classified by two judges. This number is called the agreement coefficient (p_o). This number is inflated by chance agreements. In other words, this number will give you a false sense of security in the reliability of your judges. So this percentage of observed agreement (p_o) is corrected for these chance agreements by subtracting the number of agreements that would be expected due to chance alone (p_{chance}). The result of subtraction in the numerator is then divided by $1 - p_{chance}$. The result of subtraction in the denominator represents the maximum possible improvement over chance agreement that the two judges could possibly make. So the result of the division represents the proportion of possible improvement in agreement beyond chance agreement actually achieved by the two judges. In the same way, kappa is calculated for each pair of judges that you have. The resulting kappa coefficients are then averaged to determine the kappa coefficient for your entire panel of judges.

Table 15.1 presents some possible results of a performance test where three judges rated each of ten test-takers.

TABLE 15.1.   EXAMPLE PERFORMANCE TEST DATA, INTER-RATER RELIABILITY.

Test-Taker	Judges		
	1	2	3
1	Master	Master	Master
2	Master	Master	Master
3	Master	Master	Non-master
4	Master	Non-master	Non-master
5	Non-master	Non-master	Master
6	Non-master	Non-master	Non-master
7	Non-master	Non-master	Non-master
8	Non-master	Non-master	Non-master
9	Non-master	Non-master	Non-master
10	Non-master	Non-master	Non-master

The easiest way to do a kappa calculation is to begin with a matrix for each pair of judges to organize your test results. This matrix will provide you with the numbers you need to calculate p_o and p_{chance} and, therefore, to calculate kappa for each given pair of judges. If you have three judges, you will need three matrices, one for each possible pairing of the judges. Therefore, if you have three judges, you will need a matrix for the Judge 1/Judge 2 pair, a matrix for the Judge 1/Judge 3 pair, and a matrix for the Judge 2/Judge 3 pair. (If you had four judges, you would need six matrices, one for Judges 1 and 2, Judges 1 and 3, Judges 1 and 4, Judges 2 and 3, Judges 2 and 4, and Judges 3 and 4.) Figure 15.1 illustrates such a matrix for Judge 1 and Judge 2 in Table 15.1 above.

The cells of the matrix are defined as: **a** equals the number of test-takers classified as masters by both Judge 1 and Judge 2; **b** equals the number classified as non-masters by Judge 1 but as masters by Judge 2; **c** equals the number judged as masters by Judge 1, but classified as non-masters by Judge 2; and **d** equals the number judged as non-masters by both judges. The numbers from the data in Table 15.1 for all three judges have been correctly placed in the three matrices below. Figure 15.2 shows the data for Judge 1 and

FIGURE 15.1.   MATRIX FOR DETERMINING P_O AND P_{CHANCE}.

		Judge 1		
		Master	Non-Master	
Judge 2	Master	a =	b =	(a + b) =
	Non-Master	c =	d =	(c + d) =
		(a + c) =	(b + d) =	

FIGURE 15.2.   EXAMPLE P_O AND P_{CHANCE} MATRIX, JUDGES 1 & 2.

		Judge 1		
		Master	Non-Master	
Judge 2	Master	a = 3	b = 0	(a + b) = 3
	Non-Master	c = 1	d = 6	(c + d) = 7
		(a + c) = 4	(b + d) = 6	

Judge 2; Figure 15.3 shows the data for Judge 1 and Judge 3, while Figure 15.4 contains the data for Judge 2 and Judge 3.

FIGURE 15.3.   EXAMPLE P_0 AND P_{CHANCE} MATRIX, JUDGES 1 & 3.

		Judge 1		
		Master	Non-Master	
Judge 3	Master	a = 2	b = 1	(a + b) = 3
	Non-Master	c = 2	d = 5	(c + d) = 7
		(a + c) = 4	(b + d) = 6	

FIGURE 15.4.   EXAMPLE P_0 AND P_{CHANCE} MATRIX, JUDGES 2 & 3.

		Judge 2		
		Master	Non-Master	
Judge 3	Master	a = 2	b = 1	(a + b) = 3
	Non-Master	c = 1	d = 6	(c + d) = 7
		(a + c) = 3	(b + d) = 7	

After the data have been organized into the appropriate matrices, we can begin to calculate p_o and p_{chance} and then kappa for each pair of judges.

The formula for calculating p_o is:

$$p_o = \frac{(a + d)}{N}$$

where **a** and **d** are obtained from the matrix and **N** equals the total number of test-takers. Substituting the data for Judge 1 and Judge 2 from the matrix, Figure 15.2, we calculate p_o as follows:

$$p_o = \frac{(3 + 6)}{10}$$

$$= \frac{9}{10}$$

p_o = .90 for the pair Judge 1/Judge 2

The formula for calculating p_{chance} is:

$$p_{chance} = \frac{\left[(a+b)(a+c)\right] + \left[(c+d)(b+d)\right]}{N^2}$$

where **a, b, c,** and **d** are obtained from the matrix and N_2 is the number of test-takers squared. Once again substituting the data from Figure 15.2, we calculate p_{chance} for Judge 1 and Judge 2 as follows:

$$p_{chance} = \frac{\left[(3+0)(3+1)\right] + \left[(1+6)(0+6)\right]}{10^2}$$

$$= \frac{\left[(3)(4)\right] + \left[(7)(6)\right]}{100}$$

$$= \frac{(12+42)}{100}$$

$$= \frac{54}{100}$$

$p_{chance} = .54$ for the pair Judge 1/Judge 2

As indicated earlier, the formula for calculating kappa is:

$$\kappa = \frac{p_o - p_{chance}}{1 - p_{chance}}$$

Therefore, substituting the values for p_o and p_{chance} for the Judge 1/Judge 2 pair determined above, we calculate kappa for this pair as follows:

$$\kappa = \frac{.90 - .54}{1 - .54}$$

$$= \frac{.36}{.46}$$

$\kappa = .7826$ or .78 for the pair Judge 1/Judge 2

The data for calculating p_o and p_{chance} for the pair Judge 1/Judge 3 are obtained from the matrix in Figure 15.3. These calculations are illustrated below.

$$p_o = \frac{(2+5)}{10}$$

$$= \frac{7}{10}$$

$p_o = .70$ for the pair Judge 1/Judge 3

$$p_{chance} = \frac{\left[(2+1)(2+2)\right] + \left[(2+5)(1+5)\right]}{10^2}$$

$$= \frac{\left[(3)(4)\right] + \left[(7)(6)\right]}{100}$$

$$= \frac{(12+42)}{100}$$

$$= \frac{54}{100}$$

p_{chance} = .54 for the pair Judge 1/Judge 3

Having the p_o and p_{chance} values for this pair allows us to calculate kappa for Judge 1 and Judge 3 as follows:

$$\kappa = \frac{.70 - .54}{1 - .54}$$

$$= \frac{.16}{.46}$$

κ = .34782 or .35 for the pair Judge 1/Judge 3

The corresponding calculations for Judge 2 and Judge 3 are as follows:

$$p_o = \frac{(2+6)}{10}$$

$$= \frac{8}{10}$$

p_o = .80 for the pair Judge 2/Judge 3

$$p_{chance} = \frac{\left[(2+1)(2+1)\right] + \left[(1+6)(1+6)\right]}{10^2}$$

$$= \frac{\left[(3)(3)\right] + \left[(7)(7)\right]}{100}$$

$$= \frac{(9+49)}{100}$$

$$= \frac{58}{100}$$

p_{chance} = .58 for the pair Judge 2/Judge 3

$$\kappa = \frac{.80 - .58}{1 - .58}$$

$$= \frac{.22}{.42}$$

$\kappa = .5238$ or $.52$ for the pair Judge 2/Judge 3

Now we have three kappa coefficients, one for each pair of judges. In order to obtain the overall kappa coefficient, the symbol for which is $\overline{\kappa_2}$ (Conger, 1980), we must average the three pairwise kappas. This calculation is shown below.

kappa for Judge 1/Judge 2 = .78
kappa for Judge 1/Judge 3 = .35
kappa for Judge 2/Judge 3 = .52
Therefore, the average kappa is:

$$\overline{\kappa_2} = \frac{.78 + .35 + .52}{3}$$

$$= \frac{1.65}{3}$$

$\overline{\kappa_2} = .55$, the kappa coefficient for all three judges

This average kappa is interpreted as the average improvement over chance agreement resulting from using the rating instrument and the trained judges. The premise behind the statistic is that if you flipped a coin instead of using trained judges armed with a rating instrument, you would obtain a predictable amount of agreement between the coin flips; kappa represents the improvement over this chance agreement resulting from using the trained judges and the rating instrument.

It is important to remember that the average kappa does **not** represent the average percentage of agreement between the judges; that figure would be obtained by averaging the three p_o figures for the three pairs rather than averaging the three kappas. Kappa is a superior measure, however, because the average percentage of agreement would be badly inflated due to chance agreements alone. Organizations that base decisions about reliability on percentage of agreement figures alone typically don't realize that many times their raters are making decisions about test-takers at levels no better than chance. Employees certainly deserve more consistency in their evaluations than can be obtained by simply flipping a coin to see whether or not they pass a performance test. It is even quite possible for kappa to assume negative values meaning that raters are operating at levels below chance agreement with one another. Such a circumstance indicates a very serious reliability and validity problem with the instrument or with the judges.

The question of how high a kappa coefficient should be is very difficult. It is so because how reliable the judges have to be depends entirely on what the organizational and personal consequences are of their being unreliable. As described in Chapter 7 in the section Criticality of Decisions and Test Length, an organization should undertake a systematic examination of what the consequences are to the organization and to the test-takers of making mistakes in master/non-master decisions. We consider an average kappa coefficient of .65 a minimum. As you can readily imagine, the value should be higher as the criticality of the performance test increases. Experience in using this statistic will help an organization determine how high the value of kappa should be; after several applications of the statistic, you will get a "feel" for what its various levels mean in terms of levels of agreement between judges.

PRACTICE

Table 15.2 (on page 331) provides a sample of possible results from a performance test where three judges rated each of twelve test-takers. Use the formulas above to calculate the average kappa coefficient $\overline{\kappa_2}$ for these three judges. Three blank matrices (Figures 15.5, 15.6, and 15.7) are provided below to assist you.

FIGURE 15.5.   BLANK P_O AND P_{CHANCE} MATRIX, JUDGES 1 & 2.

		Judge 1		
		Master	Non-Master	
Judge 2	Master	a =	b =	(a + b) =
	Non-Master	c =	d =	(c + d) =
		(a + c) =	(b + d) =	

Figure 15.6. Blank P_O and P_{CHANCE} Matrix, Judges 1 & 3.

Judge 1

		Master	Non-Master	
Judge 3	Master	a =	b =	(a + b) =
	Non-Master	c =	d =	(c + d) =
		(a + c) =	(b + d) =	

Figure 15.7. Blank P_O and P_{CHANCE} Matrix, Judges 2 & 3.

Judge 2

		Master	Non-Master	
Judge 3	Master	a =	b =	(a + b) =
	Non-Master	c =	d =	(c + d) =
		(a + c) =	(b + d) =	

Table 15.2. Sample Performance Test Data, Inter-Rater Reliability.

	Judges		
Test-taker	1	2	3
1	Master	Master	Master
2	Master	Master	Master
3	Master	Master	Master
4	Master	Master	Master
5	Master	Non-master	Master
6	Master	Non-master	Non-master
7	Non-master	Non-master	Non-master
8	Non-master	Non-master	Non-master
9	Non-master	Non-master	Non-master
10	Non-master	Non-master	Non-master
11	Non-master	Master	Master
12	Non-master	Non-master	Master

FEEDBACK

The three matrices above should have been completed as follows in Figures 15.8, 15.9, and 15.10 respectively:

FIGURE 15.8. ANSWER FOR P_O AND P_{CHANCE} MATRIX, JUDGES 1 & 2.

Judge 1

		Master	Non-Master	
Judge 2	Master	a = 4	b = 1	(a + b) = 5
	Non-Master	c = 2	d = 5	(c + d) = 7
		(a + c) = 6	(b + d) = 6	

Figure 15.9. Answer for P_O AND P_{CHANCE} MATRIX, JUDGES 1 & 3.

Judge 1

		Master	Non-Master	
Judge 3	Master	a = 5	b = 2	(a + b) = 7
	Non-Master	c = 1	d = 4	(c + d) = 5
		(a + c) = 6	(b + d) = 6	

FIGURE 15.10. ANSWER FOR P_O AND P_{CHANCE} MATRIX, JUDGES 2 & 3.

Judge 2

		Master	Non-Master	
Judge 3	Master	a = 5	b = 2	(a + b) = 7
	Non-Master	c = 0	d = 5	(c + d) = 5
		(a + c) = 5	(b + d) = 7	

The kappa coefficients for each of the three pairs of judges should have been calculated as shown below.

For the pair Judge 1/Judge 2:

$$p_o = \frac{(4+5)}{12}$$

$$= \frac{9}{12}$$

$$p_o = .75 \text{ for the pair Judge 1/Judge 2}$$

and

$$p_{chance} = \frac{\left[(4+1)(4+2)\right]+\left[(2+5)(1+5)\right]}{12^2}$$
$$= \frac{\left[(5)(6)\right]+\left[(7)(6)\right]}{144}$$
$$= \frac{(30+42)}{144}$$
$$= \frac{72}{144}$$

$p_{chance} = .50$ for the pair Judge 1/Judge 2

so kappa can be calculated as follows:

$$\kappa = \frac{.75-.50}{1-.50}$$
$$= \frac{.25}{.50}$$

$\kappa = .50$ for the pair Judge 1/Judge 2

For the pair Judge 1/Judge 3:

$$p_o = \frac{(5+4)}{12}$$
$$= \frac{9}{12}$$

$p_o = .75$ for the pair Judge 1/Judge 3

and

$$p_{chance} = \frac{\left[(5+2)(5+1)\right]+\left[(1+4)(2+4)\right]}{12^2}$$
$$= \frac{\left[(7)(6)\right]+\left[(5)(6)\right]}{144}$$
$$= \frac{(42+30)}{144}$$

$p_{chance} = .50$ for the pair Judge 1/Judge 3

so kappa can be calculated as follows:

$$\kappa = \frac{.75 - .50}{1 - .50}$$

$$= \frac{.25}{.50}$$

$$\kappa = .50 \text{ for the pair Judge 1/Judge 3}$$

For the pair Judge 2/Judge 3:

$$p_o = \frac{(5 + 5)}{12}$$

$$= \frac{10}{12}$$

$$p_o = .8333 \text{ or } .83 \text{ for the pair Judge 2/Judge 3}$$

and

$$p_{chance} = \frac{\left[(5 + 2)(5 + 0)\right] + \left[(0 + 5)(2 + 5)\right]}{12^2}$$

$$= \frac{\left[(7)(5)\right] + \left[(5)(7)\right]}{144}$$

$$= \frac{(35 + 35)}{144}$$

$$= \frac{70}{144}$$

$$p_{chance} = .4861 \text{ or } .49 \text{ for the pair Judge 2/Judge 3}$$

so kappa can be calculated as follows:

$$\kappa = \frac{.83 - .49}{1 - .49}$$

$$= \frac{.34}{.51}$$

$$\kappa = .6666 \text{ or } .67 \text{ for the pair Judge 2/Judge 3}$$

Averaging the three kappa values gives you the overall kappa coefficient as follows:

$$\overline{\kappa_2} = \frac{.50 + .50 + .67}{3}$$

$$= \frac{1.67}{3}$$

$$\overline{\kappa_2} = .5566 \text{ or } .56, \text{ the kappa coefficient for all three judges.}$$

CALCULATING AND INTERPRETING PHI (ϕ)

Phi is a correlation coefficient used to determine the relationship between two dichotomous variables, that is, two variables each of which has only two values. As such it is an appropriate statistic to use for calculating the level of agreement between two judges, each of whom have assigned test-takers to master/non-master classifications. Here again, we recommend that you use more than two judges to establish the reliability of your performance testing system. Phi can be extended to more than two judges by averaging the phi coefficients obtained for each possible pair of judges in a process analogous to that described for kappa above.

One begins to calculate phi by constructing a matrix to summarize the judgments made by each possible pair of judges. As with kappa above, if you have three judges you will need three matrices, one each for the pair Judge 1/Judge 2, the pair Judge 1/Judge 3, and the pair Judge 2/Judge 3. Figure 15.11 illustrates how the matrix for Judge 1 and Judge 2 would look. **Note:** The matrix for phi is constructed differently from the matrix used to determine p_o and p_{chance} values for calculating kappa. The matrix

FIGURE 15.11.   MATRIX FOR CALCULATING PHI.

		Judge 1		
		Non-Master	Master	
Judge 2	Master	B =	A =	(A + B) =
	Non-Master	D =	C =	(C + D) =
		(B + D) =	(A + C) =	

for phi must be set up in exactly the way shown in order for the formula to provide the correct result.

The three matrices for calculating the phi coefficient on the data in Table 15.1 above would be completed as follows in Figures 15.12, 15.13, and 15.14 for the pairs Judge 1/Judge 2, Judge 1/Judge 3, and Judge 2/Judge 3 respectively.

FIGURE 15.12. MATRIX FOR CALCULATING PHI, JUDGES 1 & 2.

Judge 1

		Non-Master	Master	
Judge 2	Master	B = 0	A = 3	(A + B) = 3
	Non-Master	D = 6	C = 1	(C + D) = 7
		(B + D) = 6	(A + C) = 4	

FIGURE 15.13. MATRIX FOR CALCULATING PHI, JUDGES 1 & 3.

Judge 1

		Non-Master	Master	
Judge 3	Master	B = 1	A = 2	(A + B) = 3
	Non-Master	D = 5	C = 2	(C + D) = 7
		(B + D) = 6	(A + C) = 4	

FIGURE 15.14. MATRIX FOR CALCULATING PHI, JUDGES 2 & 3.

Judge 2

		Non-Master	Master	
Judge 3	Master	B = 1	A = 2	(A + B) = 3
	Non-Master	D = 6	C = 1	(C + D) = 7
		(B + D) = 7	(A + C) = 3	

The formula for calculating phi is:

$$\phi = \frac{(AD) - (BC)}{\sqrt{(A + B)(C + D)(A + C)(B + D)}}$$

The next step in the calculation of phi for the three judges is to calculate phi for each of the possible pairs. These calculations are illustrated below.

For the pair Judge 1/Judge 2:

$$\phi = \frac{\left[(3)(6)\right] - \left[(0)(1)\right]}{\sqrt{(3)(7)(4)(6)}}$$

$$= \frac{(18 - 0)}{\sqrt{504}}$$

$$= \frac{18}{22.45}$$

ϕ = .8017 or .80 for the pair Judge 1/Judge 2

For the pair Judge 1/Judge 3:

$$\phi = \frac{\left[(2)(5)\right] - \left[(1)(2)\right]}{\sqrt{(3)(7)(4)(6)}}$$

$$= \frac{(10 - 2)}{\sqrt{504}}$$

$$= \frac{8}{22.45}$$

ϕ = .3563 or .36 for the pair Judge 1/Judge 3

For the pair Judge 2/Judge 3:

$$\phi = \frac{\left[(2)(6)\right] - \left[(1)(1)\right]}{\sqrt{(3)(7)(3)(7)}}$$

$$= \frac{(12 - 1)}{\sqrt{441}}$$

$$= \frac{11}{21}$$

ϕ = .5238 or .52 for the pair Judge 2/Judge 3

To find the phi coefficient for the entire panel of three judges, the three pairwise phi coefficients must be averaged. Unfortunately, the averaging of correlation coefficients presents some problems. Correlation coefficients are not separated from one another by equal metric units as are, for example, the numbers from one to ten. In fact, differences between large correlation coefficients are greater than differences between small ones (Guilford & Fruchter, 1978). In other words, the correlation coefficients .95 and .99 are further apart than the correlation coefficients .15 and .19. So, sometimes simply figuring the average of correlation coefficients results in a distorted number.

The most reasonable advice is that if your phi correlation coefficients for your pairs of judges are close to one another in value and are not very large, you can obtain the overall phi (or average phi, $\bar{\phi}$) *by calculating a simple average*—adding the phi coefficients up and dividing by the number of pairs. However, while you hope that the phi coefficients are similar, indicating agreement among the pairs, you also hope that the phi coefficients are large, indicating agreement between members of every pair. Therefore, if you are successful in achieving high agreement levels between your judges, you may find the average of your phi coefficients is distorted.

Happily, there is a procedure for correcting average correlation coefficients for this distortion. The process is quick and easy. Each phi coefficient is converted to what is called a *Fisher's Z coefficient* using a simple table (Guilford & Fruchter, 1978). Zs can be safely averaged. So you add up the Z coefficients and divide by the number of coefficients. This average Z is then converted back to a correlation coefficient resulting in a corrected average phi coefficient ($\bar{\phi}_{corrected}$) for your panel of judges.

This process is illustrated using the three phi coefficients just calculated for the data from Table 15.1. For purposes of comparison, we will first calculate the simple average of these coefficients.

The simple average of the phi coefficients resulting from the data in Table 15.1 is:

$$\bar{\phi} = \frac{.80 + .36 + .52}{3}$$
$$= \frac{1.68}{3}$$
$$\bar{\phi} = .56$$

The corrected phi average is computed by first converting each phi into a Z coefficient using Table 15.3 on the next page.

TABLE 15.3. CONVERSION TABLE FOR ϕ (r) INTO Z.

r	Z	r	Z	r	Z	r	Z	r	Z
.000	.000	.200	.203	.400	.424	.600	.693	.800	1.099
.005	.005	.205	.208	.405	.430	.605	.701	.805	1.113
.010	.010	.210	.213	.410	.436	.610	.709	.810	1.127
.015	.015	.215	.218	.415	.442	.615	.717	.815	1.142
.020	.020	.220	.224	.420	.448	.620	.725	.820	1.157
.025	.025	.225	.229	.425	.454	.625	.733	.825	1.172
.030	.030	.230	.234	.430	.460	.630	.741	.830	1.188
.035	.035	.235	.239	.435	.466	.635	.750	.835	1.204
.040	.040	.240	.245	.440	.472	.640	.758	.840	1.221
.045	.045	.245	.250	.445	.478	.645	.767	.845	1.238
.050	.050	.250	.255	.450	.485	.650	.775	.850	1.256
.055	.055	.255	.261	.455	.491	.655	.784	.855	1.274
.060	.060	.260	.266	.460	.497	.660	.793	.860	1.293
.065	.065	.265	.271	.465	.504	.665	.802	.865	1.313
.070	.070	.270	.277	.470	.510	.670	.811	.870	1.333
.075	.075	.275	.282	.475	.517	.675	.820	.875	1.354
.080	.080	.280	.288	.480	.523	.680	.829	.880	1.376
.085	.085	.285	.293	.485	.530	.685	.838	.885	1.398
.090	.090	.290	.299	.490	.536	.690	.848	.890	1.422
.095	.095	.295	.304	.495	.543	.695	.858	.895	1.447
.100	.100	.300	.310	.500	.549	.700	.867	.900	1.472
.105	.105	.305	.315	.505	.556	.705	.877	.905	1.499
.110	.110	.310	.321	.510	.563	.710	.887	.910	1.528
.115	.116	.315	.326	.515	.570	.715	.897	.915	1.557
.120	.121	.320	.332	.520	.576	.720	.908	.920	1.589
.125	.126	.325	.337	.525	.583	.725	.918	.925	1.623
.130	.131	.330	.343	.530	.590	.730	.929	.930	1.658
.135	.136	.335	.348	.535	.597	.735	.940	.935	1.697
.140	.141	.340	.354	.540	.604	.740	.950	.940	1.738
.145	.146	.345	.360	.545	.611	.745	.962	.945	1.783
.150	.151	.350	.365	.550	.618	.750	.973	.950	1.832
.155	.156	.355	.371	.555	.626	.755	.984	.955	1.886
.160	.161	.360	.377	.560	.633	.760	.996	.960	1.946
.165	.167	.365	.383	.565	.640	.765	1.008	.965	2.014
.170	.172	.370	.388	.570	.648	.770	1.020	.970	2.092
.175	.177	.375	.394	.575	.655	.775	1.033	.975	2.185
.180	.182	.380	.400	.580	.662	.780	1.045	.980	2.298
.185	.187	.385	.406	.585	.670	.785	1.058	.985	2.443
.190	.192	.390	.412	.590	.678	.790	1.071	.990	2.647
.195	.198	.395	.418	.595	.685	.795	1.085	.995	2.994

Each phi coefficient is located in the column labeled r; the r is a standard statistical notation designating a correlation coefficient. The corresponding Z coefficient is read from the column labeled Z.

Using the table, we determine that:
phi of .80 equals Z of 1.099 (for the pair Judge 1/Judge 2)
phi of .36 equals Z of .377 (for the pair Judge 1/Judge 3)
and
phi of .52 equals Z of .576 (for the pair Judge 2/Judge 3)
Calculating the simple average of the Zs follows.

$$\bar{Z} = \frac{1.099 + .377 + .576}{3}$$
$$= \frac{2.052}{3}$$
$$\bar{Z} = .684$$

Now we return to the table to convert our average Z back into a phi coefficient. We discover that the value .684 does not appear exactly in the table; the table doesn't break Zs down that finely. So we choose the Z value in the table closest to our average Z, which is .685. The phi corresponding to this value is .595. Therefore,

$$\bar{\phi}_{corrected} = .595 \text{ or } .60$$

Notice that the corrected phi is larger than the simple average phi. This comparison illustrates the distortion in uncorrected average correlation coefficients.

The answer to the question of how high an average phi correlation coefficient should be is tempered by the same considerations that determine how high an average kappa coefficient should be. How reliable the judges must be depends on the consequences of their being incorrect in their decisions. In general, a phi below .75 should be considered unacceptable. For critical objectives, phi coefficients above .95 should be expected.

PRACTICE

Using the performance test results appearing in Table 15.2 and the formulas and procedures described above, practice calculating the simple average and the corrected average phi coefficients for these test data. Three blank matrices (Figures 15.15, 15.16, and 15.17) are provided below to assist you.

FIGURE 15.15.   BLANK MATRIX FOR CALCULATING PHI, JUDGES 1 & 2.

		Judge 1		
		Non-Master	Master	
Judge 2	Master	B =	A =	(A + B) =
	Non-Master	D =	C =	(C + D) =
		(B + D) =	(A + C) =	

FIGURE 15.16.   BLANK MATRIX FOR CALCULATING PHI, JUDGES 1 & 3.

		Judge 1		
		Non-Master	Master	
Judge 3	Master	B =	A =	(A + B) =
	Non-Master	D =	C =	(C + D) =
		(B + D) =	(A + C) =	

FIGURE 15.17.   BLANK MATRIX FOR CALCULATING PHI, JUDGES 2 & 3.

		Judge 2		
		Non-Master	Master	
Judge 3	Master	B =	A =	(A + B) =
	Non-Master	D =	C =	(C + D) =
		(B + D) =	(A + C) =	

FEEDBACK

The three matrices above should have been completed as shown in Figures 15.18, 15.19, and 15.20, respectively:

FIGURE 15.18. ANSWER MATRIX FOR CALCULATING PHI, JUDGES 1 & 2.

Judge 1

		Non-Master	Master	
Judge 2	Master	B = 1	A = 4	(A + B) = 5
	Non-Master	D = 5	C = 2	(C + D) = 7
		(B + D) = 6	(A + C) = 6	

FIGURE 15.19. ANSWER MATRIX FOR CALCULATING PHI, JUDGES 1 & 3.

Judge 1

		Non-Master	Master	
Judge 3	Master	B = 2	A = 5	(A + B) = 7
	Non-Master	D = 4	C = 1	(C + D) = 5
		(B + D) = 6	(A + C) = 6	

FIGURE 15.20. ANSWER MATRIX FOR CALCULATING PHI, JUDGES 2 & 3.

Judge 2

		Non-Master	Master	
Judge 3	Master	B = 2	A = 5	(A + B) = 7
	Non-Master	D = 5	C = 0	(C + D) = 5
		(B + D) = 7	(A + C) = 5	

The phi calculation for the pair Judge 1/Judge 2 is:

$$\phi = \frac{\left[(4)(5)\right] - \left[(1)(2)\right]}{\sqrt{(5)(7)(6)(6)}}$$

$$= \frac{(20 - 2)}{\sqrt{1260}}$$

$$= \frac{18}{35.5}$$

$$\phi = .5070 \text{ or } .51 \text{ for the pair Judge 1/Judge 2}$$

The phi calculation for the pair Judge 1/Judge 3 is:

$$\phi = \frac{\left[(5)(4)\right] - \left[(2)(1)\right]}{\sqrt{(7)(5)(6)(6)}}$$

$$= \frac{(20 - 2)}{\sqrt{1260}}$$

$$= \frac{18}{35.5}$$

$$\phi = .5070 \text{ or } .51 \text{ for the pair Judge 1/Judge 3}$$

The phi calculation for the pair Judge 2/Judge 3 is:

$$\phi = \frac{\left[(5)(5)\right] - \left[(2)(0)\right]}{\sqrt{(7)(5)(5)(7)}}$$

$$= \frac{(25 - 0)}{\sqrt{1225}}$$

$$= \frac{25}{35}$$

$$\phi = .7143 \text{ or } .71 \text{ for the pair Judge 2/Judge 3}$$

The simple average of these phi coefficients is:

$$\bar{\phi} = \frac{.51 + .51 + .71}{3}$$

$$= \frac{1.73}{3}$$

$$\bar{\phi} = .5767 \text{ or } .58$$

The corrected average phi for the three judges is calculated by first transforming the phi coefficients to Zs:

phi of .51 equals Z of .563 (for the pair Judge 1/Judge 2)

phi of .51 equals Z of .563 (for the pair Judge 1/Judge 3)

and

phi of .71 equals Z of .887 (for the pair Judge 2/Judge 3)

The simple average of the Zs is:

$$\bar{Z} = \frac{.563 + .563 + .887}{3}$$

$$= \frac{2.013}{3}$$

$$\bar{Z} = .671$$

Converting the average Z back into a phi, you should have found that Z of .671 has a corresponding phi value of .585; therefore,

$$\bar{\phi}_{corrected} = .585 \text{ or } .59$$

Notice that because the original phi values were not terribly high or terribly different, the difference between the simple average phi and the corrected phi is extremely small.

REPEATED PERFORMANCE AND CONSECUTIVE SUCCESS

As discussed in Chapter 7, one issue in creating cognitive tests is how many items should appear on a test. The point was made that the more items included on the test, the more reliable the test would be. This is so because test items are, in effect, like samples of behavior; the more samples of test-taker behavior you examine, the more accurate your assessment of his or her competence will be. A parallel issue exists in performance testing, although it is not so frequently discussed. That issue is: "How many times should a test-taker be asked to demonstrate a behavior on a performance test before we can make an accurate assessment of his or her mastery of the task?"

The danger in making a mastery/non-mastery decision on the basis of a single performance trial is that some tasks can be performed correctly due to chance. Some skills are so essential and the consequences of error in making the master/non-master decision are so severe, that repeated performance trials with consecutive successes are warranted. Robert Lathrop (1983) described in detail a process for determining how many performance demonstrations are required to make a master/non-master decision at a given criterion level (for example, mastery = 80 percent or mastery = 70 percent), with a pre-specified level of confidence. His work makes clear several important (and sobering) points for performance test designers to remember:

- The higher you set the criterion for mastery status, the more quickly you can identify non-masters, but the greater the number of performance trials required to establish mastery. For example, if the criterion for mastery is performing correctly 80 percent of the steps in a procedure, you will be able to detect non-masters in fewer trials than if the criterion were 70 percent; however, more performance trials are required to establish mastery at a criterion of 80 percent than at a criterion of 70 percent.
- The lower you set the criterion for mastery status, the more quickly you can identify masters, but the greater the number of trials required to establish non-mastery. For example, if the criterion for mastery is performing correctly 80 percent of the steps in a procedure, you will be able to identify masters in fewer trials than if the criterion were 90 percent; however, more performance trials will be required to establish non-mastery at a criterion of 80 percent than at a criterion of 90 percent.
- The greater the precision you desire in making master/non-master decisions, the more trials will be required to establish either mastery or non-mastery. It is possible to establish independently the levels of error you can tolerate in false positive (erroneously classifying a non-master as a master) and false negative (erroneously classifying a master as a non-master) errors. Willingness to tolerate fewer mistakes of either kind will increase the number of performance trials required.
- Statistically speaking, given the high criterion levels typical of corporate performance tests and typically acceptable error rates, it is impossible to classify an individual as a master or a non-master on the basis of a single performance trial. It may be possible to establish non-mastery in only two trials, but it typically requires at least four or five performance trials to establish mastery.

- Consecutive success is extremely important in the performance testing of critical skills. The effect of a single failed attempt to perform the task is a dramatic increase in the number of additional successful performance trials required to establish the mastery of the test-taker.

   The advice that follows from statistical arguments like Lathrop's is as follows:

- Be sensitive to the possibility (even the likelihood) of error in performance testing; scrutinize tasks with the intention of identifying those likely to be performed correctly by chance. Such tasks are candidates for repeated performance trials.
- Insist on two or more consecutive successful demonstrations of tasks required for the health and safety of clients or employees and tasks essential for organizational survival.
- Remember that, while lowering the criterion for mastery makes it easier to identify masters, the criterion for mastery should rightfully be determined by what level of competence is required to do the job. Changing such a criterion, or cut-off score, should never be taken lightly (see Chapter 13).
- Be alert for tasks that must be performed under a variety of different conditions. If these different conditions influence the likelihood of the task's being performed correctly, it is advisable that the test-taker be asked to demonstrate his or her competence under all conditions essential to successful completion of the task on the job.
- Be especially careful of broadly stated, critical objectives such as, "Given appropriate warning indicators in a simulated nuclear power plant, identify the source of radiation leakage." If, on a performance test for this objective, the test-taker is confronted with only a single warning indicator pattern, how do the test designers know that he or she can respond correctly to different patterns? Such objectives require a variety of task demonstrations in order to be assessed with confidence.
- For performance tests of critical tasks, be certain that you have formally established the reliability of your rating instruments

and your raters and based the performance test on a thorough and accurate job/task analysis.

PROCEDURES FOR TRAINING RATERS

If you think back to a recent Olympics gymnastics or diving competition, you have probably had three observations about the rating process: (1) The judges are very consistent in rating the performances of the athletes, (2) your assessments of the athlete's performance ("easily a 9.5," "Blew that one, probably a 9.1") were probably close to the judges', and (3) if one judge is consistently different from the other judges, you begin to wonder about the judge's skill or motivation. These insights provide an important perspective on why you need to train your raters and how to train them.

For professional and legal reasons, raters need to make consistent and accurate ratings. Good Olympic judges have a combination of experience and training that can serve as a model for any rating situation. There are some simple steps you can follow to train your raters to these high standards:

1. Bring together those people who are familiar with the skill or product to be rated and who will later be asked to serve as raters.
2. Plan a rater training session at which you will have available a sample of performances or products that are to be rated. In an ideal setting you would have a model case performance (or product) where all the attributes of a correct performance are present, a clear non-example of the performance (or product), and a range of stimuli between these two extremes— perhaps with the most common errors illustrated. This training session can be based either on a live performance or on a high-fidelity media simulation, for example, a DVD of an assembly process. If the rating is of a product, the product itself should be present.
3. The raters should be presented with the first stimulus, usually the model case performance. All raters then use the checklist to review the performance or product. If the performance is mediated, the DVD can be stopped and an action discussed.

If the performance is live, plan to record the actions (for example, a tape recording of an air traffic controller's interchange), so that raters can discuss specific behaviors that may not be clear.

4. Provide the next stimulus, often the non-example, and have the raters assess the performance (or product) as they would during an actual testing session. Again, record the activities if they are live.

5. Ratings for each behavior should be tabulated as a percentage of agreement and posted for the group to see. Raters then share their assessments, step-by-step, with the other raters. Points of contention (low percentages of agreement) should be reviewed and discussed until all the raters understand the reasoning behind the correct assessment.

6. A new stimulus is presented, ratings tabulated and shared, and then discussed. This cycle is continued until the judges have reached a high degree of consistency (90 percent).

7. Ten final trials are then presented to the group for the documented inter-rater reliability, that is, the average kappa or average phi.

8. Document the final measures of inter-rater reliability and collect the stimulus materials.

This entire process will rarely take more than a day's effort. In one particular experience, we established a high inter-rater level of agreement with eighteen judges from around the nation in less than a morning. *Remember though, you are establishing the reliability of the rater and the rating instrument in tandem. The rating instrument by itself cannot be considered reliable in the sense that a cognitive test can be.* When the raters move into the field to conduct performance assessments, don't assume there is no need for further follow-up. After a period of time (perhaps six months), collect copies of the ratings where multiple judges have observed the same stimulus and calculate the inter-rater reliability coefficient. If your levels of consistency have dropped below the allowable range, then you should bring the raters together for a refresher course.

Finally, when you need to train a new rater, you can use the stimulus materials (if appropriate) that were originally generated for the initial rater training session. After each stimulus you can compare the new rater's judgments to those of the original group until the new rater has reached or exceeded the originally established level of agreement.

WHAT IF A RATER PASSES EVERYONE REGARDLESS OF PERFORMANCE?

We have seen instances of performance testing wherein one rater passes every test-taker regardless of the quality of performance. Clearly, this raises a flag for the organization regarding the validity of the rater, and we offer some advice for this situation. First, we look at what happens to the phi reliability coefficient under this circumstance; the discussion illustrates some of the important properties of the phi coefficient. Briefly stated, phi is sensitive not only to the agreements between raters but to the master/non-master composition of the group being tested, and the subsequent ability of the raters to agree on *both* mastery and non-mastery performances. An extended example follows for readers who find themselves with this particular dilemma.

Assume the rater Klaus passes every test-taker; therefore, his correlation with anyone else's ratings will always be 0. If we calculate Klaus' reliability coefficients, we would find:

- Klaus' phi coefficient with any other rater is 0.
- Klaus' κ (kappa) coefficient with any other rater is also 0.

However, neither of these coefficients would equal 0 if Klaus had failed any one test-taker, regardless of which one it was. Beyond that, which of the test-takers Klaus fails determines the value of the coefficients.

Before looking at additional examples, we want to comment on the meaning of a zero-order correlation coefficient. Remember that the correlation of any factor that has no variability (that is, all data points are alike) with any other factor will always be 0. In the case of Klaus' ratings, it is as if correlations are "unimpressed" with raters who cannot make distinctions among test-takers. In the eyes of phi, so to speak, Klaus is not rating any behavior on the part of test-takers; rather he is passing whatever he sees. (The phi would similarly be 0 if Klaus failed every test-taker he rated.)

Because Klaus is an invalid rater, his relationship to any other rater is 0. Consider an even more extreme case—Klaus's sightless sister Klaustine also passes every test-taker. Their percent of agreement is 100 percent; their phi coefficient is 0. Phi gives no "credit" for two invalid raters who agree.

Now, for some examples:

Consider the case of Klaus paired with Lisa. The percent of agreement between Klaus and Lisa is 80 percent. Figure 15.21 portrays this relationship between Klaus and Lisa. The calculation that follows indicates that the numerator will be 0 regardless of what the denominator is, so the phi value will equal 0; this will be the case for every rater paired with Klaus. (Kappa also results in 0.)

FIGURE 15.21.   KLAUS AND LISA PHI CALCULATION WHEN KLAUS PASSES
ALL TEST-TAKERS.

		Lisa		
		Non-Master	Master	
Klaus	Master	B = 2	A = 8	A + B
	Non-Master	D = 0	C = 0	C + D
		B + D	A + C	

$$\phi = \frac{(AD) - (BC)}{\sqrt{(A+B)(C+D)(A+C)(B+D)}}$$

$$= \frac{(0-0)}{\sqrt{whatever}}$$

$$\phi = 0$$

Now consider improvement in the Phi coefficient if Klaus agreed with Lisa on one of the two test-takers that Lisa failed. The matrix and calculation in Figure 15.22 illustrate that the phi jumps to a whopping .67. (Kappa for these data equals .62.) The percent of agreement also increases to 90, but as subsequent examples will show, the improved phi is a function of the agreement *on failure*.

FIGURE 15.22. PHI WHEN KLAUS AGREES WITH LISA ON ONE PERFORMER
SHE FAILED.

		Lisa		
		Non-Master	Master	
Klaus	Master	B = 1	A = 8	(A + B) = 9
	Non-Master	D = 1	C = 0	(C + D) = 1
		(B + D) = 2	(A + C) = 8	

$$\phi = \frac{(8-0)}{\sqrt{(9)(1)(8)(2)}} = \frac{8}{\sqrt{144}} = \frac{8}{12} = .67$$

For the next example, let's keep the original percent of agreement unchanged at 80. Consider what the value of phi would be if Klaus and Lisa agreed that only one of the test-takers they both passed had, in fact, failed. Figure 15.23 shows how that data would be placed in the phi matrix. Notice that in this case the percent of agreement is unchanged from the original data—still 80. The difference is that in this situation phi "knows" that Klaus can detect a failing test-taker because he fails the same test-taker that Lisa failed; hence their phi correlation is vastly improved (.51 instead of 0), even though their percent of agreement stays the same. The

FIGURE 15.23. PHI WHEN KLAUS AND LISA AGREE ONE PREVIOUSLY PASSED
PERFORMER FAILED.

		Lisa		
		Non-Master	Master	
Klaus	Master	B = 2	A = 7	(A + B) = 9
	Non-Master	D = 1	C = 0	(C + D) = 1
		(B + D) = 3	(A + C) = 7	

$$\phi = \frac{(7-0)}{\sqrt{(9)(1)(3)(7)}} = \frac{7}{\sqrt{189}} = \frac{7}{13.7} = .51$$

difference is the presence of the one agreed-upon failing test-taker. (The corresponding kappa value for these data is .41).

Now let's see what would happen to their phi coefficient if Klaus had failed one of the test-takers that Lisa had passed. The data appear in Figure 15.24. This time, of course, their percent of agreement drops to 70; that is, they now agree that only seven of the ten test-takers passed. The calculation below the table shows that phi is no longer zero as it was when Klaus passed everyone. But now phi is worse than 0; it has dropped to −.17. Phi "recognizes" that Klaus is no longer blindly passing everyone, but the negative value indicates that he now actively disagrees with Lisa on what constitutes failure. In other words, as a pair Klaus and Lisa are even less reliable than before. (The kappa coefficient on these data is −.15.)

FIGURE 15.24.   PHI WHEN KLAUS FAILS ONE PERFORMER LISA PASSED.

		Lisa		
		Non-Master	Master	
Klaus	Master	B = 2	A = 7	(A + B) = 9
	Non-Master	D = 0	C = 1	(C + D) = 1
		(B + D) = 2	(A + C) = 8	

$$\phi = \frac{(0-2)}{\sqrt{(9)(1)(8)(2)}} = \frac{-2}{\sqrt{144}} = \frac{-2}{12} = -.17$$

We would argue that Klaus is an invalid rater. Even if you were to plant a known failing performance among the rated test-takers, Klaus can't spot it or won't report it if he does. Either way, his ratings are invalid.

WHAT SHOULD YOU DO?

Some organizations would be tempted to throw out Klaus' ratings when reporting inter-rater reliability for this performance test. Here is our advice in order of desirability—from a measurement point of view, anyway:

- Decide that Klaus should not be performing this function. If you have tried to remediate him to improve his ability to spot a failure, and he still can't or won't, this job is not for him.
- Let the organization take its psychometric lumps for continuing to allow Klaus to rate. Add in a 0 for Klaus' correlations and include his presence in your total if you are averaging raters' performance. This will lower your average, but the resulting overall figure is more accurate and therefore more defensible—after all, Klaus is an invalid rater.
- Use only a percentage of agreement to determine inter-rater reliability and report the range of agreement among raters, for example, "percent of inter-rater agreement ranged from .82 to .98." Your figures will be inflated by chance agreement but at least you aren't throwing out any data.

WHAT IF YOU GET A HIGH PERCENTAGE OF AGREEMENT AMONG RATERS BUT A NEGATIVE PHI COEFFICIENT?

In general, people tend to equate a high percent of agreement as leading to a high phi. Oddly enough, it is possible to find yourself in a situation in which you have a generally positive degree of agreement among the judges, but end up with a negative phi. (This last situation is similar to what happened with Klaus and Lisa in Figure 15.24, where there is a 70 percent agreement with a phi of $-.17$). Let's consider a new pair of raters, Gina and Omar, with a phi of $-.17$. Gina and Omar's percent of agreement is 70 percent, but their phi reflects the fact that they can agree only on test-takers they think should pass; they are incapable of agreeing on test-takers who should fail.

- Each test-taker that Omar fails, Gina passes.
- Each test-taker that Gina fails, Omar passes.

Phi will exact a heavy toll on this pair.

As we saw with Klaus and Lisa earlier, if Gina and Omar could agree on just one failing test-taker, maintaining their agreement on the seven they believe to have passed, their percent of agreement would increase by a modest 10 percent to 80 percent agreement, but the effect on the Phi coefficient is a big jump to .51. (See Figure 15.23).

Now, what if Omar and Gina had improved their percent of agreement to 80 percent, not by agreeing on a failing test-taker as above, but by agreeing on one more passing test-taker; that is, instead of agreeing on seven passes, they agree on eight passes, but don't improve in their ability to agree on failing test-takers. The calculation in Figure 15.25 illustrates that their phi improves only from $-.17$ to $-.11$. In other words, phi is not "impressed" by further agreement on passing test-takers; it is agreement on *failure* that is required to prove the reliability of the pair.

FIGURE 15.25.   PHI WHEN GINA AND OMAR AGREE ON ONE MORE
PASSING PERFORMER.

		Gina		
		Non-Master	Master	
Omar	Master	B = 1	A = 8	(A + B) = 9
	Non-Master	D = 0	C = 1	(C + D) = 1
		(B + D) = 1	(A + C) = 9	

$$\phi = \frac{(0-1)}{\sqrt{(9)(1)(9)(1)}} = \frac{-1}{\sqrt{81}} = \frac{-1}{9} = -.11$$

Just for the sake of completeness, move just one test-taker in the table above into the "D" cell. The resulting table is displayed in Figure 15.26. In this circumstance Gina still fails one test-taker whom Omar passes, and Omar still fails one test-taker whom Gina passes, just as above, but they have agreed on one failing test-taker. Just as the logic of phi would predict, they get a boost in their phi coefficient to .375 (.38, if rounded) due to their demonstrated ability to agree at least once on what constitutes failure.

FIGURE 15.26. PHI WHEN GINA AND OMAR AGREE ON ONE FAILING PERFORMER.

		Gina		
		Non-Master	Master	
Omar	Master	B = 1	A = 7	(A + B) = 8
	Non-Master	D = 1	C = 1	(C + D) = 2
		(B + D) = 2	(A + C) = 8	

$$\phi = \frac{(7-1)}{\sqrt{(8)(2)(8)(2)}} = \frac{6}{\sqrt{256}} = \frac{6}{16} = .375 \text{ or } .38$$

Notice that, at .375, phi is smaller than in the situation below, Figure 15.27, (identical to the third matrix produced for Klaus and Lisa earlier) where the percent of agreement is still at 80, but Gina and Omar are more consistent in how they disagree—both of their disagreements are about test-takers that Gina passes and Omar fails.

FIGURE 15.27. PHI WHEN GINA AND OMAR ARE MORE CONSISTENT
IN DISAGREEING.

		Gina		
		Non-Master	Master	
Omar	Master	B = 0	A = 7	(A + B) = 7
	Non-Master	D = 1	C = 2	(C + D) = 3
		(B + D) = 1	(A + C) = 9	

$$\phi = \frac{(7-0)}{\sqrt{(7)(3)(9)(1)}} = \frac{7}{\sqrt{189}} = \frac{7}{13.7} = .51$$

In conclusion, phi has properties similar to other correlation coefficients; it is sensitive to consistencies between the two raters—even consistencies in disagreement—and a shift in a single rating has a bigger impact on the coefficients when the total sample size (that is, the number of test-takers being rated) is small. However, phi is identical to all other correlation coefficients in rendering a value of 0 if there is no variance in one of the factors being correlated.

CHAPTER SIXTEEN

REPORT SCORES

CRT Versus NRT Reporting

Summing Subscores

What Should You Report to a Manager?

Is There a Legal Reason to Archive the Tests?

A Final Thought About Testing and Teaching

Now that the testing process is complete, you need, finally, to turn your attention to reporting the scores. Reporting the test scores is a politically volatile issue in the testing process and probably will be raised at the beginning of the test-development effort if the stakeholders believe the test will actually be used to make decisions.

If you have followed the process described in this book, you have created a valid and defensible test. With such a test you can trust the results and people can be properly identified as having the necessary skills or not. Many organizations take comfort in the error associated with poor test construction, that is, if everyone feels the test really doesn't measure what is needed on the job, then nobody has to feel bad or worried if he or she can't perform on the test. After all, most thinking goes, you can pick up what you need "on the job." But a well-designed test is like an accurate thermometer; you may think you feel OK, but the measuring device shows a fever and identifies a need for treatment. Nobody argues with a thermometer in the physician's office, but everyone will argue about a test in an organization.

CRT Versus NRT Reporting

As you enter into what we hope will be constructive discussions about the use of test scores in the organization, please keep in mind the fundamental assumption of criterion-referenced testing—you can only make one judgment about a test-taker's performance: Either he or she was classified as a master or was not. This assumption is easily lost on managers who want to use the test scores as a means of sorting people for merit or other purposes. The raw scores of test-takers should **not** be reported in the CRT environment. Nor should class averages.

You cannot use the CRT process to make any distinction beyond the master/non-master decision. Much to the consternation of many managers, there is no acceptable legal, professional, or ethical argument that someone with a score of 82 should be treated differently from someone with a score of 95 if both are above the cut-off point. But there can be a big difference in the consequence to two people if the cut-off is 80 and one scores 78 and the other 82.

Summing Subscores

We have encountered organizations in which managers have remained adamant that a single score for each test-taker, the cut-off score for the course, and the class average be reported for each course. During discussion, we usually find that a manager's review of the course content leads to a conclusion that some units should be worth more than others and an appropriate weight should be assigned to each unit before determining the final score. We are going to show you a scheme for weighting, but not before we make three points:

- If you are into these kinds of discussions, realize you are probably making increasingly political decisions that stray from the original purpose of CRT. Most of the time change is incremental in organizations, and you may feel the greater good is derived from ushering testing beyond its current state of invalidity to at least a more systematic course of continual improvement, and the compromises to reach that goal are defensible.

- *We don't believe in weighting tests by assigning a multiplier.* The issue of weighting a test by a certain amount (or test items for that matter) often comes up, and we advise against it. A simple analogy should help here. If you had a jar of jelly beans of three colors and you had to guess what the proportion of red, blue, and white beans were in the jar, which strategy would you prefer to use? (1) Reach in once, count the beans' color proportions and multiply your findings by three or (2) reach in three different times and then make your estimate based on the total proportion of your sample? For example, if you reached in only once, you might have grabbed two white and one red. If you reached in three times, you might grab two white and one red, then one white and two blue, and then two blues and one red. In the latter case, you might more safely conclude the proportions were 33 percent white, 22 percent red, and 44 percent blue instead of 66 percent white and 33 percent red. Weighting multiplies error, and if you remember from our very first words in Chapter 1, "All the procedures we will discuss and recommend are tied to a simple assumption: The primary purpose of test development is the reduction of error."

  If you seek to weight some objective because you feel it is more important than other components of the test, the weighting should be accomplished by adding more items to assess the objective or unit (reaching in more times to the jelly bean jar), rather than by assigning a multiplier. So if you feel Objective 1 should be worth 50 percent of the score, write 50 percent of the items to assess it. Don't write one item and multiply by 50.

- When student scores vary more on one test than on another, the tests with higher variation in scores will have greater effects on a final grade. This phenomenon is described by Francis (2006) regarding the typical university practice of weighting tests to reach a final course grade. The statistical issue he describes centers around the role of variation of scores among tests:

  > When you multiply or divide test scores to change their weight or value, you artificially increase (when you multiply) or decrease (when you divide) the size of the standard deviation and its

influence in weighting the test or grading assignment independent of the instructor's intended weight. (p. 22)

Because we expect CRTs to have small and similar standard deviations as a consequence of mastery, this issue may not typically affect CRT score combinations. However, this is an issue that might be considered more seriously in high-stakes tests in order to reduce error in the final test decision for a test-taker. Correcting the problem of weights requires a somewhat complicated statistical process using transformed T-scores (see Francis, 2006, p. 20).

The combined cut-off score for a course. The overall, combined cut-off score for a course is determined by a simple process:

1. Assign a weight to each unit test in the course.
2. Multiply each individual test's cut-off score by the weight assigned to that test.
3. Add up the weighted cut-off scores to determine the overall, combined course cut-off score.

Table 16.1 shows an instance in which there were three major tests in the course. The first test was assigned a weight of .40, the second, .30, and the third .30. The respective cut scores were .90, .85, and 1.0 (all items must be mastered). The overall course cut-off score would be approximately 92 percent.

TABLE 16.1. CALCULATION OF THE OVERALL COURSE CUT-OFF SCORE.

Unit	Test Weight	Cut-Off	Weighted Cut-Score
1	.40	.90	36%
2	.30	.85	26%
3	.30	1.00	30%
			92%

The combined individual performance score. The overall, combined score for a person who has taken several tests within a course is determined by a process similar to the combined course cut-off score:

1. Assign a weight to each unit test in the course.
2. Multiply each individual's test score by the weight assigned to that test.

3. Add up the weighted individual scores to determine the person's overall, combined performance score.
4. Compare the individual score to the course cut-off to determine if the test-taker achieved mastery.

Table 16.2 continues an instance in which three major tests in the course were weighted .40, .30, .30 with respective cut-off scores of .90, .85, and 1.0 (all items must be mastered). The test-taker scored 85 percent, 80 percent, and 100 percent. The individual's overall score would then be approximately 88 percent—a nonmastery judgment if the overall combined course cut-off score were 92 percent.

TABLE 16.2. CALCULATION OF AN INDIVIDUAL'S WEIGHTED PERFORMANCE SCORE.

Unit	Test Weight	Individual Score	Weighted Individual Score
1	.40	.85	34%
2	.30	.80	24%
3	.30	1.00	30%
			88%

WHAT SHOULD YOU REPORT TO A MANAGER?

This question is actually one that should be addressed at the beginning of the test-development process so that all the test's stakeholders have a shared understanding of how the scores will be used. In general, though, we think there are some minimal types of information that would help the organization make decisions surrounding the test-taker's performance:

• Report the test-taker's score as mastery or not.
• Describe the test measures that were used to assess the skills or knowledge.
• Indicate what, if any, remediation options are available for test-takers who do not meet mastery. Typically, remediation means on-the-job supervision and coaching, repeating a

course, or individual study of areas that need improvement, followed by retesting.

• Provide the name of the person the manager can call if he or she has questions about the test.

IS THERE A LEGAL REASON TO ARCHIVE THE TESTS?

Is there a legal reason to save tests? This question is frequently asked during the completion of the CRTD process. We asked Patricia Eyres the question (personal communication, 2002) and here is what she said:

> On the answer to your question: Unlike tax or financial documents, there are no "specific" federal requirements on how long tests and related test papers are kept. Most states don't have specific standards either. Each organization should have its own document-retention policies, and should enforce them consistently. Most employers maintain employment-related documents for the longest period of time that is relevant in their state for discrimination or other employment-related lawsuits. HOWEVER, once an organization knows or reasonably should know that a claim, lawsuit or investigation "may" be forthcoming, it "must" take immediate and effective steps to suspend its regular document disposal policies to retain documentation that "may" be relevant to that claim/investigation/lawsuit. Failure to do so is the big "O" [obstruction of justice]. Deliberate destruction of documents under these circumstances is a felony. Accidental or negligent destruction of documents under these circumstances can result in civil penalties, fines, and severe sanctions in civil litigation. It's a no-no.

In light of this advice, it would seem wise to check with your legal department if you have any questions—and especially if you are developing a high-stakes test.

A FINAL THOUGHT ABOUT TESTING AND TEACHING

In the tension that can exist between the test designer trying to do a job well and the manager who also wants to do well, we feel there is usually common ground to be shared. While a test score often brings with it the baggage of early schooling experience, it need not divide the organization (subordinate versus supervisor, management versus union), but rather create a bridge toward common organizational goals. We think, in the best of all worlds, the common good can be found in understanding and supporting the two roles inherent in the CRT process. This book is about testing, but the tensions and mistrust often surface when the organization overlooks the role of teaching. The CRT process is based on an assumption of mastery learning, and so often the resistance one finds to testing comes when people feel there is an imbalance in roles—too much challenge through good testing but not enough support through good teaching. We think organizations that bring both factors to the table are the ones that will prosper.

PART FOUR

LEGAL ISSUES IN CRITERION-REFERENCED TESTING

CHAPTER SEVENTEEN

CRITERION-REFERENCED TESTING AND EMPLOYMENT SELECTION LAWS[1]

PATRICIA S. EYRES

---

[1] Portions of this chapter were adopted from the first edition of *Criterion-Referenced Test Development*.

WHAT DO WE MEAN BY EMPLOYMENT SELECTION LAWS?

The legal principles of employee selection apply whenever a test-taker is being evaluated by any job-related opportunity measures that could lead to future assignments, skill-building opportunities, and so forth. For legal purposes the term "selection" is not limited to pre-employment selection.

WHO MAY BRING A CLAIM?

Essentially, to bring a claim to Federal courts under *The Uniform Guidelines on Employee Selection* (1978), Title VII of the Civil Rights Act (1964), or the Americans with Disabilities Act (1990) a person must have "standing." Standing is conferred only to those defined as protected groups under the particular act. For example, in the area of equal employment opportunity or employees with disabilities, the courts will not entertain a claim from a person unless he or she falls within a protected group as defined by these regulations. Under Title VII, everyone has standing based on gender, because the law protects both men and women when their gender is used as a basis for an adverse employment action. Nothing prohibits a claim by males, although it might be hard to establish an adverse impact on men.

Likewise, people who are discriminated against by reason of their race or ethnicity have standing under Title VII. This would seem to include anyone whose race or nationality is used as a basis for the employment decision or for whom the employment practice has an adverse impact—even if the person is the majority race in the particular workforce. However, the cases that have created precedent in the area of adverse impact involve people of color, so (practically speaking) the standards have been limited to minorities. It would be awfully difficult for a person from the majority race/ethnicity to prove adverse impact.

In the area of disability, only people who are covered under the Americans with Disabilities Act ("ADA") have standing. This is a big group: anyone who has a "covered disability" and is otherwise qualified to "perform the essential functions of the job, with or without reasonable accommodation" (42. U.S. Code, Section

12101, ADA Title 1, Section 101(9)). Thus, a non-disabled person has no standing under the ADA, even if she has been excluded because of a testing decision.

While the above discussion relates to federal employment laws (and by extension to state anti-discrimination statutes), outside of the discrimination arena, an employee could file a lawsuit under the common law of many states for other alleged wrongs stemming from a testing decision. Potential examples include the following situations:

- A test administered unfairly or inconsistently in violation of an employer's established policies; any employee governed by the policies would have redress.
- A tort claim for defamation or invasion of privacy under state law for untruthful or improper publication of the test results.
- An alleged unfair employment practice in administration of the test that precluded an otherwise qualified employee from participating in the test.

Any state court action under these theories would carry a significant burden of proof for the employee, and the standards would vary from state to state. Unfortunately, for most employers who would be the defendants in such a suit, the "significant burden of proof" may be easier to prove than expected. Given that most tests are developed and delivered in a haphazard manner with little documentation to support the process, and given that there is an established test development process outlined in the testing literature, the *Guidelines,* and the ADA, demonstrating deviation from benchmark testing standards may not be difficult.

Under the ADA, disability is defined as a "substantial limitation of a major life activity." Certainly this is a large group of potential test-takers. However, many states have even broader definitions of disability than does the ADA. For example, under the California Fair Employment and Housing Act, "disability" is defined as "any limitation of a life activity, or a limitation that makes achievement of a life activity more difficult." The California legislature broadened the law in three ways that may affect testing situations. First, they removed the word "substantial" relative to a limitation of a major life activity. Second, they specifically defined "working" as a major life activity (something the ADA does not do). Other states, such as Maine, have followed California's lead and others are expected to do so in the coming years.

Finally, the California legislature established a separate legal claim for damages for an employer's "failure to engage in the interactive process with an employee or applicant with a known disability to determine if a reasonable accommodation is required." This means that in every test situation, an organization within California must undertake an individual examination of whether the employee or applicant requires a reasonable accommodation in the testing process.

A SHORT HISTORY OF THE *UNIFORM GUIDELINES ON EMPLOYEE SELECTION PROCEDURES*

In reality, there is no unified code of laws regarding testing. However, there is a set of guidelines that have come to be viewed with "great deference" by the courts and have come to have the effect of law. These guidelines are the *Uniform Guidelines on Employee Selection Procedures* (*Uniform Guidelines*) adopted by the Equal Opportunity Commission. The *Uniform Guidelines* were an outgrowth of Title VII of the Civil Rights Act of 1964 and were designed to protect individuals from employment discrimination.

The *Uniform Guidelines* provide definitions of discrimination and adverse impact, information on how adverse impact is determined, standards for conducting validity studies, and related validation issues such as the use of alternative selection methods, cooperative validation studies, fairness evidence, and the kinds of documentation of adverse impact and validity evidence the user needs to collect and maintain (Nathan & Cascio, 1986, p. 12).

The *Uniform Guidelines* cover all employers employing fifteen or more employees, labor organizations, and employment agencies. They also cover contractors and subcontractors to the federal government and organizations receiving federal assistance. They apply to all tests, inventories, and procedures used to make employment decisions. Employment decisions include hiring, promotion, referral, disciplinary action, termination, licensing, and certification. The *Guidelines* have significant implications for personnel assessment.

The *Uniform Guidelines* were quickly adopted by federal agencies and thus became the *de facto* standard for evaluating testing decisions that led to discriminatory hiring patterns. Shortly thereafter, in 1979, a set of ninety questions and answers were issued to clarify common questions about the meaning of the *Uniform Guidelines*. An additional three questions and answers were added in 1980 (U.S. Equal Opportunity Commission). These questions did not alter the meaning of the *Uniform Guidelines*, but were purely an attempt to make them more understandable.

Theoretically, the *Uniform Guidelines* are concerned only with issues of discrimination in hiring. In reality, they have served as the focal point for many court decisions on testing, criterion-referenced and otherwise (for example, performance appraisals, assessment centers, and so forth). Because of the legal precedents they have created, an understanding of the *Uniform Guidelines* is the single most useful legal perspective of a test designer. While there has been some controversy about the usefulness of *the Uniform Guidelines* (Ballew, 1987; Smith, 1985), there really is no other single, workable alternative to guide test development from a legal perspective. Any in-house legal counsel will know of the *Uniform Guidelines*, although how thoroughly and in what realm an organization chooses to follow them will depend as much on organizational culture as anything else.

PURPOSE AND SCOPE

The *Uniform Guidelines*, whose full text can be found in Title 29 of the Code of Federal Regulations, Section 1607.16Q, are designed to promote the goal of equal opportunity of employment regardless of "race, color, sex, religion, or national origin" (p. 11,997). They were designed to provide a uniform set of standards for the development of any form of test that would affect employment opportunities, that is, standards that are consistent with generally accepted practices of psychological test construction, and apply to all selection procedures including "the full range of assessment techniques from traditional paper-and-pencil tests, performance tests, training programs, or probationary periods and physical, educational, and work experience requirements through informal or casual interviews and unscored[2] application forms." (p. 11,997)

The *Uniform Guidelines* apply to nearly any organization as a result of a wide range of federal laws and regulations; they cover employee selection for:

> hiring, retention, promotion, transfer, demotion, dismissal or referral. [And apply to the use of] job requirements (physical, education, experience), and evaluation of applicants or candidates on the basis of interviews, performance tests, paper-and-pencil tests, performance in training programs or probationary periods, and any other procedures used to make an employment decision whether administered by the employer or by an employment agency. (p. 11,997)

The *Uniform Guidelines* are designed to encourage the fair treatment of protected groups in our society, but they are not sanction for incompetence. To disproportionately screen out a group is unlawful, unless:

> the process or its component procedures have been validated in accord with the Guidelines, or the user otherwise justifies them in accord with Federal law. (p. 11,997)

In other words, a reliable and valid test will always stand up in court. The systematic design of tests, as *CRTD* has described it, should lead not only to a legally defensible position, but to professional and ethical behavior.

One of the basic principles of the *Uniform Guidelines* is that it is unlawful to use a test **or selection procedure** that creates adverse impact, unless justified by objective business needs. Adverse impact occurs when there is a substantially different rate of selection in hiring, promotion, or other employment decisions that work to the disadvantage of members of a race, sex, ethnic group, or people based on disabilities.

If an assessment process results in adverse impact, the employer is required to eliminate it or justify its continued use.

---

[2]Unscored refers to unrated or unmeasured—for which there is no scoring rubric

The *Guidelines* recommend the following actions when adverse impact occurs:

- Modify the assessment instrument or procedure causing adverse impact.
- Exclude the component procedure causing adverse impact from your assessment program.
- Use an alternative procedure that causes little or no adverse impact, assuming that the alternative procedure is substantially equally valid.
- Use the selection instrument that has adverse impact if the procedure is job-related and valid for selecting better workers, and there is no equally effective procedure available that has less adverse impact.

Note that for the continued use of assessment instruments or procedures that cause adverse impact, courts have required justification by business necessity as well as validity for the specific use.

An assessment procedure that causes adverse impact may continue to be used only if there is evidence that:

- It is job-related for the position in question.
- Its continued use is justified by business necessity.

Demonstrating the business necessity of using a particular assessment instrument involves showing that its use is essential to the safe and efficient operation of the business and there are no alternative procedures available that are substantially equally valid to achieve the business objectives with a lesser adverse impact.

LEGAL CHALLENGES TO TESTING AND THE UNIFORM GUIDELINES

Legal challenges to employment tests have generally centered on arguments that the tests (1) had an adverse or differential effect on minorities and (2) were not demonstrably valid predictors of the employee or candidate's job performance. In 1971, the U.S. Supreme Court ruled that even if an employer did not intend to discriminate by the use of tests, any test that had an adverse effect on women or minority groups would have to be validated as being job-related in order to avoid a finding of illegal discrimination by the employer.

One of the first cases to focus on specific employment testing discrimination, *Myart v. Motorola* (1966), was decided in Illinois. Leon Myart, a black applicant for a job at a Motorola factory, alleged that the hiring practices at Motorola were racially discriminatory in that he had been asked to take a qualifying test that contained questions requiring familiarity with a predominantly white, middle-class culture. A hearing examiner for the Illinois Fair Employment Practices Commission agreed that the test was discriminatory, but the Illinois Supreme Court overturned the examiner's ruling. Nevertheless, news reports on this case alerted the public to the issue of testing and discrimination.

Griggs v. Duke Power Company (1971) drew even greater attention to the issue of testing and discrimination. Until the passage of Title VII, the Duke Power Company openly practiced racial discrimination, employing black workers only in the labor department, where they were paid less than workers in other, all-white departments. After Title VII rendered such practice illegal, the company opened up job opportunities in all departments to blacks, but established a new set of hiring requirements, including a high school diploma and satisfactory scores on two aptitude tests, the Wonderlick Personnel Test and the Bennett Mechanical Aptitude Test. Blacks argued that the tests and the diploma requirements had an adverse effect, were arbitrary, and were not job-related. The trial court ruled that the tests did not violate Title VII because Duke Power did not have a discriminatory intent, but the U.S. Supreme Court disagreed. It stated that Title VII was concerned with consequences of employment practices, not with motivation, thereby drawing an important distinction between intent and effect.

Although *Griggs v. Duke Power Company* left companies free to use tests, it limited the use of tests that have an adverse impact on minorities by its holding that Congress has forbidden giving testing or measuring procedures controlling force[3] unless they are demonstrably a reasonable measure of job performance.

---

[3]Controlling force means the primary basis upon which an individual is selected or excluded.

The *Uniform Guidelines* and the seminal U.S. Supreme Court cases of *Griggs v. Duke Power Company* (1971) and *Albemarle Paper Company v. Moody* (1975) form the foundation for cases involving tests and selection/performance criteria. Essentially, these cases involve a three-step inquiry to determine whether a test creates a discriminatory adverse impact on an identifiable protected group (such as women, the disabled, or minorities).

1. First, the complaining party bears the initial burden of showing that the test at issue selects the protected class at a significantly lower rate than their counterparts. The *Uniform Guidelines* use what is known as the "four-fifths" rule. If the pass rate for the protected group is 80 percent or less than the pass rate of the non-protected group, the test has an adverse impact. Although this may be difficult to prove in practice, it is accomplished through simple statistical evidence. If the plaintiff does not meet this burden, the court never reaches the question of the test's validity.
2. Where the plaintiff meets the burden of showing a statistical disparity, one that disproportionately excludes identifiable groups based on race, gender, or disability, the burden then shifts to the defendant (the employer and/or training department) to validate its test—that is, to show that the test is job-related. When challenged, if you fail to establish that your test is job-related, the test is unlawful.
3. If you establish job-relatedness in a criterion-referenced test, the plaintiff may then attempt to rebut your proof by showing that the particular test in question is not required by business necessity because an alternative selection/evaluation device exists that would meet the employer's objective with less of an adverse impact.

In order to show "job-relatedness" (p. 11,998) you must show that the test is "demonstrably a reasonable measure of job performance" *Griggs v. Duke Power Company* (401 U.S. 421 1971), or "bears a demonstrable relationship to successful performance on the job for which it is used" *Walls v. Mississippi State Department of Public Welfare* (730 F.2d 306, 316 1985). Careful and systematic analysis is required to establish job-relatedness. For example, in

Albemarle Paper Company v. Moody, the employer claimed its test was valid because its retained psychologists found a "significant correlation" between the test scores of current employees and their supervisors' ratings of their performance. The U.S. Supreme Court rejected this defense, specifically finding the test invalid because of the absence of a systematic job analysis (422 U.S. 405, 419 1975).

REASONABLE RECONSIDERATION

Finally, if a candidate for an employment opportunity receives an unacceptable score which disqualifies him or her for an opportunity, the *Uniform Guidelines* require employers to provide "a reasonable opportunity for re-testing and reconsideration." The EEOC's emphasis has been in pre-employment selection, but the principle is equally applicable to employees who are disqualified from further advancement or barred from the worksite because they cannot pass compliance training tests. In these situations, it is helpful to the defense against a discrimination claim to provide reasonable opportunities for re-testing, particularly where the training or testing might be culturally biased or where a reasonable accommodation is appropriate.

IN CONCLUSION

Careful and systematic development of criterion-referenced tests, in accordance with the model in this book, is your best defense against disparate impact claims. Don't avoid the use of written policies. Enhance your ability to defend against discrimination charges by putting employees on clear notice of their rights and responsibilities and by providing identifiable benchmarks of your organization's expectations. Clear, consistently enforced policies tend to limit the suspicion and distrust that lead to discrimination claims.

BALANCING CRTS WITH EMPLOYMENT DISCRIMINATION LAWS

Use of any kind of test has the necessary effect of excluding some candidates or employees from job opportunities. If the test tends to weed out more women, minorities, or other identifiable groups protected under the employment discrimination statutes, it may have an unlawful "adverse impact" on a protected class of candidates for an employment opportunity.

Adverse impact can occur when an employment policy or practice (the test) is neutral by its terms, but it nevertheless has a discriminatory effect on an identifiable protected group. For example, a height requirement of six feet for a law enforcement job is neutral on its face; anyone who meets the minimal requirement can be considered regardless of gender or racial identity. But the neutral standard may fall more harshly on (thereby disproportionately excluding) women and Asian or Latino men who can't meet the minimum standard but who could perform the essential functions of the police officer position.

In the testing arena, a test with neutral scoring requirements and inflexible administration may nevertheless have an adverse impact on test-takers whose first language is not English, or on candidates with a cognitive disability. If the test screens for job-related knowledge rather than replicating a specific job task, the organization must remove obstacles to candidates' success when they have an adverse impact. This can be accomplished through the same types of reasonable accommodations in the test facility as would be available and appropriate on the job. Adverse impact usually occurs in two settings:

- Where an employer has no intent to unlawfully discriminate, but establishes pre-placement procedures which are not related to a business necessity and that have a disproportionately adverse impact on disabled individuals. For example, establishing a "neutral" post-training test that is given in a location that precludes or limits physically disabled applicants, when the disability does not limit the person's ability to perform the essential functions of the job with a reasonable accommodation.
- Setting seemingly neutral substantive qualifications which have an adverse impact on minorities (such as advanced academic degrees or extensive experience beyond that reasonably necessary to perform the job), women (arbitrary height requirements that disproportionately exclude), or disabled

(such as requirements for reading and writing ability to take a test, when reading and writing is not required for the job). In order to prevent adverse impact, these requirements must be job-related.

Each of the above testing situations requires careful analysis, clear objectives, neutral and consistently applied performance standards, and fair administration. In order to meet long-standing and emerging legal requirements, you must develop, administer, and validate tests to assure that they serve a business purpose and do not discriminate. The tests with the most legal risks are:

- Knowledge-based and skill-based tests that appear neutral and objective, but which unfairly exclude minority and disabled workers because they fail to measure job-related skills or are not accurate predictors of success on the job.
- Tests that require a reasonable accommodation for candidates with special needs, such as disabled and multi-lingual persons.

To successfully defend a test, it will be necessary for your organization to establish that it is job-related and consistent with business necessity. However, keep in mind that job-relatedness is a *necessary* but not *sufficient* condition to successfully defend a test. A *necessary* and *sufficient* defense will also require documentation of a systematic test design process and demonstration of accommodation of special needs.

WATCH OUT FOR BLANKET EXCLUSIONS IN THE NAME OF BUSINESS NECESSITY

As noted above, the ADA permits employers to use qualification standards that screen out certain disabled individuals, as long as the standards relate to an essential job function and are justified by "business necessity." However, the courts are increasingly willing to scrutinize whether your organization's policies and practices for "business necessity" go too far.

Employers who apply immutable qualification standards to all employees and applicants in particular positions can no longer do so without running afoul of the ADA when those standards are, in effect, a blanket exclusion of individuals with disabilities. In particular, it is not lawful to use hearing and vision tests to reduce safety risks that potentially screen out disabled employees.

In *Bates v. UPS* (2006), decided on October 10, 2006, the Ninth Circuit Court of Appeals tightened the already stringent standards for employers who use such across-the-board qualification standards in the name of safety. The Ninth Circuit Court of Appeals recently determined that showing justification by "business necessity" requires an individual assessment of each applicant or employee in order to determine whether reasonable accommodation might permit the applicant or employee to safely perform the job. This decision is binding on the states within the Ninth Circuit (Western U.S.) and potential persuasive authority in other jurisdictions.

In *Bates v. UPS*, the Court held that the employer, UPS, violated the ADA by requiring that all of its drivers pass the Department of Transportation's (DOT) hearing test required for drivers of vehicles over 10,000 pounds. UPS sought to use the DOT hearing test for drivers of vehicles under 10,000 pounds to screen for safety risks. The court found that because not all UPS vehicles are rated at over 10,000 pounds, UPS could not rely on the DOT's hearing standard as a qualification for all its drivers. In so ruling, the Court held that UPS failed to satisfy its burden under the business necessity defense, despite evidence showing that hearing-impaired drivers pose an additional safety risk in any vehicle.

The Court determined that an employer cannot automatically rely on a government safety standard beyond its intended scope in order to satisfy the business necessity defense. Rather the employer must show either:

- "substantially all [excluded individuals with disabilities, that is, hearing impaired drivers] present a higher risk of accidents than other non-excluded individuals," or
- "there are no practical criteria for determining which [excluded individuals with disabilities] present a higher risk and which do not."

UPS didn't show persuasively that hearing-impaired people were more likely to have accidents, just as it didn't show that there was no other way to determine whether or not hearing-impaired drivers present a heightened risk.

The court found that, even if UPS was able to present evidence that hearing impaired drivers present a greater safety risk than other drivers, UPS would also have to show that risk was higher than the accident risk already accepted by the company. For example, because UPS had in place policies that allow for drivers who have had accidents to continue as UPS drivers, UPS would have to show that hearing-impaired drivers have an even higher risk than other drivers who have displayed a propensity to have accidents.

ADVERSE IMPACT, THE BOTTOM LINE, AND AFFIRMATIVE ACTION

The *Uniform Guidelines* do not require that validated tests be used in all situations. Such procedures are desirable, but that evidence of validity will need to be provided only when the selection procedure adversely affects those of a given race, gender, or ethnic group. However, mounting case law would appear to support the need for evidence of reliable and valid tests should a hiring decision based on a test be challenged.

ADVERSE IMPACT

Adverse impact is a specific term in the *Uniform Guidelines* and is defined by:

1. A selection rate of less than 80 percent for a given race, gender, or ethnic group in comparison to the highest selection rate in the pool;
2. When a given group is more than 2 percent of the labor force in the labor area.

For example, if the local labor force were 70 percent white and 30 percent black, you would need to maintain records for these two groups. Assume there were 120 applicants for a job, eighty white and forty black, equally divided by gender, and you hired each applicant who passed a required test. If you hired forty-eight whites (60 percent) and twelve blacks (30 percent), you would not be in compliance with the *Uniform Guidelines* because the black hire rate at 30 percent is less than 48 percent (48 percent being 80 percent of the highest selection rate of 60 percent—for whites). Table 17.1 summarizes this situation.

TABLE 17.1. SAMPLE SUMMARY OF ADVERSE IMPACT FIGURES.

Gender/Race		Black	White	Total
Male	Pass	6	24	30
	Fail	14	16	30
Female	Pass	6	24	30
	Fail	14	16	30
Totals	Pass	12	48	60
	Fail	28	32	60
		40	**80**	**120**

In this example, the black selection rate is 30 percent (12/40) while the white selection rate is 60 percent (48/80). Under the definition of adverse impact, any selection rate that is less than 80 percent of the highest rate is discriminatory. Since the highest selection rate for races is for whites at 48/80 or 60 percent, then 80 percent of 60 percent equals 48 percent. Therefore, any hiring rate less than 48 percent will be viewed as racially discriminatory. In this instance, the hiring rate for blacks is 30 percent and would thus be in violation of the *Uniform Guidelines*. There is no difference in the hiring rate by gender, both rates being 30/60 or 50 percent, so no adverse impact based on gender would be indicated.

PRACTICE

Review Table 17.2 to determine whether there is evidence of adverse impact by race or gender. Again, assume that you hire each applicant who passes your test.

TABLE 17.2. SUMMARY OF ADVERSE IMPACT FIGURES FOR PRACTICE.

Gender/Race		Black	White	Hispanic	Total
Male	Pass	20	5	5	30
	Fail	30	10	10	50
Female	Pass	10	10	0	20
	Fail	20	10	10	40
Totals	Pass	30	15	5	50
	Fail	50	20	20	90
		80	**35**	**25**	**140**

FEEDBACK

There is evidence of adverse impact by race, but no evidence of adverse impact by gender; the test discriminates against Hispanics. The impact is determined as follows:

1. Determine the passing ratio for each protected group.
   Passing ratio for blacks   = 30/80 or 38 percent
   Passing ratio for whites   = 15/35 or 43 percent
   Passing ratio for Hispanics   = 5/25 or 20 percent
   Passing ratio for males   = 30/80 or 38 percent
   Passing ratio for females   = 20/60 or 33 percent
   The highest passing ratio by race is 43 percent; by gender, 38 percent.

2. Determine the minimal selection rate for each protected group. To do this for race, you multiply the highest selection rate (in this case, that for whites at 43 percent) by 80 percent or .80.
   a. Selection rate by race = 80 percent of 43 percent
   $$= .80 \times .43$$
   $$= .344 \text{ or } 34 \text{ percent}$$

   At 20 percent, the Hispanic selection rate is below the minimal selection rate of 34 percent; therefore, adverse impact is indicated. At 38 percent, the black selection rate is above the minimal selection rate required and, therefore, would not be seen as evidence of adverse impact.

3. To determine the minimal selection rate for gender, you multiply the highest selection rate (in this case, that for males at 38 percent) by 80 percent or .80.
  b. Selection rate by gender = 80 percent of 38 percent
$$= .80 \times .38$$
$$= .304 \text{ or } 30 \text{ percent}$$
The selection rate for females at 33 percent is above the minimal selection rate of 30 percent and would not be seen as evidence of adverse impact.

The Civil Rights Act of 1991, which amended Title VII of the Civil Rights Act of 1964 (42 U.S. Code, Section 703) prohibits adjusted scoring, the use of different cut-off scores for different groups of employees, or other alteration of employment-related tests results based on race, color, national origin, religion or gender. This practice was called "race norming" or "within-group scoring" and was historically used to ensure a minimum number of minority job applicants and employees.

With the ban on differential adjusted scoring, employers are free to select the most capable candidate, provided the person meets the minimum qualifications for the job. However, the 1991 amendments clearly provide that employers may be liable for damages if their selections result in adverse impact through disproportionately greater negative impact on any one protected group. This puts a premium on detailed job analysis and criterion-referenced testing, to assure that a broad cross-section of qualified candidates are accorded equal opportunities to demonstrate their abilities to perform job-related tasks. In turn, this should lead to selection of a representative workforce based on race, nationality, and gender.

THE BOTTOM LINE

The "bottom line" is a specific term in the *Uniform Guidelines* that refers to the principle that federal agencies will not seek enforcement actions against an organization provided that the total selection procedure does not have adverse impact, that is, a selection differential exceeding 80 percent of the highest protected group's rate. The 80 percent level is a "rule of thumb" and:

> is not intended as a legal definition, but is a practical means of keeping the attention of the enforcement agencies on serious discrepancies in rates of hiring, promotion, and other selection decisions. (*Uniform Guidelines*, p. 11,998)

However, this does not necessarily mean that the organization will not be challenged, even if the average selection rate of all tests meets the 80 percent rule. In *Connecticut v. Teal* (cited in Smith, 1985, p. 23) the Supreme Court found that, while a particular company's total bottom line was acceptable, the results of a specific test that had an adverse impact on blacks was discriminatory. Nor is the bottom line limited only to the 80 percent rule; the courts have often required evidence of statistical significance in addition to the differential selection rates among protected groups.

Adverse impact, the 80 percent rule, is best measured against the "total selection process" for a given job, that is, all steps leading to the final choice of an applicant for a given job. If there are a series of tests—medical, psychological, etc.—used to make the final hiring decision, only the final outcome for the hiring decision need be determined and compared to 80 percent. Adverse impact does not have to be calculated for each step along the way. Nor does adverse impact have to be determined if the number of selections is too small to warrant. (The definition of "too small" is not provided in the *Uniform Guidelines*, although they do note that the regulations apply to most organizations with more than fifteen employees for more than twenty weeks a year.) However, records on employment decisions must be kept on

> groups for which there is extensive evidence of continuing discriminatory practices. ... For groups for which records are not required, the person(s) complaining may obtain information from the employer or others (voluntarily or through legal process) to show that adverse impact has taken place. (*Uniform Guidelines*, p. 12,000)

The specific collection of adverse impact data is a matter of organizational policy that should be developed by the legal department. There are a number of tough questions that you as an instructional designer or test developer are probably not in a position to resolve, but can at least raise with the appropriate division, for example:

- Are data to be collected for each course? Promotion? New hires?
- Who are the protected groups for whom the data are to be collected? Blacks, Whites, Hispanics, American Indians, Asian/ Pacific Islanders?
- What are the boundaries of the applicant pool from which the employer draws candidates, such as the geographic region, representative academic institutions or trade/industry organizations?
- What is the proportion of these groups in the labor force?
- While an annual summary of hiring decisions is usually required by the EEOC, should they choose to explore an organization's procedures for employee selection, how often should the data be compiled, for example, quarterly, semi-annually, yearly?
- Who will be responsible for collecting the data and reporting it?

AFFIRMATIVE ACTION

The *Uniform Guidelines* are reasonably straightforward about their relationship to affirmative action policies. They:

> encourage the development and effective implementation of affirmative action plans or programs in two ways. First, in determining whether to institute action against a user on the basis of a selection procedure which has adverse impact and which has not been validated ...(and) Second ... do not preclude the use of selection procedures, consistent with Federal law, which assist in the achievement of affirmative action objectives (*Uniform Guidelines*, Section 17, p. 12,001).

The *Uniform Guidelines* (Section 6A) allow the use of "lawful" alternative selection procedures that eliminate adverse impact if the employer does not demonstrate the validity of the initial testing process, but do "not impose a duty to adopt a

hiring procedure that maximizes hiring of minority employees"
(p. 12,004). The search for alternatives is required only during
the "validity study" (Smith, 1985) for the test, that is, during the
job analysis, planning, and test validation stages. Smith (1985)
notes that:

> the search for alternatives (testing strategies) is required only
> during the course of a validity study, and there need be only a rea-
> sonable investigation ... reasonable, in most circumstances [is] a
> search of the published literature. Investigation of the unpublished
> literature is required only when adverse impact is high and valid-
> ity is low. ... The legal standard of *Moody,* under which a plaintiff
> can prove discrimination by showing that an alternative serving
> the employer's legitimate business needs but with lesser adverse
> impact exists, is not changed by the guidelines of the questions
> and answers. (p. 23)

Section II of the *Uniform Guidelines,* however, concludes with
the following:

> Nothing in Section 6A should be interpreted as discouraging the
> use of properly validated selection procedures, but Federal equal
> employment opportunity law does not require validity studies to be
> conducted unless there is adverse impact. (p. 12,001)

There may be a temptation by some to review this final passage
and conclude that the easiest way out is to set the cut-off score low
enough that nearly all applicants pass the test. However, Cascio,
Alexander, and Barrett (1988) observed:

> The courts have recognized this to be an exercise in futility; if
> an organization is unable to weed out those individuals who are
> minimally qualified, what possible justification is there for the use
> of a test in the first place? In fact, one could argue that selectees
> should be drawn at random from those who score above the cut-off
> score. ... Setting a very low cut-off score (one that might be called
> "arbitrarily low," or as one court said, "a remarkably humble level,"
> since a person could pass the test by responding randomly) tends,
> in the opinion of the court, to destroy the credibility of the entire
> testing process. (pp. 6–7)

RECORD-KEEPING OF ADVERSE IMPACT AND JOB-RELATEDNESS OF TESTS

The *Uniform Guidelines* and Subsequent Regulations 2 require that all employers maintain a record of their employment-related activities, including statistics related to testing and adverse impact. Filing and record-keeping requirements for large employers (those with over one hundred employees) are generally more extensive than those for employers with one hundred or fewer employees. To learn more about the specific requirements, refer to EEOC regulations on record-keeping and reporting requirements under Title VII, and the ADA, 29 CFR part 1602, and the *Uniform Guidelines*.

ACCOMMODATING TEST-TAKERS WITH SPECIAL NEEDS

Tests should evaluate the abilities of your employees to perform the tasks of the job, not disabilities or disorders. The Americans with Disabilities Act (ADA) requires you to conduct tests in a place and manner accessible to persons with disabilities. Candidates with impaired sensory, motor, or speaking skills should be offered modified tests or appropriate auxiliary aids to accommodate their disabilities, such as taped examinations, interpreters, and Braille or large-print exams. In order to meet these legal requirements, you are justified in asking for advance notice of the accommodations required and may also request proof of the participant's special needs.

When your company hires a qualified disabled employee and provides a reasonable accommodation to perform an essential job function, that employee must also receive appropriate reasonable accommodations for on-the-job and classroom training, and for testing/evaluation following the training. For example, a dyslexic candidate who will not be required to read on the job, or who will be accommodated on the job, cannot be forced to take a pen-and-paper "test" following training without a similar reasonable accommodation. To so require would create a disparate impact on learning disabled employees, thereby denying an equal employment opportunity. This is true even if the testing policy is facially neutral and applied to all candidates. The ADA's requirement for a reasonable accommodation would apply.

Reasonable accommodation is defined as a change in the job application and selection process, a change in the work environment or the manner in which the work is performed, that enables a qualified person with a disability to enjoy equal employment opportunities. Under this Act, qualified individuals with disabilities must be provided reasonable accommodation so they can perform the essential job functions, as long as this does not create undue hardship to the employer.

Undue hardship is defined as significant difficulty or additional expense and is determined based on a number of factors. Some factors that are considered are the nature and net cost of the accommodation, the financial resources of the facility, the number employed at the facility, the effect on resources and operations, the overall financial resources of the entire organization, and the fiscal relationship of the facility with the organization. An accommodation that is possible for a large organization may pose an undue hardship for a small organization.

In designing reasonable accommodations, you should first determine the reason for the test. Once you know the objective for measuring "successful performance" on the test, you can evaluate alternatives for measuring the knowledge, skill, or abilities of the disabled test-taker.

Candidates are tested for several reasons. First, tests are used as a teaching tool during the training itself. The facilitator may use quizzes or other evaluation vehicles to assess the level of knowledge of participants at the outset of the training. In this sense, the test becomes part of the design process, to assure that the training addresses the needs of the group and individual participants. In order assure that the training meets the needs of all participants, including the disabled, the test should be designed to measure objective skills that are reasonably related to success in the training. Disabled participants are entitled to reasonable accommodations to allow them to achieve the benefits of tests as a teaching tool.

Second, organizations use evaluation mechanisms to determine whether participants have retained information presented during a training program or on-the-job instruction and can apply the information to their job tasks. In these situations, the test-taker is rarely competing with other employees. Nevertheless, the results of the test may be used to determine whether candidates are capable of being placed into certain jobs. If the test is measuring job knowledge—rather than replicating a skill the employee must perform on the job—a reasonable accommodation may be required. If disabled participants are unable to complete the test, but could perform effectively on the job, the test may violate the ADA unless a reasonable accommodation is provided. This is particularly so in the safety area, where employers are required by occupational safety laws to prevent employees from working in an environment where they cannot do so safely. Thus, the disabled employee who cannot pass or complete the test itself—but could perform safely—must be provided with an alternative testing method to ascertain his retention and understanding of the safety training.

Third, testing assures that employees can perform specific skills, both hard skills (specific job tasks) and soft skills (analysis, application of principles). A qualified disabled employee is one who can perform the essential functions of the job, with or without a reasonable accommodation. Although this type of test is also not a "competitive" process per se, disabled participants do not have a truly equal opportunity unless they are provided with the same level of reasonable accommodation that would be appropriate to assist them in performing the essential functions of the job.

Finally, tests are administered to narrow the field of qualified candidates for limited opportunities, which is a competitive process. Candidates are excluded based on competitive rankings. If an applicant can prove that the testing was not administered equitably for all applicants, it may result in an ADA violation. (Adapted from Eyres, 1998, pp. 167–169.)

In general, it is the responsibility of the individual with a disability to inform her employer that an accommodation is needed. However, you may ask for advance notice of accommodations required, for the hiring process only, so that you may adjust your testing program or facilities appropriately. When the need for accommodation is not obvious, you may request reasonable documentation of the applicant's disability and functional limitations for which he or she needs an accommodation.

TESTING, ASSESSMENT, AND EVALUATION FOR DISABLED CANDIDATES

Tests and evaluation of candidates should mirror the tasks those candidates will be expected to perform on the job. If the candidate cannot perform an essential function of the job safely and effectively, she is *not* a qualified disabled employee. Tests are only unlawful in this context if they measure marginal, rather than essential functions, or if they set performance standards artificially high as a "pretext" to exclude disabled employees.

An obligation to reasonably accommodate a disabled test-taker's needs may include any of the following:

- Making existing facilities accessible for the test.
- Acquisition or modification of equipment or devices for the test.
- Appropriate adjustment or modification of policies, examinations, and test materials.
- Providing qualified readers and interpreters (for sight or hearing impaired test-takers).

Several types of disabilities covered under the ADA are affected by tests:

- Learning disabilities, such as dyslexia and attention deficit disorder, which impact the ability to perform effectively in a timed testing situation;
- Sensory impairments, primarily sight and hearing, which affect the ability to read test questions and hear the instructions;
- Motor coordination and dexterity challenges, which impact the ability to sit, use a writing implement, or respond on a computer-based test;
- Medical conditions, such as diabetes, epilepsy, asthma, or conditions triggered by environmental conditions, which may require breaks during lengthy test situations.

The following checklist may be used to determine when and how to consider reasonable accommodations in the testing process to assure an equal employment opportunity.

General Issues for All Disabilities

1. Prepare in advance for special testing procedures. If possible, inform participants at the time of enrollment that there will be a test, and fully describe what is required to pass, and how performance will be measured. If this is not feasible, make the announcement at the earliest possible time after training commences.
2. Ask participants to advise you of any special requirements they may have to take the test, so that you have time to arrange for access, facilities, and related physical layout issues.
3. All tests should measure objective, job-related knowledge, tasks, and skills. This will assure that all participants, disabled and otherwise, are being measured on the appropriate standards that will predict their success on the actual job.
4. Tests should use a variety of formats, including true/false, multiple-choice, and narrative. With computer-based tests, strive for a variety of interactive methods to test multiple skills.
5. Provide separate instructions for each type of question.

Learning Disabilities

1. Remember that if the employee is not going to be required to read, analyze, synthesize information, recall information, and respond on the job within the same time parameters as the test vehicle, you are not replicating on-the-job performance. In these situations, a reasonable accommodation to take the test or demonstrate knowledge/skill should be considered.
2. Consider verbal tests, where appropriate, to assure that reading difficulties do not adversely affect the candidate.
3. If you know in advance that additional time will be needed for a learning disabled candidate, establish the ground rules in advance. While it is not necessary—and may be inappropriate—to advise other employees why the disabled employee is being given additional time, let them know that a reasonable accommodation has been requested and granted.
4. Make every effort to remove distractions and pressure from the test room.
5. If you don't know the need in advance, and the participant requests additional time or it becomes obvious during the test

that more time is needed, discreetly inquire how much time is needed.

6. Remember that it is not necessary to reduce the performance standards or to adjust the passing score as a reasonable accommodation. Learning disabled employees are not illiterate or dumb, and a reasonable accommodation is only designed to allow them to meet the performance standards. Set your standards as high as possible, and then design procedures to meet the timing needs of the candidate, always maintaining the objective of measuring proficiency or anticipated success on particular jobs.

- If the test-taker cannot read, but can write well, provide the test questions in a pre-recorded format on a cassette tape or audio file, or supply a monitor to read the questions during the test. If a monitor is used, place the test-taker in the room so that distractions to other participants are minimal.
- Conversely, if the learning disability precludes writing clearly, allow the participant to respond to the questions verbally or to record answers onto a cassette for later transcription.

7. In some situations, take-home tests may be an accommodation. If the instructor is not required to monitor the test, this can be an option. You can take steps to provide a different test from the other participants, but you should rely on the integrity of the accommodated candidate.

8. For math tests, allow calculators when possible. Design the test to reveal both the conceptual skills and the correct answers.

Visual Impairments

1. Discuss with the test-taker how to best test his or her job knowledge or skill.
2. If the visually impaired candidate or applicant is accustomed to a reasonable accommodation on the job, such as a magnifying instrument, Braille materials, or a reader, permit the same accommodation in the testing situation.
3. Consider verbal tests or pre-recorded questions and answers.

4. If other participants are permitted access to materials during the test (the standard "open book/open note" format), strive to replicate that benefit for the visually challenged participant.

Hearing Impairments

1. Provide all instructions in writing, preferably transcribed exactly as those presented orally. If this is impossible, or if the test is interactive, consider an interpreter who can translate into American Sign Language.
2. If an interpreter is used, take steps to minimize distractions to other participants.
3. Consider providing additional time for the test-taker to demonstrate proficiency with job tasks.

Mobility Impairments

1. If the candidate has trouble writing, consider oral tests or tape-recorded questions and answers.
2. If physical agility is required, make sure the test reflects a job-related function, which is an essential function of the job. If the function is marginal to the job, and the candidate cannot perform, this cannot be used to exclude him/her from the opportunity, because it violates the ADA.
3. If the candidate will be using a reasonable accommodation on the job to perform physical tasks, allow the same accommodation in the test setting. This may require testing in the job environment rather than in the test room.
4. Consult with the candidate in advance, or at the earliest time, to determine what type of accommodation will be helpful.

Medical Issues

1. Always consult with the test-taker regarding his or her needs within the physical facility and the administration of the test. If the test is lengthy, a diabetic may need to have food or a beverage in the room, or take a break to test blood sugar levels. If so, provide an opportunity to extend the test by the amount of time needed for breaks.
2. If the conditions are an issue for candidates with extreme allergies or other conditions affected by the test environment,

make the determination of an alternative test site in advance. If the need for an accommodation does not become apparent until the test is under way, be flexible and prepared to make adjustments as needed. The tester may need to be excused if she becomes ill during the test, and an alternative time and location set to repeat the test. Again, while you cannot completely eliminate the potential for abuse, you should rely on the integrity of the candidate and monitor with appropriate observations and medical certifications, where necessary (Eyres, 1998, pp. 167–171).

TEST VALIDATION CRITERIA: GENERAL GUIDELINES

Validation techniques discussed in the *Uniform Guidelines* have more to do with psychometric testing procedures than with legal analyses. However, the threshold legal question will be whether the test in fact measures what it is supposed to measure. The *Uniform Guidelines* adopted standards of validity utilized by the American Psychological Association in its *1974 Standards for Education and Psychological Tests*. But of these standards, only content (Does the test match the job?) and criterion (Does the test sort known masters and non-masters?) would be appropriate for CRTs. *If a test does have an adverse impact on any protected group, it will require validation in order to be defensible to legal challenge.*

Validation of the test should be conducted before the test is implemented. If you determine that a test does have an adverse impact without the evidence of validity, and you continue to use the test

until the procedure is challenged, (users) increase the risk that they will be found to be engaged in discriminatory practices and will be liable for back pay, awards, plaintiff's attorney's fees, loss of Federal contracts, subcontracts or grants, and the like. Validation studies begun on the eve of litigation have seldom been found to be adequate. (*Uniform Guidelines*, p. 12,002)

In conducting a validity study, you should also attend to a number of other issues.

- A validity study must not only be job-specific, but also may need to be location-specific. In other words, the *Uniform Guidelines* do not assume that a study conducted in one location, for example, New York City, will be a fair test for workers in another location, for example, Carbondale, Illinois. To be safe, the validity study should be conducted as a joint venture with other members of the organization who will be affected by the results of the test. Paraphrasing the *Uniform Guidelines,*

  > Results from one site may be used elsewhere: (1) if the original study has been shown to be valid, (2) the job(s) are closely matched, (3) there is evidence of fairness in the original study, (4) any variables that might affect fair use in the new location have been considered. (p. 12,006)

- The same method for determining validity does not have to be used for all parts of a test.

  > For example, where a selection process includes both a physical performance test and an interview, the physical test might be supported on the basis of content validity, and the interview on the basis of a criterion-related (concurrent validity) study. (*Uniform Guidelines*, p. 12,003)

- Users do not have to develop the test themselves. If another test will meet all standards, then it is appropriate to use that test. However, in the event of a challenge, proof will rest with the organization using the test, even if a test manual claims validity for the test.
- Establishing the validity of the test is a necessary but not sufficient step in the selection process. The test in use must be the test as validated.

  > For example, if a research study shows only that, at a given passing score the test satisfactorily screens out probable failures, the study would not justify the use of substantially different passing scores, or of a ranked list of those who passed. (*Uniform Guidelines*, p. 12,003)

While the choice of a validation technique can be made based on its appropriateness for the type of selection and its technical and administrative feasibility, the content for the test should be drawn only from knowledge, skills, or abilities associated with the job and should not test for behaviors that an employee "will be expected to learn on the job" (*Guidelines*, p. 12,004).

> The phrase "on the job" is intended to apply to training which occurs after hiring, promotion, or transfer. However, if an ability, such as a language, takes a substantial length of time to learn, is required for successful job performance, and is not taught in advance, a test for that ability may be supported on a content validity basis. (*Guidelines*, p. 12,007)

Therefore, while the test should not cover skills to be learned after the job has been taken, in some circumstances the test can appropriately assess abilities that a candidate must bring to the job.

Ranking of performers on a test is acceptable only if there is a demonstrated statistical relationship between the rank and levels of performance, that is, ranking must rest on an inference that higher scores on the procedure are related to better job performance.

- For example, for a particular warehouse worker job, the job analysis may show that lifting a fifty-pound object is essential, but the job analysis does not show that lifting heavier objects is essential or would result in significantly better job performance. In this case a test of ability to lift fifty pounds could be justified on a content validity basis for a pass/fail determination. However, ranking of candidates based on relative amount of weight that can be lifted would be inappropriate.
- On the other hand, in the case of a person to be hired for a typing pool, the job analysis may show that the job consists almost entirely of typing from manuscript and that productivity can be measured directly in terms of finished copy. For such a job, typing constitutes not only a critical behavior, but it constitutes most of the job. A higher score on a test that measured words per minute typed, with adjustments for errors, would therefore be likely to predict better job performance than a significantly lower score. Ranking or grouping based on such a typing test would therefore be appropriate under the *Uniform Guidelines* (p. 12,005).

TEST VALIDATION: A STEP-BY-STEP GUIDE

1. OBTAIN PROFESSIONAL GUIDANCE

To ensure both the effectiveness and legality of post-training tests, consider retaining competent professionals, whether they are outside consultants or a part of your organization, to design and administer tests. Expertise needed includes:

- *Test development expertise.* Professionally competent staff or consultants should develop and supervise the tests. This training does not require a degree in psychometrics or a related field but may rely on academic training or related experience.
- *Content expertise.* The degree and kind of expertise needed will vary with the complexity and level of the contemplated tests. Sometimes expert knowledge comes from conferences or interviews with those directly associated with the job, such as candidates, current employees, and supervisors. At other times, experts from specific professional fields might be used.
- *Legal expertise.* Since the *Uniform Guidelines* were drawn up in consultation with professional psychological associations and were highly influenced by APA standards, it is quite likely that a competent testing psychologist will be familiar with the requirements of the *Uniform Guidelines.* It is helpful, however, to have legal guidance if you are using a test for the first time or you have a significant percentage of multi-national, multi-lingual, or multi-abled test-takers. A legal expert should be highly knowledgeable about litigation in the field of testing and the business goals.

The *Uniform Guidelines* encourage, but do not require, professional supervision of an employment testing program. They note, however, that professional supervision will not be considered a substitute for documented evidence of validity.

2. SELECT A LEGALLY ACCEPTABLE VALIDATION STRATEGY FOR YOUR PARTICULAR TEST

Content and criterion validation approaches are currently accepted for demonstrating the validity of using a test to make an employment decision, including post-training placement decisions. Although treated as separate approaches in the *Uniform Guidelines,* both approaches are closely linked.

While both approaches to validity are considered substantively valid, the EEOC's *Uniform Guidelines* require only that one be used when showing the job-relatedness of a test that would otherwise violate Title VII.

To meet EEOC requirements, an employer using a test can select any validation method that is appropriate for the type of test, the job, and the employment situation and is technically or administratively feasible.

3. UNDERSTAND AND EMPLOY STANDARDS FOR CONTENT-VALID TESTS

The *Uniform Guidelines* impose specific standards on content-valid testing. The standards are summarized in the following checklist:

Job Analysis

- A content validity study must include an analysis of the important work behaviors required for successful job performance.
- The analysis must include an assessment of the relative importance of work behaviors and/or job skills.
- Relevant work products must be considered and built into the test.
- If work behaviors or job skills are not observable, the job analysis should include those aspects of the behaviors that can be observed, as well as the observed work product.

For Tests Measuring Knowledge, Skill, or Ability

- The test should measure and be a representative sample of the knowledge, skill, or ability.
- The knowledge, skill, or ability should be used in and be a necessary prerequisite to performance of critical or important work behavior.
- The test should either closely approximate an observable work behavior, or its product should closely approximate an observable work product.

- There must be a defined, well-recognized body of information applicable to the job.
- Knowledge of the information must be a prerequisite to the performance of required work behaviors.
- The test should fairly sample the information that is actually used by the employee on the job, so that the level of difficulty of the test items should correspond to the level of difficulty of the knowledge as used in the work behavior.

For Tests Purporting to Sample a Work Behavior or to Provide a Sample of a Work Product

- The manner and setting of the test and its level and complexity should closely approximate the work situation.
- The closer the content and the context of the test are to work samples or work behaviors, the stronger the basis for showing content validity.

4. EVALUATE THE OVERALL TEST CIRCUMSTANCES TO ASSURE EQUALITY OF OPPORTUNITY

Consider how the test will be used. Test evaluation must take into account how the test will be used. A professional job analysis should be performed to identify the tasks involved in the job and the knowledge, skills, abilities and other characteristics required.

Have job experts take the test. An employer proposing to adopt a test should administer the test to in-house experts who are familiar with the job, and weigh their opinions carefully.

Consider test reliability. Reliability refers to the consistency, the dependability, or the repeatability of test results. A test that does not measure abilities consistently has little or no value. Reliability measures that were discussed in previous chapters will provide more evidence of a test's worthwhileness in addition to the basics of content validity.

Consider fairness. The ideal test should not only be fair to all groups and individuals, but should also appear fair, so that test-takers will accept the test and not feel uncomfortable taking it. A test is considered fair if, among other things, it has clear rules for administration and scoring so that results may fairly be compared with each other; it is free of cultural, racial, or gender stereotypes and does not emphasize one culture over another; and it does not eliminate people with a disability, such as weak language skills or blindness, from a wide spectrum of jobs that they are capable of performing well.

Weigh potential adverse impact. If minorities, women, persons over forty, or disabled candidates tend to do poorly on a test, the employer has an obligation under equal employment opportunity laws to look for an alternative selection procedure that will do a comparable job of selecting capable employees, but will have less adverse impact.

Consider practicality. Practical considerations, including cost, ease of administration, special equipment needed, and ease of scoring, are always factors in deciding which test to use. For example, extremely long tests are difficult for both the test-taker and the test administrator, even though they usually are more reliable than extremely short tests.

Evaluate the test developer. An employer should obtain the test author's résumé and list of publications if considering using outside expertise.

KEYS TO MAINTAINING EFFECTIVE AND LEGALLY DEFENSIBLE DOCUMENTATION

WHY DOCUMENT?

Businesses lose lawsuits when their documents are turned against them in the courtroom. The outcome of civil lawsuits is increasingly affected by evidence from business records generated over years, even decades. Damage awards have soared, some due to explosive content of business communications or gaps in documentation.

Many managers and test developers today are slowly becoming aware of the legal pitfalls inherent in generating written communications and business records—ranging from informal internal memos and e-mail to draft test instruments to data collection for test validation studies—which may later be used in litigation against the company. Worse yet, those who are informed are often pressured into over-documenting, avoiding written communications, or using ambiguous language due to fear of lawsuits.

Test developers and administrators must be able to generate and use documentation in the normal course of business without compromising sound business practices. This includes knowing when and how to document their actions with data collection and analyses, implementation plans, external communications, and internal correspondence without unnecessary fear of putting anything in writing.

WHAT IS DOCUMENTATION?

Documentation is a written record of an event, discussion, or observation by one or more individuals. Most organizations rely on documentation to record their activities and those of their employees. Any written information, whether formally or informally generated, can be considered documentary evidence if it is pertinent to a legal action or a regulatory proceeding. This applies to Occupational Safety and Health Administration (OSHA) inspections, investigations, and enforcement proceedings, as well as criminal prosecutions for violation of statutes and/or civil lawsuits for damages by an injured person.

WHY IS DOCUMENTATION AN ALLY IN DEFENDING AGAINST CLAIMS?

A written record of events is the best evidence of what occurred. Many times in litigation—particularly in civil lawsuits for damages arising out of a workplace accident—the events leading up to the alleged unlawful actions took place months or years before the evidence is actually presented in court. For example, in a lawsuit alleging failure to adequately train a worker whose error caused the accident, the training may have occurred long before the accident. Assuming the worker claims he was not trained, the burden shifts to the employer to establish that the training did occur. Will a manager remember exactly when this particular employee was trained, what content areas were included in the training, how the employee grasped the material, and other important points?

Further, suppose the employee's primary language is not English. Will the manager or trainer remember what steps were taken to assure that the employee understood the training, particularly the information regarding the hazards he would face on the job? These are critical elements that will be at issue in either an OSHA inspection or a civil lawsuit following a workplace accident.

Leaving this vital information to human memory is risky. Moreover, the manager or trainer who did the training may have retired or moved to another area. In the absence of a written record of the training that took place, the employer's defense is significantly weakened. Leaving this vital information to human memory is risky. Moreover, the individual who designed or scored the test may have moved to another area or retired.

How Is Documentation Used?

Compliance Documentation

The *Uniform Guidelines* provide specific requirements for documenting test development and administration. The primary purpose for maintaining documentation of training and other aspects of compliance is to present it to an inspector at the time of a regulatory visit to your place of employment. Complete, legible, concise, and easy-to-understand documentation provides the best opportunity to avoid costly enforcement proceedings.

- *Records concerning impact.* Each user should maintain and have available for inspection records or other information that will disclose the impact that its tests and other selection procedures have on employment opportunities of persons by identifiable race, gender, or ethnic group in order to determine compliance with these guidelines. Where there are large numbers of applicants and procedures are administered frequently, such information may be retained on a sample basis, provided that the sample is appropriate in terms of the applicant population and adequate in size.
- *Applicable race, gender, and ethnic groups for record-keeping.* The records called for are to be maintained by gender, and the following races and ethnic groups: blacks (Negroes), American Indians (including Alaskan Natives), Asians (including Pacific Islanders), Hispanic (including persons of Mexican, Puerto Rican, Cuban, Central or South American, or other Spanish

origin or culture regardless of race), whites (Caucasians) other than Hispanic, and totals. The race, gender, and ethnic classifications called for by this section are consistent with the Equal Employment Opportunity Standard Form 100, Employer Information Report EEO-1 series of reports. The user should adopt safeguards to ensure that the records required by this paragraph are used for appropriate purposes, such as determining adverse impact or (where required) for developing and monitoring affirmative action programs, and that such records are not used improperly.

- *Documentation of validation studies.* Section 15 of the *Uniform Guidelines* sets forth in great detail the documentation of impact validity evidence required for users of selection procedures. For criterion-related (concurrent) validity studies, organizations should include specific information reflecting at least the following:
  - Users, locations, and dates of the study.
  - An explicit definition of the reason the study was conducted (including data about the potential disparate impact).
  - Job analyses based on specific performance-based criteria and predictors for success in the job or group of jobs.
  - Criterion measures for selection of candidates, including objective and/or subjective scoring, a full description of all criteria on which data were collected, and means by which they were observed, recorded, evaluated, and quantified.
  - If rating forms were used, all documentation reflecting the forms and instructions for raters.
  - Documents reflecting all steps taken to ensure that criterion measures are free from factors that would exclude individuals from opportunities by altering their scores on a non-job-related basis.

Test developers and those conducting validity studies should consult the *Uniform Guidelines* for more specific documentation requirements, or obtain professional advice. [*Uniform Guidelines,* 29 C.F.R. Section 15A(1)-(12).]

Documentation to Avoid Regulatory Penalties or Lawsuits

Many times, a lawsuit can be avoided by demonstrating to the potential adverse party that the employer's position will be unbeatable. In these instances, the documentation (or a portion of it) can be turned over to the adverse party in advance of any proceedings. This is valuable if it prevents the litigation. However, legal counsel should always be consulted—first, because some of the documentation may be privileged and should not be produced, and second, because this is usually a strategic issue that may affect any litigation that is filed.

Use of Documentation in Court

In most judicial proceedings, written documentation is not introduced by itself. Rather, oral testimony about an event will be given. Testimony will include that of witnesses from the adverse parties (for example, an injured employee and a manager from the employer organization) and from independent witnesses with no stake in the litigation. The trier of fact—judge, jury, arbitration panel, or others—will be asked to weigh the testimony and reach a determination.

Very often, memories of the witnesses about the same events will differ substantially. This is usually the result of human memory frailties or honest mis-recollection. However, sometimes witnesses attempt to testify about personal memory when in fact they did not actually observe or participate in the events. Sometimes, witnesses may even be untruthful.

Documentation to Refresh Memory

When recollections vary, the trier of fact must determine whom to believe. This is the crucial issue of credibility. Many times, a witness whose memory is imprecise can still be very credible if his or her memory is refreshed by reviewing documents he or she personally prepared closer to the time of the original events. This documentation is used to refresh memory.

Documentation to Attack Credibility

Documentation may also be used to discredit the credibility of a witness. Suppose an injured employee testifies that he was never trained on a hazard of his job and, as a result of that lack of training, he failed a test that kept him out of a job classification with higher pay and advancement opportunities. Suppose further that, under questioning, the employee contends he specifically remembers that he was not at work the day training took place, and was never offered an alternative opportunity. But his employer has documentation reflecting the date, location, and substance of this employee's training. When confronted with the documentation, the employee's credibility as a witness may be adversely affected.

Likewise, if the employee has kept documentation and the employer has not, the manager testifying for the employer may have diminished credibility. This may affect the outcome of the proceeding.

Disclosure and Production of Documentation

In litigation, organizations and individuals must comply with broad requirements for identification, disclosure, and production of relevant documents. These business records are subject to a very broad relevancy standard, for example, all records—tangible or in electronic form—that are relevant to the subject matter of the lawsuit or calculated to lead to the discovery of admissible evidence or witnesses. This means production of the documents that prove or disprove an issue in contention, and those that may reveal the identity of another document or the name of an additional witness.

In extreme situations, the alteration or destruction of such business documents is a felony; it's called "obstruction of justice." At least one former executive of Texaco Corporation was indicted by a New York grand jury for obstruction of justice in connection with the willful destruction of documents relevant to a pending race discrimination class action. Obstruction of justice occurs when documentation is destroyed or withheld in contemplation of or after the filing of litigation. Essentially, it is a fraud against the court system. Thus, when no litigation is pending or contemplated, even willful tampering with documentation may not be criminal. But it is never, never appropriate.

Even when not criminal obstruction, destroying documents can lead to adverse consequences in litigation. Even in the absence of civil penalties and criminal sanctions, destruction of documents, tampering with evidence, or fabricating documentation is improper. The following guidelines should be followed in connection with the handling of documentation to assure that you and your organization balance legal and ethical obligations:

- Fully understand your company's records retention policies. Follow those policies consistently. Violation of company policy may give rise to disciplinary action.
- Notify all appropriate company representatives of the obligation to identify and take reasonable steps to preserve potentially relevant documents.
- Consultants and independent speakers should develop a records retention policy you can consistently enforce. Don't make it too cumbersome. Establish objective indicia regarding which documents you keep, and those you do not. The policy should be business related, but still allow you to justify in later litigation why you did not retain a particular item. This limits the inference that you destroyed something not helpful to your position.
- Understand the range of documents that may become "documentation" in litigation. A few examples:
  - tests and criterion-referenced validation studies
  - raw data used for validation studies
  - qualification standards, job descriptions, and selection criteria for test developers and/or raters
  - materials relating to the analyses and activities undertaken during test development
- Maintain consistent procedures for developing and recording relevant information in your documentation.
- Do not back-date, fabricate, destroy, or in any way alter documentation once it is generated. This is both unethical and a prescription for disaster if you are ever asked under oath to explain the evolution of particular documentation. If something needs to be clarified, create a new memorandum explaining the clarification and the basis for it, and date the new document with the current date.
- Be careful when preparing e-mail and other electronic documents. Remember that they can be easily transmitted inadvertently, with adverse consequences when they become a business

record. Once transmitted, or part of a system-wide back-up of data, these become business record, which must be maintained in accordance with your company's record-retention policies.

PAY ATTENTION TO DOCUMENT RETENTION POLICIES AND PROTOCOLS

Record-keeping is the cornerstone of most compliance programs. Adherence to stringent record retention and disposal policies is important for your testing and employment selection policies. Good record-keeping maintains continuity for your business practices, and documentation is then available to defend against challenges, as noted above.

Organizations involved in civil lawsuits, such as employment litigation or contract matters, have a duty to preserve all business records that may be relevant to the litigation. This isn't new law. Once it becomes apparent that a lawsuit or investigation may be launched, all potentially relevant documents are subject to disclosure. Failure to produce the documents when lawfully requested results in significant consequences, including negative publicity, unfavorable results in the case itself, monetary fines, disapproval by the jury, or adverse court orders from the judge (including default and entry of a liability judgment). Failure to produce relevant documents after a court order has been entered is contempt of court, with a host of additional penalties.

The duty to preserve evidence is significantly impacted by the role of electronic evidence. Communications that used to take place by telephone and in meetings are now conducted through text messaging—e-mail, PDA, IM systems, and even cell phone text messages. So conversations—including those about your organization's test design and administration process—that were rarely captured are now routinely housed on hard drives, servers, attachments, and hyperlinks.

Most organizations have document retention policies that facilitate disposal of documents, when they are no longer needed in the ordinary course of business. They can, of course, recycle their back-up tapes of electronic documents, including e-mail, on the schedules required by their retention/disposal policies.

Exception: when a company learns about any kind of potential claim or litigation, it must immediately suspend the disposal schedule for all documents relevant, or potentially relevant, to the potential litigation. This is called a "litigation hold." Failure to preserve the electronic records (as well as hard-copy records) can result in a judicially imposed sanction called "spoliation of evidence." This results from a judge's determination that a party to a civil lawsuit had a duty to preserve evidence relevant to the proceeding and failed to do so.

The duty to preserve data is triggered when a party knows or reasonably should know that the data is relevant to pending, imminent, or reasonably foreseeable litigation. Spoliation can occur without a specific intent to obstruct the proceeding and without gross negligence. It is simply failure to preserve evidence after the duty to preserve arises. If a party to a civil action negligently fails to retain evidence that it has a duty to preserve (by deletion, shredding, file purging, or other loss), a court can grant a wide array of "spoliation sanctions," including:

- An award of costs to the person or company (usually the opposing party) that was seeking the evidence during pre-trial discovery. These costs can include attorneys' fees, investigation fees, and court costs in seeking a court order to obtain the missing evidence;
- An "adverse inference" instruction to the jury that the missing or destroyed evidence was unfavorable to the party that failed to preserve it;
- An order precluding the spoliating party from introducing witnesses or evidence to support their position on the merits of the action;
- The ultimate sanction of default against the party that failed to preserve the evidence, which includes entry of judgment against it. This means the case ends adversely to the party bypassing a trial on the factual merits of the case.

One high-profile case underscores the legal risks to companies that fail to preserve all e-mail and other electronic files. Sanctions for spoliation can be so severe that they effectively destroy what might be a good defense of the suit on its merits. In *Zubulake v. UBS Warburg*, (2004) the plaintiff filed a complaint for sex discrimination. Throughout the pre-trial discovery process, she insisted that the evidence she needed to prove her case existed in e-mail sent among various UBS managers and stored on the company's computers. What started as a standard civil action for employment discrimination action was soon transformed into lengthy, very expensive, and precedent-setting battles over the production of electronic evidence. In a series of written decisions, a federal judge in New York changed the legal landscape for how electronic evidence is identified and produced, how the cost of producing large amounts of back-up tapes is allocated among the parties, and ultimately the duty to preserve e-mail and back-ups once litigation is anticipated or commenced.

In analyzing whether sanctions were appropriate for "spoliation" of relevant evidence," the judge first addressed the question of when the duty to preserve arose, concluding: "The obligation to preserve evidence arises when the party has notice that the evidence is relevant to litigation or when a party should have known the evidence may be relevant to future litigation." In this case, the Court held that UBS's duty to preserve was triggered four months prior to the plaintiff's initial complaint to the EEOC and ten months prior to the filing of the lawsuit. The court based its conclusion on a series of e-mails indicating that the key players recognized the possibility that the plaintiff might sue. Accordingly, she concluded that UBS failed in its duty to preserve the evidence.

Bottom line: your organization should enact and enforce appropriate retention policies for all documentation relating to test design, validation, or administration.

USE EFFECTIVE WORD MANAGEMENT IN YOUR DOCUMENTATION

Word management utilizes techniques for developing documentation and supporting evidence that works for the company and individual witnesses, not against them in the courtroom. Use of word management principles and effective documentation techniques should assist you in preparing business communications. Word management is:

- The discipline of writing documents, including test development criteria, validation criteria, data collection and analysis information, test administration procedures, and scoring materials, to avoid misunderstanding of those documents in future litigation to which the employer is a party.
- Drafting business records with an awareness that the document may ultimately be read and judged by untrained persons outside the company who serve as jurors.

Principles of Word Management

- Write with accuracy and precision. This refers to precision that is so factual and unambiguous that it leaves no room for differing interpretations of the essential facts. This does not mean word parsing or drawing language so narrowly that it is intended to mislead.
- Avoid connotations that may be misleading to someone not familiar with the industry. Be factual with all memos, letters, and other business communications.
- When writing about activities or events, stay within your personal knowledge, expertise, and responsibility. Don't speculate or guess as to the meaning of any aspect of a business transaction with which you are not personally familiar.
- Eliminate all inflammatory, offensive, or otherwise inappropriate content.
- Define or clarify technical terms involving crisis management, special care or skills, training practices, medical terms, or other specialized language. Always consider the purpose of the communication. For example, if you are writing to someone outside the company to require some action, use terminology that is easily understood. Remember that a lay juror, arbitrator, or judge from outside the industry may later be asked to consider the effect of your internal and external communications.
- Close the loop on all significant issues raised in writing. If information is requested of you, provide it promptly or notify the person of any foreseeable delays. If an action is requested

in writing, and the resolution is not reflected in writing, the company runs the risk that its actions may later be mischaracterized.

- Minimize handwritten comments and rapid e-mail replies that may not be well thought out. These types of communications are often incomplete or misleading.
- Control copy distribution of all sensitive records or confidential/proprietary data. Understand the scope and limitations of attorney-client privileges. Be sensitive to confidentiality, when appropriate. When in doubt, consult the legal department or human resources.
- Be consistent in your documentation techniques.

How to Write with Accuracy and Precision

- Avoid speculation and exaggeration.
- Avoid slang or shortcuts in terminology. Minimize unnecessary technical jargon; attempt to show the meaning of the term in its technical context.
- Minimize conclusionary language, such as "malingerer," "team player," or "slow learner," especially if used without a description of the underlying factual basis for the evaluation.
- Avoid subjective terms when describing people, when those terms may be misleading to a lay person serving as a juror.
- Avoid relative terms, such as "frequent," "excessive," or "substandard," unless you also give context. Think about your objective for the communication and how you intend it to be read and acted on. If someone reading the communication could ask "Relative to what standard?" the writing is non-specific. Use objective facts and examples instead.
- When writing memos, letters, e-mail, and other communications, state the facts of the situation clearly and objectively.
- Include all details: date, time, location, names of persons involved, witnesses, and conditions of the work environment.
- Be honest in assessing the situation (do not rely on second- or third-party information unless it is specified as such).
- Describe all actions and conclusions objectively, including the date, the decision or action reached, and any subsequent action to be taken or recommended.

USE OBJECTIVE TERMS TO DESCRIBE EVENTS AND COMPLIANCE

Make the effort to assure that your documents are correctly interpreted by a jury, even years after the underlying events have occurred. If your documents can be taken out of context by your adversary, or your records express opinions on the ultimate facts in dispute—without all the relevant facts—your position may be adversely affected. Avoid subjective or relative terms, which at best are ambiguous and at worse misconstrued. Your documentation should have all of the following elements:

Objectivity	Be specific and factual. Use the five "W's" (who, what, when, where, and why) as guidelines to think about the message you are creating.
Consistency	The same basic information *always*!
Reliability	Created from personal knowledge.
Relevancy	Job-related or training-related data.
Verification	Witnesses and documents are identified.
Credibility	Truthful and trustworthy.

AVOID INFLAMMATORY AND OFF-THE-CUFF COMMENTARY

Inflammatory or loose language in business records can undermine even the most effective testing and compliance programs. Consider *Thigpen v UPS* (2006). In 2006, a Florida state jury awarded Mr. Thigpen $6,000,000 for wrongful termination, concluding that he had been fired in retaliation for filing a workers' compensation claim. Mr. Thigpen was a long-term UPS driver. UPS claimed he was fired because he hadn't been documenting his stops properly.

The case hinged on an e-mail in which UPS supervisors were told to "target injury repeaters" for termination. Mr. Thigpen argued that he was harassed by his supervisors after the e-mail was sent and ultimately fired on false charges of dishonesty. Following the termination, he had trouble finding work because he was branded as dishonest.

UPS claimed the e-mail referred to the company's desire to reduce injuries through training and discipline and that this driver wasn't targeted by the e-mail since his injury record was not as bad as that of co-workers who were, in fact, targeted. Mr. Thigpen had been injured seven times in twenty years with UPS.

This "explanation" of what the e-mail "really meant" was a hard sell to the jurors, who believed the driver's version of the story. After a four-day trial, jurors needed fewer than three hours to conclude that UPS unlawfully retaliated against Mr. Thigpen. He received $669,661 in economic damages and $5.3 million in non-economic damages for the mental anguish he suffered.

DEVELOP AND ENFORCE EFFECTIVE DOCUMENT RETENTION POLICIES

The question is really not "to keep or not to keep?" but rather "to create or not to create?" Once a document is created, it then falls within the parameters of the existing records-retention policies of your organization. Many organizations have special training or instruction on the preparation of business records. This could be classified as the "do's and don'ts" of preparing company records.

The general belief is that instructing employees on how to draft specific types of documentation or format business-related documentation is best done in memoranda or policies *separate* from the organization's document-retention and disposal policies. The general subject matter of records preparation tends to follow the lines that any document created is of necessity going to be seen by people outside the company—by vendors, government agencies, adverse parties in litigation, regulatory investigators, competitors, and the press. Instructions in preparation of records tend to be specific in counseling against using words like "top secret," "destroy or shred when done," "confidential," or "secret." The general rule of thumb is to ask whether the company would be embarrassed if the record were to be seen by someone in the general public.

Instructions regarding the preparation of records should reflect that your record-keeping is in compliance with sound business practices. Pay attention to detail when preparing records to prevent ambiguities that might be difficult to overcome at a later date. In general, a later attempt to clear up any confusing language or impression created by the original document will be unsuccessful.

The length of time you keep records is subject to the needs of your particular organization. Regulatory documents should, at a minimum, be kept for the period of time set forth in the governing statute or regulation. While this is a minimum requirement, retention time may be extended by company policies for good business reasons. Once such a retention policy is adopted, it should be followed consistently. Otherwise, you may find yourself explaining in court why a seemingly relevant document was discarded, lost, or destroyed in violation of your own company's retention policies, even when the government did not require you to retain the material. The trier of fact may draw adverse inferences because the document no longer exists.

Review your personal record-keeping and your training department's record-retention policies to ensure that they accurately reflect your current business needs, while remaining effective to bolster a defense that you did everything required to meet your legal duties. Consult with your management or legal counsel if you have any questions about the company's overall requirements. A detailed analysis of document retention should be coordinated to guarantee that retention or non-retention meets reasonable standards and can be supported by testimony from your company's representatives, if necessary.

With the increased scrutiny of computer records in litigation, it is important for records policies to adequately address the non-retention and proper disposal of non-essential computer business records. This will require detailed review of all computer data systems on a periodic basis to capture newly created information. A planned, cohesive records policy is essential to prevent adverse assumptions about the absence of documents.

MAKE SURE YOUR DOCUMENTATION IS COMPLETE

Your documentation is your strongest ally in a regulatory proceeding or lawsuit. There is no substitute for clear, comprehensive files. If you have missing pages, illegible photocopies, or otherwise incomplete records, your documentation loses its positive impact. Remember that you may be required to produce your original files for inspection. It is best to use ink on handwritten materials, clearly label file folders, and use complete dates (with the month, day, and year).

MAKE SURE YOUR DOCUMENTATION IS CAPABLE OF "AUTHENTICATION"

To submit documentation to a regulator or to introduce it as evidence in a courtroom, you must establish that it was created as a business record, on or about the date it bears. This includes all evidence, including hard copies, electronic files, photographs, audiotapes, and videotapes, and other tangible items. While the parties may "stipulate" (agree) that the evidence is authentic, a difficult adversary has the option to require you to call a knowledgeable witness to authenticate, or verify, when and how the documents were created. This may be the photographer or videographer, or the individual who actually generated the documents.

Because it can be troublesome when an authenticating witness is unavailable, it is prudent to develop consistent methods for creating records maintained in the ordinary course of business. This provides flexibility and veracity when you offer documents in your own defense.

Develop productive documentation procedures to meet the needs of the particular department. Once you adopt procedures, strive for consistent enforcement. Keep informed about emerging statutory documentation requirements. When in doubt about the applicability of a statute to your industry, consult legal counsel.

IN CONCLUSION

Use documentation whenever there is an appropriate business need for it, but draft it with these principles in mind:

- Have a clear view of your objectives and design the document so that it will best help you accomplish those objectives.
- Draft it as if a jury were looking over your shoulder. Eliminate anything that is superfluous, inappropriate, or might give someone reading it a basis to mischaracterize your intent.

IS YOUR CRITERION-REFERENCED TESTING LEGALLY DEFENSIBLE? A CHECKLIST

The most effective method for avoiding claims of negligent retention and other legal problems is to be sure that all tests and other evaluation procedures are administered in accordance with objective testing guidelines. Although you can't guarantee a litigation-free workplace, this should help to reduce the number of legitimate charges of unfair employment practices based on post-training evaluation and testing.

☐ All tests should be validated and administered in full compliance with the *Uniform Guidelines on Employee Selection* procedures.
☐ All tests must be job-related based on objective task, skill, or knowledge requirements.
☐ Except under specific circumstances in which you can demonstrate that an available position is a stepping stone to other positions in the same job family, tests must be conducted and results evaluated only as they pertain to the presently available opportunity.
☐ Employees and candidates should be fully advised of the purpose of any test, how it will be conducted, the conditions under which it will be administered, the role it will play in the selection process, and who will have access to test results.
☐ If an organization administers employment tests:
   ☐ Does the test administrator always give the same instructions to each applicant?
   ☐ Are these instructions clear to the applicants being tested?
   ☐ Does the test administrator understand the test and the testing process well enough to answer questions clearly?
   ☐ Can the test administrator communicate clearly and unambiguously?
   ☐ Is each applicant given the same amount of time to complete the test?
   ☐ If a reasonable accommodation makes it necessary to extend the time given a test-taker, is it appropriate?
   ☐ Is the test administrator sensitive to special problems (for example, anxiety about tests, confusion about the use of

answer sheets, language problems) that some people might have, and does he or she take steps to minimize these problems?

☐ Are testing facilities adequate with regard to:
  ☐ Lighting?
  ☐ Space?
  ☐ Temperature?
  ☐ Noise level?
  ☐ Interruptions or distractions?
  ☐ Minimal distraction by interpreters?

☐ When testing is completed:
  ☐ Are the answers checked for scoring accuracy?
  ☐ Is there a procedure whereby applicants can learn how they performed on the test?
  ☐ Is there a process by which applicants can review the results of their employment test or request a re-test? Are the circumstances objectively described?
  ☐ Are tests, answer sheets, test scores, and scoring keys available to authorized and trained personnel?

☐ Are tests constructed so that:
  ☐ Instructions and questions are written at an appropriate language level for the test-taker?
  ☐ The mechanics of the test can be easily handled by all applicants? If not, have reasonable accommodations been considered?
  ☐ The time limits are reasonable?
  ☐ Success on the test is not highly influenced by previous testing experience (for example: there are no clues in questions or format or one question does not answer another)?

☐ When selecting or screening candidates for future success in training or task proficiency:
  ☐ Is there a clear, specific description of the job? Is it objective and able to be consistently enforced?
  ☐ Have the tests been proven to produce success by a statistical study showing a significant relationship between test scores and job proficiency (that is, concurrent validity), or do studies from other companies show test validity for similar jobs?

☐ Do these studies show that the tests do not discriminate against minorities and other protected groups?

☐ If a test measures skills (such as typing or physical tasks) that will be required immediately on a job, does the job description clearly indicate that the applicant will need these skills?

☐ If asked to discuss the employment testing program, could the employer show:
  ☐ A copy of the test(s) that the organization uses?
  ☐ A test manual or similar document giving general information and administrative and scoring instructions for each test?
  ☐ The instructions given the examinee, time limits, scoring procedures, and how scores from tests and parts of tests are weighed when no manual exists?

☐ Can the employer describe:
  ☐ How the tests were administered?
  ☐ How the tests were scored?
  ☐ How the tests were used in the selection decision?

☐ Does validity documentation show:
  ☐ When the studies were made?
  ☐ Which people were studied (the sample)?
  ☐ The sample size?
  ☐ The criterion for successful performance?
  ☐ The validity coefficients or other validity information?
  ☐ The minority and other protected groups studied and whether their results were similar to those of the total sample?

☐ In general:
  ☐ Are the same standards applied to every test-taker?
  ☐ What percentage of total applicants pass? What percentage do not pass?
  ☐ What percentage of minority applicants and applicants from other protected groups pass?
  ☐ What percentage of applicants are screened out before tests are administered?
  ☐ What percentage self-select out of the test?

☐ What percentage of minority applicants and applicants from other protected groups are screened out before tests are administered?

A FINAL THOUGHT

Legal challenges to your testing program are neither inevitable nor insurmountable. It isn't necessary to avoid all risk, as to do so could paralyze you and stifle valuable programs within your organization. You can manage your testing program within legal limits without falling hostage to the law if you are risk-aware, design effective criterion-referenced tests, develop consistent documentation techniques, and enforce appropriate policies. You can protect yourself and have the best opportunity for a solid defense by approaching test design, scoring, and administration with consistent procedures.

CRTD AS ORGANIZATIONAL TRANSFORMATION

> *Warren Buffett has written that "yardsticks seldom are discarded while yielding favorable readings," but when readings are unfavorable, "a more flexible measurement system often suggests itself: Just shoot the arrow of business performance into a blank canvas and then carefully draw the bull's-eye around the implanted arrow."*
> GEORGE WILL, 2006

In these final remarks, we share with you some observations about the consequences of implementing sound criterion-referenced testing in an organization—consequences beyond the benefits we have already presented. Far from being merely the last step in the instructional design model or the feedback loop in an abstract systems model, criterion-referenced testing has profound organization-wide implications.

One consequence of doing criterion-referenced testing (Level 2 evaluation) correctly may well be reduced demand for evaluation of transfer of training outcomes to the job (Level 3 evaluation) and evaluation of return on investment (Level 4 evaluation) (Shrock, 1999). Very often Level 3 and Level 4 evaluations are requested when management becomes dissatisfied with the performance of trained employees. Managers wonder why employees undergo expensive and time-consuming training only to perform badly on the job. Performance technologists know that failure to perform can result from a variety of factors—poor training being only one. Valid Level 2 assessment helps to address this problem in two ways.

First, following the guidelines in this book will result in testing that matches job responsibilities. When implemented, these tests will have the effect of pressuring instruction to become more job-related and relevant to the workplace. Expectations are clear and employees more motivated to reach them. It will become apparent when training is off the mark or ineffective. Job-related training, of course, transfers much more readily to practice than marginally applicable instruction or training that requires a great deal of interpretation or extrapolation on the job. Thus Level 2 testing prevents the problems that Level 3 evaluation seeks to illuminate.

Second, if factors other than training are to blame for poor on-the-job performance, good Level 2 assessment is perhaps the best way to demonstrate that fact. Given the politically disadvantageous position of training departments in many organizations, it is perhaps predictable that training is likely to be seen as the culprit; organizational and managerial shortcomings are less tidy to finger and usually more explosive to confront. Good Level 2 testing helps to identify the sources of performance problems in an organization.

The significance of this latter point should not be underestimated. In our opinion, many organizations take great comfort in not knowing who or what is to blame for performance problems. Since sources cannot be reliably identified, no one can fairly be held accountable. In this regard, serious, valid Level 2 testing will face obstacles in some organizations. Some managers will buy into assessment until they discover that it reveals organizational or managerial problems. For example, we encountered one very large corporation with numerous regional offices that invested in the creation of a sophisticated appraisal instrument for measuring soft skills attainment among recent hires. During implementation it became apparent that all new hires were achieving well except those from one region. Clearly, the data suggested that the regional manager had not supported new employees as required. This revelation was entirely attributable to the use of an appropriately created and validated organization-wide Level 2 test. However, this knowledge created the discomfort of having to deal with the manager's incompetence.

The lesson is that systems theory is powerful. Once the outcomes assessment has wide organizational support, it affects problem identification (or needs analysis) in interesting and surprising ways. Once we know how to assess what people can and cannot do, we can manipulate organizational factors—any and all of them—to maximize performance. Without this knowledge, we strive endlessly in the dark to hit a moving target, perhaps engaging periodically in a debate about what the target is.

Taken in its comprehensive, defensible form, testing is organizational transformation (Coscarelli & Shrock, 1996). More than just a step in the training process, it is a performance technology in its own right—one that has been accepted as a theoretical given for decades but which is only now beginning to realize its potential to improve human performance.

REFERENCES

Advanced Distributed Learning. (1999, April). *The DoD advanced distributed learning strategic plan.* Washington, DC: Department of Defense. Retrieved from www.adlnet.gov/downloads/156.cfm

AERA/APA/NCME Joint Committee. (1999). *Standards for educational and psychological testing.* Washington, DC: American Psychological Association.

Albemark Paper Co. v. Moody, 422 U.S. 405 (1975)

Americans with Disabilities Act. (1990). Public Law No. 101–336, Title 42 U.S. Code, Section 12101 et. seq.

Anderson, L.W., Krathwohl, D., Airasian, P.W., Cruikshank, K.A., Mayer, R.A., Pintrich, P.R., Raths, J., & Wittrock, M.C. (2001). *A taxonomy for learning, teaching, and assessing: A revision of Bloom's Taxonomy of Educational Objectives.* Boston, MA: Allyn & Bacon.

Association of Test Publishers. (2002). *Guidelines for computer-based testing.* Washington, DC: Author.

Baker, F. (2001). *The basics of item response theory.* College Park, MD: ERIC Clearinghouse on Assessment and Evaluation, University of Maryland.

Ballew, P.J. (1987). Courts, psychologists, and the EEOC's Uniform Guidelines: An analysis of recent trends affecting testing as a means of employee selection. *Emory Law Journal, 36,* 203–252.

Barrett, R.S. (1981). Is the test content-valid: Or, who killed Cock Robin? *Employee Relations Law Journal, 6*(4), 584–600.

Barritt, C., & Lewis, D. (2000, April). *Reusable learning object strategy: Definition, creation, process, and guidelines, Version 3.1.* White paper published by Cisco Systems. Retrieved from http://reusablelearningobjects.org/Docs/Cisco_rlo_rio_v3–1.pdf on December 8, 2006.

Bates v. United Parcel Service, 272 F.3d 1249 (9th Cir. 2006).

Bemis, S.E., Belenky, A.H., & Soder, D.A. (1983). *Job analysis: An effective management tool.* Washington, DC: The Bureau of National Affairs.

Berk, R.A. (Ed.). (1980). *Criterion-referenced measurement: The state of the art.* Baltimore, MD: Johns Hopkins University Press.

Berk, R.A. (Ed.). (1984). *A guide to criterion-referenced test construction.* Baltimore, MD: Johns Hopkins University Press.

Berk, R.A. (Ed.). (1986a). *Performance assessment methods and applications.* Baltimore, MD: Johns Hopkins University Press.

Berk, R.A. (1986b). A consumer's guide to setting performance standards on criterion-referenced tests. *Review of Educational Research, 56*(1), 137–172.

Berk, R.A. (1989). Criterion-referenced measurement. In *The international encyclopedia of education* (pp. 1108–1118). New York: Elsevier.

Blair, D. (1996, October). Personal communication to William Coscarelli.

Bloom, B., & Krathwohl, D. (1956). *Taxonomy of educational objectives.* New York: David McKay.

Brennan, R.L. (1972). A generalized upper-lower item-discrimination index. *Educational and Psychological Measurement, 32,* 289–303.

Browning, A.H., Bugbee, A.C., Jr., & Mullins, M.A. (Eds.). (2006). *Certification: A NOCA handbook.* Washington, DC: National Organization for Competency Assurance.

Burton, S.J., Sudweeks, R.R., Merrill, P.F., & Wood, B. (1991). *How to prepare better multiple-choice test items: Guidelines for university faculty.* Provo, UT: Brigham Young University Testing Services and the Department of Instructional Science. Retrieved November 23, 2006, from http://testing.byu.edu/info/handbooks/betteritems.pdf.

Campbell, C.P., & Hatcher, T.G. (1989). Testing that is performance based and criterion-referenced. *Performance and Instruction, 28*(5), 1–9.

Cascio, W.F., Alexander, R.A. & Barrett, G.V. (1988). Setting cutoff scores: Legal, psychometric, and professional issues and guidelines. *Personnel Psychology, 41,* 1–24.

Case, S.M., & Swanson, D.B. (2001). Constructing written test questions from the basic and clinical sciences. Philadelphia: National Board of Medical Examiners. Retrieved November 23, 2006, from www.nbme.org/about/itemwriting.asp.

Center on Education and Training for Employment, College of Education, The Ohio State University. (1995, March). *DACUM Research Chart for Computer Applications Programmer.* Columbus, OH: Author.

Conger, A.J. (1980). Integration and generalization of kappas for multiple raters. *Psychological Bulletin, 88*(2), 322–328.

Cohen, J. (1960) A coefficient of agreement for nominal scales. *Educational and Psychological Measurement, 20,* 37–46.

Coscarelli, W.C., & Shrock, S.A. (1996). How to transform an organization through criterion-referenced testing. In M. Silberman (Ed.).

The 1996 McGraw-Hill team and organization development sourcebook. New York: McGraw-Hill, pp. 209–217.

Coscarelli, W., Robins, D., Shrock, S., & Herbst, P. (1998). The certification suite: A classification system for certification tests. *Performance Improvement, 37*(7), 13–18.

Coscarelli, W., & Shrock, S. (2002). The two most useful approaches to estimating criterion-referenced test reliability in a single test administration. *Performance Improvement Quarterly, 15*(4), 74–85.

Coscarelli, W., Barrett, A., Kleeman, J., & Shrock, S. (2005). The problem of the saltatory cut-off score: Some issues and recommendations for applying the Angoff to test item banks. In M. Danson (Ed.), *Proceedings of the Ninth CAA Conference,* July 2006. Loughborough University: Loughborough, England. Retrieved December 14, 2006, from www.caaconference.com/pastConferences/2005/proceedings/ CoscarelliW_BarrettA_KleemanJ_ShrockS.pdf

Cronbach, L.J., Schonemann, P., & McKie, D. (1965). Alpha coefficients for stratified-parallel tests. *Educational and Psychological Measurement, 25*(2), 291–312.

Desmedt, J., & Yelon, S. (1991). Comprehensive open skill test design. *Performance and Instruction, 30*(10), 16–28.

Dick, W., & Hagerty, N. (1971). *Topics in measurement: Reliability and validity.* New York: McGraw-Hill.

Donath, C. (2005). Test item writing best practices: Useful and practical considerations. Waltham, MA. Retrieved December 14, 2006, from http://e-learning.umh.ac.be/file.php/1/Guide_pratique_pour_ la_conception_de_tests.pdf

Drake Prometric. (1995). *Certification for computing professionals.* New York: McGraw-Hill.

Educational Testing Service. (2003). *Fairness review guidelines.* Princeton, NJ: Author.

Eyres, P. (1997). *The legal handbook for trainers, speakers, and consultants.* New York: McGraw-Hill.

Eyres, P. (2002, January). Personal communication to William Coscarelli.

Fabrey, L. (1996). Introduction to the Standards for Accreditation of National Certification Organizations. In A.H. Browning, A.C. Bugbee, Jr., & M.A. Mullins (Eds.), *Certification: A NOCA handbook.* Washington, DC: National Organization for Competency Assurance, pp. 1–40.

Feldt, L.S., & Brennan, R.L. (1989). In R.L. Linn (Ed.), *Educational Measurement* (3rd ed.) New York: Macmillan.

Francis, R.W. (2006, Fall). Common errors in calculating final grades. *Thought & Action, 22,* 15–22.

Gael, S. (Ed.). (1988). *The job analysis handbook for business, industry, and government.* (Vols. I and II). New York: John Wiley & Sons.

Gagné, R.M. (1985). *The conditions of learning* (4th ed.). New York: Holt, Rinehart & Winston.

Gallagher, D.G., & Veglahn, P.A. (1986, October). Arbitral standards in cases involving testing issues. *Labor Law Journal, 37,* 719–730.

Griggs v. Duke Power Co., 401 U.S. 421 (1971).

Gronlund, N. E. (1988). *How to construct achievement tests.* Englewood Cliffs, NJ: Prentice-Hall.

Guilford, J.P., & Fruchter, B. (1978). *Fundamental statistics in psychology and education* (6th ed.). New York: McGraw-Hill.

Haertel, E. (1985). Construct validity and criterion-referenced testing. *Review of Educational Research, 55*(1), 23–46.

Hale, J. (2000). *Performance-based certification: How to design a valid, defensible, cost-effective program.* San Francisco, CA: Pfeiffer.

Hambleton, R.K., & Novick, M.R. (1973). Toward an integration of theory and method for criterion-referenced tests. *Journal of Educational Measurement, 10,* 159–170.

Hambleton, R.K. (1994). Criterion-referenced measurement. In *The international encyclopedia of education* (pp. 1183–1189). New York: Elsevier.

Hambleton, R.K. (2001). Setting performance standards on educational assessments and criteria for evaluating the process. In G.J. Cizek (Ed.), *Setting performance standards: Concepts, methods, and perspectives.* (pp. 89–117). Mahwah, NJ: Lawerence Earlbaum Associates.

Haney, C. (1982). Employment tests and employment discrimination: A dissenting psychological opinion. *Industrial Relations Law Journal, 5*(1), 1–86.

Henderson, J.P. (1996). Job analysis. In A.H. Browning, A.C. Bugbee, Jr., & M.A. Mullins (Eds.), *Certification: A NOCA handbook* pp. 45–65. Washington, DC: National Organization for Competency Assurance.

Hunt, M., & Metcalf, L. (1968). *Teaching high school social studies.* New York: Harper & Row.

Hurtz, G.M., & Auerbach, M.A. (2003). A meta-analysis of the effects of modifications to the Angoff method on cutoff scores and judgment consensus. *Educational and Psychological Measurement, 63*(4), 584–601.

Impara, J.C., & Plake, B.S. (2000). A comparison of cut scores using multiple standard setting methods. Paper presented at the Large Scale Assessment Conference. Snowbird, UT. Retrieved December 14, 2006, from www.education.ualberta.ca/educ/psych/crame/files/RickerCSSE2003.pdf

Jonassen, D.H., Hannum, W.H., & Tessmer, M. (1989). *Handbook of task analysis procedures*. New York: Praeger.

Kane, M. (1994). Validating the performance standards associated with passing scores. *Review of Educational Research, 64*(3), 425–461.

Keller, W.L. (1981, January). Defending before the EEOC. *For the defense*, 10–23.

Kelley, T.L. (1939). The selection of upper and lower groups for the validation of test items. *Journal of Educational Psychology, 30*, 17–24.

Kirkpatrick, D. (1994). *Evaluating training programs: The four levels*. San Francisco, CA: Berrett-Koehler.

Kleiman, L.S., & Faley, R.H. (1985). The implications of professional and legal guidelines for court decisions involving criterion-related validity: A review and analysis. *Personnel Psychology, 38*, 803–833.

Kleiman, L.S., & Faley, R.H. (1978). Assessing content validity: Standards set by the court. *Personnel Psychology, 31*, 701–713.

Lathrop, R.J. (1983). The number of performance assessments necessary to determine competence. *Journal of Instructional Development, 6*(3), 26–31.

Lathrop, R.J. (1986). Practical strategies for dealing with unreliability in competency assessments. *Journal of Educational Research, 70*(4), 234–237.

Lexile Framework for Reading. (2006, December 6). Retrieved from www.lexile.com

Livingston, S.A. (1972). Criterion-referenced applications of classical test theory. *Journal of Educational Measurement, 9*(1), 13–26.

Livingston, S.A., & Zieky, M.J. (1982). *Passing scores*. Princeton, NJ: Educational Testing Service.

Lynn, M.R. (1986). Determination and quantification of content validity. *Nursing Research, 35*, 382–385.

Mager, R.F. (1962). *Preparing instructional objectives*. Belmont, CA: Fearon.

Merrill, M.D. (1983). Component display theory. In C.M. Reigeluth (Ed.), *Instructional design theories and models: An overview of their current status*. Mahwah, NJ: Lawrence Erlbaum Associates.

Microsoft. (1995). *Microsoft certified professional program corporate backgrounder*. Redmond, WA: Author.

Millman, J. (1989). If at first you don't succeed: Setting passing scores when more than one attempt is permitted. *Educational Researcher, 18*(9), 5–9.

Mills, C.N., & Melican, G.J. (1988). Estimating and adjusting cutoff scores: Features of selected methods. *Applied Measurement in Education, 1*(3), 261–275.

Moroz, R. (2004). "Show," don't "tell." *Education 315 Student Manual*, College of Education and Human Services. Unpublished manuscript, Southern Illinois University, Carbondale, IL.

Motorola, Inc. v. Illinois Fair Employment Practices Commission, 34 III, 2d 266, 215 NE2d286 (1966).

Nathan, B.R., & Cascio, W.F. (1986). Introduction: Technical and legal standards. In R.A. Berk (Ed.), *Performance assessment methods and applications* (pp. 1–50). Baltimore, MD: Johns Hopkins University Press.

No child left behind. (2001). Public Law No. 107–110. Title 20 US Code 6301.

Noonan, J.V., & Sarvela, P.D. (1988). Implementation decisions in computer-based testing programs. *Performance & Instruction, 27*(6), 5–13.

Norton, R.E. (1997). DACUM handbook. Columbus, OH: Center on Education and Training for Employment, The Ohio State University.

Okey, J.R. (1973). Developing and validating learning hierarchies. *Audio-Visual Communications Review, 21*(1), 87–108.

Oshima, T.C., McGinty, D., & Flowers, C.P. (1994). Differential item functioning for a test with a cutoff score: Use of limited closed-interval measures. *Applied Measurement in Education, 7*(3), 195–209.

Robertson, R. (1999). In-house certification: More performance bang for your buck? *Performance Improvement, 38*(9), 26–34.

Russell, J.S. (1984). A review of fair employment cases in the field of training. *Personnel Psychology, 37*, 261–276.

Ruyle, K.E. (2001). Meet me in RIO: Implementing reusable information objects for web-based training and performance support. Paper presented at the Annual Meeting of the International Society for Performance Improvement, San Francisco, CA.

Sarvela, P.D. (1986). Discrimination indices commonly used in military training environments: Effects of departures from normal distributions. Paper presented at the Annual Meeting of the American Educational Research Association, San Francisco, CA.

Shrock, S.A. (1999). Level 2 assessment may eliminate the demand for ROI. *Performance Improvement, 38*(6), 5–7.

Shrock, S.A., & Coscarelli, W.C. (1998). Creating certification tests that measure curriculum outcomes. The 1998 annual: *Volume 1, training* (pp. 275–294). San Francisco: Pfeiffer.

Shrock, S.A., Coscarelli, W.C., & Burk, J. (1993). *Bloom's Taxonomy on the battlefield: A scenario of how Bloom's levels occur in a combat environment.* Unpublished manuscript, Southern Illinois University, Carbondale, IL.

Singer, R. (1975). *Motor learning and human performance.* New York: Macmillan.

Smith, C., Jr. (1985a, September 16). The EEOC's standards for employment testing. *The National Law Journal*, pp. 22–23.

Smith, C., Jr. (1985b, September 30). Testing must relate to specific job requirements. *The National Law Journal*, pp. 26–27.

Stepke, K. (1987, September/October). How to develop effective (and legal) personnel tests. *Legal Administrator*, 6, 28–34.

Stenner, A.J., & Wright, B.D. (2002). Readability, reading ability, and comprehension. Paper presented at the Annual Conference of the Association of Test Publishers, San Diego, CA.

Subkoviak, M.J. (1988). A practitioner's guide to computation and interpretation of reliability indices for mastery tests. *Journal of Educational Measurement*, 25(1), 47–55.

Swaminathan, H., Hambleton, R.K., & Algina, J. (1974). Reliability of criterion-referenced tests: A decision-theoretic formulation. *Journal of Educational Measurement*, 11, 263–267.

Swezey, R.W. (1981). *Individual performance assessment: An approach to criterion-referenced test development*. Reston, VA: Reston.

Taylor, R.G., & Lee, E. (1995). A review of the methods and problems of measuring reliability for criterion referenced tests and items. *Journal of Instructional Psychology*, 22(1), 88–95.

Thalheimer, W. (2006, November 21). Personal communication to William Coscarelli.

Thigpen v. United Parcel Service, Case No. 02-13221 (Broward Circuit Court 2006).

Thomas, S. (1996). Future trends in credentialing. In A.H. Browning, A.C. Bugbee, Jr., & M.A. Mullins (Eds.), *Certification: A NOCA handbook*. Washington, DC: National Organization for Competency Assurance, pp. 275–296.

Thompson, D.E., & Thompson, T.A. (1982). Court standards for job analysis in test validation. *Personnel Psychology*, 35, 865–874.

Title VII of the Civil Rights Act (1964), Public Law No. 88–352, Title 42 U.S. Code, Section 2000e-2000e-17.

Uniform guidelines on employee selection procedures. (1978). *Federal Register*, 43, 38290–38309.

Uniform Guidelines on employee selection adoption of questions and answers to clarify and provide a common interpretation of the Uniform Guidelines on Employee Selection Procedures. (1979). *Federal Register*, 44, 11996–12009.

Uniform Guidelines on employee selection adoption of additional questions and answers to clarify and provide a common interpretation of the Uniform Guidelines on Employee Selection Procedures. (1980). *Federal Register*, 45, 29530–29531.

United States Nuclear Regulatory Commission. (2005). Operator licensing examination standards for power reactors, *NUREG-1021, Appendix B, Rev. 9*. Retrieved November 29, 2006, from www.nrc.gov/reactors/operator-licensing.html

Walls v. Mississippi State Department of Public Welfare, 730 F.2d 306 (1985).

Waltz, C.F., & Bausell, R.B. (1983). *Research in nursing*. New York: McGraw-Hill.

Wang, C. (2000). How to grade essay examinations. *Performance Improvement, 39*(1), 12–15.

Wang, N., Schnipke, D., & Witt, E. (2005). Use of knowledge, skill, and ability statements in developing licensure and certification examinations. *Educational Measurement, 24*(1), 15–26.

Will, G. (2006, October 1). Education's moving target. *The Washington Post*, p. B07.

Wynd, C.A., Schmidt, B.S., & Schaefer, M.A. (2003). Two quantitative approaches for estimating content validity. *Western Journal of Nursing Research, 25*(5), 508–516.

Zieky, M., & Livingston, S. (1977). *Manual for setting standards on the basic skills assessment tests*. Princeton, NJ: Educational Testing Service.

Zubulake v. UBS Warburg, 2004 WL 1620866 (S.D.N.Y, 2004).

INDEX

Discrimination issues (continued)
  avoiding blanket exclusions, 378–380
  balancing CRTs with employment laws on, 376–378
  "four-fifths" rule, 375
  Title VII (Civil Rights Act of 1964) on, 368, 370, 374
  See also EEOC (Equal Employment Opportunity Commission); Legal citations
Distractor patterns
  described, 48, 215, 249–250
  guidelines for writing for, 160–161
  organizing the, 161–162
Diversity issues. *See* Minority populations
Documentation
  of adverse impact and job-relatedness of tests, 387
  "authentication" standard of, 415
  compliance, 402–403, 412
  used to defend against legal claims, 401–402
  definition of, 401
  effective word management in, 409–413
  functions of, 402–407
  illustration of CRTD process and, 68*fig*
  keeping complete, 414–415
  legally defensible, 400–415
  list of questions/issues to address in, 64–68
  planning, 44
  reasons for, 57–58
  retention policies and protocols for, 407–409, 413–414
  standards for, 63–64
  test security plan, 68–73
  See also Communication
Documentation word management
  avoiding inflammatory/off-the-cuff commentary, 412–413
  described, 409–410
  using objective terms, 412

principles of, 410–411
  writing with accuracy and precision, 411
Donath, C., 266
Drag and Drop test item, 129
Drake Prometric, 8
Duke Power Company, Griggs v., 374–375

E
Ebel's method, 266
Educational Testing Service, 7, 159
EEOC (Equal Employment Opportunity Commission), 376, 385, 387, 398, 409
  See also Discrimination issues; *The Uniform Guidelines on Employee Selection Procedures*
Employment selection laws
  affirmative action allowed by, 385–386
  balancing CRTs with discrimination and, 376–378
  checklist for CRTs legally defensible under, 416–419
  described, 368
  legal claims made under, 368–370
  See also Legislation; *The Uniform Guidelines on Employee Selection Procedures*
Entry tests, 30–31
Environmental Protection Agency (EPA), 59
Equal Employment Opportunity Commission (EEOC), 376, 385, 387, 398, 409
Equivalence reliability
  calculating, 299–300
  described, 19
  determining, 51
Equivalency tests, 31
Error of standards, 320
Errors
  misclassification, 267–268, 284–285
  rating, 320–322
  standard error of measurement, 282–284

ABOUT THE AUTHORS

Sharon A. Shrock graduated from Indiana University in 1979 with a doctorate in instructional systems technology. She was on the faculty at Virginia Tech before moving to Southern Illinois University at Carbondale, where she is currently a professor of curriculum and instruction, as well as the coordinator for the Instructional Design and Technology Programs. She specializes in instructional design and program evaluation and has been an evaluation consultant to international corporations, school districts, and federal instructional programs. She is the former co-director of the Hewlett-Packard World Wide Test Development Center.

Dr. Shrock is a past president of the Association for Educational Communications and Technology's Division of Instructional Development. She was a member of the International Society for Performance Improvement's (formerly the National Society for Performance and Instruction) Senior Advisory Panel and has served on the editorial boards of most of the major academic journals in her field.

She is senior author of *Criterion-Referenced Test Development* and has written extensively in the field of testing and evaluation. With over one hundred presentations in her career and more than fifty articles, she has seen her research and evaluation work published in major instructional design and technology journals, including *Educational Communications and Technology Journal, Performance Improvement Quarterly,* and the *Journal of Educational Computing Research.*

In 1991 she won the Outstanding Book award for *Criterion-Referenced Test Development* from AECT's Division of Instructional Development and from the National Society for Performance and Instruction. She also won ISPI's Outstanding *Performance Improvement*

Quarterly article. In 1992 she was co-recipient of Indiana University's L.C. Larson Alumni Award for "outstanding leadership in instructional systems." She was the 1992 recipient of SIUC's Outstanding Contribution to Graduate and Professional Education Award. In 1994 she received the SIUC College of Education Teacher of the Year Award. E-mail her at sashrock@siu.edu.

William C. Coscarelli graduated from Indiana University in 1977 with a Ph.D. in instructional systems. He then joined the faculty at Southern Illinois University at Carbondale, where he is a professor in the instructional design specialization of the Department of Curriculum and Instruction. He also served as the co-director of the Hewlett-Packard World Wide Test Development Center. He has spent sabbaticals as a visiting scholar at the National Center for Vocational Education at Ohio State, a lecturer in Holland, England, and Ireland, and most recently at Bonn, Cologne, and Cairo.

Dr. Coscarelli has been elected as president of the Association for Educational Communications and Technology's Division for Instructional Development, appointed as founding editor of *Performance Improvement Quarterly,* and elected as the first vice president of publications for the International Society for Performance Improvement. He also served as president of ISPI (formerly the National Society for Performance and Instruction), an international association dedicated to improving performance in the workplace.

He is author of the *Decision-Making Style Inventory,* co-author (with Gregory White) of *The Guided Design Guidebook,* and second author (with Sharon Shrock) of *Criterion-Referenced Test Development Technical and Legal Issues.* He has made more than one hundred presentations in his career and written more than sixty articles.

He has won the outstanding book award for *Criterion-Referenced Test Development* from two professional societies and is a co-recipient of the L.C. Larson Indiana University Alumni Award for "outstanding leadership in instructional systems." He also received ISPI's Distinguished Service Award. He can be reached at coscarel@siu.edu.

Pfeiffer Publications Guide

This guide is designed to familiarize you with the various types of Pfeiffer publications. The formats section describes the various types of products that we publish; the methodologies section describes the many different ways that content might be provided within a product. We also provide a list of the topic areas in which we publish.

FORMATS

In addition to its extensive book-publishing program, Pfeiffer offers content in an array of formats, from fieldbooks for the practitioner to complete, ready-to-use training packages that support group learning.

FIELDBOOK Designed to provide information and guidance to practitioners in the midst of action. Most fieldbooks are companions to another, sometimes earlier, work, from which its ideas are derived; the fieldbook makes practical what was theoretical in the original text. Fieldbooks can certainly be read from cover to cover. More likely, though, you'll find yourself bouncing around following a particular theme, or dipping in as the mood, and the situation, dictate.

HANDBOOK A contributed volume of work on a single topic, comprising an eclectic mix of ideas, case studies, and best practices sourced by practitioners and experts in the field.

An editor or team of editors usually is appointed to seek out contributors and to evaluate content for relevance to the topic. Think of a handbook not as a ready-to-eat meal, but as a cookbook of ingredients that enables you to create the most fitting experience for the occasion.

RESOURCE Materials designed to support group learning. They come in many forms: a complete, ready-to-use exercise (such as a game); a comprehensive resource on one topic (such as conflict management) containing a variety of methods and approaches; or a collection of like-minded activities (such as icebreakers) on multiple subjects and situations.

TRAINING PACKAGE An entire, ready-to-use learning program that focuses on a particular topic or skill. All packages comprise a guide for the facilitator/trainer and a workbook for the participants. Some packages are supported with additional media—such as video—or learning aids, instruments, or other devices to help participants understand concepts or practice and develop skills.

- *Facilitator/trainer's guide* Contains an introduction to the program, advice on how to organize and facilitate the learning event, and step-by-step instructor notes. The guide also contains copies of presentation materials—handouts, presentations, and overhead designs, for example—used in the program.

- *Participant's workbook* Contains exercises and reading materials that support the learning goal and serves as a valuable reference and support guide for participants in the weeks and months that follow the learning event. Typically, each participant will require his or her own workbook.

ELECTRONIC CD-ROMs and web-based products transform static Pfeiffer content into dynamic, interactive experiences. Designed to take advantage of the searchability, automation, and ease-of-use that technology provides, our e-products bring convenience and immediate accessibility to your workspace.

METHODOLOGIES

CASE STUDY A presentation, in narrative form, of an actual event that has occurred inside an organization. Case studies are not prescriptive, nor are they used to prove a point; they are designed to develop critical analysis and decision-making skills. A case study has a specific time frame, specifies a sequence of events, is narrative in structure, and contains a plot structure—an issue (what should be/have been done?). Use case studies when the goal is to enable participants to apply previously learned theories to the circumstances in the case, decide what is pertinent, identify the real issues, decide what should have been done, and develop a plan of action.

ENERGIZER A short activity that develops readiness for the next session or learning event. Energizers are most commonly used after a break or lunch to stimulate or refocus the group. Many involve some form of physical activity, so they are a useful way to counter post-lunch lethargy. Other uses include transitioning from one topic to another, where "mental" distancing is important.

EXPERIENTIAL LEARNING ACTIVITY (ELA) A facilitator-led intervention that moves participants through the learning cycle from experience to application (also known as a Structured Experience). ELAs are carefully thought-out designs in which there is a definite learning purpose and intended outcome. Each step—everything that participants do during the activity—facilitates the accomplishment of the stated goal. Each ELA includes complete instructions for facilitating the intervention and a clear statement of goals, suggested group size and timing, materials required, an explanation of the process, and, where appropriate, possible variations to the activity. (For more detail on Experiential Learning Activities, see the Introduction to the *Reference Guide to Handbooks and Annuals,* 1999 edition, Pfeiffer, San Francisco.)

GAME A group activity that has the purpose of fostering team spirit and togetherness in addition to the achievement of a pre-stated goal. Usually contrived—undertaking a desert expedition, for example—this type of learning method offers an engaging means for participants to demonstrate and practice business and interpersonal skills. Games are effective for team building and personal development mainly because the goal is subordinate to the process—the means through which participants reach decisions, collaborate, communicate, and generate trust and understanding. Games often engage teams in "friendly" competition.

ICEBREAKER A (usually) short activity designed to help participants overcome initial anxiety in a training session and/or to acquaint the participants with one another. An icebreaker can be a fun activity or can be tied to specific topics or training goals. While a useful tool in itself, the icebreaker comes into its own in situations where tension or resistance exists within a group.

INSTRUMENT A device used to assess, appraise, evaluate, describe, classify, and summarize various aspects of human behavior. The term used to describe an instrument depends primarily on its format and purpose. These terms include survey, questionnaire, inventory, diagnostic, survey, and poll. Some uses of instruments include providing instrumental feedback to group members, studying here-and-now processes or functioning within a group, manipulating group composition, and evaluating outcomes of training and other interventions.

Instruments are popular in the training and HR field because, in general, more growth can occur if an individual is provided with a method for focusing specifically on his or her own behavior. Instruments also are used to obtain information that will serve as a basis for change and to assist in workforce planning efforts.

Paper-and-pencil tests still dominate the instrument landscape with a typical package comprising a facilitator's guide, which offers advice on administering the instrument and interpreting the collected data, and an initial set of instruments. Additional instruments are available separately. Pfeiffer, though, is investing heavily in e-instruments. Electronic instrumentation provides effortless distribution and, for larger groups particularly, offers advantages over paper-and-pencil tests in the time it takes to analyze data and provide feedback.

LECTURETTE A short talk that provides an explanation of a principle, model, or process that is pertinent to the participants' current learning needs. A lecturette is intended to establish a common language bond between the trainer and the participants by providing a mutual frame of reference. Use a lecturette as an introduction to a group activity or event, as an interjection during an event, or as a handout.

MODEL A graphic depiction of a system or process and the relationship among its elements. Models provide a frame of reference and something more tangible, and more easily remembered, than a verbal explanation. They also give participants something to "go on," enabling them to track their own progress as they experience the dynamics, processes, and relationships being depicted in the model.

ROLE PLAY A technique in which people assume a role in a situation/ scenario: a customer service rep in an angry-customer exchange, for example. The way in which the role is approached is then discussed and feedback is offered. The role play is often repeated using a different approach and/or incorporating changes made based on feedback received. In other words, role playing is a spontaneous interaction involving realistic behavior under artificial (and safe) conditions.

SIMULATION A methodology for understanding the interrelationships among components of a system or process. Simulations differ from games in that they test or use a model that depicts or mirrors some aspect of reality in form, if not necessarily in content. Learning occurs by studying the effects of change on one or more factors of the model. Simulations are commonly used to test hypotheses about what happens in a system—often referred to as "what if?" analysis—or to examine best-case/worst-case scenarios.

THEORY A presentation of an idea from a conjectural perspective. Theories are useful because they encourage us to examine behavior and phenomena through a different lens.

TOPICS

The twin goals of providing effective and practical solutions for workforce training and organization development and meeting the educational needs of training and human resource professionals shape Pfeiffer's publishing program. Core topics include the following:

> Leadership & Management
>
> Communication & Presentation
>
> Coaching & Mentoring
>
> Training & Development
>
> e-Learning
>
> Teams & Collaboration
>
> OD & Strategic Planning
>
> Human Resources
>
> Consulting

What will you find on pfeiffer.com?

- The best in workplace performance solutions for training and HR professionals

- Downloadable training tools, exercises, and content

- Web-exclusive offers

- Training tips, articles, and news

- Seamless on-line ordering

- Author guidelines, information on becoming a Pfeiffer Affiliate, and much more

Discover more at www.pfeiffer.com